Brendan Scott

The Struggle for a Socialist and Secular Ireland

by

John P. Swift

Umiskin
Press

Hardback ISBN 978-1-8381112-0-5

Paperback ISBN 978-1-8381112-1-2

Umiskin Press acknowledge the co-operation of the individual authors,
and the Irish Labour History Society, Beggars Bush.
No part of this publication may be copied, reproduced,
or transmitted in any form or by any means,
without the written permission of the publisher.
The copyright of the text and index is the original work of the author,
and the copyright resides with him.

A limited edition of
?? Hardbacks and ??? Paperbacks

Typeset in 10.5pt New Baskerville on 12.5 body.

Layout and Printing by
CRM Design + Print Ltd
Dublin 12

Produced by trade union labour in Ireland

Permission to reproduce copyright material is gratefully acknowledged.
Every effort has been made to trace copyright holders but if any have been inadvertently
overlooked the necessary arrangements will be made at the first opportunity

Contents

In Memoriam

Mary Burke, from Clonmel, was Chair of the first ITGWU Women's Affairs Committee in 1982, serving on the Committee until 1990 when she became Chair, SIPTU Interim National Women's Committee, 1990-1992, and Chair, SIPTU National Women's Committee, 1993-1995. Quietly determined, her gentle manner masked a steely and committed champion for gender equality and social justice.

Jack Charlton, from the Northumberland mining community of Ashington, enjoyed a career as a professional footballer with Leeds United, 1952-1973, before managing Middlesbrough, Sheffield Wednesday and Newcastle United, an apprenticeship for his ten-year management of the Republic of Ireland, 1986-1996. The country's pride and excitement generated by the team's qualification for Euro 88 in Germany and World Cups in Italy 1990 and USA 1994 were incalculable. Charlton remained true to his working class roots, noticeably when supporting the 1984-1985 British Miners' Strike.

Mike Cooley, born in Tuam in 1934, after an apprenticeship in the Irish Sugar Company studied engineering in Germany, Switzerland and England. Active in TASS (Technical, Administrative & Supervisory Section), his leadership of the Lucas Aerospace Plan – an imaginative project to resist redundancies threatened by defence cuts by manufacturing alternative, socially useful products – led him to original thinking in computer-aided design and human interaction with technology. He was central to the Greater London Enterprise Board (1992) and AI & Society (1987) creating thousands of jobs. His globally influential publications included *Architect or Bee?* (1980), *Delinquent Genius: The Strange Affair of Man & His Technology* (1992, republished 2018); and *The Search For Alternatives: Liberating Human Imagination* (2018). The Coooley Archive is held in Waterford Institute of Technology.

Brendan Halligan, Labour Party Political Director, 1967-1968, and General Secretary, 1968-1980, was a key strategist and close ally of Brendan Corish. He was elected Senator, 1973-1976; TD, Dublin South West, 1976-1977; and MEP for Dublin, 1983-1984. Founder and President, Institute of International & European Affairs, he published many policy reflections with Scáthán Press, including his reminiscences of his times with Corish.

Brian Hogan, described as 'Dublin's most prolific commercial architect for three decades', designed many significant buildings in the capital and was long-serving architectural advisor to SIPTU, especially on the futuristic, carbon-neutral deigns for the new Liberty Hall.

John Hume, a long-standing member of the ITGWU/SIPTU Derry Branch, was a founder member of the Social Democratic & Labour Party and central to the Peace Process and Good Friday Agreement for which, with David Trimble, he was awarded the Nobel Peace Prize in 1998.

Peter Keating was an official of the Marine, Port & General Workers' Union and Workers' Union of Ireland, always on the left and involved in many progressive campaigns, particularly the long struggle to save Clondalkin Paper Mills which he described in his *Clondalkin, A Workers' Victory,* (Communist Party of Ireland, Dublin, 1983).

Margaret MacCurtain [Sister Benvenuta] was Prioress, Sion Hill Convent, 1984-1989, and lectured in Irish History at UCD, 1964-1994, becoming Professor, School of Irish Studies, Dublin, 1972-1989, and was founding Principal, Ballyfermot Senior College. A leading women's historian, she was active in the Irish Labour History Society, particularly in organising their ground-breaking Conference on 'Women in Labour History' in 1975.

Fergus McCabe, from Marino, was a committed community worker and leading figure in the Inner City Organisations Network, CityWide Drugs Crisis Campaign and Community Work Ireland. He was involved with Young People at Risk, the National Substance Misuse Strategy Committee and National Oversight Group of the National Drugs Strategy.

Angela (Nolan) McQuillan was the energetic, final Secretary, Ireland-USSR Society, 1985-1991, her Russian language skills complementing her commitment to deepening understanding of the Soviet Union in Ireland. From Roscommon, she was married to John 'Jack' McQuillan, Clann na Poblachta/Independent/National Progressive Democrats/Labour TD for the county, 1948-1965, and formed lifelong friendships with Noël & Phyllis Browne.

Colm Ó Bríain was deeply active in theatre and the arts, serving as Arts Council Director, 1973-1983; founding the Project Arts Centre, 1967, and the National Association of Drama for Young People, 1980, as well as working for RTÉ, the Abbey Theatre and the National College of Art and Design. He was Labour Party General Secretary, 1983-1985, overseeing organisational reforms, appointment of the Party's first Youth Officer, and serving as Special Adviser to Minister for the Arts, Michael D. Higgins.

Ken Quinn, a butcher and lifelong Larkinite, was active in the Workers' Union of Ireland Meat Federation before becoming a FWUI/SIPTU official in Dublin, Clonmel, Waterford and Wexford. A founder member of the Socialist Workers' Movement, he was brother of the long-standing FWUI/SIPTU National Trustee Jim Quinn.

Edwina Stewart, a lifelong member of the Communist Party of Ireland, acquired her communism from her activist parents Eddy and Sadie Menzies, and developed it alongside her husband, James (Jimmy) Stewart, CPI General Secretary, 1984-2001. Edwina was Secretary, Northern Ireland Civil Rights Association, 1969-1977; served on the CPI National Executive from 1970.; and was an influential, pioneering voice for women's rights, anti-sectarianism; peace; and class politics.

Foreword

Brendan Scott: An Ever Present, Past & Future Tense

On the first day that I started work in the Education & Training Department of the Irish Transport & General Workers' Union (ITGWU) in September 1974, my fellow Tutor Des Geraghty handed me a bundle of cyclostyled notes written by someone called Brendan Scott. They dealt with economics and politics and what I later discovered to be a draft of *Labour and Socialism*.[1] I was impressed, the content being close to positions that I had developed while active in Clann na hÉireann and reading *Rosc Catha*, *United Irishman* and the *Irish Democrat*. There was an elegant, accessible style to the writing which – as I soon discovered – translated easily to the classroom, an acetate slide and overhead projector. I drew on them for years.

I was anxious to meet the author of this work whom everyone that I talked to spoke of so highly. I was disappointed to discover that he had died on 19 September 1973, not least as I was commonly told – for long afterwards – 'you'd have got on well with Brendan Scott', 'it's a pity you never met Brendan Scott' and so on. He became a subject of fascination. I asked all those that I met in the movement had they known him and what could they tell me. Eventually, memories faded and he slipped from view, the fate we all face. I never forgot him though despite never having met him.

When a few of us re-launched a Labour Party Branch in Howth in the early 1980s – with the consent of the Sutton Branch we were members of – we decided at our inaugural meeting that the branch should have a name that reflected our essential views. Angela 'Angie' Ó Laoire suggested 'Scott Gilmore' and that is what the branch became. We were subsequently often asked by Labour Party Head Office and others, 'Who was Scott Gilmore?' Our reply was that Scott Gilmore was four people – Brendan Scott, George, Harry and Charlie Gilmore!

George Gilmore, when I briefly knew him, walked with the aid of sticks, a rucksack behind him, and lived at the Slads on Howth Summit. I found him to be a somewhat silent, aloof man but he once allowed me engage him in a lengthy conversation about his involvement in the Republican Congress.[2] He wrote of those experiences and remained a Connollyite, encouraging me to hold firm to socialist republican values.[3] Harry I never met but understand that he shared his brother's views. Charlie was a gregarious presence around Howth when I moved there in 1981, famous for his nautical cap and sailing the beautiful hooker *St John* with her maroon sails. Charlie often shared documents which he produced over a pint from a jacket pocket. I encouraged him to tell the story of his part in the defence of Connolly House in 1933, a tale he told with relish and a promise that he 'would do it again if needed'.[4]

Members who knew Brendan Scott – and quite a few did – argued for the branch simply to be named after him but the Gilmores were well-known, lived on the peninsula and the combination of names distanced the branch from the divisions and dissension of its previous, divided and ultimately expelled existence in the Conor Cruise O'Brien period. We sought approval to use Scott's name from his wife, Carol Ann, who gave it readily but gathering material on his life proved problematic.

Our difficulty underlines the value of what John P. Swift has done in reconstructing as much of Brendan Scott's life and writings as he could. Swift previously wrote an acclaimed biography of his father, Bakers' Union leader John Swift, under the title *An Irish Dissident*.[5] It is a title that might equally apply to Scott. What Swift's study of Scott's life demonstrates is the dynamic swirl of dissidence that emerged in the 1960s with many of its activists engaged simultaneously in trade unions; labour and socialist politics; civil rights and republicanism; housing action; gender equality and challenging Catholic social doctrine and sectarianism; anti-imperialism and support for liberation movements in Africa, Asia, Central American and elsewhere; opposing Apartheid in South Africa; peace and nuclear disarmament; extending friendship to and understanding of the Soviet Union; traditional music, folk song and rock; youth movements; and even the beginnings of what would now be called environmentalism. Forensic tests would discover Scott's DNA permeating most of these activities.

So many names of those involved with Scott in the Labour Party – directly and in Left pressure groups within the party, Irish Anti-Apartheid Movement, Ireland-USSR Society, Dublin Housing Action Committee and more, went on to become senior figures in the trade union movement, politics, journalism or the arts. What Scott's destiny was will never be known but his influence on all the others mentioned was significant and unanimously acknowledged by them in contemporary tributes – like those by Kader Asmal and Noël Browne for example – or in interviews with Swift for this study.

After being handed those notes, Brendan Scott became an ever-present in my life, a figure of fascination, an inspiration through his writings and deeds. Swift's study answers many questions, raises others, explains personal and political linkages that I had wondered about, and deepens my regret that I never had the opportunity to meet and work with Scott. I did argue with Swift that he surely had better choices for someone to write a 'Foreword' to his study of Scott other than me as I had never known him. Swift knew, however, that I was aware of Scott, seeing him as my template as worker educationalist.

I thus read Swift's life of Scott with intense interest, gathering an understanding and deeper appreciation of its subject, his immense, wide-ranging and selfless activism. He was and remains a personally inspiring figure. But then too, so is the author. I was privileged to know his parents

John and Harriet Swift (née Hendy), regularly visiting their home in Dundrum – usually to 'receive instruction' from a Marxian catechism from John. My engagement in labour history owes much to him. 'Young John' was a long-standing ITGWU/SIPTU colleague, an inspiration behind the creation of the Musicians' Union of Ireland – as well as historian of the hugely impressive history of musicians' unions – and a constant, respected political comrade.[6] I could not refuse his request and have been enriched by it.

There are those that might question 'why write a biography of a largely forgotten, relatively minor figure like Scott?'[7] Well, as has been argued here and will become apparent below, for those who knew him he was no minor figure. Even if he was – by standards that judge significance only by elected position, leadership role or major published work – not hugely significant, his thinking, speaking and writing was at the heart of many broad, challenging debates that questioned the unthinking orthodoxy of the time. Oh, that such intellectual leadership for alternative, socialist thought was available today to infuse the working class movement with perspectives of internationalism, global environmental awareness and, above all, hope and belief that things can be changed, permanently, for the better!

So, the book is not about what Scott could or might have been but what he was and is. In short, where is the Brendan Scott we need today? That alone is reason for Swift to write the book and for us to read it. Scott would derive little satisfaction from reading his own biography – he shunned any limelight – but would seek to know what actions, organising activities and political engagements it moved its readers to.

If you wish to honour Scott's memory, do as he would do: commit to the cause of liberating and uniting humanity. In that respect, Scott's significance is his ever presence in both past and future tenses: truly a substantial legacy.

Francis Devine,
Musicians' Union of Ireland,
September 2020

Notes

1   'Left Archive: *Labour and Socialism* by Brendan Scott (1973), with an appreciation of Brendan Scott by Dr. Noel Browne, c. 1973 June 22, 2015', https://cedarlounge. wordpress.com/2015/06/22/left-archive-labour-and-socialism-by-brendan-scott-1973-with-an-appreciation-of-brendan-scott-by-dr-noel-browne-c-1973/. The document is reproduced in facsimile here https://cedarlounge.files.wordpress.com/ 2015/06/labour-and-socialism.pdf [both retrieved 12 September 2020].

2   Anthony Coughlan, George Gilmore – Protestant Republican, *Village*, (n.d), https://villagemagazine.ie/george-gilmore-protestant-republican/;   Diarmuid Ferriter, 'Gilmore, George (1898-1985), republican socialist', *Dictionary of Irish Biography, vol. 4*, (RIA/Cambridge University Press, Cambridge, 2009), pp. 99-100. George Gilmore, *The Irish Republican Congress*, (Cork Workers' Club, Historical reprints 4, Cork, 2011), 1934 edition available at www.connollyassociation.org.uk/

irish-republican-congress/irish-republican-congress/; https://cedarlounge.files.
wordpress.com/2011/08/mail0077.jpg; *Labour & the Republican Movement*, (Sinn
Féin, Dublin, 1966), available at https://cedarlounge.wordpress.com/2011/08/29/
left-archive-labour-and-the-republican-movement-by-george-gilmore-introduction-
by-peadar-odonnell-sinn-fein-december-1966/ [both retrieved 12 September 2020].

3 NUIG's Hardiman Library holds the papers of George Gilmore, G41, http://vm-
server52.nuigalway.ie/col_level.php?col=G41 [retrieved 12 September 2020].

4 Brian Hanley, 'The Storming of Connolly House', *History Ireland*, vol. 7 (2), Summer
1999, pp. 5-7, and reproduced here http://irelandscw.com/docs-CHsiege.htm
[re5trieved 12 September 2020].

5 John P. Swift, *John Swift: An Irish Dissident*, (Gill & Macmillan, Dublin, 1991). Swift's
production of the quarterly Musicians' Union of Ireland (MUI) Newsletter *Sound
Post* from Spring 2003 to the present is a significant achievement.

6 John P. Swift, *Striking a Chord: A Trade Union History of Musicians in Ireland*, (Watchword, Dublin, 2012).

7 His biography does not appear in the *Dictionary of Irish Biography* but should do so
after Swift's work is published.

Preface

Ever since the death of Brendan Scot at the age of forty in 1973, I had periodically considered researching and writing an article or a pamphlet about his life and times. My reluctance to proceed was based on what turned out to be an unfounded belief that there would be insufficient records to document his life. Eventually, in early 2018, on the occasion of the funeral of Brendan Scott's wife, Carol Ann Scott (née O'Rourke), with whom I had worked in the trade union movement, I made myself known to their eldest son, Eoin Scott, with a view to discussing the possibility of writing an article or pamphlet on his father.

Subsequently Eoin Scott and his siblings, Melanie Scott and Ivan Scott, provided me with unlimited access to Brendan Scott's papers, which included significant published and unpublished articles and speeches he had written. Further relevant material was sourced from others who were friends or colleagues of Brendan Scott. The Labour Party records deposited in the National Library in recent years were an invaluable source of information, as were many other labour movement records in the Irish Labour History Society's Archive and in private collections. A parallel trawl of other sources of information on Brendan Scott, including the national, regional and left-wing press proved to be a great deal more productive than I had anticipated. I also gleaned much from my interviews with Eoin, Melanie and Ivan Scott and with many others, including former colleagues and friends of Brendan Scott.

By the end of 2018, it had become evident that the project I had undertaken could not be confined to an article or a pamphlet and that there was sufficient material for a book.

Despite all the overlaps in the activities in which Brendan Scott was engaged, I have attempted to approach his biography chronologically as far as possible.

Readers should note that the John Swift mentioned in the narrative of this book refers, not to the author, but the author's father, John Swift (1896-1990), the former General Secretary of the Irish Bakers', Confectioners' and Allied Workers' Amalgamated Union and colleague of Brendan Scott in many progressive organisations and campaigns, including the Labour Party, the Liaison Committee of the Left – Labour Party (LCLL) and the Ireland-USSR Society.

John P. Swift
October 2020

Acknowledgements

For their assistance in researching this biography of Brendan Scott, I thank the staffs of the following institutions: the Central Statistics Office, the National Archives, the National Library, Trinity College, Dublin, Library, University College, Dublin, Library, Dublin City Library and Archive, Dún Laoghaire Public Library (Lexicon), the Irish Labour History Society Archive, RTÉ Photographic Archive, SIPTU Library, the Registry of Friendly Societies and UCD Freedom of Information Office.

I also thank the following individuals for their assistance with this project: Susan Boland (née O'Rourke), Ethel Buckley, Frank Buckley, Charles Callan, Alicia Carrigy (née Edwards), Pat Carroll, Aidan Clarke, Sandra Collins, Fergal Costello, Orla Cullen, John Cunningham, Fergus D'Arcy, Francis Devine, Michael (Mick) Dowling, Gerard Duffy, Patsy Duffy (née Burke), Tony Dunne, Sean Edwards, Eamonn Farrell, Eithne FitzGerald (née Ingoldsby), Eric Fleming, Ita Gannon (née McGrath), Jack Gannon, Des Geraghty, Tom Geraghty, Niall Greene, Brendan Halligan, John Horgan, Máirín Johnston (née Mooney), Jean Kennedy, Gearóid Kilgallen, D. R. O'Connor Lysaght, Padraig Mannion, Donal McCartney, John McDonnell, Helen McGinley (née Bonar), Kieran Jack McGinley, Catherine McGuinness (née Ellis), John Medlycott, Bob Mitchell, David Neligan, Sam Nolan, Michael (Mick) O'Reilly, Pádraig Ó Snodaigh, David Patterson, Ed Penrose, Richard Pine, Michael Quinn, Pearl Quinn, Dermot Quish, Mary Sealy (née Simms), Adrienne Swift (née Walker), David Swift, Justin Swift, Neville Swift, Robert Swift, Yseult Thornley, Julian Walton and Michael Williams.

For identifying material and sources that I might otherwise have missed, I am grateful to Charles Callan, Pat Carroll, Fergal Costello, Fergus D'Arcy, Francis Devine, Ita Gannon, Jack Gannon, Des Geraghty, D. R. O'Connor Lysaght, Kieran Jack McGinley, John Medlycott and Richard Pine. For placing at my disposal relevant documents and/or publications and/or photographs, I am grateful to Ethel Buckley, Brendan Byrne, Charles Callan, Pat Carroll, Fergal Costello, Fergus Darcy, Francis Devine, Michael (Mick) Dowling, Eamonn Farrell, Ita Gannon, Jack Gannon, Des Geraghty, Niall Greene, Máirín Johnston, Gearóid Kilgallen, John McDonnell, John Medlycott, Ed Penrose, Pearl Quinn, Eoin Scott, Melanie Scott, Ivan Scott, Yseult Thornley and Julian Walton.

For reading draft chapter(s) of my manuscript, I am grateful to Fergal Costello, Jack Gannon, Ita Gannon Gearóid Kilgallen, Eoin Scott, Melanie Scott and Ivan Scott; for reading the entire text, I thank David Patterson and Adrienne Swift. I am grateful to all of them for their many useful comments and observations. I am particularly indebted to the labour historians, Charles Callan, Francis Devine, and Kieran Jack McGinley,

Principal, Umiskin Press, who also read the entire text, making many pertinent observations. In researching this book, their general advice, assistance and support were invaluable. Needless to say, any errors or omissions are entirely my responsibility. Francis Devine is also thanked for contributing *September Song, 1973*, his poetical tribute to Brendan Scott and the Foreword of this book.

For photo enhancing and editing I thank David Swift and Justin Swift; for typing Appendices 3 and 5, I thank Sandra Collins; for other general technical assistance, I am grateful to Orla Cullen, Justin Swift, Neville Swift and Robert Swift.

Special thanks are due to Eoin, Melanie and Ivan Scott for answering my interminable queries. Incidentally, following in their parents' footsteps, Eoin Scott, a member of the Labour Party, and Melanie Scott have been and are actively involved in many progressive causes and campaigns.

I thank Kieran Jack McGinley and Umiskin Press for accepting my manuscript for publication. I also thank Christy Hammond and his colleagues at CRM Design and Print for their contribution to the design and production of this book.

Finally, I would like to thank my wife, Adrienne, and our five sons, David, Justin, John, Neville and Robert, for their support and encouragement in relation to this project.

John P. Swift
October 2020

Abbreviations

AC	Administrative Council (Labour Party)
AGM	Annual General Meeting
ARIAM	Associate Royal Irish Academy of Music
ASTI	Association of Secondary Teachers Ireland
ASTMS	Association of Scientific, Technical and Managerial Staffs
ATGWU	Amalgamated Transport and General Workers' Union
BA	Bachelor of Arts
BBC	British Broadcasting Corporation
BICO	British and Irish Communist Organisation
CC	Catholic Curate
CCL	Citizens for Civil Liberties
CIA	Central Intelligence Agency
CIU	Congress of Irish Unions
CND	Campaign for Nuclear Disarmament
CORL	Campaign to Oppose Repressive Legislation
CPI	Communist Party of Ireland
CPSU	Communist Party of the Soviet Union
CSEU	Civil Service Executive Union
CSO	Central Statistics Office
CUS	Catholic University School
CYM	Connolly Youth Movement
DCL&A	Dublin City Library & Archive
DCTU	Dublin Council of Trade Unions
DL	Democratic Left
DTUC	Dublin Trade Union Council
DHAC	Dublin Housing Action Committee
Dr.	Doctor
DRC	Dublin Regional Council ([Labour Party)
DSP	Democratic Socialist Party
EEC	European Economic Community
GIO	Guild of Insurance Officials
GPO	General Post Office
HTAI	History Teachers' Association of Ireland
IAAM	Irish Anti-Apartheid Movement
IALSO	Irish Association of Labour Student Organisations
IBCAWAU	Irish Bakers', Confectioners' and Allied Workers' Amalgamated Union
ICO	Irish Communist Organisation
ICTU	Irish Congress of Trade Unions
ILHS	Irish Labour History Society
IMETU	Irish Municipal Employees' Trade Union
INTO	Irish National Teachers' Organisation
IPA	Institute of Public Administration
IRA	Irish Republican Army
IRFU	Irish Rugby Football Association
ITGWU	Irish Transport and General Workers' Union
ITUC	Irish Trade Union Congress
IVV	Irish Voice on Vietnam
IWL	Irish Workers' League

IWLM	Irish Women's Liberation Movement
IWP	Irish Workers' Party
LCLL	Liaison Committee of the Left (Labour Party)
LRAM	Licentiate Royal Academy of Music
LRIAM	Licentiate Royal Irish Academy of Music
MA	Master of Arts
MC	Master of Ceremonies
MEP	Member of the European Parliament
MP	Member of Parliament (UK)
NATO	National Association of Tenants' Associations
NATO	North Atlantic Treaty Organisation
NEC	National Executive Committee
NICRA	Northern Ireland Civil Rights Association
NILP	Northern Ireland Labour Party
NLF	National Liberation Front (Vietnam)
NLI	National Library of Ireland
NPD	National Progressive Democratic (Party), commonly known as the National Progressive Democrats or NPDs
NUVB	National Union of Vehicle Builders
OP	Order of Preachers or Dominican (formal name of the Dominicans)
POOA	Post Office Officials' Association
QUB	Queen's University, Belfast
RIA	Royal Irish Academy
RTÉ	Raidió Teilifís Éireann
RUC	Royal Ulster Constabulary
SC	Senior Counsel
SDLP	Social Democratic and Labour Party
SJ	Society of Jesus
SIPTU	Services Industrial Professional and Technical Union
SMB	Foreign Missions Society (Switzerland), commonly known as the Bethlehem Fathers
SPD	Social Democratic Party of Germany
SPI	Socialist Party of Ireland
TB	Tuberculosis
TCD	Trinity College Dublin
TD	Teachta Dála (a member of Dáil Éireann)
TV	Television
UCD	University College Dublin
UIO	Union of Insurance Officials
UK	United Kingdom
UMDC	United May Day Committee
UN	United Nations
UNESCO	United Nations Educational, Scientific and Cultural Organisation
US	United States [of America]
USA	United States of America
USSR	Union of Soviet Socialist Republics
UUP	Ulster Unionist Party
VAT	Value Added Tax
WLM	Women's Liberation Movement
WP	Workers' Party
WUI	Workers' Union of Ireland

List of Photographs

Photograph Credits

No.	Photographer	Source
Front cover		RTÉ Photographic Archive
1.		Scott Family Collection
2.		Scott Family Collection
3.		Scott Family Collection
4.		Scott Family Collection
5.		Yseult Thornley Collection
6.		Scott Family Collection
7.		Yseult Thornley Collection
8.		Scott Family Collection
9.		Scott Family Collection
10.		Scott Family Collection
11.		Scott Family Collection
12.		John Medlycott Collection
13.		SIPTU
14.		*Irish Independent*/Swift Collection
15.		RTÉ Photographic Archive
16	Fergal Costello	Máirín Johnston Collection
17.	Fergal Costello	Máirín Johnston Collection.
18.		Eamonn Farrell Collection
	George Jeffares	Swift Collection
20	George Jeffares	Brendan Byrne Collection
21.	John P. Swift	Swift Collection
22.		*Irish Socialist*/Swift Collection
23.		Gearóid Kilgallen Collection
24.		Scott Family Collection
25.		Eamonn Farrell Collection
26.		Yseult Thornley Collection
27.	David Swift	Swift Collection
28.		Scott Family collection
29.		*Liaison*/Irish Labour History Society Archive
30.	Francis Devine	Francis Devine Collection

For

Adrienne
David, Justin, John, Neville & Robert

Umiskin Press, Ireland

Umiskin Press is a not-for-profit publishing house, publishing commissioned and non-commissioned works mainly, though not exclusively, works of labour history, Labour interest, trade union issues, biography, poetry, cultural and social matters. Umiskin is a townland in Kilcar, County Donegal, birthplace of the McGinleys.

Dr. Kieran Jack McGinley is the Principal of Umiskin Press having previously been Chairman of Watchword Ltd., and is the immediate Past President of the ILHS 2014 - September 2020.

WILLIAM WALKER
Social Activist & Belfast Labourist
1870–1918

Mike Mecham
Foreword by Alvin Jackson

Umiskin's recent publications were three volumes of *Left Lives in Twentieth Century Ireland* co-edited by Francis Devine and McGinley (Vol 1+2; Devine & Smylie (Volume 3 - April 2020); Mike Mecham's William Walker, Social Activist & Belfast Labourist (1870-1918) October 2019; Devine & Sean Byers: William Walker Centenary Essays (2018).

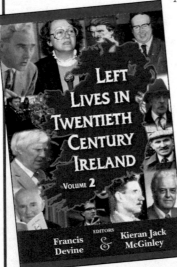

LEFT LIVES IN TWENTIETH CENTURY IRELAND
VOLUME 2
EDITORS
Francis Devine & Kieran Jack McGinley

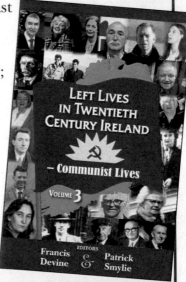

LEFT LIVES IN TWENTIETH CENTURY IRELAND
– Communist Lives
VOLUME 3
EDITORS
Francis Devine & Patrick Smylie

Umiskin Press publishes limited editions of hardback and paperback volumes of between 150 and 500 per print run.

CHAPTER 1

From Easkey to London

Brendan Scott, a teacher by profession, was a visionary socialist, secularist, human rights activist and internationalist. Throughout his short life he campaigned relentlessly for social justice, human rights and a socialist and secular Ireland. A radical member of the Labour Party, he was a committed, consistent champion of left unity. From the mid to the late 1960s, a time of major political, economic and social change in Ireland, Scott was an influential figure in Labour's adoption of a radical socialist programme. In terms of policy, this transformed possibly the most conservative Labour Party in Western Europe into arguably the most radical one. When, in the early 1970s, Labour distanced itself from its core socialist policies, clearing the way for a Fine Gael-Labour Coalition Government, Scott was a key opponent of that development.

Aside from his involvement in the labour movement, Scott was active in a number of other progressive organisations, among them the Irish Anti-Apartheid Movement and the Ireland-USSR Society, of which he was Secretary and Vice-President, respectively; the Irish Voice on Vietnam and the Dublin Housing Action Committee.

Of outstanding integrity and ability, Scott was a charismatic figure with an engaging personality and keen sense of humour. Intelligent, knowledgeable, articulate and modest, he had a profound knowledge of such subjects as philosophy, history, politics, education and literature. Constantly in demand as a platform speaker, he was also an accomplished writer. Some of his writings on historical, political and other topics appeared in the national and left-wing press. His most significant written work, his pamphlet, *Labour and Socialism* (Appendix 1), completed in January 1973, was published posthumously within a month of his death.

Born in the Atlantic coastal village of Easkey, County Sligo, on 8 May 1933, Brendan Michael Dominic Scott, to mention his full name, was the eldest of two sons[1] of Martin Scott (1893-1970) and Sarah (Colleen) Scott, née Kilduff (1895-1968). A native of Killeenduff, County Sligo,[2] Brendan's father, a postman, was a participant in the War of Independence and, as a result of his involvement in either that event or possibly the Civil War, fled to America.[3] Back in Ireland, he married Colleen Kilduff, a native of Easkey, in 1930, and the couple settled in Easkey.[4] A National School teacher in the village of Cloonin Mór, some eight miles from her home, Colleen, a shopkeeper's daughter, was a major influence on Brendan.[5] Brendan's parents were Fianna Fáil voters and the family religion was Roman Catholic.[6]

Brendan Scott commenced his formal education at Easkey National School. Remarkably, at Easkey's 'Gaelic' revival movement's annual Feis in 1943, in a competition for over fourteen-year-olds, Scott, then aged ten, shared second prize in one of the categories of Irish language awards.[7] Prior to completing his primary education, Scott won a scholarship to the Patrician College, Ballyfin, County Laois.[8] During his time there, he was a member of the College's Dramatic Guild, participating, for example, in 'a most impressive production' of the drama, *Franciscan Spring*, in December 1950, 'before a great audience, which included many clergy.'[9] He was then seventeen. Throughout his life, he retained an interest in theatre, performing periodically in various productions over the years. In an observation on this particular interest of Scott's, his friend and colleague, Ruarc Gahan,[10] later said: 'He…had a remarkable gift for spoof, and indeed considerable potential as an actor.'[11]

On concluding his schooling, in 1952, Scott declined a scholarship to All Hallows College, Drumcondra,[12] in favour of a Sligo County Council scholarship to University College, Dublin (UCD).[13] A year later he was awarded a UCD scholarship, his subjects being history, Irish and English.[14] The Sligo County Council scholarship was renewed in September 1954[15] and extended for a further year in October 1955.[16] However, in September 1956, presumably for financial reasons, the Council declined to renew the scholarship for a further year.[17] After attaining an Honours BA degree in History in 1955,[18] Scott obtained a History MA the following year.[19] He found employment as a part-time history tutor in UCD.

In the mid-1950s, the by then politically radicalised Brendan Scott met his future wife, Carol Ann O'Rourke, an undergraduate at UCD. Subsequently, Carol Ann's parents had reservations concerning their proposed marriage. Aside from misgivings about Brendan's lack of permanent, full-time employment, they were less than enthusiastic about his radical politics. Nevertheless, Brendan, then twenty-three, and Carol Ann, twenty, married in St. Joseph's Church, Glasthule, County Dublin, on 18 March 1957. Their wedding reception, held in the Royal Marine Hotel, Dún Laoghaire, was followed by a honeymoon in the West of Ireland.[20] The best man, David Thornley,[21] a distant cousin of Carol Ann's, was later a presenter of RTÉ's flagship, current affairs television programme, *Seven Days*, Associate Professor of Political Science at Trinity College, Dublin (TCD) and a Labour Party TD. That would appear to have been the high point of the relationship between Brendan Scott and David Thornley, the former subsequently taking a socialist and secular path, the latter a nationalist-republican one.

Almost four years younger than Brendan, Carol Ann was born in Dublin on 2 January 1937. She was the eldest of four children of Martha O'Rourke (née Carroll), a civil servant up to the time of her marriage, when she was obliged to resign, and Dermod O'Rourke, an architect. At the time of Brendan and Carol Ann's marriage, the O'Rourke family, which was also

Roman Catholic, resided at 4 Arkendale Road, Glenageary, County Dublin. Educated at Loreto College, St. Stephen's Green, Carol Ann was studying for a BMus at UCD when she met Brendan. However, after becoming pregnant with their first child, Eoin, she did not complete the course. Less than three months following her marriage, while still an undergraduate at UCD, Carol Ann won the Murray Cup for Senior Piano at the Sligo Feis Ceoil. The *Irish Independent* Music Critic, Mary MacGoris, was impressed: 'Carol Ann Scott gave a lovely performance of Ravel, but her Bach and selections of Mendelssohn were equally fine.'[22] Five years later, she won the premier award, the Delaney Memorial Cup.[23] Later, her piano studies at the Royal Irish Academy of Music (RIAM), Dublin, with Rhona Marshall and Dorothy Stokes, culminated in three teaching diplomas: ARIAM, LRIAM and LRAM, London. Carol Ann went on to have a successful music teaching career in Sutton Park School and in the RIAM.[24] Brendan and Carol Ann had three children, Eoin, Melanie and Ivan, born, respectively, in 1957, 1958 and 1967.

With Brendan and Carol Ann expecting their first child prior to their marriage, a difficult situation in the Ireland of the 1950s, particularly for Carol Ann's devout Catholic mother, the Scotts moved to London in 1957.[25] Another reason for relocating was the absence of suitable employment in Ireland. Residing initially at 8 Tayfare Street, Streatham, the Scotts re-located to 45 Telford Avenue, Streatham, in July 1957 and subsequently to 6 Handen Road, Lee.[26] In London, Brendan obtained a teaching post at a Secondary Modern School, augmenting his income by working as a barman in the evenings.[27] For some of their time in London, the Scotts shared a flat with Aidan Clarke,[28] a son of the poet, Austin Clarke, and a future Professor of History and Vice-Provost of TCD.[29]

Two years later, in 1959, following Brendan's appointment as a geography teacher at Sutton Park School,[30] the Scott family returned permanently to Dublin.[31] At Sutton Park, Brendan also taught 'some Latin'[32] and in one particular year successfully taught five subjects to Leaving Certificate honours level.[33] Residing initially with Carol Ann's parents in Glenageary, the family moved around 1963 to their own house at 14 Maywood Grove, in the Dublin suburb of Raheny, remaining there until around the late 1960s when they relocated to 8 Shielmartin Drive, Sutton.[34] Back in Dublin, Scott resumed his formal education at UCD, obtaining a Higher Diploma in Education in 1960.[35]

Sutton Park School was established in 1957 by mainly Protestant business people in Howth and Sutton who did not wish to have their children educated in Roman Catholic schools. Originally catering for day pupils and boarders, it is now a day school. It was and remains a private, progressive, pupil-centred, co-educational, first and second level school. Although, formally, multi-denominational in character, Sutton Park is, effectively, non-denominational.[36] Much of the credit for its liberal ethos is attributable to the original Headmaster, Ruarc Gahan, and his many progressive colleague teachers, including Brendan and Carol Ann Scott.

In their early teaching years at Sutton Park, Brendan and Carol Ann twice visited alternative or 'free' schools in Britain that were providing 'democratic' education, namely Summerhill in Suffolk and Kilquhanity in Scotland.[37] Founded in 1921 by Alexander Sutherland Neill, with the belief that the school should be made to fit the child, rather than the other way around, Summerhill is an independent, fee paying, co-educational, boarding school. It was then run as a democratic community, the running being conducted at school meetings open to all staff and pupils, where everyone had an equal vote. These meetings served as both a legislative and judicial body. Members of the community were free to do as they pleased, so long as their actions did not cause any harm to others, according to Neill's principle 'Freedom, not Licence.' This extended to the freedom for pupils to choose which lessons, if any, they attended. The philosophy of Kilquhanity School, which was founded by John Aitkenhead and his wife, Morag Aitkenhead (née MacKinnon), in 1940, was heavily influenced by the writings of Neill, the founder of Summerhill, where Aitkenhead had worked, that is to say, 'children learn best with freedom from coercion.'

Exchange visits between Sutton Park School and British liberal schools were initiated by Ruarc Gahan in 1959, when H. B. Jacks, Headmaster of Bedales School, in the village of Steep, in Hampshire, addressed a Sutton Park parents' meeting.[38] In 1967, another parents' meeting was addressed by Michael Duane, 'a charismatic advocate of progressive and non-authoritarian education' and former Headmaster of Risinghill, an early comprehensive school in Islington, London.[39] Other Sutton Park parents' meetings were addressed by the aforementioned A. S. O'Neill of Summerhill, in 1968[40] and John Aitkenhead of Kilquhanity, in 1971.[41] Under Ruarc Gahan's leadership, some of the educational experiments initiated in these British schools were implemented in Sutton Park.[42]

At Sutton Park, Scott and his teaching colleagues were members of the trade union, the Association of Secondary Teachers Ireland (ASTI). Although Scott appears to have been uninvolved in national union affairs, probably because Sutton Park was a relatively small school,[43] he was for a period the local ASTI union representative and was in office during the three-week national teachers' strike in February 1969.[44] At issue was the ASTI's refusal to accept the recommendations of the Ryan Tribunal on teachers' pay. The Tribunal's principal recommendation, the introduction of a common basic salary for all teachers, did not find favour with the secondary teachers.

Although no longer the local union representative, Scott found himself informally in a similar position in September 1970 when the School's Board of Directors sacked the Headmaster, Ruarc Gahan. In a written account of that event, in which he contended he had been dismissed 'over some triviality', Gahan went on to say:

> After my dismissal I walked straight over to the house of my friend and colleague Brendan Scott, who had worked with me at Sutton Park for eleven years. The

next morning Brendan saw to it that the entire staff was alerted, and a staff meeting was arranged for mid-day...I related the circumstances of my dismissal and withdrew. The staff decided unanimously to withhold their services until I was reinstated...Surprised by the solid support for me, the directors eventually felt the need for a face-saving formula...I was reinstated subject to two conditions: I would not be present during the financial part of Board meetings (which had always bored me anyway), and I would always be accompanied at Board meetings by a member of staff, who was to see that I did whatever the Board told me to do.[45]

Beyond Sutton Park School, while a lecturer in Methodology of History at St. Patrick's College, Maynooth, in the early 1970s, Scott represented staff at conferences with the employer, the Catholic bishops.[46]

Notes

1   Brendan Scott's younger brother was Basil Scott.
2   Melanie Scott, email to the author, 31 December 2019.
3   Interview with Eoin and Melanie Scott, 23 August 2019.
4   Melanie Scott, email to the author, 31 December 2019.
5   Interview with John Medlycott, 1 November 2018; Melanie Scott, email to author, 30 May 2020, in which she stated: 'As Eoin [Scott] said Colleen...Scott was a huge influence on our father, Brendan Scott – both through her intellect and her personality. We believe she was the person who pushed for him to be educated at a boarding school to try to ensure he reached his educational potential and have no doubt she taught him a lot in his early years using her teaching abilities. I clearly recall that he was devastated when she died.'
6   Interview of Eoin and Melanie Scott, 23 August 2019.
7   *Western People*, 3 July 1943.
8   Interview with Gerard Duffy (first cousin of Brendan Scott), 25 February 2019.
9   *Leinster Express*, 16 December 1950.
10 For further information on Ruarc Gahan see Ian Blake, 'Irish Schools: Sutton Park School', *Irish Times*, 26 May 1965; Ruarc Gahan *Sutton Park School: The First Fifteen Years, A personal memoir*, undated, 1975.
11 Ruarc Gahan, 'Brendan Scott: An Appreciation', *Irish Times*, 24 September 1973.
12 Interview with Eoin Scott, 15 January 2010.
13 *Ballina Herald*, 11 October 1952.
14 *Irish Independent*, 1 August 1953.
15 *Ballina Herald, Western People*, 11 September 1954.
16 *Ballina Herald*, 8 October 1955.
17 *Sligo Champion*, 8 September 1956.
18 *Ballina Herald*, 3 December 1955.
19 UCD (Freedom of Information) email to the author, 23 January 2019.
20 *Irish Times*, 19 March 1957.
21 ibid., 19 March 1957. For further information on David Thornley (1935-1978) see Yseult Thornley (Editor), *Unquiet Spirit: Essays in Memory of David Thornley* (Liberties Press, Dublin, 2008); Charles Callan and Barry Desmond, 'David Thornley (1935-1978)' *A Biographical Dictionary of Irish Labour Party Deputies, Senators, MPs and MEPs* (Watchword, Dublin, 2010), pp. 247-249; Edward Thornley, *Lone Crusader: David Thornley and the Intellectuals* (Ashfield Press, Dublin, 2012).
22 *Ballina Herald*, 4 May 1957.
23 *Irish Press, Irish Independent*, 26 April 1962.
24 John [P.] Swift, 'Carol Ann Scott (née O'Rourke) (1937-2018)', *Sound Post*, Volume

16, No. 2, Summer 2018, p. 18. In the mid-1970s, Carol Ann Scott married Brian Grimson, an English teacher at Mount Temple School, Dublin. After a couple of years or so, the couple separated and later divorced. Carol Ann Scott, who was later involved in the Divorce Action Campaign, died aged 81 on 31 January 2018.

25   Interview with Susan Boland, née O'Rourke (a sister of Carol Ann Scott), 7 March 2019.

26   Melanie Scott, email to the author, 9 May 2019.

27   Interview with Aidan Clarke, 14 January 2019.

28   Interviews with John Medlycott, 1 November 2018, and Aidan Clarke, 14 January 2019.

29   Kieran Jack McGinley, email to the author, 14 July 2020.

30   For further information on Sutton Park School see Ian Blake, 'Irish Schools: Sutton Park School', *Irish Times*, 26 May 1965; Ruarc Gahan, *Sutton Park School*, op. cit.

31   Ruarc Gahan, *Sutton Park School*, op. cit., p.12; Melanie Scott, email to the author, 13 August 2018.

32   Interview with John Medlycott, 22 November 2018.

33   Ruarc Gahan, 'Brendan Scott: An Appreciation', *Irish Times*, 24 September 1973.

34   Melanie Scott, email to the author, 13 August 2018.

35   *Irish Independent*, 11 July 1960.

36   Interview with Eoin Scott, 2019.

37   Eoin Scott, email to the author, 25 February 2020.

38   Ruarc Gahan, *Sutton Park School*, op. cit., p. 29.

39   ibid.

40   ibid., pp. 29-30.

41   Ruarc Gahan, *Sutton Park School*, op. cit., p. 30.

42   ibid.

43   ibid., p. 1. The total number of pupils at the school increased from 28 in 1957 to 228 by 1972.

44   Interview with John Medlycott, 22 November 2018.

45   Ruarc Gahan, *Sutton Park School*, op. cit., pp.34-35.

46   Interview with Pat Carroll, 30 October 2018.

CHAPTER 2

Political Awakening

The first couple of decades of Brendan Scott's life coincided with one of the most reactionary periods in European history. In the very year of his birth, Hitler came to power in Germany. By then, Italy and Portugal were already fascist states and Spain followed suit in 1936. That decade also saw the start of the Second World War, with all its appalling consequences including the Holocaust. In Ireland, the early 1930s witnessed the rise of the fascist Blueshirts, which, in 1933, merged with Cumann na nGaedheal and the National Centre Party to form Fine Gael. Economically, a policy of protectionism pursued by successive Irish Governments resulted in decades of stagnation, with high levels of unemployment and emigration. A virtual theocracy from the 1930s to at least the mid-1960s, Ireland was a deeply conservative and insular society. The Catholic Hierarchy wielded enormous power and influence in almost every aspect of life. In pursuing its objectives, the Hierarchy had recourse to a host of Catholic action lay groups, which harassed the few who dared to challenge Church rulings. Underpinning this reactionary society were the anti-socialist Papal Encyclicals, including *Quadragesimo Anno* and *Rerum Novarum* and, of course, the sectarian Irish Constitution of 1937. One of the most influential figures in drafting the Constitution was John Charles McQuaid, soon to become Catholic Archbishop of Dublin. The Dáil had sight of this document only after it had been submitted for papal approval![1]

None of the political parties, including Labour, was prepared to challenge the influence and power of the Catholic Hierarchy in social and political matters. For example, in 1939, following indirect pressure from the Hierarchy, the Labour Party amended its constitution to conform to Catholic teaching, removing a key section calling for public ownership of all essential sources of wealth and the establishment of a Workers' Republic.[2] Twelve years later, Labour again bowed to clerical pressure in relation to the Mother and Child Scheme. Introduced by Dr. Noël Browne,[3] Minister for Health in the First Inter-Party Government, the scheme contained proposals for free ante and post-natal care for mothers and the extension of free healthcare to all children under sixteen years of age. However, when the Hierarchy said in a statement: 'They must regard the scheme proposed by the Minister for Health as opposed to Catholic social teaching,'[4] Browne's Cabinet colleagues withdrew their support for these measures. Addressing the Dáil on the matter, on 17 April 1951, William Norton,[5] Tánaiste and Leader of the Labour Party, stated:

> If this question is raised as one in which the Bishops are to be on one side and
> the Government on the other side, I say, on behalf of the Government, that issue

is not going to arise in this country. This Government will not travel that road…
There will be no flouting of the authority of the Bishops in the matter of Catholic
social or Catholic moral teaching.[6]

Days earlier, completely isolated by his Government colleagues, including
Norton, Browne, then a member of Clann na Poblachta, resigned as
Minister for Health.

However, Browne did not distinguish himself on this matter. In the course
of his resignation speech in the Dáil, on 12 April 1951, he said: 'I as a
Catholic accept unequivocally and unreservedly the view of the Hierarchy
on this matter.'[7] The question could reasonably be asked: What then had
he been fighting for? Asked some twenty years later in a RTÉ television
interview why he had made this statement, he replied that he had done so
'for tactical reasons'[8] Elaborating a fortnight later at a Dublin meeting of
Labour Party members, Browne said that he was unable to criticise the
Church publicly in 1951 because he felt that there was little support for his
policy, but today [1971] support for a critical approach to the political
policies and actions of the Catholic Church had grown by leaps and bounds.
'I was afraid frankly, before, to criticise,' he said.[9]

For secularists such as Scott, Browne's capitulation on this issue must have
been perplexing, to say the least. That said, with the notable exception of
Browne, no member of Dáil Éireann was prepared to challenge the
Hierarchy on any issue that conflicted with the teachings of the Catholic
Church. On the contrary, politicians vied with each other to proclaim their
allegiance to the Hierarchy, none more so than the leaders of the Labour
Party. Brendan Corish,[10] Norton's successor as Labour Party Leader, was no
less subservient to the Catholic Hierarchy than his predecessor. In 1953, for
example, in the Dáil, Corish stated:

> I am an Irishman second; I am a Catholic first…If the Hierarchy give me any
> direction with regard to Catholic social teaching or Catholic moral teaching, I
> accept without qualification in all respects the teaching of the Hierarchy and the
> Church to which I belong.[11]

Catholic Church influence, of course, was not confined to the Labour Party.
It was prevalent in virtually every aspect of Irish life, including the trade
union movement. In 1950 'Holy Year', for instance, a delegation from the
all-Ireland Irish Bakers', Confectioners' and Allied Workers' Amalgamated
Union (IBCAWAU) paid an official visit to Pope Pius X11.[12] More significant
delegations to the Vatican that year were those of the Workers' Union
of Ireland (WUI),[13] and the breakaway Congress of Irish Unions (CIU),
whose principal affiliate was the Irish Transport and General Workers'
Union (ITGWU), another all-Ireland union.[14] Another manifestation of
sectarianism was the blessing by Catholic clerics of union headquarters,
including the IBCAWAU's Four Provinces House, Harcourt Street in 1948,[15]
the Workers' Union of Ireland's (WUI's) premises in Parnell Square in
1954,[16] and the ITGWU's re-constructed Liberty Hall, on May Day 1965, a
day described by the Union, not as May Day, but the Feast of St. Joseph the

Worker! In that particular case, the blessing was conferred by no less a figure than the Catholic Archbishop of Dublin, John Charles McQuaid.[17]

More significant that the foregoing manifestations of sectarianism was the support provided by many unions to the Catholic Workers' College.[18] Founded by the Jesuits, in Dublin, in 1951,[19] the College's aims and objectives had their inspiration in Catholic social principles originally expressed in the encyclicals of Popes Leo X111, Pius X1 and Pius X11.[20] When re-named as the College of Industrial Relations in 1966, one of its founders, Father Edward Kent, SJ, left no ambiguity concerning its ideology: 'It is unnecessary to say that the teaching and influence of the College is and will always be the teaching of the Church.'[21] Nevertheless, the ITGWU and the WUI were among many union affiliates of that body and sponsors of their members' participation in its courses.

Prior to the establishment of the Catholic Workers' College, courses in workers' education had been held in University College, Cork (UCC) under the direction of the College President, Professor of Theology, Alfred O'Rahilly, a committed corporatist. In Dublin, Father Edward Coyne, the noted Jesuit sociologist, had started night classes for young workers in UCD. As in Cork, Father Coyne's courses followed Catholic anti-socialist doctrine. All these initiatives by the Catholic authorities were to counter the influence of the non-sectarian People's College Adult Education Association, commonly known as the People's College, which was founded by the Irish Trade Union Congress (ITUC) in 1948.[22]

Taken together, events and developments of this kind made a deep impression on Scott, influencing his political thoughts and actions for the remainder of his life. Of independent mind, he was influenced mainly by Marx, Lenin and Connolly. Among political figures he most admired were Aneurin (Nye) Bevan[23], the Welsh-born, British Minister for Health and Housing who introduction the National Health Service after the Second World War; and Dr Noël Browne, the former Irish Minister for Health.

Informed by extensive reading of such subjects as philosophy, history, politics, literature and education, Brendan Scott's political awakening commenced as an undergraduate at UCD. He subsequently wrote widely on such matters and was constantly in demand as a platform speaker, capable of holding an audience in the palm of his hand with his wit and eloquence.[24] At Labour Party Conferences from the mid-1960s to the early 1970s, delegates would constantly be drifting in and out of the hall during most of the deliberations, except, of course, during the keynote addresses of the Party Chairman and the Party Leader. But apart from the occasional guest speaker, there were two other exceptions. When word circulated that either Noël Browne or Brendan Scott was about to speak, there would be a rush back to the hall to hear them.[25]

Scott's admiration for Browne was based on Browne's leading contribution to the eradication of tuberculosis (TB), his efforts to introduce the Mother and Child Scheme and his persistent, but often lone, advocacy of a radical socialist, secular and liberal society. Unlike Scott, Browne was reputed to be temperamental, unpredictable and egotistical. By virtually all accounts, working politically with Browne could be challenging, and not just for his moderate and right-wing opponents in the Labour Party. Matt Merrigan,[26] one of his most loyal, left-wing colleagues and admirers over many years, put it like this:

> He [Noël Browne] was difficult to work with as an equal. He was petulant and dismissive if differences emerged between him and us to the extent of walking out of meetings. Those who loved him did so from afar. Nearer the person it was toleration, and sometimes that was stretched to the limit.[27]

If Scott had difficulty with these aspects of Browne, he kept them to himself, remaining focused on the socialist and secular agendas.

Too much has been made of the fact that, in the course of his Dáil career, Browne served as an Independent and as a member of five political parties: Clann na Poblachta, Fianna Fáil, National Progressive Democrats, Labour Party and Socialist Labour Party. What is seldom mentioned, however, is that prior to becoming a member of Fianna Fáil in 1953, Browne's efforts to join Labour were successfully resisted by the Labour Leader, William Norton.[28] Furthermore, Browne's eventual admittance to the Labour Party in 1963 was initially opposed by both Norton and his successor, Brendan Corish.[29]

Politicians should be judged, not by the number of political parties they have been members of, but rather the policies they promoted, their efforts to implement those policies and their achievements. For most of his lengthy political career, irrespective of which party he belonged to, Browne campaigned consistently for a radical socialist, secular and liberal society. In pursuance of those objectives, with the honourable exception of his colleague, John (Jack) McQuillan,[30] he received little or no support from the Parliamentary Labour Party. Moreover, unlike several of his former Labour colleagues, Browne remained loyal to the labour movement for the remainder of his life. In that respect, he stands up rather well compared to several of his former Parliamentary Party colleagues, including John O'Connell, Michael O'Leary[31] and Conor Cruise O'Brien,[32] all of whom abandoned, not just the Labour Party but, more important, the labour movement, to join, respectively, Fianna Fáil, Fine Gael and the UK Unionist Party. Another defection to Fianna Fáil, was the Labour TD, Patrick Norton[33], a son of the former Labour Leader, William Norton.

Notes

1   *Irish Times*, 2 July 1987.
2   *Standard*, 21 April 1939.
3   For further information on Noël Browne (1915-1997) see Noël Browne, *Against the Tide* (Gill and Macmillan, Dublin, 1986); Joe Deasy, 'Noel Browne', *Saothar* 22, 1997, pp. 9-11; John Horgan, *Noël Browne: Passionate Outsider* (Gill and Macmillan, Dublin,

2000); Charles Callan and Barry Desmond, 'Noël Browne (1915-1997), *Irish Labour Lives*, op. cit., pp. 24-26.

4 Noël Browne, *Against the Tide*, op. cit., p. 175.

5 For further information on William Norton (1900-1963) see Charles Callan and Barry Desmond, 'William Norton (1900-1963)' *Irish Labour Lives*, op. cit., pp. 199-203; Francis Devine, *Communicating the Union: A History of the Communications Workers' Union* (Communications Workers' Union, Dublin, 2015).

6 Dáil Debates, Vol. 125, Col. 951, 17 April 1951.

7 ibid., Vol. 125, Col. 668, 12 April 1951.

8 *Irish Times*, 4 May 1971.

9 ibid., 17 May 1971.

10 For further information on Brendan Corish (1918-1990) see Brendan Halligan (Editor), *The Brendan Corish Seminar Proceedings* (Scáthán Publications, Dublin 2006); Charles Callan and Barry Desmond, 'Brendan Corish (1918-1990)', *Irish Labour Lives*, op. cit., pp. 50-52; Tony Brown, 'Ambition to Serve', *Saothar* 43, 2018, pp. 113-116; Brendan Halligan, 'A Noble Adventure': The New Republic Speech in Retrospect' in Francis Devine and Kieran Jack McGinley (Editors), *Left Lives in Twentieth Century Ireland*, Volume 2 (Umiskin Press, Dublin, 2019), pp. 66-73; Niall Greene, 'The Administrative Committee of the Labour Party in the 1960s' in Francis Devine and Jack McGinley (Editors), *Left Lives in Twentieth Century Ireland*, Volume 2, op. cit., pp. 74-79; Tony Brown, 'Brendan Corish on Social Welfare, Combating Poverty and Social Inclusion' in Francis Devine and Kieran Jack McGinley (Editors), *Left Lives in Twentieth Century Ireland*, Volume 2, op. cit., pp. 80-95.

11 Dáil Debates, Vol. 138, Col. 839, 29 April 1953.

12 IBCAWAU, minutes of NEC meeting, 21-24 November 1950.

13 *Irish Catholic Directory*, 1951.

14 *Standard*, 27 October 1950.

15 *Standard*, 24 December 1948; IBCAWAU, Resident Management Committee, minutes of meeting, 20 December 1948; *Irish Catholic Directory*, 1950. The *Standard* and the *Irish Catholic Directory* state that the 'dedication' of Four Provinces House was at the request of the IBCAWAU's NEC. There is no evidence in the Union's records to support that claim.

16 *Irish Catholic Directory*, 1955.

17 *Liberty*, May 1965.

18 For further information on the Catholic Workers' College see John Swift 'The launching of the People's College', *Irish Socialist*, No. 261, February 1985, p. 7; John P. Swift, *John Swift: An Irish Dissident* (Gill and Macmillan, Dublin, 1991), pp. 91, 130; Aidan Seery and Liam McKenna, S. J., 'The Catholic Workers' College Dublin – a personal history', *Saothar* 39, 2014, pp. 45-53; Francis Devine, 'The Catholic Workers' College: Some Data From 1951-1961', *Saothar* 40, 2015, pp. 88.

19 John Swift, 'How Larkin Died on his Knees', *Irish Socialist*, No. 265, January 1985, p. 5; 'The launching of the People's College', op. cit.; *Growth from Strength*, unpublished report of the working party to advise the Jesuit Provincial on the future of the College of Industrial Relations, 1 May 1983, p. 13.

20 *Growth from Strength*, op. cit.

21 ibid., p. 18.

22 John Swift, 'The Launching of the People's College', op. cit.

23 For further information on Aneurin (Nye) Bevan (1897-1960) see Michael Foot, *Aneurin Bevan*, Volume 1 (MacGibbon & Kee, London, 1962), Volume 2 (Davis-Poynter, London, 1973).

24 Interview with Pat Carroll, 11 May 2018.

25 ibid., 30 October 2018.

26 For further information on Matt Merrigan (1922-2000) see Matt Merrigan *Eagle or Cuckoo?: The Story of the ATGWU*, Edited and introduced by D. R. O'Connor Lysaght

(Matmer, Dublin, 1989); Ben Kearney, 'Matt Merrigan', *Saothar*, 25, 2000, pp. 13-16; Matt Merrigan, *Eggs and Rashers: Irish Socialist Memories*, Edited and Introduced by D. R. O'Connor Lysaght (Umiskin Press, Dublin, 2014).

27 Matt Merrigan, *Eggs and Rashers: Irish Socialist Memories*, op. cit. p. 116.

28 *Irish Times*, 12 October 1967; Noël Browne, *Against the Tide*, op. cit., p. 221.

29 *Irish Times*, 12 October 1967.

30 For further information on John (Jack) McQuillan (1920-1998) see Charles Callan and Barry Desmond, 'John McQuillan (1920-1998)', *Irish Labour Lives*, op. cit., p. 182.

31 For further information on Michael O'Leary (1936-2006) see Brendan Halligan, 'Michael O'Leary', *Saothar* 31, 2006, pp. 14-17; Charles Callan and Barry Desmond, 'Michael O'Leary (1936-2006)', *Irish Labour Lives*, op. cit., pp. 222-224.

32 For further information on Conor Cruise O'Brien (1917-2008) see Anthony J. Jordan, *To Laugh or To Weep: A Biography of Conor Cruise O'Brien* (Blackwater Press, Dublin, 1994); Conor Cruise O'Brien, *Memoir: My Life and Themes* (Poolbeg Press, Dublin, 1999); Charles Callan and Barry Desmond, 'Conor Cruise O'Brien (1917-2008)', *Irish Labour Lives*, op. cit., pp. 60-61.

33 For further information on Patrick Norton (1928-1999) see Charles Callan and Barry Desmond, 'Patrick Norton (1928-1999)', *Irish Labour Lives*, op. cit., pp.197-198.

CHAPTER 3

Oases of Free Expression

For socialists and secularists such as Scott, a refuge from the oppressive, conservative conformity of Irish society in the late 1950s and early 1960s was the 1913 Club, a left-wing forum of free expression. On his return to Dublin in 1959, Scott joined the Club.[1] Formed in September 1957[2] 'to lay the foundations of a left-wing party,'[3] the 1913 Club's founding Chairman was the future Labour Party TD, David Thornley, while the founding Secretary was the historian, Owen Dudley Edwards.[4] Other early members of the Club included the Geraghty brothers, Sé, Tom and Des; John Horgan,[5] later a journalist , author, Senator, Labour TD and MEP, Professor of Journalism at Dublin City University, biographer of Noël Browne and founding Press Ombudsman; and Aidan Clarke,[6] later Professor of History and Vice-Provost of TCD. The Club's weekly meetings were normally held in the basement of 33 Kildare Street, Dublin.[7]

At the inaugural public meeting of the Club, in Moran's Hotel, Dublin, on 21 February 1958, the founding Chairman, David Thornley, said the Club was a new political discussion group formed mostly by young graduates and undergraduates of UCD and TCD. The members of the Club believed that the revolution envisaged in the programme of the First Dáil aimed at the establishment of national independence and the creation of a socially just democracy. Believing that only the first ideal had been pursued, the Club aimed at helping to achieve the second ideal by non-party discussions of social and economic problems. Thornley added that the year 1913 had been chosen because it was felt that it was the last year when the two ideas had run together.[8]

In that pre-television era, the Club had little difficulty attracting high-profile speakers. For example, Thornley's address at the inaugural public meeting was followed by a 'brains trust' in which the speakers, replying to questions from the audience, included the TDs, Noël Browne and Jack McQuillan, both Independent; and the future Fianna Fáil Taoiseach, Charles Haughey. Addressing that meeting, Browne expressed the view that in the past Fianna Fáil and Fine Gael had differed radically but in recent times there had been a reversion of the progressive momentum of Fianna Fáil and a tendency of Fine Gael to become slightly more progressive.[9]

On 13 March 1958, the journalist and future Deputy Editor of the *Irish Times,* James Downey,[10] delivered a paper, 'Labour in Ireland – has it failed?', at which the other speakers were Senator Owen Sheehy Skeffington,[11] Desmond Ryan, Noel Hartnett and the Secretary of the Dublin Building Trades Operatives, A. H. Nelson. It was on that occasion that Sheehy

Skeffington declared: 'It was obvious, that the labour movement had failed to implement its own policies.' The Labour Party, he said, lacked three things – principle, policy and courage. He added, that he would like to see a labour movement growing up which would work for a planned economy and which would not be afraid to call itself socialist.[12] Three months later, on 15 May, Aubrey McElhatton, presented a paper on 'Irish Industrial Development'. On that occasion, the other speakers were the TDs, Noel Lemass (Fianna Fáil), Jack McQuillan (National Progressive Democrats), and the writer and republican socialist, Peadar O'Donnell.[13]

On 8 June 1960, the journalist and broadcaster, Proinsias Mac Aonghusa, delivered a paper on 'The Press in Politics.'[14] A month later, on 15 July, Brendan Scott (1913 Club) was one of four speakers at a symposium on 'Republican Labour', at which the Club Chairman, William Fuge, presided. The other speakers were Seán MacBride,[15] Leader of Clann na Poblachta and former Minister for Foreign Affairs; Donal Nevin,[16] Labour Party; and Professor David Greene, Professor of Irish, TCD. Scott's contribution appears to be unrecorded. In his address, MacBride called for the creation of a 'Third Force' which would rally together the more progressive and nationalistic – meaning all republican – elements in the country. Referring to the formation of the Irish Congress of Trade Unions (ICTU) the previous year, he said that the emergence of a united trade union movement had established the basis of such a force. In an apparent response to MacBride, Nevin, then Research Officer of the ICTU, said that the only real party in the country was the Labour Party. 'The labour movement was the repository of all that was best in Irish republicanism, from Tone, Emmet, Lalor to Pearse and Connolly. It must pursue an independent role in politics and have a radical social and economic programme.'[17] On 9 November, Charles Coonan read a paper on 'The Webbs, Socialist Pioneers'. Other speakers in late 1960 included the journalists, James Downey, on 'Social Crisis in the Irish Countryside' and Liam MacGabhann on 'America – A New Outlook.'[18]

Early the following year, on 20 January 1961, in Moran's Hotel, Thornley presided at a symposium on Ireland's foreign policy. The other speakers were the TDs, Lionel Booth (Fianna Fáil), Patrick Lindsay (Fine Gael) and Brendan Corish (Labour Party Leader), Senator Eoin Ryan (Fianna Fáil), Seán MacBride and James Downey.[19] The following month, at its annual general meeting (AGM), the Club passed a resolution recording the Club's pleasure at the 'unity statement' by the Labour Party the previous September and expressed the hope that on the basis of this statement the members of the Labour Party, Clann na Poblachta and the National Progressive Democrats would work together to achieve an association among the progressive forces in Ireland which would serve to advance the principles of democratic socialism. Also at that AGM, the 1913 Club expressed its 'profound disquiet' at the murder of the Congolese independence leader and first Prime Minister, Patrice Lumumba, and urged the Minister for External Affairs to ensure that the Irish troops in the Congo were used to carry out the purposes of the original UN General

Assembly resolution on the Congo and under no circumstances to help to uphold any regime which had not the democratic support of the Congolese people.[20]

In its programme for April 1961, the Club listed a lecture on the Trade Unions by the future Labour Leader, Michael O'Leary.[21] MacBride and Greene were again the speakers, along with Abe Gangat, Secretary of the Afro-Asian Students' Association, at a meeting on human rights under the auspices of the Club, on 31 May 1961.[22] There appears to be no evidence of the Club's existence after that date, probably a consequence of the advent of television.

Three years earlier, in 1958, the 1913 Club gave birth to a new, left-wing, progressive, secular political party, the National Progressive Democratic Party, commonly known as the National Progressive Democrats (NPD). Founded by the hitherto Independent TDs, Noël Browne and Jack McQuillan; and Noel Hartnett and Laurence Roche, the party was launched by Browne and McQuillan, in Moran's Hotel, Dublin and in Roscommon, on 16 May 1958.[23]

At a meeting of Browne's supporters, on 3 July 1958, a group of NPD supporters broke away from the leaders following a dispute about whether the National Executive of the party should be elected by the meeting or appointed by Browne. While the agenda of the meeting listed the election of a National Executive, the party was then confined to Browne, McQuillan and Noel Hartnett, an unsuccessful by-election candidate, no members having been enrolled, despite offers of support. Since the meeting comprised only a limited number of NPD supporters, Browne proposed that he should appoint an Executive Committee for a period of a year and that during that period the committee would seek support throughout the country, formulate policies and enrol members. Following the adoption of Browne's proposal by a majority of those present, Thornley was one of about a dozen who withdrew from the meeting. In a press interview the following day, Thornley stated that he was finished with the party and would no longer support Browne. Basing his belief on the democratic aims of the party, he told the meeting that an Executive Committee should be elected by a meeting and not appointed by a leader. Thornley had other significant misgivings about the running of the NPDs, including the manner in which the candidate, Noel Hartnett, in the recent Dublin South-Central Constituency by-election, had been chosen and the fact that the election itself had been fought 'on a personality basis.' Thornley had been the Direction of Elections in that by-election.

These developments were considered at a meeting of the committee of the 1913 Club on 4 July 1958, when a resolution was carried formally withdrawing confidence in Browne and the NPD. In a statement, the committee added that, at the outset of the recent Dublin by-election campaign, issues had arisen which caused grave disquiet. No efforts were made to enrol members or to set up a democratic organisation in the party.

The candidate was chosen by Browne without consultation with the supporters, who first learned of his choice in the newspapers. In the absence of any fundamental policy, the election was fought entirely 'upon personalities and catch-penny issue[s],' a technique which lost the new party much of the support it might otherwise have gained.[24]

Many years later, Browne offered an alternative account of this rift between himself and Thornley:

> Thornley was annoyed when the NPD submitted Noel Hartnett instead of himself as a candidate in a Dublin by-election. Soon after Noel's failure to win the seat David, with the help of right-wing allies, made an abortive attempt to take over the party. Unsuccessful, he resigned and publicly declared his disgust with our politics. In the process he did much damage to our new small group.[25]

During this particular period, Brendan Scott was in London but no evidence has emerged that he was ever a member of the NPDs, which was disbanded in 1963 when its two TDs, Browne and McQuillan, joined the Labour Party.

Complementing the 1913 Club was the monthly, independent socialist paper, *The Plough*. Although not among the named contributors to accessible issues of *The Plough*,[26] Scott was a regular reader of this publication following his return from Britain in 1959. It is also possible that he wrote some of the uncredited articles that appeared in its pages, for example, 'Wanted – Education for Workers',[27] 'Church and State in Education',[28] and 'Summary of Labour's Policy on Education.'[29] If Scott did, in fact, pen such pieces, his uncharacteristic anonymity may have been to pre-empt possible objections from the parents of Sutton Park pupils.

An important forum for socialists of all hues, *The Plough* originated at a meeting of some three dozen liberal-minded citizens in Dublin, in 1957. A committee was elected to consider the possibility of launching a paper 'in which ideas would be discussed on their merits and questions – political, social, educational, etc. investigated in a spirit of impartial enquiry.' A recruitment leaflet was produced which was critical of aspects of Irish society. It was stated that the paper would have no connection with any political parties. The signatories of the leaflet were Brendan Behan, Louie Bennett,[30] Michael Dillon, James Gilbert, David Greene, May Keating (née Walsh)[31], Arnold Marsh, Mary [Maisie] McConnell, Matt Merrigan, Máirtín Ó Cadhain, James Plunkett and Owen Sheehy Skeffington.[32]

Initially an eight-page publication, *The Plough* was later reduced to six pages and later still to four. Priced at four pence, it was sold in many newsagents, including Eason's.[33] Its original legend, 'Ireland's Progressive Paper'[34] was replaced in May 1958 by 'Independent-Socialist-Irish'[35] and again in the 1960s by 'The Forum of the Left in Ireland.'[36] *The Plough* was published by Comhar Fhollseacháin Teo (Co-Operative Publications Limited),[37] initially at 23 Parliament Street, then 19 Parliament Street and occasionally at 33 Kildare Street, Dublin, the normal meeting place of the 1913 Club. *The Plough* also ran a weekly discussion group[38] and a lending library, which was open on Wednesday and Friday evenings,[39] at its Parliament Street office.

The first monthly edition of *The Plough* was published in September 1957, the last in 1965. It was claimed that the paper was run by a committee of non-aligned socialists,[40] including Paddy Bergin,[41] Paddy Carmody,[42] Cartan Finegan, Tim Graham, May Keating, Maisie McConnell (Editor),[43] Norah O'Neill[44] and Joan O'Mara. Although some of the aforementioned may have been 'non-aligned', it is likely that Bergin and McConnell were then Labour Party members while Carmody was a member of the Irish Workers' League, a forerunner of the Communist Party of Ireland.[45]

Much of *The Plough*'s success was attributable to three of its committee members, May Keating, Maisie McConnell and Norah O'Neill. May Keating was the wife of the painter, Seán Keating, and mother of the future Labour Party TD and Minister, Justin Keating. A lifelong socialist, she was for many years centrally involved in left-wing politics in Dublin. On her demise, in 1965, she was described by an anonymous contributor as 'one of the *Plough's* staunchest, most consistent and most reliable supporters…It was she who gave us…the idea…for collecting the money necessary to launch *The Plough*; it was she who gave us its title; it was she who obtained for us the design… And these were only a few of the initial contributions she made.'[46] Maisie McConnell was the Editor of *The Plough* throughout its existence. An active member of the Labour Party, she was also a member of the Liaison Committee of the Left - Labour Party or LCLL[47] (of which Scott was a founding, prominent and influential member) and a founder Committee member of the Irish Labour History Society (ILHS) in 1973.[48] Production and management of *The Plough* was in the capable hands of Norah O'Neill, a civil servant. She later regularly boasted that it was sold in London and on Times Square, New York, within days of its publication in Dublin. Many years later, O'Neill was an effective 'Business Editor' of *Saothar*, the annual journal of the ILHS.[49]

In February 1961, *The Plough* defined its purpose and its role thus:

What Is "*The Plough*"?

The Plough is an Independent, Socialist Irish paper, which has been published monthly over the past four years by Co-Operative Publications Ltd.

Although a political paper it is not attached to any political party or group and its policy is directed by the members of the Co-operative Society.

The policy has been to encourage and foster co-operation between the left wing forces in Ireland and to the consciousness that Socialism is an alternative to Capitalism.

The Plough does not advance any rigid line of Socialism but feels that its present function is to provide a platform to the various groups and individuals who analyse the weaknesses of our society and propound their ideal of Socialism.

The Plough is

INDEPENDENT: Its independence is expressed in its elected editorial committee comprised of individuals, not representatives of any party or sect, who view Socialism in its historical, contemporary and theoretical context.

"*The Plough*" receives no subsidy or allowance from any organisation and is neither influenced by the endorsement or disapproval of any political party.

SOCIALIST: As a Socialist paper "*The Plough*" finds inspiration in the writings of James Connolly.

It believes that the welfare of society can only be judged by the condition of its poorest member.

Believing in equal opportunity for all and special privilege for none, it will fight racial and religious discrimination and gladly give voice to other countries in their fight.

IRISH: "*The Plough*" believes in the sanctity of the Irish nation.

Only under Socialism may a nation attain full stature and as political and economic independence is necessary for it to function, *The Plough* demands the re-unification of the Six Counties with the rest of Ireland and the creation of a Workers' Republic.[50]

Among named contributors to *The Plough* were Brian Behan, Paddy Bergin, Andrew (Andy) Boyd,[51] Desmond (Des) Branigan,[52] Deasún Breathnach, Fenner Brockway, MP, Christy Brown, Noël Browne, TD, Hubert Butler, Austin Clarke (a poem), Peadar Cowan, Beatrice (Betty) de Courcy Ireland (née Haigh), R. M. Fox, George Gilmore,[53] David Greene, Roy Johnston,[54] Justin Keating,[55] Loretta Keating (née Wine), Mary Manning, Proinsias Mac Aonghusa, Frederick May, Matt Merrigan, Jack McQuillan, TD, M. Mhic Suibhne (widow of Terence MacSwiney), Ewart Milne, John (Jack) Murphy,[56] TD, Seán O'Casey (two letters, Vol. 1, Nos. 2 and 5), Senator Owen Sheehy Skeffington and David Thornley (a short story).[57]

In 1961, 'The Common Market – Destiny or Disaster?' was the topic of an overflowing public meeting sponsored by *The Plough*, in the Abbey Lecture Hall, Dublin. Chaired by Cartan Finegan of the *The Plough*, the speakers were Noël Browne, Andy Boyd and John de Courcy Ireland.[58] Referring to the economic state of Ireland, Browne said: 'The left wing in Ireland could not escape responsibility for the state of affairs. It sought escape from social revolution by joining the republican movement and in latter years divided itself into splinter groups, unable to recognise and fight the main enemy. They indulged in intrigue instead of coming out into the open and publicly declaring their socialism.'[59]

To stimulate debate on Irish society, a series of interviews for *The Plough* was conducted by committee member, Cartan Finegan. Interviewees included Brian Behan, Noël Browne,[60] Desmond Greaves, Denis Larkin,[61] James Larkin, Junior,[62] Seán MacBride and Michael O'Riordan.[63] In 1965, an entire edition of the publication was devoted to the issue of apartheid in South Africa.[64]

Following a gradual decline in quality and size, *The Plough* ceased publication in 1965. The death of May Keating that year[65] and the advent of television on a mass scale, undoubtedly contributed to its demise.

Notes

1 *Liberty*, Vol. 28, No. 3, October 1973, p. 12.
2 Interview with Aidan Clarke, 14 January 2019.
3 *Irish Examiner,* 5 July 1958.
4 Interview with Melanie Scott, 6 May 2019. Melanie Scott had recently been provided with this information by Owen Dudley Edwards.
5 John Horgan, *Noël Browne: Passionate Outsider* (Gill and Macmillan, Dublin, 2000), p. 189.
6 Interview with Aidan Clarke, 14 January 2019.
7 Interview with Tom Geraghty, 7 November 2018.
8 *Irish Times,* 22 February 1958.
9 ibid.
10 For further information on James Downey (1933-2016) see James Downey, *In My Own Time: Inside Irish Politics and Society* (Gill and Macmillan, Dublin, 2009).
11 For further information on Owen Sheehy Skeffington (1909-1970) see Andrée Sheehy Skeffington, *Skeff: A Life of Owen Sheehy Skeffington* (Lilliput Press, Dublin, 1991).
12 *Irish Times,* 14 March 1958.
13 *Dublin Evening Mail,* 15 May 1958; *Irish Times,* 16 May 1958. For information on Peadar O'Donnell (1893-1986) see Michael McInerney, *Peadar O'Donnell: Irish Social Rebel* (O'Brien Press, Dublin, 1974); 'Peadar O'Donnell: Commandant General, Irish Republican Army', in Uinseann Mac Eoin (Editor), *Survivors* (Argenta Publications, Dublin, 1980), pp. 21-34.
14 *Irish Times,* 8 June 1960.
15 For further information on Seán MacBride (1904-1988) see Uinseann Mac Eoin (Editor), *Survivors,* op. cit., pp. 105-133.
16 For further information on Donal Nevin (1924-2012) see Donal Nevin (Anon) *1913 Jim Larkin and the Dublin Lock-Out* (WUI), Dublin, 1964); Donal Nevin (Editor), *Trade Union Century* (Mercier Press, Dublin, 1994); Donal Nevin (Editor), *Lion of the Fold* (Gill and Macmillan, Dublin 1998); Donal Nevin (Editor), *James Connolly: A Full Life* (Gill and Macmillan, Dublin, 2005); Donal Nevin (Editor), Between Comrades: James Connolly Letters and Correspondence 1889-1916 (Gill and Macmillan, Dublin, 2007); Donal Nevin (Editor), *James Connolly: Political Writings 1893-1916* (SIPTU, Dublin, 2011); Donal Nevin (Editor) *Writing of James Connolly: Collected Works* (SIPTU, Dublin, 2011); Francis Devine, 'Donal Nevin (1924-2018)', *Saothar* 39, 2014, pp. 119-122.
17 *Irish Independent, Irish Press, Irish Times,* 16 July 1960. See also *The Plough,* Vol. 3, No. 7, August 1960, p. 5, which makes no reference to Brendan Scott being among the speakers.
18 *The Plough,* Vol. 4, No. 1, January 1961, p. 3.
19 *Irish Times,* 21 January 1961; *The Plough,* Vol. 4, No. 2, March 1961, p. 4.
20 *Irish Times,* 17 February 1961.
21 *The Plough,* Vol. 4, No. 4, April 1961, p. 5.
22 *Irish Times,* 1 June 1961.
23 ibid., 17 May 1958; John Horgan, *Noël Browne: Passionate Outsider,* op. cit., pp. 193, 199.
24 ibid., 5 July 1958.
25 Noël Browne, *Against the Tide,* op. cit., p. 253.
26 The author did not have access to a full run of *The Plough.* In early 2020, having been available the previous year, *The Plough* was unavailable in the NLI. In 2019, although listed in the DCL&A catalogue, it could not be found. However, 38 of roughly 80 editions of *The Plough* were available in the ILHS Archive.
27 *The Plough,* Vol. 2, No. 1, January 1960, p. 4.
28 ibid., March 1962, p. 1.

29 ibid., October 1964, p. 4.
30 For further information on Louie Bennett (1870-1956) see Kevin Myers, 'An Irishman's Diary', *Irish Times*, 13 March 1990; Mary Cullen Owens, *Louie Bennett* (Cork University Press, Cork, 2001).
31 For further information on May Keating (d. 1965) see 'A Friend of "the Plough", *The Plough*, March 1965, p. 1; Éimear O'Connor, *Seán Keating: Art, Politics and Building the Irish Nation* (Irish Academic Press, Dublin, 2013).
32 Éimear O'Connor, *Seán Keating: Art, Politics and Building the Irish Nation*, op. cit., pp. 101-102.
33 *The Plough*, Vol. 3, No. 2, February 1960, p. 6.
34 ibid., Vol. 1, No. 2, November 1957 to Vol. 1, No. 6, April 1958.
35 ibid., Vol. 1, No. 7, May 1958 to Vol. 4, No. 6, September 1961.
36 ibid., Vol. 1, No. 7, May 1958.
37 ibid., May 1964, p. 4.
38 ibid., Vol. 1, No. 8, June 1958, p. 1.
39 ibid., Vol. 2, No. 2, February 1959, p. 7.
40 ibid., Vol. 4, No. 2, February 1961, p. 1.
41 For further information on Paddy Bergin (1913-1991) see Francis Devine, 'Paddy Bergin', *Saothar* 16, 1991, pp. 4-5; Charles Callan and Barry Desmond, 'Patrick Bergin (1913-1991)', *Irish Labour Lives*, op. cit, pp. 11-12.
42 For further information on Paddy Carmody (1927-1979) see Mick O'Reilly, *From Lucifer to Lazarus* (Lilliput Press, Dublin, 2019); Francis Devine & Patrick Smylie (Editors), 'Paddy Carmody, 1927-1979: An Unorthodox Communist', *Left Lives in Twentieth Century Ireland – Communist Lives*, Volume 3, (Umiskin Press, Dublin, 2020), pp. 157-168.
43 Niamh Breathnach, 'Norah O'Neill', *Saothar* 28, 2003, p. 20.
44 For further information on Norah O'Neill (1916-2002) see Niamh Breathnach, 'Norah O'Neill', *Saothar* 28 2003, op. cit., pp. 19-21, which inaccurately records Norah O'Neill's birth year as 1921. Norah O'Neill stated she was born in 1916.
45 Mick O'Reilly, 'Paddy Carmody, 1927-1979: An Unorthodox Communist', op. cit., p.157.
46 *The Plough*, March 1965, p. 1.
47 Barry Desmond, *Finally and In Conclusion: A Political Memoir* (New Island, Dublin, 2000), p. 57.
48 *Civil Service review*, Christmas 1973, front cover photograph of founding ILHS Committee, including Maisie McConnell (front row, extreme left) (Civil Service Executive Association).
49 Charles Callan, email to the author, 1 October 2018.
50 *The Plough*, Vol. 4, No. 2, February 1961, p. 1.
51 For further information on Andrew (Andy) Boyd (1921-2011) see Andrew Boyd, *The rise of the Irish Trade Unions 1729-1970* (Anvil Books, Dublin, 1972); Francis Devine, 'Andrew Boyd (1921-2011)', *Saothar* 37, 2012, pp. 137-140.
52 For further information on Desmond (Des) Branigan (1918-2016) see Francis Devine and Gerard Madden, 'The greatest trade union leader in Ireland today: the life of Des Branigan (1918-2016)', *Saothar* 43, 2018, pp. 135-139.
53 For further information on George Gilmore (1898-1985) see George Gilmore, *1934 Republican Congress* (Dochas Co-op. Society, Dublin, undated, circa 1970).
54 For further information on Roy Johnston (1929-2019) see Roy H. W. Johnston, *Century of Endeavour: A Biographical & Autobiographical View of the Twentieth Century in Ireland* (Tyndall Publications, Carlow, in association with Lilliput Press, Carlow, 2003).
55 For further information on Justin Keating (1930-2009) see Charles Callan and Barry Desmond, 'Justin Keating (1930-2009)' *Irish Labour Lives*, op. cit., pp. 130-131; Francis Devine, 'Justin Keating', *Saothar* 35, 2010, pp. 100-102; Barbara Hussey and Anna

Kealy (Editors), *Nothing is Written in Stone: The Notebooks of Justin Keating* (Lilliput Press, Dublin, 2017).

56 John (Jack) Murphy (1915-1985) was a prominent unemployed campaign activist in Dublin in the 1950s and was elected as an Independent Unemployed TD in 1957. He resigned his seat in 1958 and emigrated to Canada but later returned to Dublin where he died in 1985.

57 *The Plough*, 1957 to 1965; Whyte's Fine Arts and Collectibles Auctioneers and Valuers, website, 8 January 2020.

58 *The Plough*, Vol. 4, No. 6, September 1961, p. 4. For information on John de Courcy Ireland (1911-2006) see Kevin Myers, 'The maritime man', *Irish Times, Weekend*, 24 August 1991; Francis Devine, 'John de Courcy Ireland', *Saothar* 31, 2006, pp. 8-14.

59 *The Plough*, Vol. 4, No. 6, September 1961, p. 4.

60 ibid., June 1965, p. 1.

61 ibid., May 1964, p. 3. For further information on Denis Larkin (1908-1987) see Charles Callan and Barry Desmond, 'Denis Larkin (1908-1987)'; *Irish Labour Lives*, op. cit., pp. 146-147.

62 For further information on James Larkin, Junior (1904-1969) see Manus O'Riordan: 'James Larkin Junior and the forging of a thinking intelligent movement', *Saothar* 19, 1994, pp. 53-68; Manus O'Riordan, 'The Voice Of A Thinking Intelligent Movement: James Larkin Junior And The Ideological Modernisation Of Irish Trade Unionism', *Studies in Irish Labour History* 2, (ILHS, Dublin, 1995); Charles Callan and Barry Desmond, 'James Larkin Junior (1904-1969)', *Irish Labour Lives*, op. cit., pp. 152-155.

63 For further information on Michael O'Riordan (1917-2006) see Michael O'Riordan, *Pages from History on Irish-Soviet Relations* (New Books, Dublin, 1977); *Connolly Column: The story of the Irishmen who fought in the ranks of the International Brigades in the national-revolutionary war of the Spanish people, 1936-1939* (New Books, Dublin 1979); Francis Devine, Micheál O'Riordan', *Saothar*, 31, 2006, pp. 14-17; Michael Quinn, *The Making of an Irish Communist Leader; The life and times of Michael O'Riordan 1938-1947* (Communist Party of Ireland, Dublin, 2011); Conor McCabe, *'Someone Who'll Carry On The Fight When I'm Gone'*, Michael O'Riordan, 1917-2005, Francis Devine & Patrick Smylie, (Editors) *Left Lives in Twentieth Century Ireland - Communist Lives*, Volume 3, op. cit., pp. 89-103.

64 *The Plough*, April 1965.

65 ibid., March 1965, p. 1.

CHAPTER 4

Campaigning for Nuclear Disarmament

Prior to enrolling in the 1913 Club, Scott had come into contact with a number of progressive forces in London, most notably the Campaign for Nuclear Disarmament (CND),[1] which was founded in November 1957. He was a participant in many of its activities, almost certainly including the first Aldermaston to London march the following year. Following his return to Dublin in 1959, Scott was a keen participant in the activities of Irish CND,[2] which had been launched the previous year. In the early period of its existence, its officers were – President: Professor Anthony Farrington, geologist and resident Secretary of the Royal Irish Academy (RIA); Vice-Presidents: R. M. Fox, the writer; Joseph Johnston,[3] Professor of Applied Economics, TCD; Professor Cormac Ó Ceallaigh, Institute of Advanced Studies; and Peadar O'Donnell; Chairman: Helen Chenevix,[4] later General Secretary of the Irish Women Workers' Union and a former President of the ITUC; and Secretary: Betty de Courcy Ireland (née Haigh). A key supporter and activist of Irish CND was the indefatigable May Keating.[5]

In what was possibly its first public demonstration in Dublin, in August 1958, Irish CND mounted a picket comprising seven women and two children outside the American and British Embassies. Helen Chenevix, one of those present, said nuclear tests should be stopped immediately.[6]

Councillor Catherine Byrne (Fine Gael), Lord Mayor of Dublin, presided at Irish CND's first public meeting, in the Royal Hibernian Hotel, Dublin, on 15 December 1958. The speakers were: Professor E. T. S. Walton, joint recipient of the Nobel Prize for Physics for his work in splitting the atom; Donal Nevin, Research Officer of the ITUC; Peadar O'Donnell and Cormac Ó Ceallaigh.[7] In his address, Walton said: 'I am satisfied that the advantages, what ever [sic] they may be, to be gained by nuclear tests, can in no way justify the risks which they inflict not alone on the present population, but on populations to come.' The following resolution, proposed by Walton, was passed unanimously:

> That this meeting expresses its grave concern at the growing nuclear danger and urges our Government to press for the immediate suspension of nuclear tests and to continue support of all policies which may lead to nuclear disarmament and the removal of the causes of war.[8]

Nevin said that the people of Ireland could feel proud of the stand which their representatives had taken in the United Nations (UN) debates on the question of nuclear disarmament. Though most people found the thought of another war was unthinkable, he thought there was a very real danger. It could, he said, be started by accident, a mistake in the identity of a dot on a radar screen.[9] Nevin was followed by Ó Ceallaigh who stated that there could be no doubting the fact that the nuclear tests raised the level of radio-activity in the world's atmosphere. One thing which had not been established, he said, was whether the effects of radiation could be withstood to a certain threshold after which they could harm or if their deleterious effects were proportional to the doses received.

In April 1959, an Irish CND deputation, composed of Chenevix, de Courcy Ireland, Nevin, Ó Ceallaigh and Dr. D. M. Smyth, Dunsink Observatory, presented a resolution to the French Ambassador protesting against French policy in regard to nuclear weapons. Carried at the Campaign's AGM, the resolution expressed dismay at the news of an approaching French nuclear weapons test and urged the French Government to reconsider its policy on nuclear armament.[10] The French Government was again in the dock on 15 February 1960 when an Irish CND public meeting, in the Royal Hibernian Hotel, passed a resolution condemning the defiance by the French Government of world opinion by testing a bomb two days earlier and demanding that no further tests be undertaken by France. Speakers on that occasion, at which Helen Chenevix presided, were Noël Browne, TD, Justin Keating, T. W. Moody, Professor of History at TCD; Donal Nevin and Stella M. B. Webb.[11] Mentioning that a number of nations were now capable of making atomic bombs, Nevin said that if these countries insisted on their prerogative of testing the bombs it was quite evident that the worst fears of scientists with regard to radiation would be realised. Moody stated that the question of any country's position in regard to nuclear disarmament could not be left solely to the Government. Stating that bombs were tested by man to facilitate the destruction of man, Browne added:

> It is monstrous that men should test these weapons and in process propagate radiation so that inevitably children, as yet unborn, would suffer in a terrible way. Because of genetic changes people would be born with various defects and deformities.[12]

The year 1960 also saw the affiliation of Irish CND to the European Federation Against Nuclear Arms, which had a membership in twelve countries.[13] On 15 May, de Courcy Ireland accompanied a delegation of trade unionists and students to Belfast to join a protest march drawing attention to increased radioactive fallout in Northern Ireland.[14]

Irish CND made further representations to the French Ambassador, in January 1961, protesting at the explosion the previous month of a French nuclear weapon on the Sahara Desert, at a time when in all other nations in the atomic block had ceased to make further tests.[15]

A protest by the Irish Students' Campaign for Nuclear Disarmament against the establishment of Polaris submarine bases was held on 1 March in Dublin. Some 200 participants delivered protest resolutions to the British, American and French Embassies and a letter of support to Frank Aiken, Minister for External Affairs, for his efforts for disarmament at the UN. It turned out to be a somewhat thankless exercise when rival students showered the protestors with tomatoes, eggs and flour bags as they marched through Grafton Street and a crowd outside Trinity College jeered and threw missiles. Some rival students shouted: 'We want more and better bombs.' Gardaí intervened after the outbreak of minor scuffles.[16]

A sizeable Irish contingent participated in the annual CND Aldermaston to London march in 1961. Some sixty protestors, mostly university students, who travelled from Dublin were joined by about ninety London-Irish on the march. Among the speakers at the public meeting in Trafalgar Square were Joan Littlewood, Bertrand Russell and Canon John Collins.[17]

In a statement, on 6 September 1961, signed by Betty de Courcy Ireland and Helen Chenevix, Irish CND expressed its conviction that the re-armament of Germany was the chief immediate cause of world tension. It urgently appealed to the Federal Government of Germany to renounce claims for frontier revision and for the right to arm its forces with nuclear weapons. The statement also expressed 'profound regret' at the Soviet Government's resumption of atomic tests and demanded that the present reserves of these weapons be abolished under supervision of a team of experts working through the United Nations. Copies of the statement were sent to the USSR's Embassy in London for transmission to Moscow.[18]

Four days later, Irish CND held a parade to protest against the resumption of nuclear tests. Cars carried placards with inscriptions such as 'No More Hiroshimas' and 'No More Soviet and US Bomb Tests.'

Led by Anthony Farrington and John de Courcy Ireland, an Irish CND deputation met officials of the Department of Foreign Affairs, in November 1961, and proposed that a plebiscite be held on Ireland's entry to the European Economic Community (EEC). The deputation said there was anxiety about the possibility of military bases being established in Ireland should Ireland become a member of the EEC and accept all of its political implications.[19]

In March 1962, Irish CND unanimously passed a resolution urging the Government to inform the UN that it would refrain from manufacturing or acquiring nuclear weapons and refuse to receive any nuclear weapons on behalf of any country.[20] A month later, on 20 April, a Dublin group of twelve members of Irish CND, led by Noël Browne, TD, and John and Betty de Courcy Ireland, joined Northern Ireland nuclear disarmers in a parade through Belfast to protest about hydrogen bomb tests and to mark the twenty-first anniversary of the blitz on Belfast, when 'hundreds of people were killed and thousands wounded.' At a meeting on Customs House Square, it was agreed to send telegrams to President John F. Kennedy, Prime Minister Harold Macmillan and Premier Nikita Khrushchev.[21]

Two months later, Irish CND wrote to the American Ambassador protesting against American nuclear tests, pointing out that in pursuing these tests, the USA was adding further to the volume of poison already lodged in the atmosphere, the water and the soil.[22]

Two months later again, led by Browne, eight 'placarded' cars were driven around Dublin city by Irish CND to mark the seventeenth anniversary of the atomic bomb explosion that devastated Hiroshima. This protest was described by John de Courcy Ireland as 'merely a quiet commemoration of Hiroshima.'[23]

An Irish CND conference, in Dublin, on 14 October 1962, passed a resolution 'deploring the contradiction between the praiseworthy stand on nuclear disarmament by Frank Aiken, the Minister for External Affairs, at the UN and the avowed acceptance by the Cabinet of the political and defence views of the EEC.'[24] Ten days later, 'a fairly large crowd' attended a meeting organised by Irish CND, at the corner of Middle Abbey Street and O'Connell Street, to protest against the USA blockade of Cuba.[25]

A day earlier, on 23 October 1962, Browne was a participant in a peaceful, but controversial demonstration against the American blockade of Cuba. When the combined, fifty-strong, Irish CND-NPD group of demonstrators, who had marched from the city centre, approached the American Embassy in Merrion Square they encountered a force of some twenty-five gardaí, including Special Branch detectives, with two alsatians. Displaying placards bearing such slogans as 'Hands off Cuba', 'Keep our Neutrality' and 'Stop War, Mr. Kennedy', the marchers were refused permission, either collectively or singly, to deliver a memorandum of protest to the embassy. When some of the demonstrators then sat on the road, scuffles ensued and some of the demonstrators were 'taken, kicked and thrown along the road' by the gardaí. At least eight of the demonstrators were attacked and bitten by the alsatians. While three of the demonstrators required hospital treatment, Browne, who was also attacked by an alsatian, was more fortunate:

> A number of guards lunged out at me with their fists. Another pulled me over and then kicked me in the back when I was on the ground. I succeeded in gaining my feet only to find an alsatian dog had been set on me, which, grabbing hold of my arm, pulled me onto the ground...I was fortunate to be wearing a heavy coat which saved me from a severe mauling from the dog.[26]

Judged by the scarcity of press reports of Irish CND activities for a number of subsequent years, it appears that the organisation went into temporary decline, possibly as a result of East-West détente.

Notes

1 *Liberty*, Vol. 28, No. 3, October 1973, p. 12; Interviews with John Medlycott, 22 November 2018, 29 January 2020.
2 Interview with John Medlycott, 29 January 2020.
3 For further information on Joseph Johnston see Roy H. W. Johnston, *Century of Endeavour: A Biographical & Autobiographical; View Of The Twentieth Century In Ireland* (Tyndall Publications, Carlow, in association with Lilliput Press, Dublin, 2003).
4 Helen Chenevix (1886-1963) was a co-founder of the Irish Women's Suffrage Federation. After joining the Irish Women Workers' Union in 1917, she served as

Joint Honorary Secretary (1918-1920), Assistant General Secretary (1920-1955), and General Secretary (1955-1957). She was President of the ITUC for 1949-1950.

5   Éimear O'Connor, *Seán Keating: Art, Politics and Building the Irish Nation* (Irish Academic Press, Sallins, County Kildare, 2013), p. 101, 312.

6   *Irish Independent*, 30 August 1958.

7   *Irish Times*, 15 December 1958.

8   *Irish Independent*, 16 December 1958.

9   ibid.

10 ibid., 28 April 1959.

11 *Irish Independent, Irish Times*, 16 February 1960.

12 *Irish Press*, 16 February 1960.

13 *Irish Independent*, 16 May 1960.

14 ibid.

15 *Anglo-Celt*, 21 January 1961.

16 *Irish Examiner*, 2 March 1961.

17 *Irish Press*, 4 April 1961.

18 ibid., 7 September 1961.

19 ibid., 22 November 1961.

20 ibid., 21 March 1962.

21 *Evening Herald*, 20 April 1962.

22 ibid., 13 June 1962.

23 *Sunday Independent*, 19 August 1962.

24 *Irish Press*, 15 October 1962.

25 *Irish Independent*, 25 October 1962.

26 *Plough*, November 1962, p. 1, 4.

CHAPTER 5

Trade Union Cultural and
Educational Endeavours

Scéim na gCeardcumann (trade union scheme), an Irish language, trade union-based cultural, educational and social organisation, which was founded by Críostóir de Baróid,[1] in 1959,[2] was based at Dún Laoi, North Mall, Cork. Among prominent members were Tadhg Harrington, later Deputy General Secretary of the Communications Workers' Union, and Tadhg Philpott, Branch Secretary of the Cork No. 4 Branch, ITGWU.[3] Scéim's aims were to spread a knowledge of the Irish language, culture and history among trade unionists. Its wide range of social, cultural and educational activities included the provision of regular Irish language classes.[4] It also established Scéim na gCeardcumann Credit Union in Cork.[5]

One of Scéim's earlier initiatives was its annual excursions, 'Lorg na Laoch' or Warrior's Path, to places of cultural and historical interest. A 1965 outing, for example, included tours of Kilmainham and Arbour Hill Gaols.[6] In 1970, Scéim launched a new campaign to popularise Irish traditional music and dance in Cork City, in conjunction with the Cork Pipers' Club. Re-established some years earlier, the Club's meetings and Irish sessions had been held in Scéim's Dún Laoi premises.[7]

Later that year, on the initiative of Scéim, forty-two Cork-area electricians, from a total of ninety volunteers, spent a weekend on Cape Clear Island wiring the homes of twenty-one of its inhabitants. This group of islanders was composed of elderly people or families not immediately in a position to pay for the installation of electricity. The ESB, which acted as contractors for the island's co-operative movement, set up a diesel-powered generator and laid cables across the island. However, the island's co-operative movement had ultimate responsibility for the project. All the necessary cable was provided free of charge by a Cork wholesale electrical firm. A press report stressed that the electricians 'will get no pay whatever for the weekend and, in fact, some of them will have to forego the opportunity of making overtime money which they would do at home.' The electricians were members of different unions, all affiliated to the Cork Council of Trade Unions, which gave the project its blessing.[8] Five years earlier, at the Council's AGM, on 28 March 1965, the outgoing President, Con O'Donovan, said the Council had always given full support to the use of Irish and through Scéim na gCeardcumann had encouraged the workers to use Irish in their everyday life.[9]

Meanwhile, on 22 November 1963, the day of American President John F. Kennedy's assassination, a Dublin branch of Scéim, later re-named Scéim na gCeardcumann (Áth Cliath), was founded at a meeting in Moran's Hotel.[10] Brendan Scott was among its members and delivered at least one lecture under its auspices.[11] Its founding Runaí was the soon to be elected Labour Party TD, Michael O'Leary. He was succeeded by Des Geraghty, traditional flute player and subsequently biographer of Luke Kelly and President of SIPTU, who later served as Cathaoirleach.[12]

In May 1964, Scéim (Áth Cliath) defined its role and outlined its aims and objects:

> Preamble: Sceim na gCeardcumann is an organisation of the modern national and Labour movements. It is a social movement dedicated to the service of Ireland; an educational movement striving to awaken national consciousness and patriotism, particularly within the ranks of organised workers; and a cultural movement conscious of the importance of the Irish language, tradition and culture to our struggle for fulfilment as a nation. The work of Sceim na gCeardcumann is based on the belief that irish workers must lay an important and distinctive part in the work of the Irish revival.

> Pending the establishment of a national organisation and constitution for Sceim na gCeardcumann, Sceim na gCeardcumann (Ath Cliath)) will co-operate with Sceim na gCeardcumann (Corcaigh) and other Sceimeanna as they may be founded in all matters of common concern by means of regular consultation, discussion and sharing of common experience. Pending this date Sceim na gCeardcumann (Ath Cliath) adopts the following statement of aims and rules of procedure:

> Name: Sceim na gCeardcumann (Ath Cliath)

> Aims and Objects: To spread a knowledge of our language, culture and history among Irish workers, manual and intellectual, in the Dublin area, to foster a national consciousness among its members, and to defend our heritage as a nation.

> Methods of Work: the holding of regular Irish classes, lectures, symposia, social functions, excursions to the Gaeltacht and places of historical and cultural interest, and the use of any other means that may seem appropriate from time to time for the attainment of the above. The Irish language should be used as far as possible in all the activities of the Sceim.[13]

Aside from Brendan Scott, other active Scéim (Áth Cliath) members included Charlie Bird, Brendan Byrne, Maura Chambers, Fergal Costello, Kevin Conneff (a member of The Chieftains), Larry Daly, Barry Desmond,[14] Paddy (Packie) Early, Jimmy Ferguson, Clare Fitzsimons (née Egan), Paddy Fitzsimons, Úna Gannon, Carmel Gannon, Ita Gannon (née McGrath), Jack Gannon, Des Geraghty, Hugh Geraghty,[15] Séamus (Sé) Geraghty, Betty Hayden (née Kelly), Mick Hayden, Dessie Hynes, Máirín Johnston (née Mooney),[16] Jimmy Kelly,[17] Jim Kemmy,[18] Matt Lacey, Raynor Lysaght (D. R. O'Connor Lysaght),[19] Pat Murphy,[20] Mick Murray, Proinsias Ó Mordha, Josephine Bean Úi Mhórdha (née Kavanagh), Mattie O'Neill[21] and future *Irish Times* columnist, Ethna Viney (née Carberry).[22]

Scéim (Áth Cliath), which published a monthly newsletter, *Treoraí*, was located at 44 Lower Gardiner Street, the headquarters of the Dublin Council of Trade Unions.[23]

At the AGM of Scéim (Áth Cliath), on 6 February 1968, the following officers were elected: John Clarke (Cathaoirleach), Deasún Mag

Oireachtaigh (Leas Cathaoirleach), Pat Murphy (Runaí), Clare Egan (Leas Runaí) and Betty Kelly (Cisteóir).[24]

Meanwhile, in 1963, in one of its earliest activities, Scéim (Áth Cliath) organised regular, twice-weekly classes on Irish culture and language.[25] Among Irish language tutors were Seán Ó Laighin (Dublin), Séamus Ó Tuathail (Dublin), Gearóid Ó Crualaoich (Cork) and Ruaidhrí Ó Tuairisg (Galway).[26] Irish language courses were held at both 20 and 35 Parnell Square while the venue for AGMs and lectures was the Kevin Barry Hall, 44 Parnell Square.[27]

In its leaflet, *Springboard Education Courses,* around 1968, Scéim (Áth Cliath) stated:

> Our unique series of education courses are provided to cater for workers with little opportunity of pursuing more specialised and comprehensive studies. Formal classes have been kept to a minimum. The standard of instruction will take into account differences in educational background for the benefit of every pupil. Classes will be conducted by people with wide experience in their field of study.

In that period, four subjects were taught: English, Gaeilge, typing and public speaking.[28] In addition to Brendan Scott,[29] many others offered their services as tutors for Scéim's educational programme.[30]

In January 1968, Scéim (Áth Cliath) gave notice of a six-part, fortnightly lecture series, *The Irish Trade Union Movement,* to be held in the Kevin Barry Hall between 30 January and 9 April. The speakers were Kader Asmal, Jack Gannon,[31] Noel Harris, Donal Nevin, Sam Nolan[32] and John Swift.[33]

Scéim (Áth Cliath) also ran céilís,[34] Irish traditional music and dancing classes, literary and historical lectures, discussions and symposiums on local and national affairs affecting trade unions, a drama circle, whose ambition was the formation of a self-sufficient workers' theatre group in Dublin,[35] a camping and hiking club, a football team and a ballad club. From 1968, weekly, Friday night ballad sessions, previously held in the rear of Lavin's pub in Church Street (since demolished), were transferred to the Kevin Barry Hall. Lavin's fame as a venue derived from flute player, John Egan's Wednesday night gigs which had commenced there many years earlier.[36] In addition to its own regular singers, other artists to appear at those Scéim (Áth Cliath) sessions included The Hamiltons, Gerry Hunt and Mick Carroll, Seán Keane, The Lindsay Folk, Denis McGrath, The McKenna Folk (popularly known as The McKennas), and Mick and Rosemary O'Connor.[37] Plans for a troop of Irish dancers, who were members of Scéim (Áth Cliath), to participate as part of a larger group of Irish dancers in a folk festival in Strakonice, Czechoslovakia, in September 1968,[38] were pre-empted by the Warsaw Pact invasion of that country the previous month.[39]

Marching under its own banner, Scéim na gCeardcumann was a participant in the annual Wolfe Tone Commemoration at Bodenstown, County Kildare, in 1967 and 1968[40] and probably in subsequent years. Among other participants in those events, which were organised by an increasingly socialist Sinn Féin,[41] later Official Sinn Féin, were left-wing members of the Labour Party, including the Young Socialists; the CPI and the Connolly Youth Movement (CYM).

Scéim (Áth Cliath) supported the 'Defence of the West: Dublin Group', which was working to help small farmers in the West of Ireland turn their holdings into viable economic units, through the co-operative system. In an appeal for volunteers, Scéim (Áth Cliath) said:

> Support can be given by…giving one's time actually working on any one of the Co-operative Schemes…To date Groups have travelled from Belfast, Derry, Dublin, Tyrone and Monaghan to help the Co-operative Movement in the West. These groups have consisted of industrial and clerical workers, men and women all giving their time free and at their own expense.[42]

To mark May Day 1968, Scéim (Ath Cliath) held a Youth Conference in Liberty Hall, on 5 May, entitled, *What did James Connolly Mean?* Chaired by Des Geraghty, the other speakers were Arthur Allen, Wallie Carpenter, Peter Graham, Liam Mac An Ultaigh, Michael (Mick) O'Reilly[43] and Yvonne Pickard.[44]

The conference was preceded the previous evening by Scéim's annual James Connolly Commemoration May Day concert. These concerts were normally held in the auditorium of the ITGWU's recently re-constructed Liberty Hall, although the first one took place in the Mansion House on 10 May 1964. In a report of that event, which had an audience of 700, it was stated:

> The star of the night was Luke Kelly. He was formerly a member of the Ronnie Drew Group. He must rank as one of the best ballad singers in either Ireland or Britain. He has a powerful voice of considerable range and he sings with great passion and without gimmicks.[45]

Heading the bill at Scéim's first Liberty Hall concert, in 1966, was the celebrated Irish traditional and folk group, The Dubliners, which, of course, included Luke Kelly. Other featured artists included Ceoltóirí an Chaisleáin, Festí Ó Conlúin, The McKennas, Bill Meek, The O'Donnells, Seósamh Ó Héanaí, The Pikemen and Prentice Folk. Proinsias Mac Aonghusa, Vice-President of the Labour Party, read from the works of Connolly.[46] All of these artists performed without a fee and many of them appeared at similar events in subsequent years.

Later that year, on 25 November, a Scéim (Áth Cliath) fund-raising concert at the Embankment, Tallaght, County Dublin, featured Luke Kelly and Barney McKenna of The Dubliners, Mick Carroll and Gerry Hunt, The Green Linnet Trio, Shay Healy, Denis McGrath, Paddy Reilly and The Shylo Folk.[47] This was a particularly successful venture as Mick McCarthy, the proprietor of the Embankment, did not charge for the use of the venue and agreed that the takings at the door would be retained by Scéim.[48]

There is little or no evidence of Scéim na gCeardcumann's existence beyond the early 1970s. A possible explanation for its demise is that many of its most active members became involved in other progressive organisations.

Notes

1   *Irish Press,* 1 September 1969.
2   *Irish Examiner,* 19 December 1963.
3   Interview with Francis Devine, 23 July 2020.
4   *Evening Echo,* 4 September 1967.
5   *Irish Examiner,* 14 May 1971.
6   *Irish Press,* 22 May 1965.
7   *Evening Echo,* 5 February 1970.
8   *Irish Independent,* 25 November 1970.
9   *Irish Examiner,* 29 June 1965.
10 ibid., 19 December 1963; Scéim na gCeardcumann (Áth Cliath), Publicity Officer, letter to Mr. J. Cassidy, September 1964.
11 Interview with Des Geraghty, 30 June 2020.
12 Brian Hanley, 'The IRA and Trade Unionism, 1922-72', in Francis Devine, Fintan Lane and Niamh Puirséil (Editors), *Essays in Irish Labour History: A Festschrift for Elizabeth and John W.* Boyle (Irish Academic Press, Dublin and Portland, Oregon, 2008), p. 167.
13 *Treoraí,* undated, circa December 1968.
14 For further information on Barry Desmond (1936-) see Barry Desmond, *Finally and in Conclusion* (New Island, Dublin, 2000); Barry Desmond, *No Workers' Republic!: Reflections on Labour and Ireland, 1913-1967* (Watchword, Dublin, 2009); Charles Callan and Barry Desmond, *Irish Labour Lives: a Biographical Dictionary of Irish Labour Party Deputies, Senators, MPs and MEPs* (Watchword, Dublin, 2010).
15 For further information on Hugh Geraghty (1945-2007) see Hugh Geraghty, *William Patrick Partridge and his times (1874-1917),* Curlew Books, Dublin, 2003); Francis Devine, 'Hugh Geraghty', *Saothar* 32, 2007, pp. 79-82.
16 Máirín Johnston (née Mooney) (1930-) was an Administrative Council member of the Labour Party in The 1960s and a National Executive Committee member and Women's Secretary of the CPI in the 1970s. She is the author of *Around the Banks of Pimlico* (Attic Press, Dublin, 1985) and of children's books.
17 For further information on Jimmy Kelly (1942-2018) see Francis Devine, 'Jimmy Kelly (1942-2018) Trade Unionist', *Saothar* 44, 2019, pp. 146-147); 'Jimmy Kelly (1942-2018)', *Sound Post,* Vol. 16, No. 4, Winter 2018, p. 16.
18 For information on James (Jim) Kemmy (1936-1997) see Francis Devine, 'Jim Kemmy', *Saothar* 22, 1997, pp. 14-18; Charles Callan and Barry Desmond, 'James Kemmy (1936-1997)', *Irish Labour Lives,* op. cit., 132-133; Brian Callanan, *Jim Kemmy: Stonemason, Trade Unionist, Politician, Historian* (Liffey Press, Dublin, 2011).
19 For information on Raynor Lysaght (D. R. O'Connor Lysaght), see D. R. O'Connor Lysaght, 'The Rake's Progress of a Syndicalist: The Political Career of William O'Brien, Irish Labour Leader', *Saothar* 9, 1983, pp. 48-62; D. R. O'Connor Lysaght (Editor), *100 Years of Liberty Hall: Papers on the history of SIPTU, given at the Irish Labour History Society Conference, 22 October 2009* (Dublin, 2013); D. R. O'Connor Lysaght, 'From the GPO to the Winter Palace: how a Workers' Revolution was lost and how a workers' revolution was won', *Saothar* 38 (Irish Labour History Society, Dublin, 2013), pp. 119-130; *From the GPO to the Winter Palace: How a Workers' Revolution Was Lost & How a Workers' Revolution Was Won* (ILHS Studies in Irish Labour History, No. 15, Dublin, 2016).

20 For information on Pat Murphy (d. 2009) see Philip O'Connor, 'Pat Murphy', *Saothar* 35, 2010, pp. 102-105.
21 For information on Mattie O'Neill (1921-1992) see Francis Devine, 'Mattie O'Neill', *Saothar* 17, 1992, pp. 7-9.
22 Interviews with Des Geraghty, 30 June and Jack and Ita Gannon, 2 July 2020; Ita Gannon, email to the author, 21 July 2020.
23 Interviews with Jack and Ita Gannon, 1 July; Jack and Ita Gannon, email to the author, 12 July 2020.
24 *Treoraí*, undated, circa March 1968.
25 *Irish Examiner*, 19 December 1963.
26 Jack and Ita Gannon, email to the author, 12 July 2020.
27 Interviews with Jack and Ita Gannon, 1 July 2020.
28 *Springboard Education Courses*, leaflet, Scéim na gCeardcumann (Áth Cliath), undated, circa 1968.
29 Interview withDes Geraghty, 30 June 2020.
30 Those who offered their services as Scéim (Áth Cliath) tutors included Kadar Asmal, Deasún Breatnach, Anthony Coughlan, Donal Foley, Jack Gannon, Una Gannon, Eoghan Harris, Noel Harris, John Horgan, Proinsias Mac Aonghusa, Deasún Mag Oireachtaigh, Mary Maher, Donal Nevin, Ita Nic Craith (Ita Gannon), Sam Nolan, Peadar O'Donnell, Cian Ó hEigeartaigh, Brendán Ó hEithir, Ruaidhrí Ó Tuairisg, Séamus Ó Tuathail, Owen Sheehy Skeffington and John Swift.
31 Scéim na gCeardcumann. *Why Carry a Union Card?* leaflet. The lecturer series on 'The Irish Trade Union Movement', comprised: John Swift (former General Secretary, IBCAWAU), on 'History- Formation – Development of the Movement', on 30 January 1968; Kader Asmal (Lecturer in Law, TCD), on 'Trade Unions and the Law, on 13 February; Donal Nevin (Assistant General Secretary, ICTU), on 'Trade Unions and the Community', on 27 February; Sam Nolan (Dublin Council of Trade Unions and Amalgamated Society of Woodcutters), on 'Unofficial Workers' Action', on 12 March; Noel Harris (Secretary, Guild of Insurance Officials), on 'The Unions in Future Society', on 26 March; and Jack Gannon (Executive, DCTU, and Plumbing Trades Union), on 'Workers' Democracy', on 9 April.
32 For information on Sam Nolan (1930-) see Brian Kenny, Sam Nolan: *A Long March on the Left* (Brian Kenny in association with Personal History Publishing, Dublin, 2010); Brian Kenny, 'A Long March' Sam Nolan, 1930-', in Francis Devine and Kieran Jack McGinley (Editors), *Left Lives in Twentieth Century Ireland*, Volume 2 (Umiskin Press, Dublin, 2019), pp. 175-194.
33 For information on John Swift (1896-1990) see John Swift, *History of the Dublin Bakers and Others* (IBCAWAU, Dublin, 1948); Michael McInerney, 'A Lifetime in the Service of Labour', *Irish Times*, 31 July 1975; RTÉ radio interview of John Swift by Pádraic Ó Raghallaigh, first broadcast between 10 August and 14 September 1976; 'John Swift' in Uinseann MacEoin (Editor), *Survivors*, op. cit., pp. 56-74; Fintan O'Toole, 'Swift and Sure', *Sunday Tribune*, 25 November 1984; RTÉ *Today Tonight* television interview of John Swift by Una Claffey, transmitted 1 July 1985; John P. Swift, 'Irish Labour's Living History', *Sunday Tribune (Colour Tribune)*, 23 August 1987; Justin Keating, untitled, *Evening Herald*, 27 March 1990; Michael D. Higgins (MDH),, 'John Swift – An Appreciation', *Irish Times*, 16 April 1990; Francis Devine, 'A Dangerous Agitator: John Swift, 1896-1990, Socialist, Trade Unionist, Secularist, Internationalist, Labour Historian,' *Saothar* 15, 1990, pp. 7-19; John P. Swift: *John Swift: An Irish Dissident*, op. cit.; John Swift, *Told in Toberona: A Memoir* (Watchword, Dublin, 2008); John P. Swift' 'A Solitary Voice That Echoes Still', in Francis Devine & Kieran Jack McGinley (Editors), *Left Lives in Twentieth Century Ireland*, Volume 1, op. cit., pp. 75-96.
34 Brian Hanley, 'The IRA and Trade Unionism, 1922-72', op. cit.
35 *Tar Iseach 1* leaflet, Scéim na gCeardcumann (Ath Cliath), circa late 1960s.
36 Ita Gannon, email to the author, 22 July 2020.

37 *Treoraí*, undated, circa April 1968.
38 ibid., undated, circa July 1968.
39 Jack and Ita Gannon, email to the author, 12 July 2020.
40 *Treoraí*, undated, circa June 1968.
41 The December 1967 edition of the *United Irishman* reported that at that year's Sinn Féin Árd Fheis, the party's constitution was amended to include the following aim: '…the establishment of a democratic socialist republic…'
42 Scéim na gCeardcumann, "Defence of the West: Dublin Group", new report, circa late 1960s.
43 For information on Michael (Mick) O'Reilly, see Mick O'Reilly, *From Lucifer To Lazarus: A Life On The Left* (Lilliput Press, Dublin, 2019).
44 Scéim na gCeardcumann, 'What did James Connolly Mean?' Youth Conference, 5 May 1968, programme. The programme was as follows: Arthur Allen (Chairman, Irish Student Movement), on 'A Student View'; Liam Mac An Ultaigh (Chief Scout, Fianna Éireann), on 'The National Question'; Peter Graham (Chairman, Young Socialists; Committee, Irish Association of Labour Student Organisations; Committee, Kevin Street Technical School Fabians), on 'Social Democracy'; Yvonne Pickard (Committee, Progressive Women's League) on 'The Women's Role'; Wallie Carpenter (Chairman, Dublin District Junior Workers' Committee, Amalgamated Union of Engineering and Foundry Workers), on 'The Trade Unions'; and Mick O'Reilly (Executive, CYM and CPI; Executive Committee, Dublin No. 2 Branch, IBCAWAU).
45 *Irish Socialist*, No. 37, June 1964, p. 1.
46 Scéim na gCeardcumann, 'James Connolly Commemoration May Day Ballad Concert', programme, 1 May 1966
47 *Treoraí*, undated, circa December 1968.
48 Ita Gannon, email to the author, 21 July 2020.

CHAPTER 6

Intimations of an
Irish Enlightenment

As a consequence of momentous developments unfolding at home and abroad, the Ireland to which Brendan Scott returned in 1959 was on the verge of major economic, social and cultural change. A beneficiary of the economic boom of the 1960s in many Western countries, Ireland also prospered from finally abandoning its decades-long, failed economic policy of protectionism. These factors and the Anglo-Irish Free Trade Agreement of 1965 resulted in significant improvements in the economy and living standards, as well as substantial reductions in both unemployment and emigration. Average annual unemployment of some 51,000 in the 1960s was 10,000 less than the previous decade,[1] while estimated, average, annual emigration fell by 57 per cent, from 40,000 in the 1950s to 17,000 in the 1960s.[2]

In what was one of the most successful periods in its history, the trade union movement recorded several remarkable achievements during the 1960s, including a reduction in the working week from 5½ to 5 days, a reduction in the weekly working hours from as much as 48 to 40 and an increase from 2 to 3 weeks in paid annual holidays. Hundreds of thousands of workers benefitted from these improvements in conditions of employment. Those advances also contributed to a surge in the affiliated membership of the ICTU, which, in the decade ending in 1970, grew by 78,000, from 432,000 to 510,000.[3]

No less significant than the aforementioned developments was the beginning of a gradual liberalisation of this country from the 1960s onwards. Major contributory factors in that trend included the Second Vatican Council which marked the beginning of the decline of the political and social influence of the Catholic Church in Ireland, the reverberations of which are still being felt; the advent of television, including British television; the introduction by Donagh O'Malley, Fianna Fáil Minister for Education, of the free secondary education scheme in 1967; and substantial growth in inward and outward tourism.

There were also progressive developments abroad, chief among them the American Civil Rights Campaign, which, of course, influenced the birth of the Civil Rights Movement in Northern Ireland. In 1968, major events took place in continental Europe, including widespread strikes and demonstrations by students and workers in France; and the 'Prague Spring', in which Alexander Dubček, First Secretary of the Communist Party of Czechoslovakia, unsuccessfully attempted to introduce democratic reforms, including a relaxation of restrictions on the media, speech and travel. There were also widely supported, international campaigns against apartheid in South Africa and American military involvement in Vietnam. In addition, there was a gradual thaw in East–West Relations, particularly between the USA and the USSR. These and other factors contributed to a more questioning, open and liberal society than had hitherto existed in Ireland.

The 1960s also witnessed the beginning of a cultural revolution, including a major resurgence of interest in Irish traditional and folk music, boosted by the formation in 1957 of Comhaltas Ceoltóirí Éireann.[4] Branches of Comhaltas were established throughout Ireland and Irish traditional and folk music became immensely popular at home and abroad. Ireland went on to produce such internationally-acclaimed groups as the Clancy Brothers and Tommy Makem, The Chieftains, The Dubliners, Planxty and the Bothy Band. Irish rock music also made its mark internationally with such acts as Rory Gallagher, Thin Lizzy, Horslips, The Boomtown Rats and, of course, the phenomenally successful U2.

Des Geraghty, former SIPTU President, traditional flute player and biographer of Luke Kelly, saw these cultural developments as part of the fundamental change then underway in Ireland. Writing specifically about the 1960s and Luke Kelly and the Dubliners in 2019, he said:

> Luke and the Dubliners were part of the peaceful revolution that began in the early 1960s and saw the people of this country begin to shake off the cobwebs of a conservative Church and State.
>
> They were worthy ambassadors for a newer era of change, a time that saw the rise of many diverse movements for equality and human rights. They helped to enliven our tradition of music and song and reawaken a latent spirit of self-confidence and pride in being, though their appeal was universal. That spirit still resonates strongly in the hearts of the people of this country.[5]

In 1966, around the time of the Jubilee of the 1916 Rebellion, there was a growing realisation that James Connolly, long overshadowed by Patrick Pearse, was by far the most significant of the leaders of that event. This led to renewed interest in Connolly's socialist writings, as did the centenary of his birth two years later. Perhaps benefiting from this and from some of the other major economic, social and cultural changes, there was a notable surge in membership of Irish left-wing parties during the mid to late 1960s. Many of the new recruits were young, active trade unionists.

Sinn Féin was a beneficiary of this development, significant numbers of young people swelling its ranks. From the early 1960s onwards, that party had been gradually transforming itself from that of a purely nationalist-republican organisation to one actively promoting socialism. Evidence of just how far that party had travelled was the public declaration by its President's, Tomás Mac Giolla,[6] in January 1969: 'The policy of the republican movement…was the establishment of a democratic socialist republic.' Elaborating, he said that this would be in line with Connolly's interpretation of socialism, that is to say, 'State ownership and co-operative control by the workers of the means of production, distribution and exchange…' Mac Giolla was delivering a lecture commemorating the First Dáil, organised by the National Commemorative Committee, in Jury's Hotel, Dublin.[7] Interestingly, Mac Giolla's statement was made less than a year before the split in Sinn Féin in December 1969.

The mid to late 1960s also saw considerable growth in the Irish Workers' Party (IWP). A double boost for the party was the formation of the Connolly Youth Movement (CYM) in 1965[8] and the Party's merger in 1970 with the Communist Party of Northern Ireland to form the present Communist Party of Ireland (CPI).[9] Originally catering for socialists of all persuasions, the CYM evolved into the youth section of the IWP in the late 1960s. By that time, the combined membership of the IWP-CYM, hitherto counted in dozens, could now be measured in hundreds.

That said, the Labour Party was by far the greatest beneficiary of recruitment to left-wing parties in the 1960s, the number of branches increasing by 50 per cent between 1965 and 1967. Significantly, by 1967, almost half the members of the Administrative Council (AC) were less than thirty-five years of age.[10] More important from Brendan Scott's perspective, many of the new recruits were radical socialists. A further boost for Labour was the affiliation of three major trade unions, namely, the Amalgamated Transport and General Workers' Union (ATGWU), the ITGWU and the WUI, bringing to seventeen the number of affiliated unions.[11] As well as that, between 1957 and 1965, Labour gained significant electoral support, its share of first preference votes increasing from 9.1 per cent in the 1957 General Election to 11.6 and 15.4 per cent, respectively, in the General Elections of 1961 and 1965. The number of Labour Party seats in Dáil Éireann rose from twelve in 1957 to sixteen in 1961 and twenty-two in 1965.

Scott's first involvement in electoral politics pre-dated his commitment to socialism. In the autumn of 1952, at the age of nineteen, he participated in the unsuccessful by-election campaign of the Fianna Fáil candidate and Lord Mayor of Dublin, Andrew (Andy) Clarkin, in the Constituency of Dublin North-West.[12] John Horgan, the former Labour TD and biographer of Noël Browne, has shed some light on Scott's association with Fianna Fáil: 'An undated list of members and visitors to cumann meetings in the Fianna Fáil archives includes, among others…Brendan Scott…'[13] Scott's flirtation with Fianna Fáil was almost certainly influenced by the fact that Noël Browne had been supporting that party since 1951 before joining it in November 1953.[14] As mentioned earlier, before enrolling in Fianna Fáil, Browne's application for membership of the Labour Party had been blocked by William Norton, the Labour Leader.[15] It was then that Browne and David Thornley, both future Labour TDs, joined Fianna Fáil,[16] only to sever their connection with that party the following year. According to Thornley, in the General Election of 1954, he was 'working his boots off in common with socialists like Brendan Scott' to help Browne, then an Independent candidate, to retain his seat. However, despite receiving a higher first preference vote than in the previous General Election, Browne was defeated by a mere 118 votes.[17]

In 2019, Owen Dudley Edwards, who 'knew Scott well' in the mid-1950s, said he 'strongly felt that Scott was never in Fianna Fáil'.[18] No evidence has so far emerged that Scott was ever a member or involved with that party after 1952.

In any event, Scott, then an undergraduate at UCD, was becoming increasingly interested in socialism and in national and international politics. In 1956, fearing war, he expressed concern about the implications of the Uprising in Hungary and the Suez Crisis.[19] Donal McCartney, Emeritus Professor of History at UCD, recalls a later, brief encounter with Scott, in November 1963:

> When arriving to give my lecture, Brendan was seated outside the lecture hall preparing to give a tutorial. He was looking very concerned and he told me that J. F. Kennedy had been shot. His comment was that he hoped the assassin(s) was in no way linked to Cuba for fear of how the US might react."[20]

A claim that Brendan Scott was a member of the Irish Workers' Party (IWP),[21] a forerunner of the Communist Party of Ireland (CPI), has been refuted by Sam Nolan, a former, longstanding, leading party figure, who has stated that Scott was never a member of either of those parties.[22] Nolan's refutation has been endorsed by many other former, prominent members of the IWP-CPI, including Fergal Costello[23] and Michael (Mick) O'Reilly.[24] The claim may have be based on the possibility that he was a subscriber to that party's monthly publication, the *Irish Socialist,* as were many others who were not party members, including, for example, John Swift. Scott was certainly a regular reader of the *Irish Socialist.* He was also a participant with communists and others in left unity endeavours and in the activities of such bodies as the Irish Anti-Apartheid Movement, the Ireland-USSR Society, the Irish Voice on Vietnam, the Dublin Housing Action Committee and the United May Day Committee.

Another possible basis for the claim that Scott was an IWP member may have been his response to an anti-Communist press article by Richard Beaumont, in 1962.[25] In his response, Scott stated:

> Sir – I am surprised, shocked and angered that a respectable paper like yours, whose duty it is to advise and instruct public opinion, should open its columns to such unfounded and disreputable generalizations [sic] as those found in Mr. Richard Beaumont's article on communism in Ireland (25/11/'62).
>
> Mr. Beaumont has good reason to mention the late Senator McCarthy, for the tactics used by the former are exactly those used by the latter.
>
> Would Mr. Beaumont answer the following questions:-
>
> (1) On what evidence does Rev. Gabriel Harty, O.P., base his statement that there were 800 Communist Party members in Dublin in 1957? Did Mr. Beaumont check this evidence? (Senator McCarthy always mentioned definite figures, also, but was rather loathe to quote his sources).
>
> (2) Does Mr. Beaumont allege that the regimes of Admiral Horthy in Hungary, the Colonels in Poland or Batista in Cuba were any better than the present regimes?
>
> If not, does he agree that the best method of checking Communism is to

improve the lot of our poor rather than starting an unnecessary "witch hunt"?

(3) Can he prove that the Unemployed Men's Association was organised by Communists?

(4) Can he prove that the Campaign for Nuclear Disarmament and other pacifist organisations are Communist 'front' groups? This was the type of allegation made by McCarthy.

(5) Who are the Communists in the Civil Service, the trade unions and the universities? How does he know? Senator McCarthy made the same allegations against the State Department.

(6) If Mr. Beaumont is not implying that the 96 strikes last year were not Communist inspired, why does he mention them?

(7) Is this the opening of a grand campaign which will smear all those who oppose Ireland's entry into the Common Market and especially Ireland's entry into N.A.T.O. as, at worst, Communists, or as best Communist dupes..?.[26]

Incidentally, in the mid-1950s, Scott apparently was a pacifist.[27] However, this was not his position later for, in the course of a speech at a public meeting on the Vietnam War in Dublin, on 6 May 1968, he declared: 'We can say that any man who has ever taken up reluctantly a gun for a good cause will know that social justice and human freedom are not hardy plants which can once planted be left to grow.'[28] On that same occasion, he stated: '...They [social justice and human rights] must be husbanded in every generation – if needs be in blood – as by the people of Vietnam to-day.'[29] Those are hardly the words of a pacifist.

If there is uncertainty as to whether Scott was an IWP member, there is no ambiguity concerning his membership of the Labour Party, which he joined in 1963,[30] the same year that Noël Browne and Jack McQuillan enrolled, having disbanded the National Progressive Democrats.[31] Originally a member of Labour's Fintan Lalor Branch, Dublin North-Central,[32] Scott played an important role in the formation the following year of the Seán Heuston Branch in the same constituency.[33] From the mid to late 1960s, Scott and Máirín Johnston, a member of the Party's Administrative Council (AC), were Chair and Secretary, respectively, of the Branch.[34] For some of this period, Johnston and Scott also served as Chair and Secretary, respectively, of the Party's Dublin North Central Constituency Council.[35] In the late 1960s, Scott and Fergal Costello, a RTÉ television camera operator, who was later Secretary of the RTÉ Trade Union Group, a member of the ITGWU's National Executive Council and Editor of the CPI's monthly organ, the *Irish Socialist*, were joint honorary editors of the Labour's Seán Heuston Branch monthly publication, *Action*.[36] It was founded by Scott.[37] Among other members of the Branch were Helen Brennan, Seán Corcoran, Tom Crean (a folk singer and later a Branch Secretary with the WUI and SIPTU), Larry Daly, Paddy and Clare Fitzsimons, (née Egan); Lily Greed, David Ingolsby, Eithne Ingolsby,[38] Geraldine Murphy and Vincent Murphy.[39]

Meanwhile, in the General Election of 1965, in the Dublin North-Central Constituency, Scott was involved in the successful campaign to elect the new, then left-wing candidate, Michael O'Leary.[40] Scott also participated in the campaign of Denis Larkin in the neighbouring Constituency of Dublin North-East, where Larkin secured the last, fifth seat by a margin of four votes. Around the late 1960s, having relocated from Raheny to Sutton, Scott transferred to Labour's Howth Branch in Dublin North-East. Throughout this period, he was one of the most able and effective voices campaigning for the transformation of the Labour Party into a radical socialist organisation. As the following independent assessment of the Labour Party, in May 1961, shows, Scott's aspiration was highly ambitious:

> ...In its 50 years of existence..., the Labour Party has given little inspiration apart from the Connolly period. It has won the reputation of "craving respectability, fearing to be Socialist, and yet failing to be anything else." It has failed to find its "one great, simple, central theme," which would enable it to have a policy on all problems that would both "satisfy the mind and stir the emotions." Until Labour gets to know itself, or rather to be itself, it will never fill a gap in Irish politics. Where two general parties already exist, Labour has to prove that it is radically distinctive.
>
> The Left wing urge the fullest adoption of the policy of public ownership would give it the central theme for all problems and would have the effect of drawing the propertied, business community into effective and intelligent politics. But there is no solid evidence that the trade unions are interested: they have become lost in the wood of wages and seem to have forgotten their social aims. The new creative vigour could effect change, but leadership so far is lacking.
>
> Labour, therefore, is just another political party – and a rather unimportant one – and leaves to Dr. Noel Browne, T.D., and Mr. Jack McQuillan, T. D., the central theme of public ownership which Labour could use with more success.[41]

Scott, undoubtedly, would have shared that analysis.

In the meantime, in 1969, Scott embarked on a new project when he was commissioned to present a pioneering, junior history series, *Telefís Scoile: Six Generations,* for RTÉ television.[42] Original scripts by Dr. L. M. Cullen were initially adapted for television by Brendan Scott and Jack White.[43] However, Scott was also commissioned as a 'scriptwriter' as opposed to an 'adhoc rewriter'[44] for at least some of series.[45] The first series of six programmes was transmitted on a fortnightly basis between 25 September and 4 December, with repeats from 3 October to 12 December 1969.[46] By the school year 1971-1972, the series had become a weekly one, running for seventeen weeks between 24 September 1971 and 18 February 1972.[47]A book by L. M. Cullen based on the series was published in 1970.[48] In 1972, a different role awaited Scott in a new RTÉ television series of knock-out intervarsity debates, entitled, *That This House...* Chaired by Ivor Kenny, the panel of judges was composed of Desmond Fisher, Chairman, Séamus Ó Buachalla and Brendan Scott.[49]

Scott's political interests and activities did not detract from his enjoyable domestic life. By all accounts his marriage to Carol Ann was a happy one and by 1967, with the birth of their third child, Ivan, their family was complete. Although a skilled swimmer as a child, Brendan had no particular interest in sport. Knowledgeable about gardening, he grew vegetables, including artichokes, in his garden. He was a great, if elaborate and occasional, cook, producing curries, courgettes and many other, what were then considered, exotic dishes. As indicated earlier, Brendan was a theatre enthusiast but, unlike Carol Ann, had no particular interest in music. Politics aside, his principal pastime was reading. In addition to the many books he read on a wide range of subjects, he was an avid reader of newspapers, particularly the *Irish Times* and the *Guardian,* and such left-wing periodicals as *The Plough, Irish Socialist, New Statesman* and *Tribune.* An oasis of tolerance and stimulating conversation, the family home had a cosmopolitan atmosphere, with people coming and going all the time, some from as far away as South Africa and the USSR. Underpinning these social occasions were the practical arrangements, including the provision of meals, undertaken by the highly competent Carol Ann, who was a 'wonderful' cook. Holidays were another important facet of family life. There were many vacations in London; in Easkey, County Sligo, the village of Brendan's childhood; in County Donegal, as guests of Douglas and Mary Sealy (née Simms), friends and colleagues of Brendan and Carol Ann at Sutton Park School, who had a holiday cottage in Killybegs; and camping holidays in France. In the summer of 1964, Brendan and Carol Ann, and four colleagues from Sutton Park School embarked on a seven-week, overland holiday to Istanbul. They had a lucky escape on the outward journey when the minibus in which they were travelling left the road during a storm in the Welsh mountains. Five members of the party, including the Scotts, sustained minor injuries but, after treatment for cuts and bruises in Bangor Hospital, the group, including the uninjured driver, Ruarc Gahan, the School's Headmaster, proceeded with their journey to Turkey.[50]

Notes

1   CSO, Unemployment Live Register, average annual unemployment, 1950-1969.
2   CSO, estimated net migration, April 1950 to March 1970.
3   Donal Nevin (Editor), *Trade Union Century* (ICTU and Radio Telefís Éireann, Cork and Dublin, 1994), p. 435.
4   AITM, Application for registry of a Trade Union, 2 December 1956; *Nenagh Guardian,* 9 May 1959.
5   *Des Geraghty,* 'Double Header' honours Luke', *Sound Post,* Vol. 17, No. 1, Spring 2019, p. 2.
6   For information on Tomás Mac Giolla (1924-2010) see Padraig Yeates, 'Tomás Mac Giolla', *Saothar* 36, 2011, pp. 127-128.
7   *Irish Times,* 21 January 1969.
8   *Irish Socialist,* No. 85, Marcgh 1969, p. 4.
9   ibid., No. 95, April 1970, p. 6; Sean Nolan (Anon) (Editor), *Communist Party of Ireland: Outline History* (Communist Party of Ireland, Dublin, undated, 1975), pp. 3-4.
10 Brendan Corish, TD, *The New Republic,* Address to the 1967 Labour Party Annual Conference (Labour Party, Dublin, 1967).
11 *Irish Times,* 24 January 1969.

12 Interview with Raynor Lysaght, 20 January 2019, in which he informed the author that Brendan Scott had told him about his involvement in the 1952 Fianna Fáil by-election campaign.

13 John Horgan, *Noël Browne: Passionate Outsider* (Gill and Macmillan, Dublin, 2000), p. 183.

14 Noël Browne, *Against the Tide*, op, cit., 1986), p. 220.

15 ibid., p. 221.

16 *Irish Times*, 12 October 1967.

17 ibid., 13 May 1971.

18 Melanie Scott, email to the author, 13 August 2018. At the author's request, she had recently asked Owen Dudley Edwards whether her father had been a member of Fianna Fáil.

19 Interview with Susan Boland (née O'Rourke), 7 March 2019.

20 Donal McCartney, email to the author, 5 December 2018.

21 Matt Treacy, *The Communist Party of Ireland 1921-2011: Vol. 1: 1921-1969*, p. 292.

22 Interview with Sam Nolan, 20 December 2019.

23 Interview with Fergal Costello, 21 December 2019.

24 Interview with Michael (Mick) O'Reilly, 21 December 2019.

25 *Sunday Independent*, 25 November 1962.

26 ibid., 2 December 1962.

27 Melanie Scott, email to the author, 3 August 2018. She had recently been informed by Owen Dudley Edwards that Brendan Scott 'was a pacifist' and had 'introduced him [Dudley Edwards] to the concept in very clear terms.'

28 Brendan Scott, hand-written notes of undated and unpublished speech, evidently delivered at a public meeting on the Vietnam War, in the Mansion House, Dublin, on 6 May 1968. [Brendan Scott Papers].

29 ibid.

30 Matt Merrigan, *Eggs and Rashers: Irish Socialist Memories*, Edited and Introduced by D. R. O'Connor Lysaght, op. cit., p. 220.

31 Noël Browne, *Against the Tide*, op. cit., p. 256.

32 Bob Mitchell, letter to the author, 23 January 2019, in which he stated: 'When Michael [O'Leary] was selected as one of the Labour candidates for Dublin North Central in anticipation of the 1965 General Election he asked me to be his agent. I moved from the Universities Branch to the Fintan Lalor Branch and went to work building up that Branch. Brendan [Scott] was one of those who joined.'; Interview with Máirín Johnston, 31 October 2019, in which she confirmed that when she joined the Labour Party's Seán Heuston Branch, in 1964, Scott was already a member. She thought it likely that Scott had earlier been a member of the Fintan Lalor Branch.

33 Mary Maher (M.M.), 'Death of Brendan Scott', *Irish Socialist*, No. 131, October 1973, p. 3.

34 Interwiews with Fergal Costello and Máirín Johnston, 31 October 2019.

35 Interview with Máirín Johnston, 30 October 2018.

36 Mary Maher (M.M.), 'Death of Brendan Scott', op. cit.; Interview with Fergal Costello, 31 October 2019.

37 Mary Maher (M. M.), 'Death of Brendan Scott', op. cit.

38 Eithne FitzGerald, née Ingolsby (1950-) is an economist, a former Labour Party TD and Minister of State. She is married to the well-known economist and *Irish Times* columnist, John FitzGerald, a son of former Taoiseach, Garret FitzGerald.TD.

39 Interview with Fergal Costello, 5 November 2018; Fergal Costello, email to the author, 24 September 2020.

40 Interview with John Medlycott, 22 November 2018.

41 *Irish Times*, 2 May 1961.

42 RTÉ, letters to Brendan Scott offering him engagements in television programmes,

24, 29 July, 29 August and 12 September 1969; RTÉ, Remittance Advice Slips, in respect of Brendan Scott, 23 December 1971 (two) and 28 February 1974 (two); RTÉ, *Telefis Scoile: Six Generations,* programmes of series, 25 September to 4 December 1969 (RTÉ, Dublin, 1969) and 24 September 1971 to 18 February 1972. (RTÉ, Dublin, 1971); Kader Asmal, 'Brendan Scott: An Appreciation', *Irish Times,* 21 September 1971; Des Geraghty (Anon), 'Brendan Scott', *Liberty,* October 1973; Mary Maher (M.M.), 'Death of Brendan Scott', op. cit.

43 L. M. Cullen, *Six Generations: Life and Work in Ireland from 1790, Based on R.T.E. Series* (Mercier Press, Cork, 1970), p. 7.

44 RTÉ, letter to Brendan Scott, 24 July 1969.

45 RTÉ letters to Brendan Scott, 29 July, 29 August and 12 September 1969; RTÉ Remittance Advice Slip, 28 February 1974 for 'Telefis Scoile Repeats', between 5 October and 23 November 1973, following Scott' death.

46 RTÉ, *Telefis Scoile: Six Generations,* programme of series, 25 September to 4 December 1969 (RTÉ, Dublin, 1969).

47 ibid., 24 September 1971 to 18 February 1972. (RTÉ, Dublin, 1971).

48 L. M. Cullen, *Six Generations: Life and Work in Ireland from 1790, Based on R.T.E. Series,* op. cit.

49 *Irish Times,* 23 February 1972.

50 *Evening Herald,* 15 July; *Irish Independent, Irish Times,* 16 July 1964.

CHAPTER 7

Promoting a Socialist and Secular Ireland

One of the more dominant developments of the late 1960s was the eruption of a major outbreak of violence, later to become known as 'The Troubles', in Northern Ireland. This followed more than forty years of discrimination against the nationalist community by the ruling Ulster Unionist Party (UUP). Compounding this injustice was the failure of successive British Governments to demand the elimination of that discrimination.

The first significant challenge to that state of affairs came from the non-sectarian Northern Ireland Civil Rights Association (NICRA), which was founded in 1967. As a result of its brief but highly effective campaign, significant concessions were extracted from the Unionists and the British Government, including the key demand of 'one man, one vote', an end to electoral gerrymandering, equal access to local authority housing and government employment, and the disbandment of the Ulster Special Constabulary, commonly known as the 'B Specials'.

However, before those reforms were implemented, peaceful civil rights demonstrations had been attacked by the Royal Ulster Constabulary (RUC) and other elements of the security forces. There was an escalation in violence when nationalist communities in Belfast and elsewhere in Northern Ireland were attacked by Loyalist paramilitaries. There followed the launch of the armed campaign by the Provisional IRA, which had emerged following a split in the republican movement in December 1969. Throughout this period, there was constant harassment of the nationalist community by the RUC and subsequently by the British Army.

Among seminal events that contributed to a major escalation of violence in Northern Ireland were the RUC's baton-charge of the peaceful civil rights march in Derry, on 5 October 1968, the introduction of internment without trial, on 9 August 1971, and 'Bloody Sunday', 30 January 1972, when the British Army shot dead thirteen innocent, unarmed civilians during a peaceful anti-internment march in Derry. A fourteenth victim died later.

Meanwhile, in the Republic, there was the 'Arms Crisis', in early 1970, when the Taoiseach, Jack Lynch, dismissed two Cabinet ministers, Charles Haughey and Neil Blayney, for alleged involvement in a conspiracy to smuggle arms to the Provisional IRA. Two days earlier, Lynch had asked the then hospitalised Minister for Justice, Mícheál Ó Móráin, to resign. At the ensuing arms trial, charges against Blayney were dropped while Haughey and other alleged conspirators were found 'not guilty'. Blayney claimed that the Government was aware of the plan; Haughey denied any involvement. In protest at the sackings of Haughey and Blayney, Kevin Boland, Minister for Local Government, resigned from the Government. He was also adamant that Lynch and most of the Cabinet were aware of the plan to import arms.

Shortly before the Arms Crisis, on 7 October 1969, Brendan Scott was one of a number of speakers at a public forum on 'Civil Rights North and South', in Dublin's Mansion House, organised by the Labour Civil Rights Group in co-operation with People's Democracy.[1] In the course of his address, Scott (Dublin Regional Council of the Labour Party), said: 'Only a socialist Ireland could provide an ideology to answer Northern workers' fears. All who drew inspiration from Connolly should draw up a blueprint for the reconciliation of Catholic and Protestant workers.'[2] Other listed speakers at that event, at which Des Geraghty, presided, were Kevin Boyle, Peter Cosgrove, Michael Farrell, Matt Merrigan, Flor O'Mahony and Cyril Toman.[3]

The Northern Ireland crisis was a contentious issue in the Labour Party, exacerbated by Conor Cruise O'Brien, the Party's controversial spokesperson. Previously an ardent anti-partitionist, he had recently adopted the 'two nations' theory.[4] But, for the vast majority of Labour members, including those on the left, O'Brien's opposition to the Provisional IRA was uncontentious. What was contentious was his unbalanced approach to the nationalist-republican and unionist-loyalist positions, in which he was generally critical of the former but could find little or no fault with the latter. He was also generally uncritical of the actions of the British Army and of the actions and inactions of the British Government in relation to that State. These difficulties could have been avoided had Labour appointed a more balanced spokesperson on Northern Ireland. In a private rebuke of O'Brien, Barry Desmond, one of O'Brien's greatest Parliamentary Party admirers, expressed concerns about public reaction to Labour's Northern Ireland policy, describing it as 'a mixture of dismissive contempt and cynical concern.' Pledging his support for O'Brien as Party spokesperson on Northern Ireland, Desmond added: '…Let us not create undue difficulties for ourselves and the Party and give unnecessary ammunition to the enemies of Labour.'[5]

While the Labour Party was overwhelmingly opposed to the Provisional IRA, five of its eighteen TDs were suspected of being fellow travellers of that organisation, namely Stephen Coughlan,[6] John O'Donovan,[7] Dan Spring,[8] David Thornley and Seán Treacy. Although unsupportive of O'Brien's 'two nations' position, another group of Labour Deputies was strongly opposed to the Provisional IRA and its campaign. In addition to the Party Leader, Brendan Corish, and Conor Cruise O'Brien, this group included Noël Browne, Frank Cluskey,[9] Barry Desmond, Justin Keating and Michael O'Leary.

Around early September 1971, in an extensive document on Northern Ireland (Appendix 2) submitted to Labour 'spokesmen', Brendan Scott said he accepted the Party's overall strategy, expressed reservations about the tactics being employed in relation to Official and Provisional Sinn Féin, speculated on possible outcomes of the crisis in the North and outlined a range of possible initiatives that might be taken by the Party and others.

In a written response to Scott's document, on 7 September 1971, Conor Cruise O'Brien said:

> ...I agree that there are many distinctions properly to be made between various categories of Sinn Feiners...However, both the Sinn Fein-I.R.A. movements have in common the essential features of being militaristic and undemocratic. For this reason I think we should mark off our own position firmly and clearly from theirs and decline all common action with them. We should not of course refuse debate with them – to subject their policies to rational criticism. I agree we should keep in mind all the time that there are some potentially valuable people in the movement - especially among the Officials but perhaps among some of the younger Provisionals also – whom we should be trying to enlighten and win over rather than antagonise. However, I think that it is necessary to risk some degree of antagonisation [sic], not certainly for its own sake but in order to make our own position so clear and logical that it will eventually have power over their minds, even if at first they find it offensive. Hence the importance of the blows I have been striking against the cult of 1916. Unless that myth is broken no progress can be made because, if 1916 was politically wise and right, then the use by a minority of the gun still remains right, since the objectives of 1916 are still unattained.
>
> I like most of your suggestions as regards what might be done. At our meeting with Congress [ICTU] representatives we may see what initiative we might obtain from them. I like the idea of trying to get a cessation of violence followed by the release of internees, though I am not very sanguine about actually getting either of these results.
>
> As regards your No. 5 – disarming all civilians – this is an attractive idea and I have in fact advocated it in the past. The British army have obviously failed to disarm even the I.R.A. and their efforts to do so have in fact worsened the situation. An effort to disarm the Protestants would similarly be resisted or evaded as the Protestants think if they are disarmed they would then be handed over to rule from Dublin...
>
> It is clear, in the present temper of the Protestant people, that the Government can make no concession on internment as long as the bombing and sniping go on. If internment is not ended, the S.D.L.P. are committed not to engage in talks about anything with "Stormont" – that is to say with the representatives of the Protestants. It is very hard to see how these courses can end in anything but sectarian civil war with the results of which you are conscious.
>
> However, we can only do our best to break the cycle and hope that revulsion from the effects of violence will come to the aid of reason.
>
> Yours sincerely,
>
> Conor Cruise O'Brien.[10]

Despite some major policy disagreements with O'Brien on Northern Ireland, several left-wing delegates, including Scott, spoke against a motion to remove him as the Party's Northern Ireland spokesperson at the 1972

Annual Conference.[11] Speaking during a debate on the Party's policy on Northern Ireland, Scott said he was worried that Labour's policy document on the North would turn out to be a public relations gimmick and suggested that delegates were trying to blame Conor Cruise O'Brien for their own past mistakes.[12]

Always wary of nationalism, particularly the sectarian, right-wing, anti-socialist variety so often found in Ireland, Scott was completely opposed to the Provisional IRA, as were the vast majority of those associated with the Liaison Committee of the Left – Labour Party (LCLL),[13] including Dermot Boucher,[14] Noël Browne, James (Jim) Kemmy and John Swift. Highly critical of the failure of the Ulster Unionist Party and successive British Governments to address discrimination against the nationalist community, the LCLL enthusiastically supported NICRA's campaign for the dismantling of that discrimination, strongly opposed the introduction of internment without trial, overwhelmingly rejected the 'two nations' theory being promoted by O'Brien and others, and vehemently condemned the Bloody Sunday murders.

Scott's particular views on NICRA were contained in a speech he made in the late 1960s:

> To-day in Ireland we have a number of parties who draw their inspiration from the thought of Connolly – the Labour Party, Sinn Féin, the Workers' Party [Irish Workers' Party], the Connolly Youth, the P. D. [People's Democracy] the Rep. Labour Party. In their hands lies a heavy responsibility. It is they which must draw up the blue print for a new Ireland – an Ireland in which the status of any worker Cath [Catholic] or Prot [Protestant] will be enhanced not depressed. It is they who must again do as Wolfe Tone did and produce the ideas for a political system which will transend [sic] religious bigotry.

> The time is short and no party is I think able to take on the work without the help of the others. During this winter let all those parties begin the great task of producing a Socialist blue print for the conciliation of Cath. [Catholic] and Prot. [Protestant] Workers…

> Those who want a united country must win the Northern Protestants or at least a significant number of them to the national position. The only way in turn to do that is to establish a democratic community – or at least as near as such as is possible in a divided Ireland – in which free and full political debate can occur, a community in which some people no longer benefit from discrimination against their neighbours, in which the great mass of Prots. [Protestants] can learn that Nats. [Nationalists] Republicans & Socialists are not all votaries of the great Beast of Babylon.

> Let us to-night try to begin this Full & free political debate.

> I think that we can all agree that the demands of the N. I. C. R. A.'s Covenant [sic] of Civil Rights are vital and are an immediate objective especially if we include one man one job and one family one home. It is not only necessary but vital that we all unite behind these demands. These are the basic minimum bricks to build the foundations but I think we must also prepare now for the next stage. Namely to prepare answers to the Protestant workers genuine questions what is in this for me what do I get out of this. [sic].[15]

In a letter to the press in August 1972, Scott and nine others, not all of them Labour Party members, made clear their views on the Provisional IRA and its loyalist counterparts:

> Dear Sir – We, the undersigned, appalled at the continuing senseless slaughter of Irish men, women and children, both Roman Catholic and Protestant; alarmed at the rapid growth of fascist elitism within both communities in the Six Counties; saddened that the noble People's Struggle of 1968-69 has been allowed to degenerate into sectarian anarchy; conscious that the real sufferers are working-class people, call upon the Provisional Alliance [sic] to cease their bombing campaign.

> Only such a cessation can allow the really important struggle for civil rights and real justice for all the people – to be resumed and prevent the struggle passing back into the hands of opportunist politicians on both sides who betrayed the people's trust in the past.

> The bombing campaign is now the greatest single factor preventing political progress North and South.

> We appeal to the Provisionals to realise that the bombing campaign cannot attain and will indeed hinder – the only worth while [sic] objective in the Six Counties, a united working class, capable of throwing off the yoke of both British capitalism and native gombeen exploitation. We pose to you James Connolly's question:

>> "When you talk about freeing Ireland do you only mean the chemical elements which compose the soil of Ireland? Or is it the Irish people you mean."

> Does your bombing campaign lessen or increase the danger of sectarian conflict? Could you build the Republic of Tone and Pearse and Connolly on a sectarian foundation?

> If you are serious about building the Republic of Tone then the only course which can be followed is that initiated by the Civil Rights struggle. Bombs are not substitutes for political thought. A people's struggle can only be waged by a united, informed people. This can only be a slow painful process and any attempt to short-cut will lead to the cul-de-sac of military dictatorship.

> Realising that a people's struggle cannot be waged by bombing campaigns, which endanger the civil population, we call upon all trade Unionists, Socialists and republicans, North and South, to join their voices with ours in urging an immediate cessation of the bombing campaign. We commend all those who, whilst maintaining their support for the people's struggle, have opposed the bombing and violence…

> We have wasted too much time already. All who identify with the workers and common people must oppose and destroy the reactionary sectarian organisations of the right, whether they be the Catholic Provos or the Protestant Orange/Unionist Vanguard. We now declare ourselves ready to play our part in association with those organisations of the people struggling for economic, social and political rights. Brendan Scott, Matt Merrigan, Terence P. McCaughey, Frank Butler, Griff Cashman, John de Courcey Ireland [sic], Séamus de Paor, Des Geraghty, Kevin P. McConnell, Des Donass [sic]. August 4, 1972.[16]

In October 1972, Brendan Scott and Tomás Mac Giolla, President of Official Sinn Féin, addressed a Wolfe Tone Society meeting on the theme 'British Responsibility'. In a resolution passed at that meeting, the Society said there was increasing evidence of British Army involvement in sectarian crimes in Northern Ireland and that the British Army and Government had continually refused to act impartially there and had permitted the build-up of a Frankenstein monster in the sectarian armed bands which were allowed the freedom of the streets. 'We urge the Irish Government to publicise abroad in every way possible the implications of present British policy and to demand that the British Army act impartially in disarming those threatening civil war, as the essential prerequisite for obtaining civil rights, democracy and peace for the Six County area.'[17]

On the first anniversary of Bloody Sunday, Brendan Scott, Kevin McCorry and Des O'Hagan were the speakers at a commemorative event honouring the fourteen victims. Held under the auspices of the Dublin Comhairle Ceanntair of Official Sinn Féin,[18] the event took place in the Mansion House, Dublin, on 30 January 1973. Brendán Ó Dúill, a member of Irish Actors' Equity Association, was Master of Ceremonies at what was mainly a musical affair, involving, among others, the McKenna Folk, Al O'Donnell, Fiddlers Green, Liam Weldon and Tony McMahon.[19] Speaking at that event, Scott said:

> We have met to commemorate the massacre of the innocent. We have met to remember the deaths of 'our people.' Let me spell out again what Socialists and Republicans mean by 'our people.' 'Our people' are not 'our people' because they are Catholic, because they are of Celtic stock, because they now believe in a United Ireland. No! Our people are the deprived people, the exploited people, the ill-housed people, the unemployed people, the people who have been promised everything and granted nothing. It would be an insult to those who died in Derry not to couple them in our rememberance [sic] with those of an other [sic] religious persuasion who, innocent non-combatants also died in a bombing campaign which has made it more difficult to achieve the ideas of Tone & Connolly. If we believe in the teaching of Tone and Connolly then we must and do couple our sorrow for Derry with our sorrow for the victims of bombs and assassins in Belfast also.
>
> To-night [sic] we should also couple with them the hundreds and thousands of 'our people' who have died in Algeria, in South Africa at Sharpville, in Aden, in Cyprus and in the death camps of Hitler's Europe...[20]

In another speech on nationalism and socialism in the late 1960s or early 1970s, Scott said:

> ...We owe the men of 13 and 16 a tribute. But we don't owe them or they never expected from us ancestor worship. The navel contemplating belief that all Ireland requires is their supreme sacrifies [sic] repeated over & over again, more shootings, more bombings, more flag draped coffins, more funeral orations...
>
> Orwell defined Nationalism as the habit of assuming that human beings can be classified like insects and that whole blocks of millions or tens of millions of people can be confidently labelled "good" or "bad" and also the habit of identifying oneself with a single nation or unit placing it beyond good or evil and recognising no other duty than that of advancing its interest. Nat. [Nationalism] is power hunger tempered by self deception.
>
> What are the great Nationalist objectives to be achieved in Ireland.
>
> (1) United Ireland (2) Economically independent Ireland (3) Gaelic Ireland.
>
> Socialism on the other hand is fundamentally an internationalist creed. It places the economic well being [sic] of human beings on a higher level than the colour of the pieces of cloth which flies over their heads.

It sees a greater step forward in the hand clasp of a Belfast docker and a Liffey docker than the shooting of an R. I. C. man. It believes that an Irish plutocrat can squeeze his workers just as hard as a British one… It believes that a decent health act and a decent education act are of far greater importance than a Republic of Ireland act. It sees that the only sane way to a united Ireland is through a united world built on the realization [sic] of a common humanity by the workers in every land. It sees that the rulers in both North & South have always successfully divested the legitimate grievances of the workers by sounding the clarions of nationalism…[21]

Writing more generally about Ireland, in early 1973, Scott said:

…I would be – and I am sure any Republican or Socialist would be – ready to fight for the rights of conscience of either Catholic or Protestant. In historic terms the Protestant ethos is more favourable to the growth of socialism as both the thesis of capitalism and the antithesis of socialism grew out of the Reformation. I think it would be an abmonation [sic] to force any Protestant group into a theocratic Catholic republic – and I think the present Irish Republic is such a state. But I feel equally strongly about the principle of Ascendancy – whether it be in Ulster or Rhodesia. Socialism cannot co-exist with this principle. The one virus which, whenever it has infected Socialism, always kills or maims it, is Nationalism. In Ireland we have the healthy differentiation between Nationalist and Republican. The Nationalist is the believer in Ascendancy – be he Northern or Southern Catholic, or Northern or Southern Protestant. The Republican in French or Irish history is the assimilationist – he believes in creating new conditions to solve old equations, e.g., Tone's famous definition of an Irishman.[22]

Specifically addressing the 'two nations' position Scott wrote:

The Two Nations theory, and especially its conclusions, strikes me as being dangerous opportunism. Pandering to Ascendancy nationalism has always led to disaster for socialism. Remember that the Hitlers, Mussolinis and Mosleys began their careers as socialists. Today, also, it is easy to involve workers in defence of Ascendancy, e.g., the "Hard-Hats" and poor whites of the States, the White miners of South Africa, the white workers of Rhodesia. Again not all the South Vietnamese army are conscripts. I would like to ask the believers in the Two Nations theory, and especially those who believe that it should lead to the support of a Northern State, the following questions:

(a) Do you believe that separate development is ever likely to lead to socialism in South Africa or Rhodesia.

(b) Are they supporting separate development in Wales, Scotland and Brittany – why the British and Irish Communist Party [sic]?

(c) If it is a question of a majority within the boundaries of the state supporting the borders of the state, then why not support Israel and Formosa?[23]

I feel that the hypothesis that all violence in the North is the result of the presence of the British Army is equally wrong. This is not 1920. Violence in the North comes from the imposition of, the reaction to, Ascendancy Orange Nationalism. It was the simple bourgeois civil rights demands which toppled the Unionist Party and opened the cracks in the structure. It was the return to armed confrontation which facilitated the rise of William Craig [founder of the Vanguard Unionist Progressive Party] and his brigades.[24]

Writing about the challenges facing socialists in the Republic of Ireland in relation to Northern Ireland, Scott stated:

I think we do not further the cause of socialism in the South – or the North – by wasting time and energy supporting or rejecting the wish fulfilments or dream fantasies of the S.D.L.P., or the pious "Hear no evil, see no evil, do no evil" conservatism of the Labour Party Establishment. We can profoundly affect the Northern situation by changing the Southern situation.

We can only do this by making a real effort to come together, plan together, at least consent to work for short term objectives together. Stalinist, Trotskyist, Independent Socialist thought they could afford the luxury of internecine squabbles in the Weimar Republic. Eventually Hitler united them – in a pile of ashes in the concentration camps.[25]

Notes

1   *Irish Times,* 7 October 1969.
2   ibid., 8 October 1969.
3   ibid., 7 October 1969.
4   ibid., 14 June 1969.
5   Barry Desmond, letter to Conor Cruise O'Brien, 31 December 1971. [O'Brien Papers, UCD, pp. 82, 226.]
6   For further information on Stephen Coughlan (1910-1994) see Charles Callan and Barry Desmond, 'Stephen Coughlan (1910-1994)', *Irish Labour Lives,* op. cit., pp. 56-57.
7   For further information on John O'Donovan (1908-1982) see Charles Callan and Barry Desmond, 'John O'Donovan (1908-1982)', *Irish Labour Lives,* op. cit., p. 217.
8   For further information on Dan Spring (1910-1988) see Charles Callan and Barry Desmond, 'Daniel Spring (1910-1988)', in *Irish Labour Lives,* op. cit., pp. 244-245.
9   For further information on Frank Cluskey (1930-1989) see Charles Callan and Barry Desmond, 'Francis Cluskey (1930-1989)', in *Irish Labour Lives,* op. cit., pp. 41-43; Dr. Kieran Jack McGinley (Editor), *Cluskey: The Conscience of Labour* (Umiskin Press, Dublin, 2015).
10   Conor Cruise O'Brien, letter to Brendan Scott, 7 September 1971. [Brendan Scott Papers].
11   Michael Gallagher, *The Irish Labour Party in transition 1957-82* (Gill and Macmillan, Dublin, 1982), p. 148.
12   *Irish Times,* 28 February 1972.
13   The Liaison Committee of the Left – Labour Party (LCLL) was an informal group of mainly non-Trotskyist socialists which existed from 1971 to 1977. Its principal activity was to campaign for the retention of the socialist policies adopted at the 1969 Labour Party Annual Conference and to oppose coalition with capitalist parties. Among it more prominent members were Matt Merrigan (Chairman), Dermot Boucher (Secretary), Pat Carroll, David Neligan and, up to his final illness, Brendan Scott. Also closely associated with LCLL were Dr. Noël Browne and John Swift.
14   Dermot Boucher (1943-2004), who was an employee of the Irish Productivity Centre, was the Secretary of the Liaison Committee of the Left – Labour Party (LCLL) from 1971 to 1977 and Editor of its publication, *Liaison,* from 1972 to 1977 (Brendan Scott was founding Editor in 1971-1972). An Executive Committee member of the Socialist Labour Party from 1977-1982, he later joined the Workers' Party.
15   Brendan Scott, untitled, hand-written speech, undated, circa late 1960s.
16   *Nationalist and Leinster Times,* 18 August 1972.
17   *Irish Times,* 10 October 1972.

18 After the split in Sinn Féin, in December 1969, the left-wing section became known as Official Sinn Féin or Sinn Féin, Gardiner Place; the right-wing breakaway became known as Provisional Sinn Féin or Sinn Féin Kevin Street.
19 *Irish Times*, 2 February 1973.
20 Brendan Scott, untitled, unpublished, hand-written speech, undated, 30 January 1973.
21 Ibid., circa late 1960s-early 1970s.
22 Brendan Scott, *Labour and Socialism* (Liaison Committee of the Left – Labour Party, Dublin, January 1973), p. 13.
23 ibid.
24 ibid., pp. 13-14.
25 ibid., p. 14.

CHAPTER 8

Solidarity

Brendan Scott enthusiastically welcomed the formation in 1970 of the Irish Women's Liberation Movement (IWLM). Short-lived, but highly influential, the IWLM was re-named later as the Women's Liberation Movement (WLM). Founded following a meeting in Bewley's Café, in Grafton Street, Dublin, the IWLM subsequently met weekly in Margaret Gaj's (née Dunlop) restaurant in Lower Baggot Street. Over 1,000 women attended its first public meeting in the Mansion House. Among more prominent members of the IWLM, many of whom were journalists, were Mary Anderson, Máirín de Burca, Nuala Fennell, Margaret Gaj, Máirín Johnston, Mary Kenny, June Levine, Mary Maher, Marie McMahon, Nell McCafferty, Mary Sheerin and Rosita Sweetman.[1]

The objectives of the IWLM were set out in its manifesto, *Chains or Change?: The Civil Wrongs of Irish Women:* equal rights in law, equal pay and the removal of the marriage bar, justice for widows, single mothers and deserted wives, equal educational opportunities, the right to contraception and one family one house. A sign of those times was the omission of any reference to the bans on divorce and abortion.

In an imaginative and highly effective protest, on 22 May 1971, forty-seven IWLM activists took the train to Belfast to import contraceptives, which were then prohibited in the Republic. Several other influential bodies were founded by members of the IWLM, including Women's Aid, the Rape Crisis Centre and the National Women's Council of Ireland.

The IWLM was also a participant in the United May Day Committee's May Day demonstrations in the early 1970s. According to Michael O'Riordan, the former General Secretary of the Communist Party of Ireland (CPI), in common with similar events overseas, May Day had been celebrated in Dublin by the labour and trade union movement for many years up to the 1930s, 'when the cold wind of anti-Socialist reaction chilled the living daylights out of the then Labour leadership.'[2]

In 1950, the Irish Workers' League (IWL), re-named the Irish Workers' Party (IWP) in 1962, forerunners of the CPI, restored the tradition and for almost the following two decades held an annual May Day rally at the corner of O'Connell Street and Middle Abbey Street,[3] where the principal speakers were Michael O'Riordan, Joe Deasy,[4] Sam Nolan and George Jeffares.[5]

Then, in 1969, on the initiative of the IWP, a United May Day Committee (UMDC) was formed. In addition to the IWP and CYM, it was representative of other socialist, republican, youth and student organisations.[6] Organised by the IWP, the 1969 event involved a march from Parnell Square to the corner of O'Connell and Abbey Streets, where a public meeting was held. Participants included the CYM and Scéim na gCeardcumann, the trade union-based cultural and educational organisation. With an attendance of 300, the meeting was addressed by speakers from the CYM, a leading, unnamed trade unionist from Northern Ireland and Sam Nolan of the IWP.[7] After leaving Middle Abbey Street, the parade continued to the Department of Labour, Mespil Road, which was being picketed by a number of union members against proposed trade union legislation. The picket was organised by the Workers' Advice Bureau.[8]

On the following Sunday, 4 May, over 200 hundred people participated in a UMDC May Day parade from Glasthule to Dún Laoghaire pier, where a public meeting was held. Organised by the Dún Laoghaire-Rathdown Branch of the Labour Party, participants included the CYM, Bray Young Socialists and members of the Christian socialist group, Grille. The speakers included Flor O'Mahony, Branch Chairman, who presided, and John de Courcy Ireland.[9]

The following year, 1970, the UMDC, comprising representatives of the CPI, CYM, Left Labour Party groups, Official Sinn Féin, the Socialist Party of Ireland (SPI) and the Union of Students in Ireland (USI), held a public demonstration in Dublin.[10] Among banners displayed at that event were those of the CPI, CYM, Labour Party (Seán Connolly Branch), Official Sinn Féin; UCD Republican Club and 'Cement Workers' Protest, Drogheda and Limerick'. Chaired by Sam Nolan, CPI and the Dublin Council of Trade Unions (DCTU), other speakers included Joe Deasy, Vice-Chairman, Southern Area Committee, CPI; Máirín Johnston, Vice-Chair, Dublin Regional Council (DRC) of the Labour Party; Mick O'Reilly, CYM; and Seamus Rhatigan, Official Sinn Féin.[11]

Separately, a Labour Party DRC May Day demonstration was held on 2 May 1970, when Maoists, Young Socialists and a parade of cement workers led by a brass band marched from Parnell Square to Foster Place, where a public meeting took place. Among the marchers were the Party Chairman, Dan Browne,[12] the General Secretary, Brendan Halligan,[13] Noël Browne, TD, and the Derry socialist, Eamonn McCann. Speakers included Vincent McDowell, a former Chairman of Labour's DRC and Jim Kemmy, the future Democratic Socialist Party and Labour TD.[14]

On May Day 1971, about 1,000 people took part in the UMDC's march from Parnell Square to the GPO. Participants included the recently-formed Liaison Committee of the Left – Labour Party (LCLL), and other left-wing Labour Party members, Official Sinn Féin, the WLM, the CPI, the CYM, the Young Socialists and Socialist Labour Alliance. Speakers included Des Bonass,[15] Labour Party AC and LCLL; Máirín de Burca, Official Sinn Féin; Mary Kenny, WLM; and Sam Nolan, CPI. All the speakers denounced the proposed introduction of the Government's Prohibition of Forcible Entry and Occupation Bill. Challenging the trade union leadership to organise its members against the Bill and entry to the EEC, de Burca demanded a massive organisation of the workers by the trade unions. 'If they do not, they will be betraying the working class, as they have so often done in the past,' she declared.[16]

A significant feature of that 1971 demonstration was the 300-member WLM contingent. Marching behind a large black and white banner, many of the women, who were pushing prams or carrying children in their arms, held placards with slogans demanding equal pay, equal opportunity, day nurseries for children and increased social benefits. Addressing those assembled at the GPO, Mary Kenny, representing the WLM, said that the trade unions had never really entered into the fight on behalf of women workers. 'Women in industry were earning only half the rate paid to men and their wages now in relation to men's wages were worse than in 1935. The great mass of unpaid women workers, the mothers rearing children in the home, were working in conditions which would not be tolerated in any factory,' she said.

The present writer recalls a UMDC march from Glasthule to Dún Laoghaire, where a public meeting was held, on the afternoon of Sunday, 2 May 1971. The speakers were Noël Browne, TD, Michael O'Riordan, General Secretary of the CPI, and Brendan Scott, LCLL. In his address, apparently the only one partially recorded, Browne called for the overthrow of capitalism and the implementation of Connolly's revolutionary socialism 'Capitalism today', he said, 'was coming to inevitable disintegration, but the workers were suffering during its decline. The Government was relying on the silence of the workers towards the growing queue of unemployed, of the healthy towards the sick, or those in houses towards the homeless. The Government was hoping that the Irish people would not care and they had not as yet shown that they did'.[17]

The CPI claimed that the 1971 Dublin UMDC march was 'as big as the Dublin Council of Trade Unions (DCTU) official Connolly [Commemoration] Day'[18] event, held annually on the Sunday closest to 12 May, the anniversary of Connolly's execution. In contrast to the IWP's and UMDC's May Day demonstrations, the DCTU Commemoration was invariably a sectarian affair in which the ITGWU and some other unions marched from their headquarters to Mass at the Church of Mary of the Angels, Church Street, and thence to Arbour Hill, where a decade of the Rosary was recited, before proceeding to a public meeting at the GPO. Those wishing to avoid this sectarianism would join the parade at Parnell Square.

On May Day 1972, the UMDC staged an anti-EEC rally at the GPO, preceded by a march by about 250 participants from Parnell Square. Speakers included Sam Nolan, CPI, who presided; Eamonn Farrell,[19] Socialist Party of Ireland (SPI); Derry Kelleher, Vice-President, Official Sinn Féin; Des Bonass, LCLL; and Ray Heffernan, CYM.[20]

A notice for the following year's event mentioned that Tomás Mac Giolla, President of Official Sinn Féin, would be among the speakers and that the march would be a demonstration of support for the British workers who had declared a one-day strike against Edward Heath's Conservative Government's pay curbs policy.[21]

Notes

1   Interview with Máirín Johnston, 14 July 2020; Máirín de Burca, email to the author, 2 August 2020.
2   *Irish Socialist,* No. 150, May 1975, p. 1.
3   ibid.
4   For further information on Joe Deasy (1922-2013) see Brian Kenny, *Joe Deasy: A Life on the Left* (Hugh Geraghty-Crumlin-Drimnagh, Walkinstown Branch, The Labour Party, Dublin, 2009); Francis Devine, 'Joe Deasy (1922-2013)', *Saothar* 38, 2013, pp. 181-184.
5   For further information on George Jeffares (1925-1995) see Joe Deasy, 'George Jeffares', *Saothar* 29, 2007, pp. 79-82.
6   *Irish Socialist,* No. 150, May 1975, p. 1.
7   *Irish Independent,* 29 April 1969.
8   *Irish Press,* 2 May 1969.
9   ibid., 5 May 1969.
10   *Irish Socialist,* No. 139, May 1974, p. 1.
11   *Irish Press,* 2 May 1970.
12   Daniel (Dan) Browne (1925-2010) was a Branch Secretary of both the National Union of Vehicle Builders NUVB) and the ATGWU, with which the NUVB merged in 1972; Chairman of the Labour Party from 1969-1971, a member of Dublin City Council from 1974-1985, serving as Lord Mayor of Dublin in 1982-1983, and the mainstay for decades of the Dublin Workingmen's Club.
13   Brendan Halligan (1936-2020), an economist, politician, public affairs consultant and academic, was Political Director of the Labour Party from 1967-1968; General Secretary, 1968 to 1980; Senator, 1973-1976, TD for Dublin South West, 1976-1977; and MEP for Dublin, 1983-1984. In 1991, he was a leading figure in the creation of the Institute of European Affairs, serving as Chair, 1985-1995, and lectured on European integration at the University of Limerick. From 2007-2014, he was Chair, Sustainable Energy Authority of Ireland. See also Brendan Halligan (Editor), *The Brendan Corish Seminar Proceedings* (Scáthán Publications, Dublin, 2006); 'A Noble Adventure': The New Republic Speech in Retrospect', in Francis Devine & Kieran Jack McGinley (Editors), *Left Lives in Twentieth Century Ireland,* Volume 2 (Umiskin Press, Dublin, 2019, pp. 66-73; 'Anon, 'Labour politician who had life-long commitment to social justice: Brendan Halligan', *Irish Times,* 15 August 2020, p. 12.
14   *Irish Times,* 4 May 1970.
15   Desmond (Des) Bonass (d. 2019), a Clerical Officer with the ATGWU, was a member of the Administrative Council of the Labour Party and an activist in the Liaison Committee of the Left – Labour Party (LCLL) from 1971-1977. From 1977-1982 he was an Executive Committee member of the Socialist Labour Party. For further information on Des Bonass see 'Des Bonass: The Matt Merrigan I knew' in Des Derwin, 'Memories of 'A Marvellous Legacy': Matt Merrigan, 1922-2000', in Francis Devine & Kieran Jack McGinley (Editors), *Left Lives in Twentieth Century Ireland,* Volume 2 (Umiskin Press, Dublin, 2019), pp. 118-122).
16   *Sunday Independent,* 2 May 1971; *Irish Times,* 3 May 1971.

17 *Irish Times,* 3 May 1971.
18 *Irish Socialist,* No. 106, June 1971, p. 1.
19 Eamonn Farrell was a Secretary of the Dublin Housing Action Committee, a member of Sinn Féin, a founding member in 1971 of the Socialist Party of Ireland (SPI), which merged with Jim Kemmy's Limerick Socialist Organisation and the British and Irish Communist Organisation (BICO) to form the Democratic Socialist Party (DSP) in 1972. Farrell was also a member of Socialist Against Nationalism and the Divorce Action Group. He ceased his political activities with the demise of the SPI and entered journalism, becoming picture editor of the *Sunday Tribune* and Editor of RollingNews.ie photo agency.
20 *Irish Press,* 2 May 1972.
21 ibid., 30 April 1973.

1. Wedding of Brendan Scott's parents, Martin and Sarah 'Colleen' Scott (née Kilduff), 30 September 1930.

2. Brendan Scott, aged about three, County Sligo, circa 1936.

3. Brendan Scott at his BA Honours in History graduation, UCD, 1955.

4. Brendan and Carol Ann Scott (née O'Rourke) at their wedding reception, Royal Marine Hotel, Dún Laoghaire, 18 March 1957.

5. Brendan and Carol Ann Scott's wedding reception, Royal Marine Hotel, Dún Laoghaire, 18 March 1957, from left: Basil Scott, Colleen Scott, Susan O'Rourke, Rev. John Bergin, C.C., Glasthule, Dorothy O'Rourke, May Keating, David Thornley, Aidan Clarke, Brendan Scott, Carol Ann Scott, Katherine Sheppard, Dermod O'Rourke, Martha O'Rourke, Winnifred Carroll, Tommy Carroll and Desmond O'Rourke.

6. The Scott family, London, summer 1958,
from left: Carol Ann, Eoin and Brendan.

7. Group pictured at unknown, possibly 1913 Club event,
in Dublin, circa 1957, from left: David Thornley, founding Chairman;
Peadar O'Donnell (republican socialist, writer); unidentified;
Noël Browne, TD, (Independent); and
Erskine Childers, TD, Minister for Lands (Fianna Fáil).

8. *Pupils and teachers of Sutton Park School, Dublin, 1961.*
Brendan Scott is seated in the second row from the front, fourth from the right.

*9. Brendan Scott,
Howth, 1961.*

*10. Brendan and
Carol Ann Scott with
their children,
Eoin and Melanie,
County Donegal,
early 1960s.*

11. Brendan Scott,
Dublin,
early 1960s.

12. Brendan Scott,
County Donegal,
circa 1968.

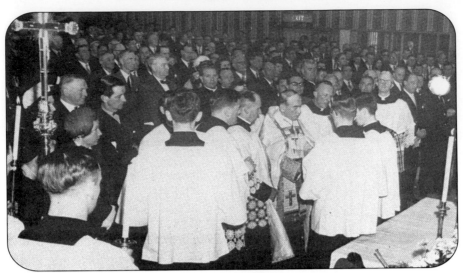

13. The 'blessing' of the re-constructed Liberty Hall, Dublin, headquarters of the Irish Transport and General Workers' Union, by the Catholic Archbishop of Dublin, John Charles McQuaid, 1 May 1965. Note the presence of Dr. Noël Browne

14. Irish Anti-Apartheid Movement, 'Brother Lend a Hand', conference for trade unionists on apartheid and South Africa and South West Africa, Shelbourne Hotel, Dublin, 9 September 1966, from left: Charles McCarthy (General Secretary, Vocational Teachers' Association), Barry Desmond (Industrial Officer, Irish Congress of Trade Unions and IAAM Secretary), and John Swift (General Secretary, Irish Bakers', Confectioners' and Allied Workers' Amalgamated Union).

CHAPTER 9

When the Talking had to Stop

The Dublin Housing Action Committee (DHAC), which came into existence in the late 1960s, was yet another body in which Brendan Scott, a member of the Committee, played a prominent role. In the first edition of its publication, *Crisis,* it was stated: 'Throughout the city of Dublin there are hundreds of flats and houses lying idle (vacant possession being more important and profitable than housing families) while 10,000 families are homeless.'[1]

Calling for a housing emergency to be declared, a prohibition on demolishing sound living accommodation and an immediate cessation to the building of 'prestige' office block projects, the DHAC inspired the formation of similar bodies in Cork, Limerick, Derry, Dún Laoghaire and elsewhere. The DHAC also pledged itself to fight for the following demands:

1. Adequate housing for the citizens of Dublin.
2. Fair rents for proper homes.
3. Protection from eviction by unscrupulous landlords.
4. An end to the scandal of empty houses.
5. Protection for squatting families.[2]

Initially, picketing Dublin City Council meetings and organised other public demonstrations, the DHAC was soon taking direct action, resisting evictions and occupying mainly vacant houses. In 1969, and possibly in other years, the DHAC had at least two publications: *Crisis,* which appeared on a bi-monthly basis, and *The Squatter.*

A non-political, non-sectarian body,[3] the DHAC sprang from Sinn Féin's Citizens Advice Bureau in 1967,[4] 'to focus attention on the plight of Dublin's homeless' and was run by 'those directly involved in the problem.' While anyone could contribute to discussions, only the homeless could vote at its meetings.[5] Any organisation wishing to affiliate could do so by writing to the Secretary.[6] Brendan Scott and Máirín Johnston, Chair and Secretary, respectively, of Labour's Seán Heuston Branch from the mid to late 1960s,[7] were the prime movers in the Branch's affiliation to the DHAC,[8] while Scott and the then homeless Paddy Behan[9] were the Branch representatives.[10] For a period, Fergal Costello also represented the Branch on the DHAC.[11]

Among chairpersons of the DHAC were Proinsias De Rossa (later President of the Workers' Party (WP) and Democratic Left (DL); a WP TD and DL TD and Minister; and a WP and Labour Party MEP); Bernard Browne[12] (a postman, a CPI member and later Branch Secretary of the Federated Workers' Union of Ireland and SIPTU); while secretaries included Dennis Dennehy (a member of the Irish Communist Organisation); and Eamonn Farrell (Sinn Féin and later a SPI and DSP member) and Seán Dunne (Sinn Féin). Affiliated organisations included the CPI, the CYM, some Labour Party branches and student bodies. Among leading activists in the DHAC's campaigns were Fergal Costello, Máirín de Burca, Austin Flannery, OP, Eric Fleming, Margaret Gaj, Máirín Johnston, Pat Murphy, Seán Mac Stíofáin, Seán Ó Cionnaith, Sam Nolan, Michael (Mick) O'Reilly, Michael O'Riordan, Ed Penrose, Brendan Scott, Michael Sweetman, SJ,[13] and Netherlands-born Stefan van Velthoven. Senator Owen Sheehy Skeffington was a supporter.

One of the DHAC's earliest activities was to oppose evictions of four families in a row of cottages at Sarah Place, Islandbridge, Dublin, in January 1968. Claiming that the dwellings were uninhabitable and would be demolished, Dublin City Council offered tenants alternative accommodation elsewhere in Dublin, including Ballymun. For some of the tenants the offer was unreasonable and unacceptable and they decided to resist eviction. Among those evicted were Josephine and Michael Eiffe, a brother and sister aged 67 and 65, who had lived all their lives at 11 Sarah Place. A Corporation offer of a one-bedroom flat in Ballymun was declined as it entailed sharing a bedroom. Contending that the pair could have slept one in the bedroom and the other in a reception room, a Corporation official said: 'They might have wished for better but what about the family of nine in one room waiting for a house in Ballyfermot and the many other large families in similar positions.'[14] What an admission of a failed housing policy!

Support for the tenants came from the DHAC. On the morning of 15 January 1968, about a dozen placard-bearing members of the DHAC and the Citizens' Advice Bureau picketed one of the cottages at Sarah Place, where evictions were imminent. At about the same time a force of about twenty-five gardaí and Corporation officials gathered at the pavement outside the cottages. Some twenty minutes later, a scuffle broke out when gardaí cleared demonstrators away from the door of one of the dwellings. Two protestors, Seán Dunne, a DHAC Executive Committee member and Chairman of the Citizens' Advice Bureau; and Séamus Ó Tuathail, a DHAC member and Editor of Sinn Féin's monthly paper, the *United Irishman*, were bundled into a garda car and taken to the Bridewell.

Forty minutes later, when the bailiffs approached the locked door with a pick-axe, another larger scuffle began, with gardaí and demonstrators struggling up and down the pavements and across the road in front of traffic. According to a press report, 'nine more of the demonstrators… were bundled struggling violently into squad cars and driven away.'

During the first scuffle, Marie Dennehy, who was living with her husband and children in a caravan, was thrown to the ground. A Dublin Fire Brigade ambulance took her to hospital where she was detained for observation.

Corporation bailiffs then hacked down the door of the cottage and started to remove furniture and other belongings into the street. They later went round to the back of Sarah Place and battened down the door of another cottage, the home of Anthony Brady, his wife and their two children, aged four years and four months. Later again, Corporation workmen began to dismantle the slate roofs of all the cottages.[15] By then, a second group of demonstrators had arrived, among them the CPI's General Secretary, Michael O'Riordan. Having establish that the workmen were trade unionists, O'Riordan, holding aloft his ITGWU membership card, persuaded them, in accordance with union policy, not to participate in the evictions. That infuriated the gardaí, particularly the officer in charge.[16]

A week or so later, in a letter to the press, the trade union position on evictions, at least in the WUI, was clearly outlined:

> Sir – Regarding the evictions which took place in Sarah place [sic] recently, I would like to clear up the position regarding the Corporation employees who ejected the unfortunate families. As far as we are concerned, no member of this union took part in this work.
>
> In September 1965, this committee which represents all Corporation workers who are members of the Workers' Union of Ireland, passed   resolution condemning the use of trade unionists for this type of work and gave instructions to our members not to participate in it. This direction has never been withdrawn. Yours etc., Tom Geraghty, Chairman, Corporation Section Committee, Workers' Union of Ireland.[17]

Immediately following O'Riordan's intervention in the evictions, twelve demonstrators, including O'Riordan, were arrested and taken to the Bridewell. During the earlier scuffles, there were shouts of 'Gestapo', 'Police Brutality', 'Black and Tans' and 'Hatchet Men'. Placards displayed such inscriptions as '10,000 homeless', 'House the people and end Dublin's shame', 'Demand end to demolition of sound houses' and 'No one shouted stop'.[18]

Later that day, the first group of nine demonstrators[19] was charged in the Dublin District Court with a breach of the peace, obstructing or impeding a sub-sheriff and with abusive and threatening words and behaviour. They were remanded for a week on their own bail of £20 each and an undertaking not to return to Sarah Place. Later still that day, a second group of twelve demonstrators[20] was charged with obstructing a sub-sheriff and with intimidation.[21]

At the second hearing of the case on 22 January, all the Sarah Place demonstrators were remanded on their own bail of £20 each. On that occasion, the Court was picketed by the CYM, Irish Student Movement and TCD Republican Club.[22]

At a third Dublin District Court hearing on 11 March, intimidation charges against Donough Dennehy, Marie Dennehy and Michael O'Riordan were dismissed by Justice Carr on the basis that there was no evidence to support such charges.[23] At yet another hearing of the Court three days later, the first group of protestors was informed by District Justice Carr that they 'went too far – they resisted the police and tried to break through the police cordon.' A fine of £1 was imposed on each of the defendants, with seven days to pay and in default to serve seven days in prison.[24] Separately, on a charge of riotous assembly and obstruction of the gardaí, Séamus Ó Tuathail was later fined £5.[25] No fines were paid by the defendants and none of the defendants was imprisoned.[26]

The DHAC's Sarah Place campaign appears to have been remarkably successful. A day following the picketing, Dublin City Council agreed to re-house three of the four families in the localities they had sought. This included the Brady family and Josephine and Michael Eiffe who had rejected offers of accommodation in Ballymun flats.[27] Moreover, following the evictions at Sarah Place when hatchets were used to break down the doors of tenants, Dublin City Council's Housing Committee decided to take direct control of the Corporation's eviction squad. The Committee unanimously passed a resolution, in the name of Councillor Liam Hayes (Fine Gael), that no eviction would take place until the case had been considered by the Committee. This ruling did not apply to evictions for non-payment of rent.[28]

Another successful and more famous DHAC campaign than that of Sarah Place involved the DHAC's Secretary, Dennis Dennehy and his family. In November 1968, Dennehy and his wife and two children squatted in a derelict house at 20 Mountjoy Square, which was owned by a businessman. In a court case the following month, Dennehy was ordered to vacate the premises. After refusing to do so, he was arrested for contempt of court and imprisoned on 3 January 1969. When he then went on hunger strike, the DHAC launched a major, successful campaign, including well-attended protest marches each evening from the GPO to Mountjoy Prison. On 18 January, in what undoubtedly was its most spectacular protest, some 2,000 DHAC demonstrators marched from Parnell Square to O'Connell Bridge, where several hundred of them sat down disrupting the traffic. This led to scuffles between the protestors and several hundred gardaí, many if not all of whom appeared without their identification numbers. Among the many peaceful demonstrators who were assaulted by the gardaí was John Feeney, the Chairman of the Christian-socialist group, Grille. Interviewed by an *Irish Times* reporter, he said that while standing on the footpath he was grabbed by four men in plain clothes who punched him. In a second incident nearby, in the presence of an inspector, the same four men, one of whom was wearing knuckledusters, punched him all over his body. In a separate incident, Sam Nolan, acting as a steward, intervened in an attempt to stop the fighting and was assaulted in the head and jaw. Fergal Costello, who remained seated on the bridge, informed the *Irish Times* journalist: 'I was kicked steadily for some time while I was sitting. One kick was so especially painful that I got myself across to the footpath. I was in extreme pain and could not walk properly. Some people helped me to a taxi.'[29] As a result of this assault, Costello was detained in the Mater Hospital for two weeks with an injured spine.[30] The *Irish Times* journalist witnessed Máirín Johnston, Secretary of the Seán Heuston Branch of the Labour Party and a speaker at the planned public meeting at the GPO, approaching a motor cycle garda, stating, 'You hit me in the face with your closed fist and I want your number', to which the garda replied: 'I don't know you.' Johnston also informed the journalist that she was kicked in the stomach by another garda during the first minutes of the battle. 'I screamed at him, "Why did you do that? I haven't done anything," and he said to me: 'Go back to your Labour Party cumann.'[31]

Support for the DHAC's key demands came from the Dublin Council of Trade Unions. At a specially convened meeting of the Council, in January 1969, the following motion, proposed by the ATGWU, was carried by 40 votes for with 6 against:

> Council is alarmed at the continuing housing crisis in the city which has led to squat-ins demonstrations and other forms of protest by several organisations and individuals, resulting in the jailing of a trade unionist, Mr. Denis Dennehy.
>
> Council should organise, as a matter of urgency, a mass demonstration of Dublin Trade Unionists to demand the declaration of a housing emergency by the Government, with the power to acquire all vacant houses and apartments, and to end the demolition by office block developers, of sound housing facilities.
>
> Council further demands an accelerated housing programme in the City and the acquisition by compulsory order of all building land in the city and county borough.

An addendum, proposed by Irish Actors' Equity Association, asking for official sites to be developed to accommodate itinerants, was incorporated in the resolution.[32]

Further support for the DHAC's demand for the declaration of a housing emergency was forthcoming at the 1969 Labour Party Annual Conference which adopted a resolution 'that a housing emergency exists' Proposing the motion, Michael O'Leary, TD, said: 'He would not like it to go out from the conference that they were not in sympathy with the Dublin Housing Action Committee. We accept that an emergency exists.'[33]

In a letter to the Editor of *Crisis* in the spring of 1969 about the wider issues raised by the DHAC's campaign, Scott stated:

> Recently all predictable establishment hacks crawled from beneath their various stones to denounce the demonstrations against the imprisonment of Denis [sic] Dennehy. We were told that the violence had come to the streets of Dublin and that this violence was directed by subversive elements with "foreign" ideas.
>
> The craw and tub thumpers conveniently forgot that violence which sucks on human misery has been with us for years – their kind of violence; the violence

which sucks on human misery to fatten speculators bank balances. It is violence to allow home grown TACA[34] speculators and foreign combines to grow fat on land and property deals while families of five and six have to eat, sleep and wash clothes in one room. One can see violence in forcing human beings to live in rat-infested Benburb Street, in Corporation Place, in Irishtown, Cathy Ní hUalachain Comes Home to roost every day in Dublin.

It is violence to see £2½ million pounds per acre i.e. £3,140 a sq. ft. for office property in Grafton Street while Nero Boland [Kevin Boland, Fianna Fáil, Minister for Local Government] fiddles with electoral boundaries in the Customs House.

It is violence to see an Insurance Company with £5¼ million invested in property while thousands of families cry out for a place to live.

Today there is "no room at the inn" for the poor family. If Joseph and Mary settled in a Dublin stable they would be arrested for squatting. "Caesar" Haughey [Charles Haughey, Fianna Fáil, Taoiseach] is only interested in establishing a money market in Dublin. There is no need for a Herod to massacre the innocents – diseases of overcrowding will see to that. The Joe Dowlings [Joe Dowling, Fianna Fáil TD] and Oliver J's [Oliver J. Flanagan, Fine Gael TD] are too busy looking for the thousands of trained Reds under their beds to see the star from the East rising above the overcrowded slums of Dublin. If the wise men come they will be advised by Brian "the lavatory lizard" Lenihan [Brian Lenihan, Fianna Fáil, Minister for Transport and Power] to leave their gifts with the customs and keep their mouths shut while in Ireland.

A society which roars for the preservation at all costs of the "sacred rights" of private property is a sick society. A society which jails men for finding a place for their families to live is a violent society. A society standing guard with bared teeth over its own vomit is a contemptible society.

The foundations of Irish society – the 1916 Proclamation and the First Dail Programme – are sound. The Fianna Fail top-stories are crumbling – the woodworm of graft and the termites of speculation have eaten into their fabric. If Erskine Childers [Fianna Fáil, Minister for Health] and his pals are still in the top-story looking with pleasure at a blank television screen, when the rotten structure crumbles no one will weep for them. All that would remain then would be to clear away the rubble and re-build on the old and strong foundations.[35]

Eventually, following a demonstration to the Mansion House, Dennehy was released and, subsequently, he and his family were provided with acceptable living accommodation. The Dennehy family was acutely aware that this successful outcome was a direct result of the DHAC's campaign:

> For over three years we existed in terrible conditions. First we lived in a shack and, later, we suffered in a 10 ft. leaky caravan without water or toilet.
>
> Now, thanks to the DHAC and the struggle of all those supporting the housing agitation in Dublin, we have a 22 ft. modern caravan on a corporation site at Queen Street. Water has been laid on by the Corporation and a flush toilet is being installed.
>
> For the first time in years, we have a fixed address, civilised conditions and security of tenure. Three years ago this was denied us and it would be denied us today as well but for the DHAC. If all the families who are paying exorbitant rent or existing in inhuman conditions joined the DHAC they too would be helped immensely in their struggle for proper homes at fair rents. In fact, if we all joined

together we wouldn't have much of a housing problem at all. It is only when we are divided and weak that the 26 Co. state and the landlords can continually crush us into the ground.[36]

Following his release from prison, Dennis Dennehy actively supported the DHAC's extensive programme of housing homeless people in vacant private property.

Another notable DHAC sit-down protest, involving hundreds of demonstrators, took place at College Green, following a public meeting at the GPO, on 27 September 1969. Having rejected instructions from the gardaí to move off the roadway, twenty-one protestors were arrested and taken to Pearse Street Garda Station.[37] After being charged, they were released from custody.[38] In subsequent hearings of the case in the Dublin District Court, fines of up to £15 were imposed on each of the defendants.[39] Máirín de Burca,[40] Eamonn Farrell[41] and the well-known journalists, Vincent Browne[42] and Kevin Myers,[43] were among those fined.

Dennis Dennehy's successor as DHAC Secretary was Eamonn Farrell, who, along with other families, was squatting in private property at 148 Pembroke Road, Ballsbridge, opposite the American Embassy. He remained there until the families were evicted in a dramatic dawn swoop by 200 steel-helmeted gardaí, many carrying protective shields, on 1 July 1970. Ten people were arrested, including de Burca and Farrell.[44] That eviction was one of the factors that signalled the end of the DHAC's campaign of housing homeless families in vacant private houses.[45]

Between the Mountjoy Square and Pembroke Road occupations, the DHAC housed many families in vacant accommodation in the city. However, the DHAC's greatest achievement was to raise awareness about the appalling housing situation, particularly in Dublin, and to prompt complacent politicians to address the housing crisis in a more meaningful way.

Meanwhile, in October 1969, aware that Conor Cruise O'Brien, TD, had expressed an interest in learning more about the DHAC, the DHAC decided that those members of the Committee who were also Labour Party members should seek a meeting with him. The members in question were Fergal Costello, Máirín Johnston and Brendan Scott.[46] Although O'Brien acceded to the request[47] and the meeting took place in Howth the following month, it was unproductive.[48]

Notes

1   BB [Bernard Browne?], 'Jumping The Queue', *Crisis*, Bulletin No. 1, circa March-April 1969.
2   *Crisis*, Bulletin No. 1, circa March-April 1969, p. 9.
3   ibid., p. 4.
4   *Nusight*, June 1968, p. 6.

5   *Action,* Vol..1, No. 1, undated, circa February 1969. [Labour Party, Sean Heuston Branch].

6   ibid., Vol. 1, No. 2, undated, 1969.

7   Interview with Máirín Johnston, 31 October 2018.

8   ibid., 30 October 2018; Mary Maher (M.M.), *Irish Socialist,* No. 131, October 1973, p. 3.

9   For further information on Paddy Behan (1938-2016) see Scott Millar, 'Paddy Behan (1938-2016)', *Saothar* 42, 2017, pp. 163-164.

10 *Action,* Vol. 1, No. 2, op. cit.

11 Fergal Costello, email to the author, 27 July 2020.

12 For further information on Bernard Browne (1944-2017) see Tony Dunne, 'Bernard Browne: Veteran activist who didn't suffer fools lightly', *Liberty,* Vol. 17, No. 1, February 2018; Tony Dunne, 'Bernard Browne (1944-2017) SIPTU', *Saothar* 44, 2019, p. 135.

13 For further information on Michael Sweetman (1914-1996), see John Cooney, 'Michael Sweetman', *Sunday Tribune,* 27 October 1996.

14 *Irish Times,* 25 January 1968.

15 ibid., 16 January 1968.

16 Interview with Eric Fleming, 16 June 2020. In an *Irish Press* report of this incident, on 9 March 1968, Detective Sergeant John Reynolds was reported to have said on 8 March 1968 that he saw Michael O'Riordan show a card or document [O'Riordan's ITGWU membership card] to one of the workers and say to him: "Stop working. I will guarantee to you the union will be after you and we will see whether you will work or not." The worker replied: "Will you get me a job? I am only earning a living." He [Detective Sergeant Reynolds] then heard Inspector O'Connor telling the picket that they were an unlawful assembly and they were taken into custody.

17 *Irish Times,* 24 January 1968.

18 ibid., 16 January 1968.

19 The first group of demonstrators charged in the Dublin District Court were: Laurence Malone, John Dunne, Séamus Ó Tuathail, Basil Keely, Patrick Doyle, Donal McNicholl, James Monaghan, Seamus Brogan and Deirdre McKenna.

20 The second group demonstrators charged in the Dublin District Court were: Anthony Hogan, Donough Dennehy, Eric Fleming, Albert Kennedy, Michael O'Riordan, Francis [Proinsias] De Rossa, Fintan Smyth, Marie Dennehy, Angela Quinn, Jean Meehan, Maureen Burke [Máirín de Burca] and Marie Gill.

21 *Irish Times,* 16 January 1968.

22 ibid., 23 January 1968.

23 ibid., 12 March 1968.

24 ibid., 15 March 1968.

25 *Irish Independent,* 23 March 1968.

26 Interview with Eric Fleming, 22 June 2020.

27 *Evening Herald,* 17 January 1968.

28 *Irish Press,* 5 February 1968.

29 *Irish Times,* 20 January 1969.

30 *Action,* Vol. 1, No. 2, op. cit.

31 *Irish Times,* 20 January 1969; *Action,* Vol. 1, No. 2, op. cit.

32 *Irish Socialist,* No. 84, February 1969, p. 1.

33 *Irish Press,* 27 January 1969; *Irish Socialist,* No. 84, February 1969, p. 1.

34 Highly controversial, TACA (Support) was set up by Fianna Fáil in the 1960s to raise funding from wealthy businessmen, particularly in the construction industry.

35 *Crisis,* op. cit., p. 5.

36 ibid., p. 32.

37 *Sunday Independent,* 28 September 1969.

38 *Irish Independent,* 29 September 1969.

39 *Irish Press,* 30 September 1969.
40 *Evening Herald,* 14 October1969.
41 ibid.
42 *Irish Press,* 30 September 1969.
43 ibid.
44 *Irish Press,* 1 July 1970.
45 Wikipedia, Dublin Housing Action Committee site, 13 November 2019.
46 Fergal Costello, letter to Conor Cruise O'Brien, TD, 28 October 1969. [Fergal Costello Papers].
47 Conor Cruise O'Brien, TD, letter to Fergal Costello, undated but circa early November 1969. [Fergal Costello Papers].
48 Interview with Fergal Costello, 30 April 2020.

CHAPTER 10

Challenging Repressive Legislation

A consequence of agitation over the housing crisis, particularly the DHAC's campaign, was the introduction by Fianna Fáil of the Prohibition of Forcible Entry and Occupation Bill, 1970. A resolution calling on the Government to withdraw the proposed legislation was passed at a public meeting, in the Mansion House, on 1 March 1970. Speakers included Ivan Cooper, the Independent Stormont MP; Professor David Greene, TCD; Matt Larkin, Chairman of the National Association of Tenants' Organisations (NATO); Tomás Mac Giolla, President of Official Sinn Féin; Seán Mac Réamoinn, the journalist and broadcaster; the Rev. Enda McDonagh, Professor of Moral Theology, Maynooth College; Donal Nevin, Assistant General Secretary, ICTU; Senator Mary Robinson, Paul Tansey, Vice-President of the Union of Students in Ireland (USI); and David Thornley, TD.

The meeting was interrupted several times from the floor by members of the Post Office Officials' Association (POOA), a breakaway body from the Post Office Workers' Union (POWU), who were protesting against what they alleged was an attempt by the ICTU to coerce them to amalgamate with the POWU. Jack McQuillan, General Secretary of the POOA and a former TD and Senator, was one of two people escorted from the hall when he shouted from the floor.[1]

The following month, a Labour Party protest meeting against the Bill was held at the GPO. The speakers were Roddy Connolly,[2] Chairman; the Leader, Brendan Corish, TD; John O'Connell, TD, and Brendan Scott. In the course of his speech, Scott appealed to the gardaí that, in the event of the Bill becoming law, they should not allow themselves to be used as hatchet men of a corrupt Government.[3] On 27 May, in a further protest against the Bill, some twenty members of the Irish Women's Liberation Movement (IWLM) paraded outside Leinster House, distributed leaflets published by Citizens for Civil Liberties (CCL) and carried placards with slogans: 'Kill the Bill', 'Homes not Jails' and 'One Family One House.'[4]

A month later again, in June 1971, a committee representing groups opposed to the Bill was formed in Dublin. Entitled the Committee to Oppose Repressive Legislation (CORL), its members were: Fergal Costello, Chairman; Bernard Browne, Chairman of the DHAC; Mary Earls, IWLM; Con Lehane, a solicitor, (CCL); Máirín de Burca, Secretary, Official Sinn Féin; and Michael Sweetman, SJ. Brendan Scott was a regular participant in CORL's activities.

In a statement, in June 1971, Costello said CORL's plans included an appeal to President de Valera, if the Bill was passed, not to sign it and, if signed, implementation of an immediate large scale infringement of its provisions. The group claimed support from many organisations including the Dublin and Dún Laoghaire Housing Action Committees, CCL, IWLM, Official Sinn Féin, the CPI, the CYM, the Dublin Flat-dwellers' Association, the National Association of Tenants' Organisations (NATO) and many other tenants' and trade union groups.

Contending that the wrong slant had been given to the proposed legislation by calling it an anti-squatters Bill, Costello said it was much more than that. It was aimed at students and workers who, in the course of legitimate protest, might decide to occupy their university or place of work. Already, he said, the committee had collected over 4,500 signatures of persons opposed to the Bill and it was intended to hold a protest march to the Dáil, where the petition would be presented to the Taoiseach, Jack Lynch, and later to the Minister for Justice, Desmond O'Malley. It is worth noting, he added, that, were the Bill law already, every person signing a similar petition would be guilty of an offence and would be liable to imprisonment and a fine. Pointing out that the Bill could become law by the end of July, Costello said the Committee would have to anticipate a situation in which it would be law and decide how then to act. Rejecting as untrue the Government's claim that the Bill was aimed at controlling queue-jumping in local authority housing, he said there was already sufficient power to control that matter under the 1970 Housing Act.

Michael Sweetman, SJ, said if the Bill became law, he would not break it on principle, but he could foresee situations in which he would act again as he had done before in assisting the Dublin Housing Action Committee.[5]

A month later, CORL mounted a sixteen-person picket on the St. Stephen's Green office of the Minister for Justice, Des O'Malley.[6] On 28 July, under the auspices of CORL, a petition signed by some 4,000 people appealing to President de Valera not to sign the Bill was handed in to Áras an Uachtaráin. The petition was presented to him by a garda superintendent after the President declined to meet a delegation. This was preceded by a march from the GPO to the Phoenix Park by 3,000 people, with contingents from the Labour Party, Official Sinn Féin, the CPI, the CYM, the IWLM, Conradh na Gaeilge and Dún Laoghaire Housing Action Committee.

Addressing those assembled in the Phoenix Park, CORL Chairman, Fergal Costello, who presided, said that over the previous six months almost every organisation in the State – except Fianna Fáil, had objected to 'this oppressive anti-worker legislation.' Continuing, he stated:

> The Minister says that those who object represent only 1 per cent of the population. Let Mr. O'Malley produce the other 99 per cent who agree with him. He can't, because they don't exist. But a few do agree with him and we can name them – they are the speculators, the river barons and the exploiting employers who keep Fianna Fail in power. This is a landlord's Bill. The introduction of the 'insidious' Bill was being followed up by an unprecedented amount of demolition in Dublin to make way for office blocks.

Costello then read aloud the text of the CORL letter to President de Valera., which pointed out that, in part, the Bill was repugnant as it curbed the freedom of the press. Matt Merrigan, Irish District Secretary of the ATGWU, said the Bill was the 'first major step on the high road to fascism in this country. It was being forced not only on the homeless, but on workers who could be arrested summarily by gardaí for occupying their places of employment.'[7]

Just over a week later, on 5 August, the journalist, Mary Anderson, and Máirín de Burca, were among four people arrested after a five-hour CORL protest against the Bill, which had just been passed in the Dáil by 68 votes to 46. Earlier, there had been scuffles between protestors and the gardaí after the former attempted to throw themselves at the vehicles of the departing ministers. After learning that the Bill had been adopted, those assembled were addressed by representatives of the CORL, the ATGWU, Official Sinn Féin, the Labour Party, NATO, Conradh na Gaeilge and the IWLM. Describing the Bill as a surrender by Fianna Fáil to the speculators, Costello said that the Bill was the most repressive piece of legislation to come before the Dáil since the infamous Criminal Justice Bill. In his address, Merrigan, said it was a shame that the organised trade union movement in Ireland had not 'opened its mouth' on a national basis against the Bill. De Burca stated that her movement would break the law at every possible opportunity to oppose this legislation and make it unworkable, while Dr. Moira Woods[8] of the Labour Party declared: 'We intend to break the law. Let Mr. O'Malley know that his prisons will not be big enough to hold all the people who will break this law.'[9] The Dublin North East Constituency Council of the Labour Party also condemned the legislation and expressed its support for CORL to oppose repressive legislation.[10]

CORL was not the only body formed to oppose repressive legislation in the late 1960s and early 1970s. In response to growing social unrest in the Republic and the outbreak of violence in Northern Ireland, the Fianna Fáil Government introduced a range of repressive legislation during that period. That in turn led to the formation of several civil rights bodies to oppose the proposed legislation. In 1968, three years prior to the founding of CORL, the Sixty-eight Group, was formed to oppose Fianna Fáil's Criminal Justice Bill. Notwithstanding his numerous other commitments, Scott was involved in the Group's campaign. At a meeting of the Group in June that year, at which Dr. Aidan Clarke, subsequently Professor of History and Vice Provost of TCD, presided, a resolution was passed calling on the Parliamentary Labour Party to oppose the measure 'with utmost vigour.' Scott, who proposed the resolution, said: 'The Bill would all but take away the right of peaceful demonstration. This was an attack on the basic constitutional right of freedom of expression.'[11]

The Sixty-eight Group appears to have been short-lived and superseded by a new civil rights body, Citizens for Civil Liberties (CCL), which was founded at a meeting in Buswell's Hotel, Dublin, on 20 February 1969. Its officers were Peadar O'Donnell (President), Con Lehane (Chairman), Rev. Terence McCaughey, a Presbyterian minister (Secretary) and Mícheál Ó Lionsigh (Treasurer).[12] Brendan Scott was an active participant in CCL's activities.[13]

The first object of CCL was to oppose the many clauses in the Criminal Justice Bill which it considered objectionable and which had not been dealt with in the Minister's proposed amendments.[14]

A pamphlet examining the undesirable implications of many provisions of the Bill was published in March by CCL. In relation to Section 28 of the Bill, the pamphlet stated that it ignored existing common law relating to contempt of court which was adequate to deal with situations envisaged. Much attention in the pamphlet was devoted Sections 30 and 31 of the Bill. Section 30, the pamphlet stated, required advance notice to be given the Garda Síochána of any public meeting or procession, except for some customary meetings. Noting that the Minister had given notice of amendment, the pamphlet said that if the Bill stood as moved every spontaneous factory-gate gathering or similar meeting would be liable to prosecution. 'Any amendment that retains the obligation to give notice in any statutory form must give rise to alarm', the pamphlet stated. Section 31, it was stated, gave power to impose conditions on any public meeting, procession or demonstration or to ban such meetings and that power extended even to local or parliamentary election meetings. There was also condemnation in the pamphlet of Section 45 which gave the Minister absolute discretion to transfer persons from civil to military custody on very vague pretexts and with no right of appeal.

The pamphlet went on to state that there was no similar peace-time legislation in Northern Ireland or in Britain and that sections of the Bill were unquestionably destructive of some basic freedoms and weakened many more dangerously. It also said that the Bill not only casually eroded such freedoms and rights, but reflected an apparent desire to make matters easier for inadequate prosecutions and to extend police powers in a completely unwarranted manner.[15]

In a booklet issued on 1 April, the Minister for Justice, Mícheál Ó Moráin, refuted many of the allegations made by the CCL.[16] Evidently, Ó Moráin also alleged that CCL had been founded following consultation with Sinn Féin. This was denied by CCL in a statement issued by its Secretary, Terence McCaughey, who said that the Minister's statement to that effect was untrue and that CCL included among its members people who belonged to all political parties, including Mr. Ó Morain's.[17] In a separate statement, Tomás Mac Giolla, President of Sinn Féin, stated: 'It is not true to say that Sinn Fein set up an organisation called Citizens for Civil Liberties…In fact so far as I understand there is no member of Sinn Féin on the executive of CCL.'[18]

A CCL public meeting on the Criminal Justice Bill, on 2 May, in the Mansion House, Dublin, attracted an attendance of over 500. Speakers included Con Lehane, CCL Chairman, who presided; Ivan Cooper, the

Independent Stormont MP; Rickard Deasy, the former President of the National Farmers' Association of Ireland; Austin Flannery, OP, St. Saviour's Dominican Church; Liam Hamilton, Senior Counsel and later Chief Justice; Terence McCaughey, CCL Secretary and Chaplin, TCD; and Michael Mullen,[19] the Labour Party TD and General Secretary of the ITGWU.

Addressing that gathering, Cooper said he was astounded that while they in Northern Ireland were fighting for their rights the Government in this part of the country had chosen a time such as this to introduce 'another Special Powers Act...' In his contribution, Hamilton stated that apart from the many features of the Bill which were welcome, it contained too many sections which were of a frightening nature, involving infringement of ordinary human rights, limitations of rights of accused persons, extension of powers of police and fundamental changes in court procedure – all designed to extend the powers of the State and limit the rights of the individual. The Chairman, Con Lehane, said that the platform of nine speakers, representing a wide cross section of people, was sufficient answer to the allegation of the Minister of Justice that the Citizens for Civil Liberties was subversive.[20]

A call to the Minister for Justice to withdraw the Criminal Justice Bill and to incorporate such of its provisions as were unobjectionable in a new Bill was made at the 1969 CCL AGM, in the Father Mathew Hall, Dublin, on 18 October. The meeting also called for the repeal of the Offences Against the State Act on the grounds that its provisions were repugnant to basic principles of law and observed and understood in normal democratic states and societies.[21]

In a resolution passed at its annual conference, on 12 December 1970, in relation to possible changes in the Irish Constitution, CCL declared its belief 'that in no circumstances should the internal discipline of one church be imported either into our constitution or into legislation thereunder.' The resolution added: 'The right of the individual, subject to public order and morality, to make its own decisions in matters affecting his own conscience of private moral code, must be recognised. To deny this right was a denial of civil liberty.'[22] Reiterating its position in a statement, in April 1971, CCL said it was now time to realise that our society was a pluralist one and legislation should be inspired by non-confessional principles. 'The imposition by legal process of the judgement of a majority on a dissenting minority in a matter of private morals was an assault on the liberty of the individual citizen,'[23] the statement said.

In a statement the following month, the Executive of CCL declared that proposals for community schools by the Minister for Education, Pádraig Faulkner, could not be accepted as 'conforming to the conception of a pluralist society.' The statement added:

> The Minister now sought to take the vocational schools from the ownership and control of the community... and to vest the legal ownership of the schools in trustees to be nominated by the Catholic Bishop of the Diocese. This proposal

would be divisive in its effect in the community, and discriminate in favour of one section of it. Mr. Faulkner's recent proposals require an abdication by the community of its rights in so far as the vocational schools were concerned, and seeks to invest those rights in an undemocratic manner in individual citizens not elected by the community nor responsible to it....[24]

In August the following year, on the first anniversary of the introduction of internment in Northern Ireland, the Executive Committee of CCL sent a telegram to Dr. Kurt Waldheim, Secretary-General of the United Nations:

> Hundreds of law-abiding citizens imprisoned now without charge or trial for one year, despite repeated promises by Heath (Edward 'Ted' Heath, British Prime Minister) and Whitelaw (William Whitelaw, Secretary of State for Northern Ireland) to end internment.

> Citizens for Civil Liberties, Dublin, urgently request you to use your influence on world opinion to induce the British Government to end this violation of human rights.[25]

Another issue on the agenda of Scott and his left-wing Labour colleagues, many of them now organised informally in the Liaison Committee of the Left – Labour Party (LCLL), was Fianna Fáil's Offences Against the State Act. Despite their abhorrence of the Provisional IRA's sectarianism and violence, the vast majority of Labour's left-wingers, including Scott, campaigned vigorously against the Act. Scott's contribution was somewhat limited due to the deteriorating state of his health. In a statement, in early June 1972, the LCLL deplored the part played by the Parliamentary Labour Party in giving Fianna Fáil the type of repressive legislation 'which even the Greek colonels do not possess.' The statement warned that these powers could be used against trade unionists and protesters on social issues. The statement, incidentally, also welcomed the recent Official IRA ceasefire.[26]

Speaking at a meeting organised by the LCLL, Dermot Boucher, Vice-Chairman of Labour's Dublin Regional Council, Secretary of the LCLL and an employee of the Irish National Productivity Centre, called on Labour TDs to 'salvage their tattered reputations" and demand the immediate repeal of the Offences Against the State Act and the Prisons Act. It was the duty of all socialists, he said, to act immediately to prevent the establishment of a police state here. Earlier, he had said that the Government's decision to re-activate Section 5 of the Offences Against the State Act presented socialists with a particularly painful dilemma:

> On the one hand, the unpalatable fact must be faced that at least a section of the republican movement has by its words and by its deeds branded itself as being unmistakeably fascist. The republican tradition does contain an ultra-nationalist strain which must surely be incompatible with socialist principles. At least some of those opposing the present Government would be twice as bitterly opposed to the establishment of a socialist government, which would ultimately have to deal with those people by one means or another. Again, it must be said, clearly and unequivocally, that the present campaign of indiscriminate terror being conducted by the Provisional IRA is morally indefensible, and cannot be justified by any political consideration...[27]

Notes

1   *Irish Times*, 2 March 1971.
2   For information on Roderick (Roddy) J. Connolly (1901-1980) see Charles McGuire, *Roddy Connolly and the Struggle for Socialism in Ireland* (Cork University Press, Cork, 2008); Charles Callan and Barry Desmond, 'Roderick J. Connolly (1901-1980)', *Irish Labour Lives*, op. cit., pp. 48-49.
3   *Irish Times*, 21 April 1971.
4   *Evening Herald*, 27 May 1971.
5   *Irish Times*, 23 June 1971
6   *Irish Press*, 24 July 1971.
7   ibid., 29 July 1971.
8   In the *Irish Press* (29 July 1971) report of this event, apparently Dr. Moira Woods was misnamed as Maura Walsh.
9   *Irish Press*, 5 August 1971.
10 *Irish Independence*, 6 August 1971.
11 *Irish Times*, 19 June 1968.
12 *Irish Independent*, 21 February 1969.
13 Interview with Eoin Scott, 15 January 2019.
14 *Irish Independent*, 21 February 1969.
15 *Irish Times*, 17 March 1969.
16 ibid., 2 April 1969.
17 ibid.
18 ibid., 1 May 1969.
19 For further information on Michael Mullen (1919-1982) see Charles Callan and Barry Desmond, 'Michael Mullen (1919-1982)', *Irish Labour Lives,* op. cit., pp. 188-189.
20 *Irish Times*, 3 May 1969.
21 *Irish Independent*, 21 October 1969.
22 *Irish Press*, 9 April 1971.
23 ibid.
24 ibid., 29 May 1971.
25 ibid., 12 August 1972.
26 *Irish Examiner,* 2 June 1972.
27 *Irish Times*, 12 June 1972.

CHAPTER 11

Confronting Racism

Scott's intensive involvement in the labour movement and in campaigns such as those of the Dublin Housing Action Committee and the Committee to Oppose Repressive Legislation did not restrict his commitment to international solidarity. The most obvious manifestation of this was the leading role he played in the Irish Anti-Apartheid Movement (IAAM) for virtually the final decade of his life.

The notorious Sharpeville massacre, in which sixty-nine unarmed people were murdered, and a further 180 injured, by the racist South African regime, on 21 March 1960, was possibly the catalyst for the founding four years later of the IAAM. A month prior to the massacre, Irish-based African students held a meeting of protest in the Mansion House, Dublin, against the policy of apartheid being enforced by the South African Government. The object of the meeting, at which there was a 'huge' attendance, was to secure support for the 'Boycott South African Goods' Campaign.[1] Hilda Larkin, a daughter of James Larkin, Junior, was appointed to represent Labour's Administrative Council (AC) at the meeting.

Following the Sharpeville massacre, the following resolution was passed at a joint meeting of the Labour Party's AC and Parliamentary Party:

> On behalf of the Irish Labour movement, the Administrative Council of the Labour Party and the members of the Parliamentary Labour Party express their horror at the killings by the South African police on Monday, March 21st, 1960, of scores of unarmed native demonstrators, and their sympathy with the victims.

The AC added that it felt that the Irish Government should continue to pursue a policy against racial discrimination through international machinery and that the Labour Party would give their full support to any such action.[2]

The IAAM was launched at a public meeting in the Mansion House, Dublin, on 22 April 1964.[3] Its aims were to inform the public about conditions in South Africa and campaign for the release of South African political prisoners. It also called for a boycott of South African goods.

A founding member of the IAAM, Brendan Scott[4] served as an Executive Committee member for eight years,[5] and was elected Joint Honorary Secretary (with Niall Greene)[6] for 1970-1971[7] and Secretary from 1971[8] until his final illness forced him reluctantly to withdraw.[9] The key figure throughout its existence was its Vice-Chairman, Dr. Kader Asmal,[10] a South African-born lecturer in law at Trinity College, Dublin. His wife, English-born Louise Asmal (née Parkinson)[11] was for many years Honorary

Administrative Secretary.[12] The principal founding officers were Ernest Wood, Senior Counsel (Chairman),[13] and Barry Desmond, Industrial Officer of the ICTU (Secretary).[14] Later chairpersons in Scott's era included the future Labour Party TD and minister, Dr. Conor Cruise O'Brien;[15] Dr. Patrick Lynch, Professor of Political Economy at UCD;[16] and Austin Flannery, OP.[17] Apart from Desmond and Greene, among Secretaries of the IAAM with whom Scott worked was Noel Harris,[18] Secretary of the Union of Insurance Staffs.[19] The IAAM also had a number of sponsors.[20]

In June 1964, Nelson Mandela, Walter Sisulu and seven others were sentenced to life imprisonment at the end of the Rivonia trial. That they did not receive the death penalty was due to a world-wide campaign and petition to the United Nations (UN) for their release. The nascent IAAM, in what was possibly its first public activity, collected thousands of signatures, including those of almost half the members of the Oireachtas. A packed protest meeting at the Mansion House, in June, addressed by leading members of the three main political parties, adopted a resolution calling for the imposition of economic sanctions against South Africa.[21] Among other activities that year, the IAAM persuaded twenty-nine Irish playwrights, among them Seán O'Casey, Samuel Beckett, Hugh Leonard, John B. Keane and Brian Friel, to refuse permission for their plays to be performed before segregated audiences in South Africa.[22]

The year 1965 saw the first IAAM South African rugby tour protest in Ireland, when some 350 demonstrators picketed the Irish Rugby Football Union's (IRFU's) Lansdowne Road venue. President de Valera and the entire Cabinet refused to attend the match on 10 April.[23] Sharpeville Day was commemorated for the first time, too, with four young people, wearing black sashes, fasting all day at Nelson's Pillar on O'Connell Street.[24] It was also that year that extensive campaigning began among parliamentarians, trade unionists, religious organisations and students, the groups that would be the backbone of IAAM support for the following thirty years.[25] In a further initiative in 1965, the IAAM widened its brief to include the related issues of South West Africa (now Namibia), and Rhodesia (now Zimbabwe) which made its Unilateral Declaration of Independence that year. In response, the IAAM promptly organised a march through Dublin to the British Embassy to deliver a letter of protest.[26]

An IAAM conference for trade unionists on apartheid and South Africa and South West Africa was held in the Shelbourne Hotel, Dublin, on 9 September 1966. Entitled 'Brother Lend a Hand', the conference urged Irish trade unions to support Africans victimised by anti-apartheid trade union legislation under the South African Government. Presiding on that occasion was James Larkin, Junior (General Secretary, WUI). In addition to Brendan Scott (Association of Secondary Teachers in Ireland), other listed speakers included Phyllis Altman (former Assistant General Secretary, South African Congress of Trade Unions); Barry Desmond (Industrial

Officer, ICTU); Brian Graham (Secretary, Draughtsmen's and Allied Trades' Association); Charles McCarthy[27] (General Secretary, Vocational Teachers' Association); Donal Nevin (Research Officer, ICTU); and John Swift (General Secretary, Irish Bakers', Confectioners' and Allied Workers' Amalgamated Union).

In the course of his address, Scott, then an Executive Committee member of the IAAM, said that though sanctions had been advised by the UN and were obviously the quickest way of bringing South Africa to a change in policy, they had not been enforced largely because of the pressures of big business. 'We who are trade unionists can possibly understand this better than most people,' he said, adding that British business investments in South Africa amounted to £1,000m and 243 American firms had financial investments totalling about $800m.[28]

Also that year, the IAAM issued a public declaration on Rhodesia signed by 125 public figures and organised a public meeting, which was attended by 900 people and addressed by Judith Todd, daughter of the former Rhodesian premier, Garfield Todd.[29] A vigil for human rights in Rhodesia was held at the British Embassy on Human Rights Day.[30] A briefing document on South West Africa and a boycott leaflet listing South African products on sale in Ireland were widely circulated.[31] A disappointment for the IAAM that year was the failure of Frank Aiken, the Fianna Fáil Minister for External Affairs, to support economic sanctions against South Africa.[32]

On 25 January 1967, Scott spoke on Rhodesia at an IAAM public meeting in the Queen's Hotel, Dundalk, County Louth. Chaired by Kader Asmal, the principal speaker was Dennis Brutus, the South African teacher, poet and sportsman, who had been imprisoned for twenty-two months, sixteen of them in the notorious Robben Island prison camp, in the same block as Mandela, Sisulu and the men of the Rivonia Trial.[33] Brutus was on a world tour seeking support for political prisoners.[34] The other speakers were Barry Desmond, IAAM Secretary, and the Rev. A. H. McElroy, President of the Ulster Liberal Party.[35]

Brutus was again the principal speaker later that month at an IAAM public meeting in Liberty Hall, Dublin. On that occasion, the other speakers were Brendan Scott, the Rev. C. Gray-Stack, Church of Ireland Dean of Ardfert; John O'Donoghue, the RTÉ television current affairs presenter; and Louise Asmal, Administrative Secretary, IAAM. The meeting passed a resolution calling on the Irish Government to take the necessary initiatives at the UN for the setting up of a commission to investigate South African prisons and requesting the release of all political prisoners in South Africa.[36]

On 26 June 1968, at an IAAM members' meeting, 900 people gathered to hear Oliver Tambo, acting President-General of the African National Congress (ANC) speak on racism. A resolution calling for Government action against South Africa was passed unanimously.[37] Also in 1968, the

IAAM persuaded the National Ploughing Association to withdraw from the world championships which were held in Rhodesia, while failing to persuade the IRFU from participating in a British Lions tour of South Africa and Rhodesia, which proceeded in May.[38]

At the IAAM's 1968 AGM, on 14 September, Scott stated that two Irish newspapers, later identified as the *Irish Independent* and *Sunday Independent,* had used advertising and propaganda material from the racist South African Government and had not given the IAAM a chance to reply to this material.[39] Incidentally, at the end of 1968, membership of the IAAM stood at 2,000.[40]

Under the auspices of the IAAM, a talk by a twenty-seven-year-old, white South African citizen, Stephanie Sachs, who as a student at the University of Cape Town had been a member of the African Resistance Movement, was held in Wynn's Hotel, Dublin, on I December 1968. Although uninvolved in any sabotage activity in South Africa, she had been arrested, beaten by her interrogators and sentenced to two years imprisonment in 1964. After serving a year of her sentence, she was released. Addressing an audience of 100 young students and a number of adults, Sachs, then residing in London, said that black South Africans had no freedom of movement in their own country and lived in abject poverty. Johannesburg, one of the richest cities in the world, she said, was kept going on the cheap labour of 700,000 Africans who had to live outside the city. She added that education for black children was neither compulsory nor free as it was for white children, that to allow a [black] African to do skilled work was an offence and that in most cases [black] Africans were paid far less than their white counterparts for doing the same work. Among other speakers at that event, which was chaired by J. A. Brooks, Headmaster of Mountjoy School, Dublin, were Brendan Scott, Bunny Carr, a RTÉ television presenter; and Brian Farrell, lecturer in Politics in UCD, author and RTÉ television current affairs presenter.[41]

In a debate at the Labour Party Annual Conference, in Liberty Hall, Dublin, in January 1969, Scott suggested that all cultural and economic relations be broken off with South Africa and Rhodesia and that no visas be granted to anyone who wished to visit those countries.[42]

Later that year, at the IAAM's AGM, Scott moved a motion that was passed without dissent, condemning the activities of the State-sponsored body, Córas Tráchtála, 'which for the past eight months has actively pursued a policy of increasing trading and financial links with South Africa.' The resolution pointed out that the increase in trade of approximately 100 per cent in the previous year would, if maintained, make it even more difficult for Ireland to disengage from South Africa. Córas Tráchtála and other Irish business organisations 'would have to bear a heavy responsibility for the treachery against the oppressed people of South Africa.' The resolution called on the Government to instruct Córas Tráchtála to stop its 'shameful collaboration'. It also asked the Government to support UN resolutions to impose economic sanctions against South Africa as so many other countries had done.[43]

As mentioned earlier, Brendan Scott and Niall Greene were elected Joint Secretaries of the IAAM at the organisation's AGM, on 26 September 1970. Their colleague officers were Austin Flannery, OP (Chairman), Kader Asmal (Vice-Chairman) and Dermot O'Connor (Treasurer).[44] A year later, at the IAAM's 1971 AGM, Scott was elected Secretary.[45]

In the meantime, in January 1971, Scott was one of five signatories of a letter to the press regarding the British Government's proposal to break the UN embargo on arms sales to South Africa:

> Sir – In a few days time the Commonwealth Prime Ministers' conference opens… and the most important item on the agenda will be Britain's proposal to break the United Nations embargo on the sale of arms to South Africa.
>
> There is no doubt that aircraft, submarines, bombs and military equipment of whatever nature could be used by the South African Government to maintain supremacy. There have been occasions in the past, for example, at Sharpeville, when British weapons were used against defenceless crowds. South Africa's pressure on Britain is not purely for military hardware – it is an attempt to purchase respectability and acceptance for what has rightly been regarded by the civilised world as the evil doctrine of apartheid. If Britain decides to sell her weapons to South Africa, there is little hope of persuading France to stop the sale of Alouette helicopters, submarines and other munitions.
>
> Our Government has called at the U. N. for a strengthening, not a reversal, of the arms embargo. We would therefore like to add our voices, as Irishmen, to the protests now being heard around the world, and which will also surely be uttered by many of the Heads of States attending the Commonwealth Prime Ministers' Conference.
>
> In our capacities as chairman of the Irish Anti-Apartheid Movement and as individual members of the three main political parties we consider that any military assistance rendered to the White minority government of South Africa will result in a tragic diminution of the authority of the United Nations and will constitute a terrible betrayal of those fighting for freedom in South Africa. We appeal, at the last minute, to the British Government to listen to the voice of reason. Father A. Flannery, O.P., Chairman, Irish Anti-Apartheid Movement; Dr. Garret Fitzgerald [sic], T.D, Fine Gael; Dr. Conor Cruise O'Brien, T.D., Irish Labour Party; Senator Eoin Ryan, S.C., Fianna Fail; Brendan Scott, Joint Hon. Secretary, Irish Anti-Apartheid Movement.[46]

A day or two later, on 9 January, in a public statement, twelve Labour members of the Oireachtas and the Independent Senator, Owen Sheehy Skeffington, deprecated the invitation to Leinster House of the Springboks, 'this racially selected group', by the Fine Gael TD, Dr. Hugh Byrne. The Labour Oireachtas members were the TDs, Corish, Browne, Cluskey, Desmond, Keating, O'Connell, O'Brien, O'Leary and Thornley and Senators James Dunne, Fintan Kennedy[47] (General President, ITGWU) and Evelyn Owens.[48]

Days later again, on 13 January 1971, seventy placard-bearing members of the IAAM, supported by the Trinity College Branch of the UN Student Association, protested outside the British and French Embassies in Dublin against the proposed sale of arms by Britain to South Africa and France's involvement with South Africa. Among those present were Austin Flannery, OP, Chairman, IAAM; Máire Cruise O'Brien (née MacEntee),[49] Irish-language writer and poet; and Donal Nevin, Assistant General Secretary, ICTU. A letter, signed by Brendan Scott, Joint Honorary Secretary, IAAM, was handed in at both British and French Embassies stating that by supplying arms to South Africa, Britain and France would be aligning themselves with the forces of white supremacy in that country.[50]

Five months later again, on 5 June 1971, in his capacity as Secretary of the IAAM, Scott announced that a conference would take place in Ireland, in September, to discuss how special training in the particular nature of regimes of Southern Africa could be given to Irish missionaries and teachers. Invitations were sent to all seminaries, monasteries and convents. The announcement was made at a special consultative session attended by three members of the UN's Special Committee on Apartheid: the Ambassador of Somalia at the UN, Abdulrahin Farah (Chairman), Barakat Anmad, from India; Yanos Varga, from Hungary, and Hishan Rifai, Secretary of the Special Committee. A subsidiary of the UN, the Committee was set up to co-ordinate UN activity against apartheid and to promote assistance to the struggle for freedom in South Africa. In what was its first visit to Ireland, the Committee met the Minister for Foreign Affairs, Dr. Patrick Hillery, members of his Department, and officers of the IAAM.[51]

The conference itself, which was opened by Michael O'Kennedy, TD, Parliamentary Secretary to the Minister for Education, took place in Gonzaga College, Dublin, on the weekend of 25-26 September 1971. The Anglican Bishop of California, Rt. Rev. Edward Crowther, who had been expelled from South Africa, was among the speakers. The other speakers were Guy Clutton-Brock of Rhodesia's Cold Comfort Farm fame; Dr. Owen Dudley Edwards, lecturer in history, Edinburgh University; Ruth First, the South African author; Dean Gunnar Helander, a Swede, who spent seventeen years in South Africa; Rev. Walter Makhulu, a native of Johannesburg; and Rev. Michael Traberr, S.M.B., a Swiss priest.[52] Among others present were the Rev. Michael Harty, Bishop of Killaloe; the Rev. Austin Flannery, OP, and Brendan Scott.[53]

Later that year, on 20 November, a resolution condemning internment without trial in Northern Ireland was carried at the IAAM's AGM. Proposing the resolution, Scott said that it would be impertinent for an organisation like the Anti-Apartheid Movement to lecture the people of Northern Ireland on how they should resolve their differences. 'But as an organisation which is proud to be associated with the men who wrote that Freedom Charter [Freedom Charter adopted in 1955 by the African National Congress], we can proudly present to the people of the North the example of those who have looked beyond the littleness of the immediate situation', he said. The AGM also passed a resolution urging a boycott on all South African products and an end to Irish investment in South Africa.[54]

Perhaps the IAAM's most effective action, at least in terms of propaganda, was its earlier campaign of opposition to the proposed international rugby match between Ireland and the racist South African Springboks, in Dublin, on 10 January 1970. Aware this event would be used by the South African regime for propaganda purposes, the IAAM mounted a dynamic campaign of opposition to the visit, which was supported by the Labour Party, the CPI, the CYM, Official Sinn Féin, the ICTU and elements in Fianna Fáil and Fine Gael. Appeals from all the major political parties and the trade union movement to the IRFU to cancel the match fell on deaf ears.

On 14 November 1969, the Labour's AC unanimously passed the following resolution:

> The Administrative Council of the Labour Party opposes and condemns the racialist policies of the South African Government as being contrary to the dignity of man and against the Christian traditions of the Irish people. It calls on the Irish Rugby Football Union to cancel all fixtures with the Springboks side. Should the I.R.F.U. fail to take this course, the Administrative Council calls on all members and supporters of the Labour Party to refuse to attend any function involving the Springboks and to support the peaceful protest of the Irish Anti-Apartheid Movement.[55]

A day earlier, at an IAAM public meeting in the Connolly Hall, Limerick, chaired by Tony Pratschke of the Labour Party, a call for Limerick City Council not to give a civic reception to the Springboks was made by the IAAM's Secretary, Barry Desmond, TD. After urging 'all self-respecting' rugby followers in Limerick to refuse to participate in any function for the South African team, he asked them to join in the protests of the IAAM at Thomond Park the following day. Kader Asmal stated that if the IRFU welcomed the South African team they would be accepting South Africa's apartheid policy in sport. Since the IRFU was unwilling to enter into any discussions about the tour, public opinion must express itself in the clear terms to compel the Union to cancel the tour, said Asmal. In the concluding contribution, Scott outlined the historical reasons why Irish people should protest against discrimination in South Africa and why they should join the IAAM in protesting against the tour.[56]

President de Valera declined the IRFU's invitation to attend the Dublin match,[57] while the Taoiseach, Charles Haughey, decided not to receive the team.[58] No Government Minister attended the match.[59]

On 10 January 1970, the IAAM's principal Springboks protest took the form of a march from Dublin city centre to Lansdowne Road, where many demonstrators blew whistles in an effort to disrupt the game. Among those in the front ranks of the march were the Labour TDs, Browne, Cluskey, Desmond, O'Brien and Thornley; Bernadette Devlin, the Westminster MP; Ivan Cooper, the Stormont MP; Donal Nevin, Assistant General Secretary, ICTU; Denis Larkin, General Secretary, WUI; and Rickard Deasy, former President, National Farmers' Association.[60] In a press report of events that day, it was stated that the protest march was the largest demonstration against the Springboks on that tour, that more than 6,000 people had joined in the protest outside the ground, and that the match had been played without interruption before a crowd estimated at 30,000 – 'very small for a home international game, and well below normal for a match against a touring team', according to a press comment.[61]

As joint Honorary Secretary of the IAAM, Brendan Scott was a key figure in the campaign against the Springboks visit. In a letter to the press, subsequent to the match, Scott wrote:

> ...For me the most vivid memory will be the scene outside the Hibernian Hotel, when the beefy might of the Irish State booted back the youth of Bogside. For what purpose? So that the ambassadors of a regime which wouldn't let its "kaffirs" or "coolies" even near the dustbins of a Grade 1 hotel, which turns alsatians loose on African children, could dine in safety and comfort with their Irish hosts.
>
> Doubtless the trade ambassadors who will soon be leaving here for South Africa will be equally well protected as they leave.
>
> Our liberty chastity was so efficient that even Joe Foyle could bless their stay in our bed. "In spite of nudging from some quarters" – and with a little help from others – we, as you say, fed, housed, transported, televised and reported them.
>
> Everyone – except, of course, the bold bad trade union barons – wins a prize. "The protesters had their day," "The rugby people had their match." The losers were four thousand miles from the party.
>
> Maybe back in Cape Town or Jo'burg they will see the reflected brilliance of our whited sepulchre. Or maybe instead they will see the flames of Watts and Harlem, the fitting funeral pyres of a liberalism which choked to death on its own casuistry.[62]

Notes

1   Labour Party, Annual Report, 1960, pp. 19-20.
2   ibid.
3   *Irish Anti-Apartheid Movement 1964-1994* (Irish Anti-Apartheid Movement, Dublin, undated, circa 1994), p. 2.
4   Kader Asmal, 'Brendan Scott: An Appreciation', *Irish Times*, 21 September 1973; Des Geraghty (Anon), *Liberty*, Vol. 28, No. 3, October 1973, p. 12.
5   Kader Asmal, Brendan Scott: An Appreciation', op. cit.
6   Niall Greene had an an extensive career in the public and private sectors, mainly in aviation-related activities. After joining the Labour Party in 1964, he was elected to the Administrative Council in 1965, serving later as Financial Secretary, Vice-chairman and International Secretary. From 1973-1974, he was an advisor to the Minister for Labour, Michael O'Leary. See also Niall Greene, 'The Administrative Committee of the Labour Party in the 1960s', in Francis Devine and Kieran Jack McGinley (Editors), *Left Lives in Twentieth Century Ireland*, Volume 2, op. cit., pp. 74-79.
7   *Irish Times*, 28 September 1970.
8   *Irish Independent*, 27 September 1971.
9   Kader Asmal, 'Brendan Scott: An Appreciation', op. cit.
10 For further information on Kader Asmal (1934-2011) see Connal Parr, 'Other People's Struggles': Kader Asmal, 1934-2011, & Louise Asmal, 1939-', in Francis Devine & Patrick Smylie, *Left Lives in Twentieth Century Ireland - Communist Lives*, Volume 3, op. cit., pp. 169-186.

11 For further information on Louise Asmal (née Parkinson) see Connal Parr, 'Other People's Struggles': Kader Asmal, 1934-2011, & Louise Asmal, 1939-', Francis Devine & Patrick Smylie, *Left Lives in Twentieth Century Ireland –Communist Lives,* Volume 3, op. cit., pp. 169-186.

12 *Irish Independent,* 15 November 1965; *Irish Times,* 13 November 1972.

13 Interview with Gearóid Kilgallen, 24 July 2018.

14 ibid.

15 *Irish Times,* 26 July 1966, 12 May 1967, 4 November 1968 and 12 June 1969.

16 ibid., 8 December 1969.

17 ibid., 26 September 1970, 13 November 1972.

18 ibid., 12 June, 26 November 1969.

19 Founded in 1919 as the Guild of Insurance Officials (GIS) and re-named as the Union of Insurance Staffs (UIS) in 1969, the union transferred its engagements to the Association of Scientific, Technical and Managerial Staffs (ASTMS) in 1970. Noel Harris was Secretary of both the GIO and UIO and Irish Secretary of ASTMS.

20 *Plough,* April 1965, p. 4. Sponsors of the IAAM included Declan Costello, the Fine Gael TD; Hilton Edwards, actor, lighting designer, producer and co-founder of Dublin's Gate Theatre; Gabriel Fallon, theatre critic, actor and director; Seán Keating, the painter; Lord Killanin, James Larkin, Junior, General Secretary of the WUI; Donal Nevin, Research Officer, ICTU; Conor Cruise O'Brien, the future Labour TD and Minister; Lord Rosse, Senator Eoin Ryan, Fianna Fáil; and Senator W. B. Stanford, Regius Professor of Greek, TCD.

21 *Irish Anti-Apartheid Movement 1964-1994,* op. cit.

22 ibid.

23 ibid.

24 ibid.

25 ibid.

26 ibid.

27 For further information on Charles McCarthy (1924-1986) see Charles McCarthy, *The Decade of Upheaval: Irish Trade Unions in the Nineteen Sixties* (Institute of Public Administration, Dublin, 1973); *Trade Unions in Ireland 1894-1960* (Institute of Public Administration, Dublin, 1977); John Horne, 'Charles McCarthy', *Saothar* 12, 1987, p. 5.

28 *Irish Times,* 31 August, 10 September 1966; *Irish Independent,* 13 September 1966.

29 *Irish Anti-Apartheid Movement 1964-1994,* op. cit.

30 ibid.

31 ibid.

32 ibid.

33 *Monaghan Argus,* 21 January 1967.

34 *Irish Anti-Apartheid Movement 1964-1994,* op. cit.

35 *Monaghan Argus,* 21 January 1967.

36 *Irish Independent,* 30 January 1967.

37 *Irish Anti-Apartheid Movement 1964-1994,* op. cit.

38 ibid.

39 *Irish Times,* 25 September 1968.

40 *Irish Independent,* 2 December 1968.

41 *Irish Times,* 30 November 1968, *Irish Independent,* 2 December, 1968.

42 *Irish Times,* 27 January 1969.

43 ibid., 29 September 1969.

44 *Irish Independent, Irish Times,* 28 September 1970.

45 *Irish Times,* 22 November 1971.

46 *Irish Independent,* 8 January 1971.

47 For further information on Fintan Kennedy (1916-1984) see Charles Callan

and Barry Desmond, 'Fintan Kennedy (1916-1984)', *Irish Labour Lives,* op. cit., pp. 134-135.

48 ibid., 10 January 1970. For further information on Evelyn Owens (1931-2010) see Charles Callan and Barry Desmond, 'Evelyn Owens (1931-2010)', *Irish Labour Lives,* op. cit., pp. 231-232; Sheila Simmons and Francis Devine, 'Evelyn Owens', *Saothar* 36, 2011, pp. 133-135; Sheila Simmons & Francis Devine, 'Evelyn Owens: Equal Rights Campaigner, Labour Court Chair', *Left Lives in Twentieth Century Ireland,* Volume 1, op. cit.,pp. 199-210.

49 For further information on Máire Cruise O'Brien (née MacEntee) see Máire Cruise O'Brien, *The Same Age As the State* (O'Brien Press, Dublin, 2003).

50 *Irish Independent,* 14 January 1971.

51 *Irish Times,* 7 June 1971.

52 ibid., *Irish Press,* 27 September 1971.

53 *Irish Independent,* 27 September 1971.

54 *Irish Times,* 22 November 1971.

55 Labour Party, AC, minutes of meeting, 14 November 1969.

56 *Irish Examiner,* 15 December 1969.

57 *Irish Times,* 4 December 1969.

58 ibid., 8 January 1970.

59 ibid.

60 *Irish Independent, Evening Herald,* 10 January 1970.

61 *Irish Times,* 12 January 1970.

62 ibid., 17 January 1970.

CHAPTER 12

An Irish Voice on Vietnam

In addition to his major involvement in the Labour Party, the Irish Anti-Apartheid Movement and the Dublin Housing Action Committee in the late 1960s and early 1970s, Scott was a leading activist in the campaign of the Irish Voice on Vietnam (IVV) against American aggression in that country and elsewhere in South-East Asia. Among IVV's officers, initially at least, were Dan Breen (Chairman), Peadar O'Donnell (Vice-Chairman) and Angela Barry (Secretary). But the central figure and, for a period, Secretary,[1] was Dr. George Jeffares, a leading member of both the Irish Workers' Party (IWP) and the Communist Party of Ireland (CPI).

Scott was a regular and enthusiastic participant in the IVV's many public demonstrations and meetings. Typically, these events took the form of a march from Parnell Square to the American Embassy in Ballsbridge, where a public meeting was held. On one such occasion, on 23 March 1968, Barry and Scott handed in a letter of protest to the Ambassador, signed by Breen and O'Donnell, likening the war in Vietnam to 'the Irish struggle for freedom, with the United States taking the role Imperial Britain took in Ireland.' The Irish people, it stated, owed it to Americans and to themselves to demonstrate against the failure of Ireland's representative to support U Thant [Secretary General of the United Nations]. It was a cause of humiliation and anger that it should appear that Ireland associated with the policies of the Johnson [Lyndon Johnson, President of the USA] administration. The letter called for the ending of the bombing in Vietnam and for negotiations with the Vietnamese freedom fighters.[2]

A month or so later, on 6 May, Scott was among the speakers at a public meeting, in the Mansion House, Dublin, at which the Irish Government was strongly criticised for failing to take a more positive line on Vietnam. Presiding at that event was Donal Nevin, Assistant General Secretary of ICTU, while other speakers were Michael O'Leary, TD (Labour Party), Senator Garret FitzGerald (Fine Gael), Senator Eoin Ryan (Fianna Fáil), George Jeffares (IVV), Cathal Goulding (Sinn Féin), Rev. Michael O'Neill and Rev. John Patterson.[3] Evidently, none of the speakers, including FitzGerald and Ryan, had any difficulty sharing the platform with Goulding, then Chief of Staff of the IRA! Although Scott's contribution appears not to have been published in the national or socialist press, his hand-written, wide-ranging address has survived:

> To-night as I listened to our distinguished speakers I wondered how many times has this hall echoed to the words of protest. How many times have men tried to light a candle here to dispel the perpetual might of indifference which protects the eyes of a smug and well-fed Western World.

Once an audience in this hall knew the sounds of war. Once people in this hall went out to light the flame of social justice. And when that flame guttered and shrunk to a mere after glow [sic] men like Breen and Peadar O'Donnell still kept it alight in their hearts. Once the audience in this hall knew the front trenches of the fight for freedom ran through the middle of Dublin but maybe as the…mob murmur to us that was long ago.

In smaller numbers they came here again when Hitler's jackboots crushed in Jewish skulls. Some men came here to protest then when Irish dons politely praised the Corporate State. When Guernica was levelled they were here. When Verwoerd, Vorster, Salazar and Smith revived the concept of the master race – the conscience of Ireland gathered here.

If we are cynical we can say that we are professional protesters always doomed to be on the weaker side. Or we can say with far more truth what any man who has ever taken up reluctantly a gun for a good cause will know – but which we need to re-affirm – that social justice and human freedom are not hardy plants which can once planted be left to grow. They must be husbanded in every generation – if needs be in blood – as by the people of Vietnam to-day. The cause of Vietnam is not merely the cause of Vietnamese freedom it is humanities fight. What this incredible people are proving with their burned and battered bodies is that the days of the mailed fist and the jack boot are numbered. They are prepared to die that the age of the armed sugar company and the slave-labour dividends will vanish from the earth.

We cannot afford to be neutral in this battle. Already the contraction of imperialism is producing the predicted effects in Britain. We have seen even London dockers lured on by piggish sworts [sic] of that Neanderthal survivor – Enoch Powell. We have smelt again the stink of Hitler in Germany.

We cannot be neutral – the smell of burning flesh from Vietnam has spoiled even the appetite for polite political platitude in even the most reality-shunning university common-room.

We cannot wash our hands in Pontius Aiken's bowl for that bowl is full not of water but of Vietnamese blood, and the dust Aiken stops his ears with is the dust of Belsen and Dachau and the crushed bones of Vietnam.

If we do not protest we are not neutral. We are committed for what Johnson [USA President, Lyndon Johnson] does in Vietnam he says he does for us – our silence will prove him right. Our silence is his mandate for murder.

Our government backs Johnson. Our foreign policy like our economic policy is in hock. The keeper of our foreign policy is bereft of ideological clothing. Having pawned his Republican garments he must skulk for most of the year, far from home, clothed only in a non-proliferating Tibetan barrel…

We would be false to the ghosts in this hall if we allow our rulers to put the conscience of Ireland in moth-balls.

To-day it is Vietnamese salmon who leap at the weirs of history. They will leap the obstacles what-ever we do – but if we allow the river of human involvement to become a muddy trickle they will bruise on the rocks of fascism. If we can only divert a tributary of Irish support into the great river of world solidarity we will help a little to ease their passage.

Let us ask them what we can do to help the freedom fighters of Vietnam and let us answer that we will do what ever [sic] they want us to do. This is the struggle they wage for us. They are the ones who pay the price of history with their napalm drenched quava-riddled corpses of their children. They are the ones who pay death's piper…

We have a duty to see that our government plays no part in any swindle which seeks to deprive them of their just demands. We have the duty of seeing that our government speaks with the voice of Tone and Lalor of Parnell and Connolly and not the ventriloquists dummy of a ventriloquists dummy of a bankrupt American administration. What the people of Vietnam want from us is not advice on how to run their revolution but concrete help – just as in 1919 we wanted concrete help – the time has come to repay some of our debt before the bar of history.[4]

Later that year, on 2 November, 1,000 people participated in an IVV march from Parnell Square to the American Embassy, where a letter was handed in, signed by Breen and O'Donnell. Welcoming the USA announcement of the halt in the bombing, the letter continued:

We are, however, disturbed by statements attributed to US officials that President Johnson reserves the right to resume the bombing whenever he decides that the peace talks are not proving 'productive'. It is also regrettable that the President should have emphasised that the presence of the NLF [National Liberation Front] representatives at the forthcoming talks 'in no way involves recognition of the NLF in any form'. This does not correspond with the realities in South Vietnam. Peace talks will only be 'productive' when the U.S. is prepared to negotiate directly with the NLF, which effectively controls the greater part of South Vietnam, and finally abandons the myth that the conflict in South Vietnam is the result of 'aggression' from the 'North' Jealous as the Irish people are for the good name and welfare of a country with which they have strong ties of blood and sentiment, this aspect of the world peace movement – the American people's own demand for the withdrawal of American forces from Vietnam – finds the most fervent response in our own country.[5]

A copy of the letter was delivered to Frank Aiken, Minister for External Affairs. An accompanying statement from Breen and O'Donnell declared: 'We confess to a sense of shame that you should be Minister for External Affairs when the Irish representatives at the United Nations play the unworthy role referred to in paragraph 1 of that letter.'[6]

On 26 June 1970, an IVV statement, signed by 105 prominent citizens in various walks of life was delivered to the Department of External Affairs. Among the signatories were the Labour TDs, Noël Browne, Brendan Corish, Conor Cruise O'Brien and John O'Connell; Senator John Horgan; the novelist and playwright, John B. Keane; Peadar O'Donnell; Sean O'Faolain, the writer; Professor Liam Paor and Dr. J. G. Simms. The statement read:

We are of the opinion that many Irish people share our growing concern over the war in Vietnam and over the fact that it has now been extended to Cambodia. We fear an even wider war.

We recall the 1954 Geneva Agreement expressly forbade the presence of foreign troops on Vietnamese territory, and we are heartened by the mounting of ever greater sections of the American people for the total withdrawal of American forces from Vietnam.

We think that many Irish people would wish the Irish Government to give its public support to that demand, thereby joining those many governments who have spoken out at American policy on Vietnam.

We urge the Government to do so.[7]

The IVV's most colourful protest against American intervention in Vietnam followed a march by over 3,000 people from Parnell Square to the USA Embassy in Ballsbridge, on 4 October 1970.[8] The demonstration culminated, not just in the usual public meeting, but a mock trial (Appendix 3) of USA President, Richard Nixon, who was on a three-day official visit to Ireland. Speaking on behalf of the IVV immediately prior to the 'trial', Jeffares criticised the Irish government for its silence on the Vietnam War. He said that he was concerned that the invitation to President Nixon and his discussions on Irish soil of the war on Vietnam might be taken as meaning that Ireland, whose name was once an inspiration for peoples fighting for their independence, has now aligned itself with their oppressors. Accusing the Nixon Administration of seeking peace only on American terms, Jeffares said that this was why the Nixon period had seen an intensification of the bombing and pacification operations in South Vietnam.[9]

Scripted by Brendan Scott, who played the role of prosecuting counsel, with Joe Deasy as defence counsel and Dr. Moira Woods as judge,[10] the mock trial audience included groups from the CPI, CYM, the Internationalists, members of the Labour Party, People's Democracy, Official Sinn Féin, the Young Socialists and anarchists.[11] A brief, vivid description of the scene was published by the *Irish Times:*

> ...A mock trial of President Nixon was then held. He was found "guilty" by acclamation of war crimes...

> ...But the several hundred demonstrators who sat down on the road, forcing gardai to quietly re-route traffic for nearly two hours, appeared to miss nothing, and neither did the RTÉ film crew. They cheered, laughed and listened attentively to the script written by Mr. Brendan Scott, of the Dublin Regional Council of the Labour Party, who took the part of the prosecutor. A number of American characters, representing ex-soldiers, delivered lines taken from actual anti-war testimony given in America.

> Others in the cast had their lines heavily leavened with satire, and sketches of the late President Eisenhower and Dr. Hillery, Minister for External Affairs, drew loud response, this latter even prompting a few grins from gardai.[12]

In an act of solidarity with anti-war demonstrations in the USA, on 22 November 1972, more than 100 people took part in an IVV picket of the American Embassy, in Dublin. A letter of protest was handed in at the Embassy:

> On this day of domestic and international protest against the continuing U.S. war upon the peoples of Indochina, we add our voice to that of the great bulk of the American people who, as repeated opinion polls have shown, favour an end to the war by the immediate and total withdrawal of American military forces.

> Now that this once silent majority has spoken, it finds the President deaf. Still bent on a military victory, he has sought to placate his people by withdrawals of U.S. ground forces, while continuing to wage the war by proxy. He has had real success in changing the colour of the corpses with which he has littered the lands of Indochina – they are all brown now. And they are even more numerous,

thanks to the heaviest bombing in history – Laos alone has been bombed every single day that Mr. Nixon has been in office.

We are heartened by the fact that the conscience of the American people has not been dulled by the reduction in U.S. casualties, and that they feel not less outraged than ourselves at the spectacle of the wealthiest country on earth employing all its advanced science and technology to scourge one of the poorest, simply because this small, brave people will settle for nothing less than the American people demanded less than two centuries ago: freedom from foreign rule.

The barbarity of American actions in Vietnam is only matched by the hypocrisy which is employed in its defence. Thus in recent days the 1954 Geneva Agreements have been invoked to justify the resumption of the bombing of the cities of North Vietnam. But it was the United States which bitterly opposed those agreements in 1954, and has never ratified them since. And it is those same Agreements which prohibit the presence of foreign troops or military bases on Vietnamese soil.

The American presence in Vietnam is as illegal in its origins as it has been calamitous in its consequences. The longer President Nixon maintains it, the more he prolongs America's dishonour.[13]

Notes

1   *Irish Times,* 11 April 1973.
2   *Sunday Independent,* 24 March 1968.
3   *Irish Times,* 7 May 1968.
4   Brendan Scott, hand-written, unpublished and undated speech evidently delivered at a public meeting on Vietnam in the Mansion House, Dublin, on 6 May 1968.
5   George Jeffares, 'Vietnam Dublin Protests', *Irish Socialist,* No. 82, December 1968, p. 3.
6   ibid.
7   *Irish Examiner,* 29 June 1970; *Irish Socialist,* No. 97, July-August 1970, p. 7.
8   *Irish Socialist,* No. 100, November-December 1970, pp. 1, 7-8.
9   *Irish Times,* 5 October 1970.
10 *Irish Socialist,* No. 100, November-December 1970, pp. 7-8.
11 *Irish Press,* 5 October 1970.
12 *Irish Times,* 5 October 1970.
13 *Irish Socialist,* No. 115, May 1972, p. 5.

CHAPTER 13

Moscow Nights

Two years after joining the Irish Anti-Apartheid Movement, Brendan Scott became a founding officer of the Ireland-USSR Society, serving as Treasurer from 1966 to 1969 and Vice-Chairman from 1969 to 1973. Scott's committee colleagues were: John Swift, General Secretary of the IBCAWAU (Chairman); Barbara Miller (Vice-Chairman); Frank Edwards,[1] a teacher and member of the Irish Workers' Party who fought with the International Brigades in the Spanish Civil War (Secretary); Nora Harkin (née McGinley),[2] an employee of the Irish Hospitals' Sweepstake (Assistant Secretary); Angela Barry, Bobbie Edwards (née Walshe),[3] an employee of the Irish Hospitals' Sweepstake and formerly Treasurer of the Spanish Aid Society; and Margaret (Daisy) McMackin, lecturer in Russian language and literature and co-founder of the Russian Department, TCD.[4] At the Committee's request, Scott drafted the Society's original Constitution, including its principal object: 'The promotion of understanding and friendship between Ireland and the USSR'[5]

Among the Society's activities were the organisation of lectures, discussions and film shows on various aspects of Soviet life. Lectures were normally delivered by Irish or Soviet speakers with special knowledge of particular subjects. In the case of Irish lecturers, their talks often followed a recent visit to the USSR. In addition to meeting and receiving Soviet groups and individuals visiting Ireland, the Society organised holidays for Irish citizens in the USSR.

Brendan Scott delivered what appears to have been the first talk, 'Pages of History,' under the Society's auspices, in Jury's Hotel, Dublin, on 22 February 1967.[6] Two years later, on 5 March 1969, having recently returned from a tour of some of the Soviet Union's educational institutes, and having lectured recently on the same subject at St. Patrick's College, Maynooth, Scott gave a talk to the Society on 'Soviet Education', in the Four Courts Hotel, Dublin.

In the course of his address, he mentioned that, in 1955, the USSR had 48 million children at school compared to 9 million in 1917, and was producing 60,000 engineering graduates annually, compared with 22,000 in the USA. He said that the atmosphere in Soviet schools was formal but friendly and it was pleasant to visit schools where children seemed uncowed, unlike those in many Irish schools where the 'legacy of British sado-masochism' was cherished. He stated that 'Incomplete' secondary schools, for children between seven and fifteen years, were co-educational, comprehensive and unstreamed area schools; all children did all subjects, including woodwork, metal-work or domestic science, art and music; less than 10 per cent of students failed to make the grade; and in the eighth grade there was a strong scientific bias in the curriculum. He said there were 180 different types of complete secondary schools at which students took a two or three-year course. The three main divisions were – secondary polytechnic, at which one third of the time was spent on the sciences and one third on work training; secondary specialised, for training in skilled occupations like electronics, forestry, book-keeping, or nursery and kindergarten teaching; and vocational technical schools at which 20 per cent of the time was spent on general education and 80 per cent on work training.

'There were 760 institutes of free higher education at which about one in four applicants were [sic] accepted. Preference was given to students with two or more years work experience. During the courses, which lasted five years, students were paid a small salary according to their progress,' he said.

Concluding his talk, Scott posed three questions:

1. Would the Russian idea of comprehensive education which does not necessitate monster schools be more suitable for Ireland, especially rural Ireland, than the present British system which seems to fascinate the Department of Education?[7]

2. Would a study of the Russian system show that children can be educated without resort to the stick, and the students can be taught to appreciate art and music and at the same time acquire skills necessary for life in a technological society?

3. Could we learn something from the Russian system of self-government in schools and thus anticipate the world movement towards greater student participation in planning their own education?[8]

Scott's colleague on that Soviet trip was Nora Harkin, the Society's Assistant Secretary, who spoke on aspects of Russian life of particular interest to women.[9]

Later that year, on 9 November, in the Four Courts Hotel, Scott gave a lecture to the Society on Lenin.[10] What he said on that occasion appears to be unrecorded. Among others who gave lectures under the Society's auspices during the mid to late 1960s were Michael McInerney, Political Correspondent of the *Irish Times,* on 11 November 1966;[11] Máire de Paor and Frances Lambert, Women's Advisory Committee of the ICTU, who gave accounts of their visit to the USSR in March 1967;[12] the author, playwright and former politician, Dr. Roger McHugh, whose lecture on 20 October 1967, was entitled, 'From Leningrad to San Francisco';[13] Ruaidhrí Roberts,[14] General Secretary of the ICTU, in late 1967;[15] and James Larkin, Junior, General Secretary of the WUI, whose theme was the role of the Soviet trade unions, on 7 February 1968. In his address, Larkin said that the Soviet trade unions appeared to have much more influence than was the case when he was in Russia forty years earlier and that he found that the trade unions were the main pillars around which the daily lives of Soviet citizens were built up. He added that in the Soviet Union no worker could be sacked without the permission of the trade union committee in the factory in which he worked. While wages in some cases seemed low and goods, especially clothing and footwear, were expensive, there were no social security deductions and all medical services were completely free. Rents were surprisingly low and covered central heating and electricity. The people generally had a sense of social discipline, courtesy and good manners,[16] Larkin said.

Strangely enough, although the Society held many public events following its founding on 14 October 1966, it was only launched officially some three years later. This may have been related to fears of anti-Soviet protests at its public events, particularly following the Warsaw Pact invasion of Czechoslovakia in August 1968. Those fears proved to be unfounded.

That intervention was condemned by many socialists and communists in Ireland and abroad. In a public statement on 21 August, the ten-member Political Committee of the Irish Workers' Party (IWP), a forerunner of the CPI, said:

> We deplore the intervention by the Soviet Union, Poland, Hungary, German Democratic Republic and Bulgaria in Czechoslovakia. It is our opinion that the intervention, far from serving the cause of Socialism, can do it immense damage, unless it is speedily ended. We, therefore, call for the withdrawal of these five countries from Czechoslovakia.[17]

A resolution to that effect was carried by 9 votes to 1, the exception being Michael O'Riordan, the Party's General Secretary.[18] The Connolly Youth Movement (CYM) also passed a resolution on 21 August condemning the invasion.[19] Subsequently, both the CPI and CYM reversed their positions on Warsaw Pact intervention. This and other matters led to a major split in the CPI, when twenty-three members, including Paddy Carmody, Joe Deasy, George Jeffares, Sam Nolan and Mick O'Reilly, resigned on 17 December 1975[20] (Appendix 4). The former CPI members then set up the Irish Marxist Society, which held lectures and published a theoretical journal.[21] Most of them later joined the Labour Party.[22] Remarkably, neither the Warsaw Pact intervention nor the later resignations from the CPI were mentioned in the IWP's monthly paper, the *Irish Socialist*.

Reporting the left's response to the invasion, the *Irish Times*, said:

> In Dublin the reaction among Labour Party members, among Socialists and among Communists was one of shock and condemnation. All of them, even those most pro-Soviet, had been reassured from the Bratislava conference that there would be no invasion. Along with French, Italian, Yugoslav, Romanian and other Communists they are urging the immediate withdrawal of Soviet troops on the principle that each country must find its own way to Socialism...'
>
> Irish Socialists and Communists believe that the terrible problem will ultimately be resolved by political pressure and negotiations between Communist countries. They all deplore and condemn the use of East German troops in the invasion, because it was one certain thing to anger the Czechs and to promote violence.

There is quite a hatred of Ulbricht [Walter Ulbricht, Leader of the German Democratic Republic] in Czechoslovakia. He is the one representative of Stalinism.'[23]

Actually, a substantial number of Irish communists and socialists were unopposed to the invasion, including John Swift and Frank Edwards, principal officers of the Ireland-USSR Society. Swift, and possibly Edwards and O'Riordan, believed that the USA and some of its Western European allies were involved in undercover operations aimed at undermining socialism in Czechoslovakia. Many CPI and CYM members were also unopposed to the invasion. If Labour Party members were opposed to the intervention, this was hardly evident at the Party's Annual Conference in January 1969:

> Some of the delegates were quite willing to talk about American imperialism, but somewhat reluctant to mention the Russian intervention in Czechoslovakia, and it was left to Dr. Conor Cruise O'Brien, the fraternal delegate from the Socialist International to condemn the "cynical" invasion of Czechoslovakia…'[24]

Opposition to the invasion of Czechoslovakia found expression at a meeting of the Irish-Czechoslovakia Society, in Dublin, on 25 August 1968, when the Lord Mayor, Frank Cluskey, TD, (Labour Party) said the meeting offered whatever moral support, assistance or encouragement it could to the Czechs in Ireland. He described the invasion of Czechoslovakia as a wanton act of aggression. Donal Nevin, Assistant General Secretary of the ICTU, said that a criminal blunder had been perpetrated on the people of Czechoslovakia, and that it was important that the voices of trade unionists and socialists be heard on this occasion. Some 200 people attended the meeting.[25]

Evidently, Brendan Scott was opposed to the intervention, for he, Joe Deasy, an IWP Political Committee member; and Roy Johnston, then an influential figure in Sinn Féin, were participants in a public demonstration in Dublin against the invasion. Apparently, this protest was a joint one of opposition to the Warsaw Pact intervention in Czechoslovakia, American aggression in Vietnam and British involvement in Northern Ireland.[26]

Over a year following the invasion, on 10 October 1969, the Ireland-USSR Society was formally launched at a public meeting in the Central Hotel, Dublin. On that occasion, a resolution that the founding Committee, formed in 1966, should continue in office for a further year was adopted. However, it appears that during the intervening period, there had been some changes. For example, Scott and Harkin, founding Treasurer and Assistant Secretary were now Vice-Chairman and Treasurer, respectively, with a new Assistant Secretary, C. O'Brien. Moreover, the other founding Committee members, had been joined by the trade union leader, Noel Harris; Angela McQuillan (née Nolan),[27] a lecturer in Russian at TCD and wife of the Labour Party TD, Jack McQuillan; and Seán O'Brien.[28] In 1970, incidentally, the Society's membership stood at 250.[29]

Lecturers at the Society's public events in the early 1970s included the Belfast author and BBC television producer, Tom Boyd, who gave a talk on

Chekhov;[30] the *Irish Times* journalist, Christina Murphy, who spoke on 1 March 1971;[31] Gerry Alexander, President of Irish Actors' Equity Association, whose theme was 'The Actor and National Culture in the USSR', on 19 January 1973;[32] and, on 28 March 1973, Uinseann Mac Eoin,[33] the architect and town planner, who gave an account of his visit to Tashkent, Alma Ata and other cities in Soviet Central Asia, in December 1972.[34]

On 29 September 1973, only ten days following the death of Brendan Scott, a key objective of the Ireland-USSR Society was fulfilled when Ireland and the USSR agreed to the establishment of diplomatic relations between the two countries.[35] That the Society had contributed to the creation of the climate for such a development was acknowledged by Dr. Garret FitzGerald, Minister for Foreign Affairs.[36]

Notes

1 For further information on Frank Edwards (1907-1983) see Uinseann Mac Eoin (Editor), 'Frank Edwards: Lieut. Waterford City Battalion IRA, Sergt. XV International Brigade, Spain', *Survivors*, op. cit., pp. 1-20; Manus O'Riordan, 'Portrait of an Irish Anti-fascist: Frank Edwards, 1907-1983', *Morgen Freiheit*, New York, 1983, reproduced by Labour History Workshop, Dublin, 1984.

2 For further information on Nora Harkin (née McGinley), see Lorna Siggins, 'An Irishwoman's Diary', *Irish Times*, 23 September 1992.

3 For further information on Bobbie Edwards, née Walshe (1910-1988) see Anon,, 'Bobbie Edwards', *Irish Socialist*, No. 305, December 1988, p. 3.

4 Ireland-USSR Society, minutes of committee meetings, 14 October, 30 December 1966, 1 April, 9 November 1967; minutes of public meeting, 10 October 1969; *Irish Independent*, 17 January 1970; Michael Quinn, *Irish-Soviet Diplomatic and Friendship Relations 1917-1991* (Umiskin Press, Dublin, 2016), pp. 205-206.

5 Ireland-USSR Society, minutes of committee meetings, 14 October, 30 December 1966, 1 April, 9 November 1967; minutes of public meeting, 10 October 1969.

6 Ireland-USSR Society, minutes of committee meeting, 8 March 1967.

7 Brendan Scott, *Summary of Lecture on Soviet Education,* at Four Courts Hotel, on 5 March 1969 [Brendan Scott Papers]; *Irish Times,* 28 February, 7 March 1969.

8 Brendan Scott, *Ssummary of Lecture on Soviet Education,* op. cit.

9 *Irish Times,* 3 March 1969.

10 *Irish Press,* 8 November 1969.

11 Ireland-USSR Society, minutes of committee meeting, 25 November 1966.

12 ibid., 12 May 1967.

13 ibid., 26 October 1967.

14 For further information on Ruaidhrí Roberts (1917-1986) see Ruaidhrí Roberts, Edited and additional material incorporated by R. Dardis Clarke, *The Story of the People's College* (People's College Adult Education Association and O'Brien Press, Dublin, 1986); Paddy Bergin, 'Ruaidhrí Roberts', *Saothar* 12, 1987, pp. 5-6.

15 Ireland-USSR Society, minutes of committee meeting, 17 January 1968.

16 *Irish Times,* 8 February 1968.

17 ibid., 22 August 1968.

18 Michael O'Riordan disclosed the result of this vote to John Swift immediately after the Warsaw Pact invasion of Czechoslovakia in August 1968; Michael Quinn, *Irish-Soviet Diplomatic and Friendship Relations 1917-1991,* op. cit., p. 236.

19 *Irish Times,* 22 August 1968.

20 The twenty three members who resigned from the IWP in 1975 were: Tony Boucher, Bernard Browne, Gerry Byrne, Paddy Carmody, Paul Clarke, Fred Collins, Brian Deasy, Joe Deasy, Eamon. Dillon, Michael (Mick) Dowling, David Fitzgerald, Johnny Flood, George Jeffares, Marion Jeffares, Jimmy Kelly, Máirín.Kelly, Peter Mew, Liam Mulready, Fred Murray, John McDonnell, Sam Nolan, Michael (Mick) O'Reilly and Naomi Wayne. (See resignation statement in Appendix 4); Mick O'Reilly, *From Lucifer to To Lazarus*, op. cit., pp 46-47, 49-50, 79-80, 82-84, 119; Helena Sheehan, *Navigating the Zeitgeist: A story of the Cold War, the New Left, Irish Republicanism and International Communism* (Monthly Review Press, New York, 2019), pp. 189-191.

21 Mick O'Reilly, *From Lucifer to Lazarus*, op. cit., p. 85.

22 ibid.

23 *Irish Times*, 27 August 1968.

24 *Irish Press*, 27 January 1969.

25 *Irish Times*, 26 August 1968.

26 Interviews with Pat Carroll, 11 May 2018, who confirmed that Scott had been a participant in the demonstration; Sam Nolan, 24 May 2018, who confirmed that Deasy had been a participant; and Mick O'Reilly, 24 May 2018, who confirmed that participants included Deasy, Scott and Roy Johnston; Michael Quinn, *Irish-Soviet Diplomatic and Friendship Relations 1917-1991*, op. cit., p. 236; Mick O'Reilly, *From Lucifer to Lazaras*, op. cit., p. 84.

27 For information on Angela McQuillan, née Nolan (d. 2020), see Michael Quinn, *Irish-Soviet Diplomatic and Friendship Relations 1917-1991*, op. cit.; Michael Quinn, 'Angela McQuillan, née Nolan', *Sound Post*, Vol. 18, No. 2, Summer 2020, p. 17.

28 Ireland-USSR Society, minutes of general meeting, 10 October 1969.

29 *Irish Independent*, 17 January 1970.

30 ibid.

31 Ireland-USSR Society, minutes of committee meeting, 7 March 1971.

32 *Report* No. 1, Ireland-USSR Society, January-March 1973.

33 For information on Uinseann MacEoin (1920-2007) see Uinseann Mac Eoin (Editor), *Survivors* op. cit.

34 *Report*, No. 1, Ireland-USSR Society, January-March 1973.

35 Michael Quinn, *Irish-Soviet Diplomatic and Friendship Relations 1917-1991*, op. cit., p. 68.

36 Nora Harkin, Angela McQuillan, Seán Edwards, Brian Kavanagh (Editorial Board), *Ireland-USSR Society: 21st Anniversary Ireland-USSR Society 1987* (Ireland-USSR Friendship Society, [sic] Dublin, 1987), p. 4.

CHAPTER 14

The Seventies will be Socialist

In the Local Elections held on 28 June 1967, the Labour Party made substantial gains, its national share of first preference votes increasing from roughly 10 to 15.1 per cent. Although its share of seats was a disappointing 10 per cent, in the election to Dublin City Council Labour's representation rose from five to thirteen seats. Limerick Corporation was another impressive result, Labour securing 26.2 per cent share of the vote, thus becoming the second largest party in that city. Writing in *Labour*, 'the official organ of the Labour Party', an unnamed 'Political Observer' said:

> The local elections of 1967 could well provide the springboard from which labour will eventually attain power. The enthusiasm of the young socialists in the capital must not be dimmed. Their work and its fruits should inspire the rest of the country.[1]

While this electoral advance put a spring in the step of delegates attending Labour's Annual Conference, in Liberty Hall, Dublin, four months later, it hardly prepared them fully for the fundamental policy change signalled by Brendan Corish, TD, the Party Leader, that henceforth the Party would be socialist.

With the slogan, 'The Seventies will be Socialist', Corish in his keynote 'The New Republic' address to that 1967 Conference distanced Labour from the two conservative parties, Fianna Fáil and Fine Gael, and outlined some of the measures that an independent, socialist party would implement:

> ...Our party...must prove to the public that it is in no way involved in supporting the status quo. It must stand aside from the other two parties which compete only to see who will get the chance to keep things as they are. It must give a socialist alternative...

> The central issue facing the electorate at the next general election is whether it wants to maintain the status quo with its perpetual emigration, standing army of unemployed, crawling rate of economic growth,...or whether it wishes...to tackle the massive problem of getting our economy on the move and putting our society in order...

> The plums of the economy have been reserved to private enterprise. The State has entered only such fields as the capitalists found unattractive from a profit point of view. They have fought every attempt to use the State as a real instrument of economic growth and have preserved for themselves the right to do as they like with wealth, irrespective of the nation's needs...

> The State must plan the economy by working towards objectives and priorities. It must extend the range of its activities, by setting up new industries...It must plan by controlling the use of capital so that investment goes into industries and types of agriculture which are the most important and most beneficial to the community...

We cannot tolerate a situation in which private interests alone determine the volume and quantity of investment in our economy – or, indeed, decide whether it will be invested here at all...

The banks, insurance companies and other financial institutions cannot be left as the preserve of private enterprise. Those who questioned our credentials as socialists have forgotten that Labour has based its economic programme since the nineteen-thirties on the necessity to bring capital within the control of the central authority...

Labour commits itself to a society which permits no class differences, in which great disparities in wealth are eliminated, and in which the resources of the nation are devoted in the first place to the needs of all the people...

Corish also alluded to some socialist beliefs and principles:

...Socialism is a belief in freedom and in the right of every man to develop as he wishes. It applies not just to political freedom but also to the principle of economic freedom which recognises that all men have a right to participate in decisions affecting their livelihood...

Socialism is a belief in equality...Capitalistic competition has allowed the aggressive and the strong to accumulate wealth with few rules to prevent them from going beyond the bounds of justice...

It is in the area of...equality that socialism most differs from capitalism...We know that one per cent of the population owns more than half the wealth in most competitive economies. Is that equality? It is ludicrous to think that a man with wealth is the equal of a man without it, because wealth brings power and great wealth brings great power...

All our policies, whether on health, education, housing, social welfare, are based on the idea of community, another of the basic socialist principles.[2]

That Corish, hitherto associated with the moderate or even the right of the Labour Party, could promote such a radical path took the majority of delegates by surprise. Many wondered had the address been drafted by other senior Labour figures, particularly Brendan Halligan, an economist with the Irish Sugar Company before being appointed Political Director of the Party in 1967 and General Secretary a year later.[3] But, there is no doubt that Corish was centrally involved in this matter and was fully committed to the new socialist direction of the Party in the late 1960s.[4]

Halligan has shone some light on the origin of Corish's address:

Corish prepared meticulously for weeks and set a pattern for all subsequent speeches. We would first talk privately and in 1967 we initially met in Hoynes Hotel in Arklow, a convenient half-way house between Wexford and Dublin, supplemented by meetings in our homes. In these opening conversations, he would settle on a theme he wanted to develop, go on to outline his thoughts, which would be transcribed and typed up. He would also consult with his intimates and sometimes with outside experts. The speech would go through many drafts, seldom less than ten.[5]

Further clarification on the origin of Corish's address has been provided by Niall Greene, a former Financial Secretary and Vice-Chairman of the Party:

Corish's 'New Republic' speech to the 1967 Annual Conference was a direct outcome of the [Administrative] Committee's work, not just because of Halligan's critical role in its construction, but because of the…need, identified by the Administrative Council, to start stating clearly what Labour stood for.[6]

Returning to Labour's 1967 Annual Conference, after delivering his address, Corish stated that, in six to nine months time, he intended to summon a Special Delegate Conference representative of all branches and trade unions to debate and decide upon the policy they were evolving. The conference would have the task of approving social and economic policies based on socialism.[7]

Corish's socialist address was, of course, music to the ears of Brendan Scott and his left-wing colleagues who had been advocating such a policy for years. The left also welcomed the reiteration of the Party's strong anti-coalition position, which had been in place since 1957. Opening the debate on coalition the future Labour Leader, Michael O'Leary, TD, later to serve in Fine Gael-Labour Coalition Governments, on one occasion as Tánaiste, and later still as a Fine Gael TD, said Labour should establish its independence for once and for all and take no ministerial office as a minority with either Fine Gael or Fianna Fáil. He did not rule out supporting a minority Government on certain conditions without taking ministerial office. Nor would he object to Labour being the dominant partner in a coalition. Declaring that the Labour Party had been ruined by the last coalition Government, he added:

> They would be cutting their own throats to accept a subordinate role in a future Government. Our role must be to polarise Irish politics, to drive the other parties into one great camp so that we will be left to represent the real interests of the people. Labour's role should be to support a minority Government which would implement Labour's short-term policies.[8]

Niall Greene, later a senior officer of the Party, said he did not believe that there was any serious or sizeable support within the Labour Party for a coalition government. 'We will never again support a coalition government if we do not fully support its policy…,' he said.[9]

Corish, too, came out strongly against coalition:

> …I do not believe that the Labour Party should be used merely as an instrument to get any party into office. What we are concerned about is who is in office and what are we to do. We must approach this on the basis of how we can best promote the Labour Party. How best can we advance the cause of Socialism? I am against coalition…[10]

By an overwhelming majority, 600 votes for with 20 against, the conference adopted a resolution reaffirming the Party's opposition to any form of coalition government involving Labour in which the commanding decisions were not of the Party's making. The resolution stressed that the Party believed that the political strategy of Labour must be guided by a policy of providing the electorate with an independent socialist alternative to the stronghold exercised in political life in Ireland by the two civil war parties, and believed that success in the realisation of this objective would be jeopardised by sharing office with either of the two treaty parties.[11]

In the ensuing debate, many delegates rejected coalition in principle. Others described Labour's participation in the Inter-Party Government, presumably that of 1954-1957, as giving 'the-kiss-of-life' to Fine Gael, adding that, but for Labour's willingness to participate in the Inter-Party Government of 1948-1951, Fine Gael as a party would have died long since. On the other hand, several speakers had no objection to coalition, provided that Labour could call the tune irrespective of its numerical strength.[12]

Among other notable resolutions adopted at the 1967 Annual Conference was one calling for the nationalisation of urban land required to fulfil the long-term needs of local authority housing development.[13]

In the elections of Labour Party officers, Barry Desmond, Industrial Officer of the ICTU, was elected Chairman, defeating Michael O'Leary, TD, by 481 votes to 166; Noël Browne was elected unopposed as Vice-Chairman; while Donal O'Sullivan (Industrial Engineering Officer, ITGWU) defeated Vincent McDowell for the position of Financial Secretary by 384 votes to 166. For the left, this was an unimpressive result, with Browne the only left-wing figure returned.

In an assessment of Corish's address to Conference, *Irish Press* journalist, Seamus Brady, wrote:

> It was undiluted stuff, straight out of Connolly, that must have made the private enterprise members of the present Labour Party stiffen in their seats...[14]

> Mr. Corish threw down a challenge to all Irish political parties – including his own Labour Party – by running up the banner of full-blooded Socialism at the opening of the Party's conference in Liberty Hall, Dublin, last night.

> In his policy speech, the best of his career, he boldly offered the outline of a new Socialist society in which capitalism would be finished, private enterprise would take second place to the State, profit would no longer be the main yardstick of investment and society would be classless, with men equal'[15]

Perceptively, noting that in spite of the great anti-coalition feeling of the gathering only two members of the Parliamentary Party had spoken in the debate, Donal Foley of the *Irish Times* was somewhat sceptical about its commitment to the anti-coalition stance: 'One indeed wondered what those wise, gnarled old heads on the platform would do if the prospect of becoming a Minister became a real one.'[16] Foley's scepticism proved to be fully justified.

Perhaps the most insightful assessment of the Conference was that of Michael McInerney, Political Correspondent of the *Irish Times:*

> ...There was an air of euphoria and sheer confidence that I have never felt before.

> It was there right from the beginning of the conference. Delegates could hardly believe their ears when they heard the radical views of Mr. James Tully, who has a most conservative reputation on home affairs, even on Vietnam, that most

thorny of subjects. His was the first contribution and set the tone of conference but it was followed by Corish's speech outlining the aim – "The new Republic in a Socialist Ireland." He said that the speech was the outcome of discussions by party leaders and backroom boys and so he could not take all the credit but it certainly was the most comprehensive, intelligent, most radical statement ever heard from a Labour leader since Connolly.

There is something strange happening here, for both these men are normally moderate and conservative and the explanation probably is that the party has been seeing "an explosion from below," a groundswell, rather than a dynamic or catalyst from the top. The new influx of skilled workers, of university people, of professional men and women has transformed what was a few years ago one of the most conservative organisations in Ireland...[17]

Despite the previous conservatism of Corish up to the mid-1960s, there had been occasional signs that he was moving towards a more open and radical position. An indication of a less timid Corish was his description of the Labour Party as a socialist Party, in 1964,[18] having previously referred to both himself and the Party as 'Christian Socialist'. However, there may also have been other, more practical reasons for Corish's apparent radicalisation. By the mid-1960s, Labour faced the prospect of additional electoral competition from Fine Gael, whose liberal policy, *Towards a Just Society*, was published in 1965. There was also competition from an increasingly more radical and confident Sinn Féin, although that Party then had an abstentionist policy in relation to Dáil Éireann. Consequently, Corish and Halligan possibly felt that for Labour to advance further, the Party would need to adopt a more distinctive, radical position.

At the Special Labour Party Conference, in Liberty Hall, in June 1968, draft socialist policy documents on a range of major issues were discussed and finalised for consideration at the next annual conference of the Party, which was held the following January. Significantly, these documents had been prepared over a considerable period by sub-committees composed almost exclusively of rank and file party members. Brendan Scott, Noël Browne and John Swift, respectively, were influential members of the sub-committees on education, health and worker democracy.

It was around this time that the Fine Gael TD, Michael O'Higgins, suggested that Fine Gael and Labour should form a united front to provide an alternative Government to Fianna Fáil. This received a cool reception from Corish: 'Fine Gael are a private enterprise party. We are socialists.'[19]

Notwithstanding the socialist aspirations expressed in Corish's *New Republic* address at Labour's 1967 Annual Conference and the discussions on the socialist policies at the 1968 Special Conference, many on the left remained sceptical that the Labour leadership would actively pursue a progressive socialist path. It seemed highly unlikely that the largely rural-based, conservative TDs would accept the democratic decisions of the Party by supporting and promoting such a radical programme. Some of the left's concerns were articulated publicly by Swift:

If Connolly's doctrines are to inspire the party, Labour must campaign earnestly for at least some of the basic things Connolly thought were essentials of socialism, such as the democratisation of education and the obligation of the State to provide free education, and, important, the means to avail of it, up and including the universities; the democratisation of production, distribution and exchange by vesting control of these functions in the elected representatives who keep them going with their labour and skill.

The Labour Party must not be afraid of political power, and must forswear any interest in running non-political government – government that leaves power to its usurpation by small cliques of monopolists, speculators and moneylenders exploiting the economy for themselves, government that abandons its power in education to private money-making and sectarian interests, government that allows the medical profession to maintain paupery [sic] in the health services and privileged medicine and care in exclusive clinics and nursing homes, government that leaves housing in the hands of a privately-run building industry, free to decide that it pays better to build luxury villas and flats in Ballsbridge or Foxrock, than homes for the needy still left in the slums.[20]

Later in 1968, Labour's future parliamentary existence was called into question when the Fianna Fáil Government, intent on retaining power indefinitely, introduced a Bill to alter the electoral system for Dáil elections from proportional representation to first past the post. This would have resulted in a Fianna Fáil Government for the foreseeable future and the virtual demise of the Parliamentary Labour Party. Scott was particularly active in Labour's campaign of opposition to the proposed measure.[21] In the referendum on this issue, on 16 October 1968, the proposal was defeated by 658,000 votes to 423,000, or 61 to 39 per cent.

Notes

1   *Labour,* Vol. 1, Nos. 5 and 6, July-August 1967, p. 1.
2   Brendan Corish, TD, *The New Republic,* Address to the 1967 Labour Party Annual Conference; *Irish Times,* 14 October 1967.
3   *Irish Press,* 24 January 1969.
4   Brendan Halligan, 'A Noble Adventure': The New Republic Speech in Retrospect', in Francis Devine and Kieran Jack McGinley (Editors), *Left Lives in Twentieth Century Ireland,* Volume 2, op. cit., pp. 66-73; Interview with Catherine McGuinness (née Ellis), 11 June 2019. From 1961-1967, while parliamentary secretary of the Labour Party, Belfast-born McGuinness, was Corish's principal speech-writer. She also drafted speeches and Dáil and Senate questions for TDs and senators. Among many other roles, she also later served as an Independent Senator and a Supreme Court judge.
5   Brendan Halligan, "A Noble Adventure": The New Republic Speech in Retrospect', op. cit., p. 67.
6   Niall Greene, 'The Administrative Committee of the Labour Party in the 1960s', in Francis Devine and Kieran Jack McGinley (Editors), *Left Lives in Twentieth Century Ireland,* Volume 2, op. cit., p. 79.
7   *Irish Times,* 14 October 1967.
8   ibid., 16 October 1967.
9   ibid.
10 ibid.
11 *Irish Examiner, Irish Times,* 16 October 1967.

12 *Irish Examiner,* 16 October 1967.
13 *Irish Times,* 16 October 1967.
14 *Irish Press,* 14 October 1967.
15 ibid.
16 *Irish Times,* 16 October 1967.
17 ibid.
18 ibid., 9 June 1964.
19 ibid., 1 June 1968.
20 John Swift, 'Looking for Connolly – 2 'Labour and the development of the State', *Irish Times,* 24 July 1968.
21 Interview with Fergal Costello, 20 March 2020

CHAPTER 15

Echoes of Connolly

Debates on socialist outline policy documents and coalition dominated the 1969 Annual Conference of the Labour Party, which commenced in Liberty Hall, Dublin, on 23 January. In his opening address, Corish captured the mood of the conference on coalition:

> ...We should now take on an independent stand to bring about a clear-cut division between Left and Right. To make that stand we could not take a short-cut by aligning ourselves with another party simply to replace one government with another. To enter coalition would be to throw into reverse the forward thrust of the nation. To enter coalition would be to say stop...In coalition there would undoubtedly be some short-term advantages and personal benefits. But we cannot, nor will not, forego the future of this country for short-term party advantage...

> We will not support a minority government of either conservative party and if there is to be a Conservative Government it will not have active support from Labour within Dail Eireann...We cannot coalesce with either of the two parties which largely represent the interests of big business and who, under the guise of economic stability, which we recognise to be no more than economic stagnation, permit the continuing sell-out of our natural resources.

> It was a good thing that in making up our minds on this complex problem that we have had the experience of two coalition Governments and of the impact that had on the people. On both occasions, in subsequent elections, the electorate showed us what they thought of us for submerging our identity. Does anyone believe that it will be any different the next time? Does anyone think that we could yet again win seats?

> I know that despite pretensions to form a government on their own that the Fine Gael Party will continue to flirt with Labour. I know what they want – they want to attain power for power's sake. They have no interest in changing the system. Their only claim is that they might make a better job with the system.

> I am against coalition. In the present context we will never be accepted as equal partners and we will not be able to get our Socialist policies through a Government dominated by Conservative Ministers...

> I am looking to the future and I cannot see how, after a Coalition Government, the Labour Party could fight an election as a party with a separate identity. Coalition would lead to another instalment in the sterile contest between Fianna Fail and Fine Gael.

> Last year, [actually, October 1967] Annual Conference rightly decided...against participating in Coalition Government in present conditions. This was a democratic choice of the entire party, which at the time I supported and will continue to uphold so long as I am leader of the party. If conference should in the future decide by democratic choice to change its mind, I will, as I have consistently done since I became a member of the Parliamentary Labour Party 24 years ago, accept that decision. But the party must appreciate that to me this

is a matter of conscience and that in such an eventually my continued support for Socialism will be from the backbenches…'[1]

According to the Political Correspondent of the *Irish Times,* this last mentioned declaration by Corish 'astonished the 900 delegates', received great applause in a standing ovation and was interpreted as putting the last nail in the 'coffin of coalition…'[2] Assessing Corish's Address to Conference, an *Irish Times* leader writer observed:

> What will come out by Sunday night it is too early to predict; for, while the new party theorists have had a good innings recently – more particularly in the organs of publicity – the more conservative element has yet to be heard, and some of these are quite as conservative as the men in the other two parties which Mr. Corish castigates.

> The two big points in Mr. Corish's address are his firm assertion that Labour will have nothing to do with the coalition or with supporting a minority Government (not for him as leader, anyway) and his pledge that the parliamentary party will be amenable to the directions of the Labour Party as a whole…

> There are only two escape clauses on this subject of coalition which the party conference may finally settle. In one phrase Mr. Corish refers to last year's decision against participating in coalition government "in present conditions", and the rest of his speech leaves little room for doubt – that is, as far as he, as leader, is concerned – for he told his audience that if the conference later decided to change its mind, he would follow that decision – but from the back benches. This may open up possibilities for ambitious men in the ranks…'[3]

Apart from the left, strong support for the anti-coalition stance was voiced by, among others, the Party Chairman and future Labour TD and minister, Barry Desmond:

> …Labour's aim now was to replace the two 'conservative parties' and to emerge as an independent party without minority or coalition support or deals after the next general election[4].

In a similar vein, Ruairi Quinn, later a Labour Party TD, Minister and Party Leader, was reported as saying:

> …In previous years Labour had given the kiss of life to Fine Gael by joining a coalition government but that must not happen again. He was interested in the long term interests of the country and not the short term interests of the Party. Labour could have a coalition in the morning, Fine Gael is leaping for it but that would be a compromise with the conservative parties.[5]

The anti-coalition composite resolution was carried by an overwhelming show of hands.[6]

Among radical socialists in the Labour Party, including Scott, there were various views on the issue of coalition. While many, probably including Scott, were opposed in principle to coalition with any right-wing parties, others held the view that provided that Labour was the senior partner in government, coalition with the likes of Fianna Fáil or Fine Gael could be considered. Some prominent left-wing Labour figures were not opposed in principle to coalition. For example, Noël Browne, Minister for Health in a former coalition government, was clearly in that category. At the same time, he was wary of coalitions with the conservative parties, particularly where Labour would be in the minority position. John Swift was among a small number who were unopposed in principle to coalition, provided that the coalition adopted radical socialist policies. In practice, this effectively was a non-coalition stance. None of the left-wing Labour members, including Scott, had any difficulty contemplating coalition with other socialist parties. However, in terms of Dail Éireann, this was a purely theoretical position as the Dáil was then bereft of potential left allies.

While Labour's reiteration of its anti-coalition position was welcomed by Scott and his left-wing colleagues, their main focus at that 1969 Annual Conference was to ensure that the outline policy documents were approved, undiluted by the more moderate Party leadership. After extensive debates, twelve 'Outline Policy' documents were adopted on agriculture, banking and finance, education, foreign policy, health, housing, industrial development, local government, marine affairs, social welfare, taxation and worker democracy.[7] Published by the Labour Party in a 150-page booklet, this set of policies is probably the most comprehensive of its kind to be adopted by any political party since the establishment of this State and, unquestionably, the most radical.

The following is a selection of brief extracts from the 'Outline Policy' document:

Banking and Financial
The Labour Party stands for the public control of all the nation's financial institutions. In particular Labour repudiates the belief that private profit should be made out of the creation and management of credit...[8] The powers of the Central Bank should be extended by making it the Government Bank in a real sense; commercial bank directors should be removed from its Board...[9] External Monetary reserves in excess of reasonable banking needs should be repatriated for investment in Ireland... Half the Board of each commercial bank should be appointed by the Government to represent the community interest...The Government should acquire a share interest in the commercial banks and expand it as required...[10] The Central Bank will become the Government Bank...; it will...be given power to make capital available for social and national development at low rates of interest...[11]

Education:
Labour would ensure that every child received free education to 16, with provision for higher education. ..[12] Instruction in religion will be a curricular subject...[13] All schools will be owned by the community and controlled by their representatives. The present primary, secondary, comprehensive and vocational systems will be abolished and replaced by a single comprehensive system... Education... will be... in most cases mainly co-educational...[14] The headmaster of each school will be the manager of that school, working under the control of the Local Education Authority....We want the school to become a community centre...[15]

A Socialist Government will establish a closely integrated flexible system of Higher Education, making full use of the present institutions, viz. the universities, the research/teaching institutes and the colleges of technology, commerce and art...To implement its socialist policy for education a Labour Government will set up a Permanent Higher Education Authority which will have responsibility for the overall planning, financing and development of Higher education...[16] The present needs in university education could best be served by establishing a University of Ireland with five autonomous, non-denominational universities, including a technological university in Limerick.[17]

Housing:
A State construction company to engage in house building; control of rents of flats and bedsitters; building land to be brought under community control; abolition of ground rents; estates of large landowners to be vested in the community; the building materials industry to be brought under control of a Department of Housing and Construction; public control of all financial institutions; 100 per cent loans for all house purchases at not more than 4 per cent interest; rent tribunal to implement rent control laws; all building societies to come under public control; a differential rents scheme which would not take account of adolescents' incomes; and local authorities to become the only purchasers of building land.

Industrial Development:
A Department of Economic Development will be established, with responsibility for devising and implementing a National Development Plan. It will be the premier department of State and all sections of present Departments, semi-State bodies and agencies associated with economic development will be brought under its control. It will become the shareholder of all State Companies and Corporations...The Development Plan will express Labour's economic strategy by setting down the type of industries to be established and areas in which they will be located in the light of future expectations of world trade and technological innovation. In general, the plan will be to create complexes of large scale technology projects based on exploitation of native resources, such as agricultural materials, minerals and the sea...The plan will be implemented by a National Planning Authority invested with the full power of the State in the planned development and utilisation of the State...A State Development Corporation will be set up with the direct responsibility for establishing and extending industries and for generally developing areas judged to have growth potential....[18] A State Export Board will be set up to engage in direct selling abroad...[19]

Social Welfare:
The objective of Labour's social welfare policy is to secure for each person a basic standard of living in terms of income and services. The factors to be taken into account in computing the basic living standard will include food, accommodation, heat, light, clothing, transport and recreation...Contributions [to a Social Fund] will be obligatory on all earning members of the community and will...be based on a percentage of income...[20] The pension level will be a percentage of the average income over the period of years immediately prior to retirement. The objective will be to provide pensions within the range of a half to three quarters of this average income. In no case, however, will a pension be allowed to drop below the level necessary to maintain the basic living standard...[21] Maternity incomes will be paid up to three months after the birth... Abandoned wives and unmarried mothers will receive incomes...[22]

Taxation:
Labour's objective will be to ensure that society's wealth is used to the best advantage of the entire community with special regard to the lower and middle income groups… A capital gains tax on profits derived from capital transactions and land speculation will be introduced with a high rate of taxation…[23] Loopholes which currently permit the avoidance of estate duty will be closed and the rates will be increased…Different rates of indirect taxation will be imposed on various classes of goods so as to eliminate the burden on lower income groups, particularly for essential commodities, through a flexible system of indirect taxation, using the valued-added tax and the elimination of the existing wholesale and retail turnover taxes. The present system of rates will be abolished… and will be replaced by tax on property from which an income is directly or indirectly derived…The existing balance between direct and indirect taxation will be altered so as to increase the proportion of revenue derived from direct taxation…[24]

Worker Democracy
Worker democracy is understood as full participation in decision-making relating to the utilisation of the resources of an enterprise or organisation. The aim of worker democracy is to make the decision-takers in the place of work and in control of the enterprise responsible to those who work in it…The Labour Party believes that statutory provision must be made to secure for all those engaged in economic life effective participation in all levels of decision-making. Such changes will be made in the regulations governing the operation of State and semi-State undertakings as will, whilst conforming with the requirement of public accountability, provide for effective participation in the decision-making processes at all levels by those engaged in these undertakings. The participation will be secured through the free election by those engaged in these undertakings of their own representatives…[25] Since political decisions, as well as economic decisions, play a central part in the use of national resources, it will require a socialist government to give effect to the principle of worker democracy.[26]

If Brendan Scott contributed to the debate on education at the 1969 Labour Conference, which is highly likely, his speech appears to be unrecorded. What was partially recorded was his contribution to the debate on foreign policy. As mentioned earlier, he recommended that all cultural and economic relations be broken off with both Rhodesia (Zimbabwe) and South Africa and that no visas be granted to anyone wishing to visit those countries. He also suggested that Irish embassies be set up in East European countries as we could not have a neutral foreign policy while all embassies were confined to the West. As previously noted, four years later, despite opposition from Britain and the USA, Ireland and the USSR agree to establish diplomatic relations.[27] It was also at that 1969 Annual Conference that future Labour TD and Minister, Dr. Conor Cruise O'Brien, said that Ireland should terminate its diplomatic mission in Portugal, then a fascist state, and open one in Cuba.[28]

One of the most controversial policy documents considered at that 1969 Annual Conference was that on Worker Democracy. Opening the debate on this topic, Michael O'Leary, TD, stated:

...Some people thought the Labour Party was riding into the Valley of Death with this document... The Irish Workers' Party, however, did not deem it authentic socialism. We are the first to say that this is no complete document. It does chart the future progress of democratisation in the workplace...We lived in strange times when the *Catholic Standard* welcomed this policy while other newspapers saw it as sinister. There is nothing sinister in the document, it was an open declaration of aims, and, in this area, the Labour Party were pioneers..."[29]

In the ensuing debate, John Swift (Fintan Lalor Branch), who drafted the original document,[30] said:

...Industrial democracy [the original title of the document] was a social concept, and that it did not mean that workers would merely have a say in their employment. It meant the full involvement of the people in the control of all the natural resources, finances, means of production and distribution. Many people think of industrial relations as simply meaning improved communications. In 40 years as a trade union official, I have never been in any doubt as to what employers were trying to communicate, and that is their presumed right to make all decisions.[31]

According to a press report, all of Labour's outline policy documents 'were accepted unanimously, apart from minor amendment'.[32]

For Scott and his left-wing colleagues, the 1969 Annual Conference appeared to represent a major advance. The socialist policies and anti-coalition position were overwhelmingly adopted. In addition, it was decided that conference decisions would be binding on all Party members, including TDs and senators. Subsequently, this democratic decision was largely disregarded by the leadership.

Commenting on the Conference, the *Irish Times* Political Correspondent, Michael McInerney, wrote:

...Constitutional proposals and resolutions agreed, plus the dogmatic statement of Mr. Corish, party leader, all now declare that decisions of the national organisation and conference – now representative of the T.D.s – will be binding on Dail deputies and senators, and it is proposed, too, that every election candidate will pledge to carry out party policy...

Some fissures were visible, however, in the weekend conference. It is clear that the revolutionary quasi-Communist left wing of the party feels that there has been "a bloody sell-out" by the leadership, and that there is incredulity and anxiety among the small conservative right wing at the radical swing to the Left and in the policies for education and health...[33]

In a telling observation on the Conference, an *Irish Times* leader writer, said: '...But it will be noted that, while conference was radical in its resolutions, it elected officers of known moderate views."[34] This clearly was a reference to the election of Dan Browne, Chairman, by 414 votes to 290 for Anthony Pratschke and 33 for Dónal McGregor; Dermot O'Rourke, Vice-Chairman; and Niall Greene, Financial Secretary.[35] Dan Browne was then the Dublin Secretary of the National Union of Vehicle Builders (NUVB); Dermot O'Rourke was described by the *Irish Times* as 'a young accountant graduate having qualified into [sic] economics two years ago...who would be said to belong to the new Socialist-Republican centre rather than the Left-wing'.[36]

In an observation on the possible implications of the major Conference decisions, the *Irish Independent* Political Correspondent, Arthur Noonan said:

> ...One powerful impression was left when the Conference concluded last night – that by some means in the 15 months since the last Conference this new policy of the far left has got itself off the harmless report sheets and on the plate of the parliamentary party as a real force. It is quite clear after this weekend that any deputy who does not subscribe to the new policy document, at least in its main principles, is at best "Independent Labour" – he is certainly not part of the present Labour Party and cannot for long shelter under its wing."[37]

Actually, the Deputies in question had nothing to fear as there was never the remotest chance of the Labour leadership disciplining its TDs, particularly those on the right.

In a thoughtful and balanced assessment of Labour's 1969 Conference, Joc Deasy, a leading figure in the Irish Workers' Party and former Labour Dublin City Councillor, said:

> ...It is sobering to reflect on the results of the elections for Chairmanship and Vice-Chairmanship. Neither Mr. [Dan] Browne nor Mr. [Dermot] O'Rourke the successful candidates are men of the Left and they defeated candidates who are far more clearly identified with Socialist beliefs. Here the trade union vote seemed to effectively assert itself and will probably do more so in the future. This is presently a fact of life and emphasises the size of the task confronting Socialists in trying to win the entire Labour Movement for Socialism and imbuing it with a clear understanding of what the term signifies; it is well to stress however that in these elections the Left did receive good support.

> The most stimulating feature of the Conference ...was the genuine feeling for Socialism and the desire to give practical application to the principles of James Connolly which activated large sections of the delegates.

> How much of this feeling extended to the platform and to the municipal and Parliamentary representatives? This is a vital question; after all in a social democratic party there lies the essential seat of power. One could not help asking, as speech after speech invoked Socialism, how any of the leaders with permanent seats on the platform would shake off the tapping of a bishop's crozier? This thought was very persistent as Noel Browne went to the rostrum to speak on the Health policy and one remembered 1951!

Acknowledging that the new policies represented 'real progress' and that it had indeed been 'a heartening conference', Deasy said it would be very dangerous to conclude that the policies represented a blueprint for socialism. However, he also acknowledged that it had been repeatedly stressed that none of the 'Outline Policy' documents represented the last word on policy.[38]

While the 1969 Labour Conference undoubtedly was a high point for Scott and his socialist colleagues, they were unconvinced that the Parliamentary Party would promote such a radical programme.

Notes

1 *Irish Times*, 25 January 1969.
2 ibid.
3 ibid.,
4 ibid., 27 January 1969.
5 *Irish Independent*, 27 January 1969.
6 *Irish Examiner*, 27 January 1969.
7 *Irish Press*, 24 January 1969.
8 Labour Party, *Outline Policy* (Labour Party, Dublin, 1969), p. 92.
9 ibid., p. 93.
10 ibid., p. 94.
11 ibid., p. 95.
12 ibid., p. 66.
13 ibid., p. 67.
14 ibid., p. 68.
15 ibid., p. 69.
16 ibid., p. 71.
17 ibid., p. 72.
18 ibid., p. 134.
19 ibid., p. 135.
20 ibid., p. 59.
21 ibid., p. 60.
22 ibid., p. 58.
23 ibid., p. 113.
24 ibid., p. 114.
25 ibid., p. 33.
26 ibid., p. 42.
27 Nora Harkin, Angela McQuillan, Sean Edwards, Brian Kavanagh (Editorial Board), *Ireland-USSR, 21st Anniversary, Ireland-USSR Society 1987*, op. cit., p. 4.
28 *Irish Independent*, 29 January 1969.
29 *Irish Times*, 27 January 1969.
30 John P. Swift, *John Swift: An Irish Dissident*, op. cit., p. 192.
31 *Irish Times*, 27 January 1969.
32 ibid.
33 ibid.
34 ibid.
35 *Irish Independent*, 27 January 1969.
36 *Irish Times*, 27 January 1969.
37 *Irish Independent*, 27 January 1969.
38 *Irish Socialist*, No. 84, February 1969, p. 1.

CHAPTER 16

Snatching Defeat from the Jaws of Victory

Between Labour's 1969 Annual Conference and the General Election in June that year, a group of up to eight of Corish's right-wing Parliamentary Party colleagues sought some dilution of the socialist policies. Apparently, in response, Corish threw his resignation on the table, where it lay for a week.[1] Corish's stand would, of course, have pleased the left. What would not have pleased them, however, was Corish's confidential appeal to businessmen for financial support for the Party:

> The 'new' Labour Party is intent on becoming the Government of this country. I know that business organisations are concerned with political developments. So called 'stable' government in Ireland has, up to now, depended on the sterility of the old politics. In the future it will depend on a clear choice being offered to our people. This choice will be between alternative paths of development for Irish society.
>
> I am asking you to support the Labour Party financially so that we can bring about a healthier political climate in this country. All contributions sent to me at this address and marked 'CONFIDENTIAL' will be seen only by my secretary and me. They will be acknowledged by return.[2]

Incidentally, there is more than a little irony in Corish's statement at a pre-Election press conference, on 3 June 1969: 'On health, Labour will restore Dr. Browne's Mother and Child Scheme with free health treatment for children up to 16 years and free maternity services.'[3] This was the same Corish who had opposed the Scheme in 1951 and, initially, Browne's admission to the Labour Party in 1963![4]

The much anticipated General Election took place on 18 June 1969. Expectations of a major Labour breakthrough had been fuelled by several leading Party figures, including the Chairman, Barry Desmond, who told delegates at its Annual Conference earlier that year that Labour's aim now was to replace the two conservative parties and to emerge as an independent party without minority or coalition support or deals after the next general election[5] Similarly, on the eve of the Election, Labour's Deputy Leader, James (Jim) Tully,[6] TD, said the Party 'will seek to form a government...We believe...we will be the majority party in the next Dail.'[7] Even in sections of the press, expectations were relatively high, one national newspaper predicting Labour would win twenty-eight to thirty seats.[8]

In fact, Labour won eighteen seats, equalling the number on the dissolution of the previous Dáil,[9] but four fewer than the twenty-two secured in the previous 1965 General Election. On the other hand, Labour's first preference vote and share of first preference votes increased appreciably.

With their focus almost exclusively on the loss of seats, the result was interpreted negatively by both the Party leadership and the press. Explaining why Labour candidates had 'polled so badly', Corish, in a RTÉ television interview, said that some of the electors had been told by Fianna Fáil speakers that some Labour Party policies were dangerous and alien to the Christian beliefs of the Irish people. He said that in the city this type of approach didn't work, but that in the country such allegations if made at an after Mass meeting or whispered by any Fianna Fáil TD at a doorstep, were very damaging and this was the approach used. Asked if Labour intended to pursue its present policies despite its 'reverses' in the election, Corish said that the policies decided at their last Annual Conference would be pursued, and although there would be reviews from time to time, he did not think it would be for the purpose of deleting anything.[10]

The *Irish Times* Political Correspondent, Michael McInerney, was un-impressed with Labour's performance:

> Suggestions about Communist influence in the Labour Party made by some Fianna Fail speakers to rural audiences affected the country vote.
>
> It looks now that the allegation of Communism against O'Brien were designed more for rural than urban consumption.
>
> While there could be some satisfaction for Labour in the fact that they will now have some of the most brilliant minds in Ireland in the Dail [presumably, a reference to the likes of Noël Browne, Justin Keating, Conor Cruise O'Brien and David Thornley] and that the Labour Party has become an urban party rather than a rural party as it was in 1961 that satisfaction cannot compensate for the disasters which they suffered in the countryside. It is clear that Labour's policies were too advanced, too sudden for rural Ireland and were not that successful in Dublin or in their urban areas outside the capital.[11]

The contention by McInerney and others that the loss of seats was largely a rejection of the socialist policies is unsustainable. Actually, there is little or no evidence that those policies damaged Labour in that General Election, including in rural Ireland where five seats were lost.[12] In a candid, internal appraisal of Labour's election performance by its General Secretary, Brendan Halligan, a more plausible range of explanations was offered:

> The factors operating against the Party's performance in the election can be summarised briefly: the deliberate weakening of the P.R. system by Fianna Fáil, the changes in boundaries, weak quality of some of the candidates, poor transferring in two key constituencies, weakened state of Party organisation in some areas, the Fianna Fáil smear campaign and Labour's electoral strategy.[13]

Many years later, Niall Greene, Financial Secretary of the Party in 1969, offered another frank evaluation of Labour's 1969 General Election performance: '…We were, of course, hammered by Jack Lynch's "Cuban communism" tour of the country's convents and by our own very poor vote management, particularly in Dublin.[14]

The nomination of two candidates in both Mid-Cork and Waterford Constituencies was certainly a strategic error, resulting in the loss of those two seats. But there were many other strategic errors, including the nomination of up to four candidates in constituencies where previously there had been one or two. Arguably, the consequential split in the Labour vote, made worse by poor transfer rates between candidates, deprived the Party of potential gains.

Although there is no denying the significance of the loss of four seats, the number of seats gained or lost is an unreliable measure of electoral support. After all, a party may receive a higher first preference vote than in a previous election and secure fewer seats, as was Labour's experience in 1969. Moreover, as a result of population fluctuations, the total number of Dáil seats varies from time to time.

A more reliable, consistent measure of support is a party's share of first preference votes cast. On that basis, Labour recorded a remarkable success in that General Election of 1969. Despite promoting the most radical policies ever adopted by a major Irish political party, policies that had been in circulation for less than five months, Labour secured its then highest ever first preference vote of 224,000,[15] an increase on the previous Election of some 31,000, the party gaining more new first preferences than Fianna Fáil and Fine Gael combined.[16] Moreover, Labour's share of first preference votes rose by 1.6 per cent, from 15.4 to 17 per cent, its highest level for forty-seven years and second highest in its history. Yet, Labour's result was described by a national newspaper as a 'crushing defeat'![17]

What the Party leadership and the press appeared to have missed entirely was that, in the twelve-year period from 1957 to 1969, Labour's first preference vote doubled from 112,000 to 224,000, its share of first preferences almost doubled from 9.1 to 17 per cent, while its number of seats increased from 12 to 18, or by 50 per cent. This was achieved by an independent Labour Party with a consistent anti-coalition policy. The specific details are as follows:

Labour Party General Election Results 1957-1969

General Election	First preference votes	Percentage of first preference votes	Seats
1957	112,000	9.1	12
1961	136,000	11.6	16
1965	193,000	15.4	22
1969	224,000	17.0	18

Sources: *Irish Independent, Irish Press, Irish Times,* 1957-1969

A notable aspect of the 1969 General Election was the dramatic increase in Labour's support in Dublin City and County, its vote rising from 50,000 in 1965 to 92,000, an increase of 42,000 or 84 per cent; its share of first preference votes increasing from 17 to 27.7 per cent; and its seats from six to ten. That outstanding achievement is hardly reconcilable with McInerney's observation that it was clear Labour's policies 'were not that successful in Dublin'![18]

The most baffling aspect of the 1969 General Election was the Labour leadership's negative response to the Party's results. Obviously surprised and disappointed that, not only had the Labour's expectation of a substantial increase in its Dáil representation not materialised, but four seats had been lost, the leadership practically disregarded the significant increases in first preference votes and share of votes. It is inconceivable that any other political party, and certainly not Fianna Fáil or Fine Gael, would have adopted such an unjustified, defeatist stance.

Why, then, did the leadership interpret the result so negatively? Was it the failure of the anticipated electoral advance to materialise, particularly in relation to seats? Or was it seen by the leadership, particularly some of the more prominent TDs, such as Keating, O'Brien, O'Leary and Thornley, as an opportunity to dispense with the core socialist policies, thus clearing the way for a Fine Gael-Labour Party coalition government? What is certain is that the 1969 General Election result had hardly been declared when, contrary to Labour policy, Parliamentary Party members were secretly, and later, openly, discussing a potential coalition government with their Fine Gael counterparts and with the press.[19]

For Scott and his left-wing colleagues, Labour's additional public support in the 1969 General Election provided a firm foundation for further advances, based on the socialist policies and anti-coalition position.

Notes

1 *Irish Independent*, 20 June 1969.
2 Brendan Corish, Leader of the Labour Party, extract from confidential letter to businessmen, appealing for financial support for the Party, 10 June 1969, cited in the *Irish Times*, 21 June 1969.
3 *Irish Times*, 4 June 1969.
4 ibid., 7 December 1963.
5 ibid., 27 January 1969.
6 For information on James (Jim) Tully (1915-1992) see Charles Callan and Barry Desmond, 'James Tully (1915-1992)', *Irish Labour Lives*, op. cit., pp. 252- 253.
7 *Irish Times*, 6 January 1969.
8 ibid., 18 June 1969.
9 *Irish Independent*, 21 June 1969.
10 *Irish Press*, 20 June 1969.
11 *Irish Times*, 20 June 1969.
12 *Irish Independent*, 21 June 1969. The five seats lost outside Dublin were Cork North-East, Laois-Offaly, Mid-Cork, North Tipperary and Waterford.

13 Labour Party, Annual Report, 1969, p. 17.
14 Niall Greene, 'The Administrative Committee of the Labour Party in the 1960s', in Francis Devine and Kieran Jack McGinley (Editors), *Left Lives in Twentieth Century Ireland*, Volume 2, op. cit., p. 79.
15 *Irish Times,* 20 June 1969.
16 ibid., 31 January 1970.
17 *Irish Press,* 20 February 1970.
18 *Irish Times,* 20 June 1969.
19 *Longford Leader,* 14 March 1970, *Irish Times,* 1 June 1970, Labour Party, AC, minutes of meeting, 17 October 1970.

CHAPTER 17

The Retreat from Liberty Hall

In the period from late 1960s to early 1970s, coalition was high on the agenda of Labour Party conferences. At the 1970 Conference, held in Liberty Hall, Dublin, in late January-early February, Labour's anti-coalition policy was confirmed, albeit with the significant 'reservation' that the Administrative Council (AC) should discuss the matter in the light of the changing political situation,[1] almost certainly a reference to the Arms Crisis and turbulent situation in Northern Ireland.

Commenting on this caveat, Michael McInerney, Political Correspondent of the *Irish Times*, was under no illusions about its implications:

> ...The rigid coalition line is gone. It is understood that the trend of the closed session [of Labour's 1970 Annual Conference] on coalition and party strategy was overwhelmingly in favour of continuance of no-coalition in the traditional sense, but there is the beginning of a lobby which would agree to some form of alliance with parties that have similar aims as Labour.[2]

As no other left-wing party had representation in the Dáil, McInerney could only have been referring to Fine Gael! Adding substance to McInerney's contention was the decision of Conference to remit three coalition motions on the agenda to the AC for consideration.[3]

That the left had good reason to fear Labour's anti-coalition policy was about to be cast aside, was evident from a press report, in March 1970:

> Strong rumours are circulating in Leinster House that a secret liaison is being established between leading members of the Labour and Fine Gael parties. The new combined group is virtually a coalition party.
>
> It has been known for some time that there are deputies who favour coalition despite the ambiguous decision of the last two Labour congresses. Most obvious of these was Dr. Noel Browne. He had confessed his willingness to coalesce when speaking on television, and indeed openly declared that he would "use" the other party in the agreement for socialistic ends.
>
> This "realism" in Labour is now, so they say, activating such deputies as Dr. Conor Cruise O'Brien, Justin Keating and Dr. David Thornley.
>
> The activity is known to Brendan Corish but his attitude is that there is not to be any restriction on canvassing for coalition provided that the verdict be given at annual congresses.
>
> Some political correspondents refer to the new group as the "television group".
>
> With the above named Labour deputies can be mentioned Garret Fitzgerald [sic] and Michael O'Higgins, whose views stressed on TV have been remarkably close to those of Cruise O'Brien and Thornley...'[4]

Noël Browne was under no illusions about the direction the Labour Party was taking. Addressing the AGM of his constituency, on 19 September 1970, he said:

> In the Labour Party the general reaction to the defeat at the last general election among our conservative colleagues who, incidentally, with characteristic moral cowardice remained silent when they believed that the new word 'socialism' would shoe-horn them, however ill-fitted, into the back seat of a ministerial Mercedes, is now hostile to socialism"
>
> Now, they want to set up a new word or formula intended to waft them into power. Clearly unprincipled opportunism is the sole political dynamic of these men and women who simply use the Labour movement to further their own political concerns.
>
> Those who are now pandering to the idea in the Labour Party that socialist policies have failed can give it up. Socialist policies haven't failed, they haven't even been tried yet.
>
> If they don't like our new socialist Labour movement then they should get into one or other of the two major conservative parties in which they will be better suited…"[5]

Turning to the Labour movement [sic] itself, he said that it was a sad truth that over the years it had appeared to resist all attempts to give leadership as a truly representative workers' party.[6]

In an apparent reaction to Browne's statement, Michael Mills, Political Correspondent of the *Irish Press,* wrote:

> …Ever since Labour issued their new socialist policies before the last general election, there has been some doubt about the commitment of all the party deputies to the policy documents. There was a general belief that while everyone was, in theory, committed to the policies, in practice some were more committed than others.
>
> In time, this came to be understood as a difference between urban and rural politicians, and it was accepted that some allowance would have to be made for the traditional Labour voter in the country who was not too enamoured of the new "socialist" tag.
>
> Dr. Browne has never been a man for compromise, however, and it is quite clear he has no intention of making any allowances for traditional Labour policies. It is all or nothing, even if it means ending up with a small nucleus of true-blue socialists.
>
> Not many of his colleagues would go along with this concept. The rural deputies, in particular, would have to be more compromising if they want to continue to be elected in their constituencies…[7]

While Labour's Dublin Regional Council (DRC) came out strongly against the Party's involvement in coalition, in October 1970,[8] it was evident that some Labour TDs were ignoring the Party's anti-coalition stand and speaking publicly about coalition. For example, in June 1970, John O'Connell, TD, was reported as saying that the opposition parties would be gravely at fault if they did not take the necessary steps to restore confidence in parliamentary democracy by taking over the reins of Government.[9] At an AC meeting, on 4 November 1970, recent statements on coalition by Deputies Keating, O'Brien and O'Leary, in the press and on radio, were brought to the attention of the meeting. It was agreed to inform them that they had contravened the recent decision by the Parliamentary Party on public statements, a decision that had been endorsed by the previous meeting of the AC.[10]

It was at that same AC meeting that Corish formally initiated the abandonment of Labour's anti-coalition policy. This he did by proposing that the following motion be tabled by the AC on the agenda of the Special Delegate Conference on coalition, to be held, in Cork, on 13 December:

> National Conference affirms that there are circumstances in which participation by the Labour Party is in the nation [sic] interest, and pending the return of a majority Labour representation in Dail Eireann, Conference directs the leaders and members of the Parliamentary Labour Party to negotiate participation in a Government that would facilitate the implementation of Labour policies.

The motion was carried unanimously.'[11]

On a lighter note, in a satirical piece entitled 'Brendan's Dilemma Solved', *Irish Times* Columnist', Donal Foley, offered Corish a solution to his imminent somersault on coalition:

> A motion will come before the national conference of the Labour Party in Cork next month calling for the abolition of the front benches in the Dail. Ministers, the motion proposes, should in future sit in the back benches, and the front benches would be occupied by the backbenchers.

> Behind the motion is a bold idea which would allow Mr. Brendan Corish to resolve his present political dilemma on the coalition issue. Mr. Corish has stated unequivocally that in the event of Labour joining a coalition Government he will go to the back benches. The Labour motion would allow him to follow this course while at the same time allowing him to take office in Government...'[12]

Although Corish's call for the endorsement of Labour's socialist policies was carried almost unanimously by the 1970 Annual Conference, at a subsequent press conference, he said that while there could not be any change in the principles which guided the policies there would be a review in the light of change and with the aim of having them more generally understood inside and outside the Party.[12] Clearly, Corish was leaving himself room to manoeuvre.

Also at that 1970 Conference a composite motion on left unity, a matter of special interest to Brendan Scott, was unanimously approved:

> Conference calls on the Administrative Council to organise unity talks in Northern Ireland, to initiate the organisation of a 32-County Labour Party and in particular to set up branches in all constituencies in Northern Ireland. An addendum, which was agreed, said as the ultimate aim of the Party – a 32 County Socialist Republic – can best be attained by establishing an all-Ireland Socialist Party, conference urges, as a first step, that the Council be reconstituted to include the People's Democracy.[14]

Moving the motion, Tony Pratschke (Limerick East Divisional Council), called on the Party to work for the setting up of a 32-County Socialist Workers' Republic and the unification of all socialist forces, North and South. He said that if Labour was to be serious about unity talks all left-wing groups, including the People's Democracy, should be invited.[15] In the ensuing debate, Brendan Scott (Seán Heuston Branch) said: 'On the motion hung not only the fate of the Conference but the fate of the Party.' He added:

> The response of the Conference would determine whether they were to have a socialist party or a social democratic wheelchair association, a secular arm of the St. Vincent de Paul.

> This vote will determine whether we are to move forward to form a socialist alliance or whether we are to return to necrophilia – "and for those who don't read the *Irish Messenger* this means digging up the already putrefying corpse of Fine Gael and making love to it." The time was past for the rhetoric of solidarity: if Labour turned away, their Northern comrades would be left to Mr. Lynch, Mr. Blayney and Mr. Boland…

> The socialists of Sinn Fein should be invited to join them, together with the People's Democracy and the Derry Labour Party, in producing a blueprint for a socialist republic.[16]

Gerry Fitt,[17] the Republican Labour MP for West Belfast, said he believed the Labour Party had a basis for entering Northern Ireland. Labour had made it clear during visits to Belfast and Derry during the crisis the previous year that they were there to alleviate and to end sectarian strife, he added.[18]

On that same weekend that Labour passed a resolution on left unity, the Northern Ireland Labour Party decided, by 21,700 votes for and 1,900 against, to merge with the British Labour Party.[19]

Scott, incidentally, was the recipient of a unique compliment at that 1970 Labour Conference. Describing her impressions of the deliberations of that gathering, the producer and director, Lelia Doolan, said: '…There were occasional flashes of insight and passion – Brendan Scott; an occasional phrase of near poetry: "You can't hang houses from parachutes. You have to stand them on land."[20] A more significant tribute to Scott at that Conference was his election to the Party's AC.[21] Also elected to the AC were three other left-wing candidates, John Byrne, Jim Kemmy and Matt Merrigan.[22] A couple of months later, Scott, along with Jim Kemmy, Stan Warren and Brendan Halligan (ex officio member) were appointed by the AC as members of a new Education Committee, effectively a sub-committee of the AC. Seven other internal committees were established simultaneously on the following matters: administration, organisation, policy, political, overseas, constitution, and annual conference.[23]

Returning to the topic of left unity later that year, Scott said that so many people on the political left in Ireland spent so much time attacking other people on the left that they had forgotten their real opponents. He was speaking at a public meeting, with an attendance of some 300, organised by the DRC of the Labour Party, on 20 August 1970, in Dublin's Mansion House. Chaired by Kader Asmal, the other speakers were Conor Cruise O'Brien and Eamonn McCann. The meeting passed the following resolution:

> This meeting of Dublin citizens, organised by the Dublin Regional Council of the Labour Party...calls for the release of Miss Bernadette Devlin, MP, and other political prisoners and further calls for the overhaul of the law enforcement system and of the system of appointment of judges, both in Northern Ireland and in the Republic, in such a way as to ensure the real and effective equality of all citizens before the law.[24]

Speaking in the debate on the resolution, Brendan Scott said: 'While remembering Bernadette Devlin, we must make a plea for the other prisoners at present in gaols as well.'[25]

Before leaving 1970 it is worth noting that that year Scott was appointed as a lecturer in Methodology of History at St. Patrick's College, Maynooth, a post he retained up to his final illness, when he was replaced by his friend and colleague, John Medlycott

Notes

1   *Irish Times,* 2 February 1970.
2   ibid.
3   *Sunday Independent,* 8 February 1970.
4   *Longford Leader,* 14 March 1970.
5   *Irish Examiner,* 21 September 1970.
6   ibid.
7   *Irish Press,* 22 September 1970.
8   *Irish Times,* 29 October 1970.
9   ibid., 1 June 1970.
10 Labour Party, AC, minutes of meeting, 17 November 1970.
11 ibid., 4 November 1970.
12 *Irish Times,* 1 December 1970.
13 Ibid., 2 February 1970.
14 ibid.
15 *Irish Press,* 2 February 1970.
16 *Irish Times,* 2 February 1970.
17 For further information on Gerry Fitt (1926-2005) see Michael Murphy, 'Gerry Fitt', *Saothar* 32, 2007, pp. 83-84; Charles Callan and Barry Desmond, 'Gerard Fitt (1926-2005)', *Irish Laboir Lives,* op. cit., pp. 102-104.
18 *Irish Press,* 2 February 1970.
19 ibid.
20 ibid., 4 February 1970.
21 *Irish Press, Irish Times,* 2 February 1970.
22 *Irish Times,* 2 February 1970.
23 Labour Party, AC, minutes of meeting, 30 April 1970.
24 *Irish Times,* 21 August 1970.
25 *Irish Press,* 21 August 1970.

CHAPTER 18

An Absence of Leadership

Socialist policies and coalition were not the only contentious issues in the Labour Party in the early 1970s. Several other controversial matters arose following reactionary public statements by Labour's Alderman, Stephen Coughlan, TD, Mayor of Limerick. The first of these issues, Coughlan's decision to welcome to Limerick the racist Springboks South African rugby team in early 1970 has been mentioned in an earlier chapter of this book.

Coughlan was at the centre of a second controversy in early 1970 after a group known as the Irish Revolutionary Youth opened a Maoist bookshop in Limerick City for the sale of Mao Tse-tung literature. Over the following month or so, there was a series of armed attacks on the shop in which a petrol bomb was hurled at the door[1] and, in a second incident, a shot was fired from a passing car through a window of the premises.[2] Instead of denouncing this violence, Limerick Corporation at its meeting on 9 March unanimously passed a resolution condemning the activities of the Maoist group and dissociated the citizens from their activities. A list of 500 signatories of local people stating they objected to the presence of the shop was handed in to the Mayor, Alderman Stephen Coughlan, TD. The list had been collected by a right-wing group called the Irish National Movement. Addressing the members of Limerick Corporation, the movement's leader, John Buckley, said:

> This Council should deal with this matter immediately before the people's hostility and resentment against this establishment and its proprietors erupts into violence which could have dire consequences...

In a more sinister development, on 11 March, the *Irish Times* Limerick correspondent received an anonymous call from a group of people asking him to issue a warning on their behalf to the Maoists. A spokesman for this group said:

> Convey to the Maoists that if they are not out of the shop in seven days they will have to face the consequences. There will be a lot of trouble. We will burn the place down.'[3]

Commenting on the shooting, Coughlan said that Limerick had always been noted for its Christian outlook, its charity, but anyone in Limerick could have seen this trouble coming. The Maoist bookshop, he said, had been a deliberate provocation, aggravated by its site in the area where the Siege of Limerick had been fought and won. Coughlan continued:

> We have an outlook which we are going to keep. The people of this city abhor the introduction of these people, who are completely opposed to our Christian

tradition. While we don't condone this violent action, it is something that we all foresaw…[4]

In contrast to Coughlan's reactionary statement, Jim Kemmy, the Chairman of Labour's East Limerick Constituency Council, a member of Labour's Administrative Council (AC) and a future Democratic Socialist Party and Labour TD, spoke out against what he called the unchristian and inflammatory action which had been taken against the Maoists and the fact that no one had used Christian arguments or attempted to have dialogue with them in an effort to refute their statements or policies. Kemmy added:

> Instead they have been savagely attacked on emotional grounds… The series of attacks on the Maoist bookshop, culminating in the shooting incident, must be condemned by all democratic and freedom-loving people. The attacks are the logical result of the recent inflammatory and bigoted statements made by the Mayor of Limerick, the *Limerick Leader* and the *Limerick Chronical* newspapers and a few lay 'popes'. By fanning the flames of bigotry these statements created the climate for the attack: their responsibility is a heavy one…

> While most Irish socialists differ from the Maoists in ideology and tactics, their right to live in Limerick and to have freedom of speech is a basic human right and legal one and is guaranteed in our Constitution….[5]

Coughlan's remarks were discussed at a meeting of the Labour Party's AC on 18 March. After the meeting, the AC issued a statement opposing the use of force as a means of securing political objectives.[6]

Three days later, on 21 March, at a meeting of left-wing Labour members, in the Baggot Inn, Lower Pembroke Street, Dublin, the AC's statement was described as a 'betrayal of the Party.' The meeting demanded the recall of the AC and publication of a new statement condemning in stronger terms the recent armed attack on the Maoist bookshop in Limerick. The meeting was composed of 'rank and file' members and among those in attendance were Noël Browne, TD, Máire Cruise O'Brien and John Swift, who presided. A message from Conor Cruise O'Brien, TD, said that the meeting had his full support and was one of the best things he had seen happening in the Party in a long time.[7]

Anti-Semitic remarks by Coughlan led to yet another contentious issue in the Labour Party, in April 1970. In an address to the convention of the Credit Union League of Ireland, Coughlan accused Limerick's former Jewish community of money-lending and extortion over half a century earlier, adding that the main action taken against them had been justified. Responding to Coughlan's outburst, the Credit Union League of Ireland unanimously adopted a resolution disassociating itself from what it described as the mayor's 'anti-Semitic remarks'.[8]

The Jewish community in Ireland reacted sharply and vigorously to Coughlan's statements.[9] In a grossly inadequate apology to the Jewish community, on 24 April, Coughlan omitted any reference to the 1904 Jewish Pogrom in Limerick and merely stated that he regretted his remarks.

Nevertheless, the apology was accepted on behalf of the Jewish community by the Chief Rabbi, Dr. Issac Cohen.[10]

Coughlan's controversial remarks, particularly those relating to anti-Semitism, caused consternation in the Labour Party, and not just on the left. Although Dan Browne and Brendan Corish, respectively, Party Chairman and Leader, publicly disassociated themselves immediately from Coughlan's anti-Semitic statement, many Labour members regarded this as an inadequate response.[11] As for the Labour members of the Oireachtas, they decided on 29 April to take no further action against Coughlan.[12] It later emerged that four of the eighteen Labour deputies, Noël Browne, Frank Cluskey, Justin Keating and Conor Cruise O'Brien, all from Dublin constituencies, had supported expulsion.[13] In a statement on 1 May 1970, Browne said he disapproved very strongly of the continued retention of Coughlan. 'I don't think his apology met the original reason for the apology', he said.[14] The other named members, who remained silent, were believed to have held similar views.[15]

A tougher line on Coughlan's anti-Semitism was taken by Labour's Dublin Regional Council (DRC), of which Brendan Scott was a member.[16] At its meeting on 29 April 1970, the Council unanimously passed a resolution calling for Coughlan's immediate dismissal from the Party, and disassociated itself from his recent pronouncements.[17] However, when the Party's AC met the following day, a motion to expel Coughlan was lost. Brendan Scott, Jim Kemmy, John Byrne and Matt Merrigan then indicated they were withdrawing from the meeting and resigning from the AC as they could not accept collective responsibility for the Council's decision. Shortly thereafter, Niall Greene, the Party's Financial Secretary, who was never associated with the left, resigned from the AC on similar grounds.[18]

The AC went on to adopt the following statement:

> That the Administrative Council unanimously endorses the repudiation made by both the Party Leader, Brendan Corish and Party Chairman, Dan Browne, of the recent anti-Semitic remarks of Alderman Coughlan, T.D., Mayor of Limerick. Such statements offend against basic human values and are especially abhorrent to the principles of which the party is founded. The meeting noted that the apology made by Alderman Coughlan had been accepted by the spiritual leader of the Jewish Community in Ireland. Accordingly, the Administrative Council decided not to proceed with the expulsion of Alderman Coughlan, The Administrative Council, however, wishes to make clear that the repetition of such views by any Party member will incur immediate expulsion.[19]

Commenting on this crisis in the Labour Party, *Irish Times* journalist, Dick Walsh, wrote:

> One of the surprises of the controversy has been the silence of many members of the Parliamentary Party and the attitudes adopted by others. Particularly those who had a few years ago been considered the young radical hope of Labour.
>
> In the Dublin Regional Council, for instance, Mr. Michael O'Leary argued strongly against any move to expel Mr. Coughlan and was later to be described by one of his less conservative colleagues as "a premature statesman".

The argument is bitter, mostly because it represents not only a conflict over Mr. Coughlan and his opinions but a deep division in Labour between right and left, in some cases between country and city. Throughout the debate, the radical pressure has come from the constituencies.[20]

A day following his resignation from the AC, Scott called for an emergency delegate convention at which all members of the Party would have a chance to voice their opinions on Coughlan's remarks.[21] Describing the resignations of the AC members as a depletion of the left-wing of the Council, Scott felt that the depletion would not result in a right-wing 'coup' by co-option of right-wingers favouring the decision taken. The tragedy of this affair, he said, was that the Party had lost two men of the calibre of Niall Greene and Maurice O'Sullivan, both of whom were 'irreplaceable'. Scott also contended that the decision of the AC did not reflect the feeling of the Party as a whole.[22]

On 4 May, a special meeting of Labour's DRC passed a resolution viewing with deep concern the circumstances that had led to the resignation of five members of the AC and called on the Leader of the Party to convene a special delegate conference of the entire Party to meet not later than by 30 June. A couple of days later, at an AC meeting, it was unanimously agreed that the AC should meet a delegation from the DRC to discuss the resolution and report back to a full meeting of the AC.[23] Following two meetings between the DRC and the Party Chair and Leader, the DRC's request for a special delegate conference was declined. At its meeting on 20 May, the AC decided that the General Secretary, Brendan Halligan, should be asked to indicate to the DRC the AC's view that at that time a special delegate conference was neither opportune nor necessary and to repeat a request to hold a special one-day conference of the Dublin membership with the Leader in attendance.[24]

The failure of the Labour leadership to expel Coughlan over his anti-Semitic remarks led to resignations from the Party, among them the aforementioned Maurice O'Sullivan, who, in a press report, was described thus:

> Mr. O'Sullivan is the right-hand research and organisational man of Brendan Halligan and one of the best directors of elections the party had had for many years. He has none of the Left labels, but is rather a firm "middle-ground" man. Apparently, the last straw for O'Sullivan was a meeting of the Parliamentary Party during the previous week when a majority could not be found for an immediate expulsion of Coughlan.[25]

There were further resignations from the Party in March 1971 when three executive members of the TCD Labour Party Branch resigned in protest against the Labour Conference decision to retain Coughlan as a party member and Labour TD. They were also critical of Labour's policy towards the cement workers' strike and 'the enthusiasm about coalescing with Fine Gael – a right-wing Blue Shirt party.' The three committee members were Hazel P. Birney (Secretary), Carol Coulter (Vice-Chairman) and Sandra M.

Lysaght (committee member).[26] Among other notable resignations were Máirín Johnston, Vice-Chair of the DRC; and Fergal Costello, Chairman of Dublin North Central Constituency Council.[27]

The Coughlan affair resurfaced at the Party's 1971 Annual Conference when, following a bitter debate, a call for his expulsion over his alleged anti-Semitic views and departure from Party policy was rejected. Corish, the Party Leader, said that any penalising of Labour's right would mean, too, the expulsion of people on the extreme left![28]

A year after all factions of the Labour Party had concluded that the Coughlan affair had run its course, Coughlan, in a press interview, on 26 March 1972, reiterated his earlier anti-Semitic remarks. At the next meeting of the AC, on 13 April, the following motion, proposed and seconded, respectively, by Des Bonass and Justin Keating, TD, was considered:

That the Administrative Council resolves to cancel the Party membership of Deputy Coughlan on the following grounds:

1. That he reiterated in an interview on March 26 allegations he originally stated in Limerick in April 1970;

2. That his reiteration of these allegations is in violation of the Administrative Council decision in April 1970 and the ruling of the Chairman, Dan Browne, at the Galway Conference 1971;

3. That Deputy Coughlan's statements are a repudiation of the disciplinary line adopted by acclamation at the Wexford conference 1972 set out in the Party Leader's keynote speech and the code of the Parliamentary Party behaviour, also set out by the Party Leader in the Oughterard speech.

4. That the Council further believes that the continued membership of Deputy Coughlan is repugnant to the essential principle of anti-sectarianism and the liberal and democratic values enunciated by the Party. Deputy Coughlan has been responsible for the defection of many worthy members of the Party in Limerick and elsewhere. In addition there is disquiet felt by at least one affiliated union, the Amalgamated Transport and General Workers' Union that the Labour Party can harbour a public representative who can express these views with impunity.

The following addendum, which was accepted and became part of the motion, was then moved by Máire Walshe, seconded by Ciaran McAteer:

That furthermore Deputy Coughlan spoke specifically against Party policy in the same issue of the *Sunday Press* on the field of Northern Ireland, as approved by Conference in Wexford, Party discipline, as mentioned by the Party Leader, Deputy Corish in his speech to the Wexford Conference and in the field of the changes in the Constitution in which Deputy Coughlan specifically insulted those members of the Party who pressed for changes to the Constitution.

The amended motion was lost by twenty votes to seven, with one abstention.[29]

Thus it was that Labour's AC reneged on its earlier decision to expel Coughlan in the event of any repetition of his anti-Semitic remarks.

Notes

1   *Irish Times,* 12 March 1970.
2   *Irish Independent,* 12 March 1970.
3   *Irish Times,* 12 March 1970.
4   ibid.
5   ibid., 14 March 1970.
6   Labour Party, Annual Report, 1970, pp. 4-5.
7   *Irish Examiner,* 23 March 1970.
8   *Irish Times,* 20 April 1970.
9   ibid., 20 April 1970.
10 ibid., 27 April 1970; Labour Party, Annual Report, 1970, pp. 4-5.
11 Labour Party, AC, minutes of meeting, 30 April 1970; Annual Report, 1970, pp. 4-5.
12 *Irish Times,* 30 April 1970.
13 ibid., 2 May 1970.
14 ibid.
15 ibid.
16 *Irish Times,* 7 October 1969, 5 October 1970.
17 ibid., 30 April 1970.
18 *Irish Press,* 2 May 1970; Labour Party, Annual Report, 1970, pp. 4-5.
19 *Irish Times,* 1 May 1970; Labour Party, Annual Report 1970, pp. 4-5.
20 *Irish Times,* 2, 6 May 1970.
21 *Evening Herald,* 1 May 1970.
22 *Irish Independent,* 2 May 1970.
23 Labour Party, AC, minutes of meeting, 6 May 1970.
24 ibid., 20 May 1970.
25 *Irish Times,* 24 April 1970.
26 *Irish Independent, Irish Times,* 5 March 1970.
27 *Irish Times,* 6 May 1970; Email from the author to Máirín Johnston, 13 November 2019 and from Máirín Johnston to the author, 22 November 2019.
28 *Irish Times,* 1 March 1971.
29 Labour Party, AC, minutes, minutes of meeting, 13 April, 1972.

CHAPTER 19

A Monumental Error

For Labour's left, no issues were as important as the retention of the socialist policies and the anti-coalition stance. However, in what Scott and his socialist colleagues considered a monumental error, a Special Party Conference, in Cork, on 13 December 1970, reversed the Party's anti-coalition position. The main motion (to which there were forty-two amendments), in the name of the Administrative Council (AC), was carried by 396 votes in favour with 204 against:[1]

> That this special meeting of national conference affirms that circumstances exist in which participation by the Labour Party in government is in both the national interest and the interest of the party, and pending the return of a majority Labour Party representation in Dail Eireann, which is our aim, conference empowers the leader and members of the Parliamentary Labour Party, subject to consultation with the Administrative Council, on the terms thereof, to negotiate participation by the Labour party in a government that would guarantee the implementation of Labour policies and to participate in such a government for such time as it is in the nation's interest to do so and for so long as Labour Party policies are being implemented.[2]

While the result could be interpreted as a triumph for the leadership, the margin of victory was inflated by the earlier walkout of some 150 anti-coalitionists, led by Noël Browne.[3] Had the anti-coalitionists voted, the margin would have been relatively narrow. Whether the walk-out was a protest or simply Dublin-based delegates rushing to catch a train, as claimed by Justin Keating at the time,[4] has never been established. In any event, Browne and Merrigan immediately appealed to the dissidents to remain in the Party.[5]

For the left, there were other concerns about the result following allegations of rigging. Dermot Boucher, a former member of the Party's Standing Orders Committee, who had been expelled during the year, said that his expulsion had followed differences within the committee during which he alleged the rigging of some rural constituencies by their deputies, in particular the Constituency of Limerick East. He also claimed that some resolutions had been reversed and that debates had been slanted to favour the policy of the party leadership. He said that, in some cases, the order of speakers had been changed and that in one instance the name of Noël Browne had been put to the end of the list while that of Conor Cruise O'Brien had been elevated to the top. 'Conference', he said, 'had been manipulated by head office...'[6]

Many years later, similar allegations were made by Des Bonass:

> We [left-wing Labour Party delegates] had a terrific campaign [against coalition]. We had a third of the votes, and we won the debate. We planned to swing other people. But they actually brought – I saw it happening – busloads from Kerry. Dan Spring, Dick Spring's father, and Stevie Coughlan organised it. The busloads never attended conference until the actual vote was taking place, and we were outvoted…[7]

Adding weight to such rigging allegations was the statement by the pro-coalition Conor Cruise O'Brien in 1999, when he recalled that, at the end of the Coalition Conference, Dan Spring, TD, approached him and said: 'That was a nice speech you made there, boy, but that was a nice two busloads of delegates I brought up from Kerry too, boy.'[8] In her book, *The Irish Labour Party 1922-73*, Niamh Puirséil was in no doubt that there was substance to allegations of rigging: 'Of course, while the rigging accusations were exaggerated, they were largely true…'[9] It is difficult to see how rigging could occur without the knowledge and acquiescence of the Party leadership.

An hour or so before the Browne-led walk-out from the Special Coalition Conference, a leaflet advertising a post-conference meeting was issued by members of the 'Socialist Labour Action group'. The leaflet stated:

> That in view of the decision taken by the special delegate conference, Socialists in the Labour Party must consider their position anew. In particular, the implementation of the 1970 conference decision to call a unity conference of Socialists North and South must be discussed. All anti-Coalition Labour Party members are urged to attend.[10]

Earlier still, on the eve of the conference, an attempt had been made to form a new socialist movement. This was spearheaded by a Northern Ireland group, including Bernadette Devlin, MP, Eamonn McCann and Michael Farrell, none of whom was committed to attend the Labour conference. They took part in a meeting that evening in University College, Cork, when the various anti-coalition groups began to build a united front and to prepare for a walk-out. It was during this meeting that Browne made his first impassioned plea to the left-wing to remain within the Party and to continue fighting for control.[11]

At a press conference following Labour's conference, Corish described the proceedings as 'an exercise in democracy' and said that the result was as he had anticipated. He emphasised that no coalition negotiations would be held before a general election and that 'Labour will fight the next election on its own policies.' Summing up his personal position, he said that he regarded the decision of the conference on the motion as 'a vote for or against the leadership of the party.' Explaining why he had proposed that the resolution be supported, Corish said:

> I had no hesitation in doing this because I have been taunted as to what I would do in the event of a change in electoral strategy. I told conference that with regard to my 1969 attitude, that as long as my informed assessment of the political situation suggested to me in the context of '69, that coalition was wrong, then, in conscience, I was bound to retire to the back-benches.

> In drastically changed circumstances, when in my judgement it is right for the party to negotiate for participation in government and to adopt this policy, I found no reason to retire to the back benches.

He then described the proposed change in electoral strategy as 'an overwhelming vote of confidence in me', adding that 'there was no reason in the world why I should resign from the leadership of the party.'[12]

In a press interview immediately after the walk-out, Noël Browne described the conference as 'a farce' and accused the Party of refusing to vote on several issues involving fundamental party policy. He continued:

> They tried to give the impression that no one was in opposition to changing this fundamental policy whereas, a very substantial minority was against coalition, including the three major unions. The party will find it difficult to operate against these trade unions who account for the majority of the organised workers in the country.

He went on to emphasise that he was not leaving the party. However, he laid equal stress on his belief that 'Corish has to live the rest of his political life with this repudiation of his statement of two years ago that he would go to the back benches if the party went into coalition.'[13]

According to a press report, the majority of the dissidents appeared to have felt that the Party had become so concerned with the structure of the political machine that what they regarded as 'real socialism' had been lost sight of. They accused the conference of voting against fundamental Labour policy by defeating an amendment containing a clause stating that the second party in any coalition should also be opposed to Irish entry to the European Economic Community (EEC). They also complained that the allotted time for speeches – three minutes each to address a resolution – was inadequate and unreasonable.[14]

For Brendan Scott and like-minded socialists, the reversal of Labour's coalition position was a severe setback, effectively involving the abandonment of such fundamental policies as the democratisation and secularisation of education and health services, State control of financial institutions, State acquisition of building land for social and affordable housing, and worker democracy.

Two days following the conference, Scott, together with anti-coalition Labour colleagues, Una Claffey and Charlie Bird, both subsequently prominent RTÉ television journalists and presenters, criticised Labour's pro-coalition policy on what was then RTÉ's flagship, current affairs television programme, *Seven Days*. At an AC meeting, on 23 December 1970, Bill Conroy, a member of the Council, said that Scott, Claffey and Bird should be censured for their *Seven Days* performance. Irreparable damage had been done to the Party by virtue of their appearance on television, he added.[15] There is no evidence that any disciplinary action was taken against the trio.

In early 1971, shortly after the reversal of Labour's anti-coalition policy, Scott was a founding member[16] of an informal left-wing group, the Liaison Committee of the Left – Labour Party (LCLL), which emerged within the Party in early 1971. Its main objectives were to ensure that Labour's 1969 socialist policies and anti-coalition stance were retained. Composed overwhelmingly of non-Trotskyist, left-wing socialists,[17] its informal nature was designed to make difficult the expulsion of its members from the Party. Officers of the LCLL were Matt Merrigan (Chairman), Jim Kemmy (Vice-Chairman) and Dermot Boucher (Secretary). It is likely that Merrigan, was elected Chairman in the belief that Labour's leadership would hesitate to expel him for fear of prompting the disaffiliation of his union, the ATGWU. Key figures in the LCLL were Merigan, Boucher, Pat Carroll,[18] David Neligan[19] and, up to his final illness, Brendan Scott. Other prominent activists included Des Bonass, John Byrne, Tom Carroll, Tony Dunne (later a WUI and SIPTU Branch Secretary), Billy Keegan and Maisie McConnell. Also associated with the LLCL were Noël Browne, TD, and John Swift.[20] However, as John Horgan has observed, 'although linked with Browne, Liaison was not in any sense led by Browne.'[21] Brendan Scott was the founding Editor of the LCLL's publication, *Liaison*[22], retaining that post up to his final illness when he was succeeded by Dermot Boucher.[23]

Concerns about the Parliamentary Party's failure to promote the more radical socialist policies were raised publicly by Swift in February 1971. Referring to the adoption of those policies at the 1969 Annual Conference, he said:

> …There has followed a conspicuous silence on the part of most of the Labour Deputies regarding the more radical texts in the policy statements. It looks as though, from the glut of policy feasting at the 1969 conference, swelling digestive upset has left many of the Party spokesmen with little wind left to talk the socialism of workers democracy.
>
> Yet over this time of muteness on the policies, our economy has suffered much from chronically bad and worsening industrial relations. For nearly six months our banking services were closed down and earlier in the year the similarly irrational industrial relations had brought a like marathon stoppage in the cement and associated building industries.
>
> Over this period it was expected that at least some of the Labour shadow ministers would have demanded in the Dail that these undertakings, so important to our economy, should, as stressed in the party's policies, be brought under public control. Many concerned observers in the Party have been wondering if its spokesmen's long silence on the policy documents is to be attributed to their pre-occupation with the prospect that their shadow ministries may soon be filled with the palpable substance of their own persons. Meanwhile, anger grows in the Party branches, particularly in Dublin, at the apparent or feared abandonment of the socialism in the policy documents.
>
> Many young enthusiasts have already withdrawn from the Party: and I fear that, unless there is soon forthcoming from the leading spokesmen some strong sign of adherence to socialist principles, these losses will be followed by others, perhaps more serious. These desertions by the young and eager may be regarded

by some as but a tumult of feathers, a happening of no more weight than the flurry of up-start fledgings [sic] taking off. For others it will be the flight of good young cockerels and pullets, forced from the coop by the cluck of matriarchal cackle. To such a view, it is not the chickens coming home to roost, but the old hens.[24]

Swift's contribution was echoed in a motion tabled by the Fintan Lalor Branch (Dublin North Central), of which Swift was a member, at the Labour Party Annual Conference, in Salthill, Galway, in late February 1971. The motion noted 'the silence and absence of any activity on the policy statements adopted in 1969.'[25] But concerns about the Labour leadership's inertia in relation to the socialist policies were not confined to the left. At a joint meeting of Labour's AC and Parliamentary Party, on 15 July 1971, Senator Evelyn Owens, who was unassociated with the left, said that at the 1969 Conference an undertaking had been given that the policy documents would be expanded on the basis of the criticism offered at that Conference. To the best of her knowledge nothing had been done in the intervening period. In her view the immediate problem was to tackle the policy documents and to update them. In response, the General Secretary, Brendan Halligan, said that Senator Owens was correct in her observations but that events over the previous eighteen months had prevented the continuation of the policy formation exercise. However, he said, a start was being made on some documents.[26]

Contraception was among other issues debated at Labour's 1971 Annual Conference. Theoretically, there was no major left-right divide in the Party on this issue. A resolution urging the Parliamentary Party to demand the repeal of legislation prohibiting the importation and sale of contraceptives and literature on family planning was passed at the Conference. The decision was virtually unanimous, opposition, as one woman delegate pointed out, coming entirely from men. Before the resolution was put to the delegates an amendment, which was accepted, said that the sections of Acts dealing with contraception clearly 'contravened the spirit and the letter of the Constitution and the idea of democratic republic, which was embodied in it.' Another amendment, which was accepted, said that the Conference recognised that family planning was a matter of individual conscience. Speakers in favour of the resolution included Conor Cruise O'Brien, Noël Browne, Dr. Máire Walshe and Carol Coulter.[27] Opposing the motion, W. J. Curran, a delegate from Carrigtwohill Branch, County Cork, stated that its acceptance meant acceptance of 'free love.' To howls of laughter and hooting, he added: 'Let's not have intimate relations with everybody's wife, and control our animal instincts.'[28]

Turning to internal Labour Party matters, the newly-formed LLCL escaped censure at the 1971 Annual Conference when Corish warned those using the Party in the pursuit of policies not conforming to those adopted and championed by Labour. Chris Glennon, Political Correspondent of the *Irish Independent*, shed some light on this matter:

Mr. Corish did not name those to whom he directed the warning, but he was not talking to the leftist groups in Labour. He was talking to people whom he feels have policies more suited to republican or militant organisations – sections of Sinn Fein or Saor Eire – and to some groups who follow a Trotskyite ideology.

He declared: "We cannot tolerate the presence within the Party of those who are like a Trojan horse in our midst and whose aim is to wreak on us as much damage as their twisted minds can imagine. There can be no more dual membership of this Party and of other parties or political groups."

On Friday night, immediately after the opening session, and again on Saturday evening at least two groups held separate meetings. The Liaison Committee of the Left attracted an attendance of about 150 to a meeting in a Salthill hotel. Their aim is to keep Labour well to the left to continue to push what they see as the true socialist policies. But they are adamant that they want to stay within the Party and they spend a good deal of their time lobbying in an effort to "capture" some of the top party posts.

They do not seriously challenge the leadership; they intend providing a continual critical analysis of it and of the operations of the Party head office.

Less humorous and less organised were the Young Socialists, who disaffiliated from the Party after the December 13 decision making way for a possible coalition. Their main strength – an ability to create a lot of disruptive noise – was not of any value as far as the Conference was concerned. Few of their members remain in the Labour Party and their activities were mainly confined to handing out literature to delegates and holding their own meetings.

Yet another group, the League for a Workers' Republic, which is on the far, far left, seemingly had not got the numbers to be very much in evidence. Neither they nor the Young Socialists find any measure of support from or even compatibility with the Liaison Committee of the Left.

The Liaison Committee could be described - certainly they would describe themselves – as the vocal socialist conscience of the Party: the other two seemed to have no substantial place in or with it...[29]

Contesting the principal officerships at that 1971 Labour Conference, the LLCL nominated John Swift as Chairman,[30] Jim Kemmy as Vice-Chairman[31] and Dudley Potter, a solicitor, as Financial Secretary.[32] In the election for Chair, Swift secured 160 votes, with 213 going to Michael D. Higgins,[33] the future President of Ireland, 'who received most of his votes from the West and other poor rural areas;'[34] and 383 to Roddy Connolly, son of James Connolly, the victor.[35] For the position of Vice-Chairman, Kemmy, who came within fifty votes of victory,[36] had two opponents: Niall Greene, who was elected, and Christopher Worth.[37] In the election of Financial Secretary Potter was defeated by Donal O'Sullivan.

Although it failed to win any of the three posts, the LCLL was not disappointed with the overall results:

The left liaison group...saw this year as a holding operation. This group which is dominated by ex-members of the AC such as Matt Merrigan, Brendan Scott and Jim Kemmy put forward a short list of six approved candidates for the AC and five for the Standing Orders Committee.

They hoped to gain a foothold in both committees so that the left wing would remain informed of all party developments and that any move to crack down on the left would be opposed. In fact two members of the short list were elected and one sympathiser which quite satisfied the group, as did the showing of Jim Kemmy in the election for the Vice-Chairman of the party.[38]

Under the heading, 'Conference may have completed Labour's transformation', Michael McInerney, *Irish Times* Political Correspondent, placed that development in context:

>...It is only a few years since a Labour Leader changed the first aim in the party Constitution at the simple request of a single bishop, or went back on a firm Labour commitment about a means test in a Health Scheme when the hierarchy breathed its disfavour, and only seven years since Corish timidly mentioned that the Labour Party was "Socialist" but "Christian Socialist!" It is also remembered that a witch-hunt expelled some genuine Labour men and women from the Party, and that Owen Sheehy Skeffington was expelled for Liberal views.[39]

Notes

1   *Irish Times*, 14 December 1970.
2   ibid.
3   ibid.
4   ibid.
5   ibid.
6   ibid., 27 February 1971.
7   Des Bonass in Des Derwin, 'Memories of 'A Marvellous Legacy': Matt Merrigan, 1921-2000', in Francis Devine and Kieran Jack McGinley (Editors), *Left Lives in Twentieth Century Ireland*, Volume 2, op. cit., p. 120.
8   Conor Cruise O'Brien, *Memoir: My Life and Themes*, op. cit., p. 338.
9   Niamh Puirséil, *The Irish Labour Party 1922-73* (UCD Press, Dublin, 2007), p. 286.
10 *Irish Times*, 14 December 1970.
11 ibid.
12 ibid.
13 ibid.
14 ibid.
15 Labour Party, AC, minutes of meeting, 23 December 1970.
16 Matt Merrigan, *Eggs and Rashers: Irish Socialist Memories*, op. cit., p.115.
17 Interviews with Pat Carroll, 30 October 2018; Niall Greene, 16 November 2018; Brendan Halligan, 16 November 2018.
18 Patrick (Pat) Carroll, a former teacher, was a member of the Vocational Teachers' Association which was re-named the Teachers' Union of Ireland in 1973. A Labour Party member, he was centrally involved in the Liaison Committee of the Left - Labour Party (LCLL) from 1971 to 1977. From 1974-1983, he served as a Dublin City Councillor. A Committee member of the Irish Labour History Society since 2012, he was also served for many years on the Committee of the Irish Anti-Apartheid Movement (IAAM), Pat Carroll is married to Joan Burton, former Tánaiste, Minister and Leader of the Labour Party. She is also a former Secretary of the IAAM.
19 David Neligan, a former dentist, was a leading figure in the Liaison Committee of the Left – Labour Party (LCLL) from 1971-1977. He was Chairman of the Resources Protection Campaign in the 1970s and Chairman of the Socialist Labour Party from 1977-1982.
20 Barry Desmond, *Finally and in Conclusion*, op. cit., p. 57. Desmond statement that David Thornley, TD, was a member of the Liaison Committee of the Left (LCLL)

has been refuted in interviews with the author by Pat Carroll, on 30 October 2018, and Yseult Thornley, daughter of David Thornley, on 1 February 2019. Surprisingly, Brendan Scott, a founder and one of the most active LCLL members, is not mentioned in Desmond's list.

21 John Horgan, *Noël Browne: Passionate Outsider,* op. cit., p. 255.
22 *Liaison,* undated, circa October 1974, p. 1.
23 Matt Merrigan, *Eggs and Rashers: Irish Socialist Memories,* op. cit., p. 206.
24 John Swift, 'Labour and Workers' Democracy – 2: The Silence on Socialism,' *Irish Times,* 23 February 1971.
25 *Evening Herald,* 23 February 1971.
26 Labour Party, AC and Parliamentary Party, joint meeting, 15 July 1971.
27 *Irish Times,* 1 March 1971.
28 *Irish Independent,* 1 March 1971.
29 ibid.
30 LCLL, John Swift, Election Address for position of Chairman of the Labour Party, 1971.
31 LCLL, Pat Carroll, Election Address for position on AC of the Labour Party, 1971.
32 ibid.
33 Labour Party, Certificate of Ballot, 1971.
34 *Connaught Sentinal,* 2 March 1971.
35 *Irish Press,* 1 March 1971; Labour Party, Certificate of Ballot, 1971.
36 ibid., 28 February 1972.
37 ibid., 1 March 1971.
38 *This Week,* Vol. 2, No. 20, 12 March 1971, p.6
39 *Irish Times,* 2 March 1971.

15. Brendan Scott, RTÉ Television scriptwriter and presenter, 1 January 1969.

16. Dublin Housing Action Committee, sit-down protest, O'Connell Bridge, Dublin, 18 January 1969, Máirín Johnston (née Mooney).

17. Dublin Housing Action Committee, public meeting, GPO, Dublin, circa late 1960s – early 1970s, platform from left: unidentified, Bernard Browne (Chairman) and Máirín Johnston.

18. Dublin Housing Action Committee, sit-down demonstration, College Green, Dublin, 27 September 1969, Eamonn Farrell (Secretary) following his arrest.

*19. Irish Voice on Vietnam, protest march, O'Connell Bridge, Dublin,
circa late 1960s- early 1970s, from left: 3rd Esther McGregor,
4th Moira Woods, 5th & 6th (with hats) John Swift father and son,
10th Máirín Johnston.*

*20. Irish Voice on Vietnam, protest march, Ballsbridge, Dublin,
circa late 1960s-early 1970s.*

21. Irish Voice on Vietnam, protest march from Parnell Square to USA Embassy, Ballsbridge, Dublin, circa late 1960s-early 1970s, from left: Brendan Scott (in dark blue shirt), Louise Asmal, and behind them (with hat), John Swift.

22. Irish Voice on Vietnam, mock trial of President Richard Nixon, at USA Embassy, Ballsbridge, Dublin, 4 October 1970, from left: Brendan Scott (mock trial script-writer and prosecuting counsel), Moira Woods (judge) and Joe Deasy (defence counsel).

*23. Irish Anti-Apartheid Movement (IAAM), churches conference,
Gonzaga College, Dublin, 25-26 September 1971,
from left: Brendan Scott, Secretary, IAAM; Dean Gunnar Helander,
Sweden; unidentified, Seán MacRéamoinn, journalist and broadcaster;
and Richard Murphy, IAAM.*

*24. Irish Anti-Apartheid Movement (IAAM), churches conference,
Gonzaga College, Dublin, 25-26 September 1971,
from left: Louise Asmal, Administrative Secretary, IAAM;
Rev. Edward Crowther, Bishop of California; Brendan Scott, Secretary,
IAAM; and Rev. Walter Makhulu, Johannesburg.*

25. United May Day Committee, May Day March,
Socialist Party of Ireland contingent,
O'Connell Street, Dublin, circa 1 May 1973.

26. Meeting of British and Irish Labour Party leaders, Dublin,
19 November 1971, from left: Harold Wilson, MP, Leader, British
Labour Party; Brendan Corish, TD, Leader, Michael O'Leary, TD,
and David Thornley, TD, Irish Labour Party.

27. Sculpture of Brendan Scott by Kieran Kelly, circa 1972.

28. The Scott family, from left: Ivan, Carol Ann, Melanie, Eoin and Brendan, at the wedding of Michael Boland and Susan O'Rourke (a sister of Carol Ann), Delgany, County Wicklow, 24 June 1972.

29. Brendan Scott, Dublin,

30. Brendan and Carol Ann Scott's tombstone, St. Fintan's Cemetery, Sutton, 23 July 2020.

CHAPTER 20

Taking a Stand

In a highly courageous, landmark speech in 1971, Noël Browne strongly condemned the political power and influence of the Catholic Church in Ireland. Speaking at a Labour Party dinner in Tramore, County Waterford, on 23 April 1971, Browne said that the policies of each government in the Republic had been strictly dominated and determined by Catholic social and economic privileges. This was achieved by the classically simple process of the systematic indoctrination used by any religious or political group to establish and perpetuate its rule on society. Browne continued:

> The most important way in which the Hierarchy determined the social and economic policies of our society was that it demanded and had been given absolute control of our educational system. The system was staffed by religious orders and, in regard to lay teachers, controlled by the fear of job patronage exercised by the religious school-managers. In this way the bishops determined and controlled social and economic policies, formulated a culture which, directly and indirectly, created and moulded the mind of the voting end-product, the Irish electorate.

> Was it any surprise to find that politicians in all parties, because of their fear of the political consequences of alienating clerical support, toed the party line as laid down by the Catholic Hierarchy, on all issues of social importance?

> The harsh truth is that the Catholic Church is one of the most dedicated, resilient, obscurantist and conservative political machines in the history of man, which only now is entering into its decline the world over. Her record of chameleon conformism to the demands of social justice – only under persistent pressure from her political surroundings and never, it would appear, from sincere convictions – would shame the political antics of the most opportunist Victorian borough councillors.

> Truly it has been said: "Give us the child and we will answer for the man, the electorate, the parliament, the Cabinet and its social and economic policies." It is simply a part of the whole self-perpetuating mechanism of Catholicism...

> In recent weeks we have seen a cardinal making lavish use of our television service..., consciously seeking to confuse the current issue of the need for a simple amendment to our laws on contraception...by warning that such a simple amendment of our laws would inevitably lead to therapeutic legal abortion, divorce, euthanasia, and the total breakdown of the moral values in Irish society. Clearly, he believes that Irishmen over whom the Catholic Church has had absolute control for centuries is separated from a libertine Hibernian Sodom and Gomorrah by a slot machine of contraceptives. What an abject confession of the failure of his priestly mission.

> Has this happened in his Northern Catholic constituents? Has it happened to our Protestant fellow-Irishmen in the South whom, he says, already have access to contraceptive devices? Cardinal Heenan praised the social and sexual morality of the Catholic Irish in contraceptive-ridden Protestant England.

To me the most grievous betrayal is the way the Hierarchy deliberately seeks to mislead our politicians about the true authority of its political beliefs as expressed in pastoral letters and elsewhere…The Hierarchy refuses to make it clear that unless a matter is clearly stated to be binding under the pain of mortal sin, then whatever view it may hold or propound on any subject should be given just as much respect or suspicion as is given to the views of any other politically committed individual in society.

Although that caveat of Browne's was problematic for secularists such as Swift, he nevertheless welcome enthusiastically the general thrust of Browne's Tramore speech.

Continuing his speech, Browne said:

It is true that in issues which closely concerned married couples and the human condition generally, its views were those of men who had deserted the field of battle as laymen knew it. As bishops, archbishops and cardinals they are isolated from the stress of earning their living, becoming unemployed, and forced to emigrate, marry, found homes and families.' Consciously or otherwise, many of them have chosen their celibate lives because they find the whole subject of sex and heterosexual relationships threatening and embarrassing. Their judgement, then, cannot be trusted on these issues.

It is now long overdue that we acknowledge the understandable ignorance of men living celibate lives: that they are not competent to advise the rest of us in the complex matters of our marriage relationships except in the narrowest limits…

As it happened to his predecessors in office, it has now fallen to Mr. Lynch [the Taoiseach, Jack Lynch] to demonstrate the independence or survile [sic] subservience of his Government on this issue.

Throughout the last fifty years not one of our republican leaders has dared to free our people from the extra-parliamentary pressure of the Catholic Church with her medical social and political attitudes. Have we not grievously suffered for it?

No-one could seriously doubt but that the Catholic Church had behaved to all our political parties in an identical way as the Orange Order in its control of the Unionist Party in the North – a sectarian and bigoted politically conservative pressure group.

It is just as undemocratic and intolerable that this should pertain in the South as our Republican political leaders have so long protested against its existence in the North.

It is time that our people got up off their knees; that both our peoples, North and South, finally took on the responsibility of governing ourselves, uniting our unhappy divided nation under a true republican unity, the common name of Irishmen.[1]

Predictably, fearing a belt of a crozier and disregarding the substantive case Browne had made, the Parliamentary Labour Party disassociated itself from the speech. Yet, it is likely that some of his colleagues, particularly Keating and O'Brien, privately agreed with his analysis of Church-State relations. In a statement on 30 April 1971, the Parliamentary Party said that it was neither accurate nor fair to condemn in a global fashion Roman Catholic clerics in the manner in which Noël Browne had done in Tramore. The statement went on:

> Parts of that speech were insulting and belittling of the Roman Catholic clergy. To suggest that any of those who chose the religious life do so out of a fear of sexual relations is an insult to men and women who regard their vocations as a service to God and humanity...Dr. Browne spoke for himself when he levelled that charge against the clergy."

> We may say that the same goes for his reference to confession, which is a Sacrament of the Catholic Church and, as such, is held sacred by Catholics. It is not the function of politicians to denigrate the beliefs or practices of any religion. No purpose is served in being insulting to the Roman Catholic Church or any other Church and we will not tolerate such statements made by members of the Labour Party which insult any religion. We regret any offence that may have been caused by those remarks. It has never been part of the Labour Party's policy to engage in anti-clericalism. It is not now, nor will it be in the future," the statement added.

The condemnation of Browne's speech was contained in a long statement on the issue of whether the ban on the importation of contraceptives should be lifted...

> ...The Labour Party has decided on its policy by the democratic decision of hundreds of delegates at its annual conference. Labour is in favour of the present law being repealed solely for the purpose of facilitating responsible family planning within the ambit of the health service. Individual conscience may dictate one's attitude on contraception, but the right of those married couples whose religion or conscience permit them to use contraceptives and to have access to them, is acknowledged.

> Labour's policy does not advocate, and the party does not support, the availability of contraceptives to the unmarried through slot machines or other such outlets. We have strictly confined ourselves to the matter of family planning...'

> ...The present debate has inevitably raised the question of Church and State. It has to be accepted that where the overwhelming majority of a people belong to one Church, that the teachings of that Church will greatly influence society in its laws and conduct. To deny that is to deny social reality...

The statement acknowledged that the Roman Catholic Church had been conservative in its attitude on important and controversial issues.[2]

Speaking on 30 April, Browne said that the Labour Party's statement had damaged its policy of being a party urging a united Ireland. It must have encouraged many people in the North, he added, to believe that its concept of a Wolfe Tone Republic, a liberal democracy, was now thrown overboard, and that they could say that instead of an independent Labour Party the Republic now had a 'Catholic Labour Party' in which no Protestants would be interested.[3]

On the 30th April, a group of liberal priests, who had recently signed a document on private morality, expressed deep disappointment at the Labour Party statement. 'It now appears that we are on our own,' they said.

'No political party is supporting us and we expected so much from Labour after the Galway conference.'[4]

It is interesting to note that the position of Labour's Parliamentary Party on Church-State relations was essentially the same as that of the former Taoiseach, John A. Costello, who, in April 1971, repeated his earlier assertion that 'a Catholic government must legislate for a Catholic majority.'[5]

On 3 May, it was reported that Browne had put a number of questions to the Party. Did it seriously contest the magnitude of the failure of the Catholic Church in Ireland, and of the Irish people as a predominately Catholic nation? 'We have failed,' Browne stated, fully to educate our young people, to care adequately for the sick, or for the aged, to provide for the homeless or the unemployed and above all to do anything with the greatest social evil of all, emigration and rural de-population...' It was difficult to believe, Browne said, that the Labour Party would deny his charges of the Catholic Hierarchy's consistent direct and indirect interference in public affairs and politics. Browne's statement concluded that once again the Irish Labour Party had told people north of the Border that Rome still ruled down here.[6]

Although a Labour spokesman claimed that reaction to its statement censuring Browne had been generally favourable, leading members in Browne's constituency were very critical of the Party's stance. They condemned the Party's claim that because the vast majority in the Republic were born Catholics, were reared, educated and lived in a Catholic environment this was bound to be reflected in the country's thinking. Such a statement implied that we have a Catholic Parliament for a Catholic people and was no different from the Unionists in the North. To imply that Browne was being sectarian, the statement said, was turning the world on its head. Was Tone sectarian when he attacked the Protestants and also the Catholic bishops as Browne had done? They also argued that the fact that the Labour Party had rushed to return to its old position of subservience to the Church, as in 1951 on the Mother and Child Scheme, and in 1957 in the Fethard-on-Sea dispute,[7] was surely a confirmation of Dr. Browne's whole argument.'[8]

Further public support for Browne came from the LCLL, which, in a statement on 3 May signed by Matt Merrigan (Chairman), Jim Kemmy (Vice-Chairman), John Byrne, Brendan Scott and John Swift, noted 'with disgust and shame' the recent attack on Dr. Browne by his parliamentary colleagues. The statement continued:

> Some of the men [Labour's Parliamentary members] remained shamefully silent during the Fethard-on Sea affair and the Mother and Child controversy now thumped their breasts publicly in chorus with Deputy Oliver Flanagan and his Fine Gael colleagues.

> These same people, who showed little sympathy or sensitivity when a handful of Maoist youths were being physically threatened in the name of religion, or when

the Jewish community was being maligned, now rushed to disassociate themselves from any attempt to discuss the role of the clerical lobby in Irish politics. Did the Parliamentary Labour Party also wish to disassociate themselves from Larkin's and Connolly's criticism of this lobby?

The Parliamentary Party should look at the resolutions passed in Galway at the annual conference this year. They were instructed by their supreme policy-making body in the Party to initiate, not merely support, legislation for family planning.

The LCLL expressed agreement with Browne's statement on the political and social issues. They believed that any church that opposed family planning legislation and, at the same time, remained silent about our terrible housing record and rudimentary health and welfare services and our conservative educational system, should and must be challenged. They congratulated and supported all the priests who had the courage to question the hierarchy's insistence on imposing its interpretation of its own social teaching on the nation, irrespective of creed. 'It was to the shame of the Parliamentary Party that it should do less than that', the statement said. The statement concluded:

> Irish politicians, particularly those in Labour, had two choices. They could either lead public opinion and initiate a real debate on the causes of our serious national problems, or they could seek the security of the middle of the herd. Dr. Browne has made his choice.[9]

A week or two later, on 15 May 1971, at a LCLL rank-and-file meeting of Party members, in Liberty Hall, Dublin, Scott called for the resignation of the Labour Leader, Brendan Corish, over the Noël Browne affair. On that occasion, Browne elaborated on his criticism of the conservative wing of the Catholic Church on social and civil questions:

> It had to be faced that the Catholic Church, like all great bodies, had many roles and facets. It was spiritual, and in that sphere, inviolable, but it was also political, and had an economic place in the community as a large property-owner and as such was interested in politics also. In its political role it was surely open to the same criticism as all other political organisations. Indeed, it should be more open to criticism because of its special nature, for it is the best organised, the most effective, and the wealthiest political 'party' in the State. It has the greatest number of full-time organisers, the most successful means of securing support of its members, it has its own appointed parliament and government and has been 100 per cent successful in pursuit of its economic, political, social, educational and civil policy since the foundation of the State. Indeed, it has even a foreign policy. In that political role it has been the most conservative 'party in the State and as such must be criticised by all who saw it as opposing civil liberties and social security.

Browne said he had now come to the conclusion that these two questions, civil liberties and social security, were the most important in the political field, for no progress could be made toward socialism until these questions were resolved; and one depended on the other.

The Church also, in its political sphere, had its right-wing and left-wing.

The courageous priests who were advocating social change and advance could be described as 'left wing'. There was also clearly a right-wing in the Church in the sense of social policies, and a 'centre.' He said that his criticism was directed at the right-wing of the Church, and not the Church as a whole, that there were progressive priests and progressive bishops, as there were progressive and reactionary laymen and that he had always held that religion was a private matter for each individual, and although he did not object to the Church expressing political views they should be treated as other politicians. Opposition to socialism was also a characteristic of the Protestant Church in the North, particularly as, like the Catholic Church, it also was a great owner of property. But churchmen who advocated social reform were always welcome in the ranks of social reformers, Browne said.[10] Browne further stated that he had made his speech with his eyes open, 'knowing it would start this debate, compelling politicians to take one side or the other.' He said he did not consider his speech as sectarian. Neither did he regard it as an attack on the Catholic Church, but rather a criticism of it.[11]

Less than a week later, on 21 May, at a special meeting to discuss the Parliamentary Party's statement on Browne's Tramore speech, Labour's Dublin Regional Council passed a resolution by a large majority supporting his stand. A statement by the ten delegates who had requested the meeting said that the Council was concerned that the Parliamentary Party's position would erode the credibility of Labour. It said that if part of the structure and philosophy of capitalism happened to be in the role of the Church's teaching and actions on social and economic affairs it was inescapable that confrontation with the Church authorities would take place from time to time. Such confrontation might find the Church resisting liberal forces in civil, political, economic and such matters. Most evidence of the unenlightened attitude of Church authorities is at hand, the statement said. The statement added that the delegates were concerned about the objective role of the Church - and its servants – in forming attitudes and imposing its will on the political process through all the institutions at its command. This includes the manipulation of Governments and political parties including the Labour Party, the statement added.'[12]

If Browne had anticipated support from the CPI, he would have been disappointed, for there was no coverage of his Tramore speech in the two subsequent editions of the party's monthly paper the *Irish Socialist*.[13] Yet, both those editions published other material relating to Browne. When the *Irish Socialist* in an editorial finally got around to commenting on the matter more than two months later, it failed to address the fundamental issues he had raised.[14] In contrast to the CPI, the CYM, in its fortnightly paper, *Forward,* published an article, albeit even later than the CPI, supportive of Browne's stance.[15]

Reviewing the controversy generated by Browne's Tramore speech almost half a century later, it is clear that in raising the key issue of Church-State relations, Browne made an important and unique contribution to Irish political life. In raising this vital matter publicly, particularly in that still clerically-controlled era of the early 1970s, Browne exposed a major impediment to the advance of social justice while laying the foundation for the gradual liberalisation of Irish society, including the separation of Church and State, which continues to the present day. Sadly, he received no support from his Labour Parliamentary colleagues. It is also worth remembering that Browne was the first, and, for many decades, the only member of Dáil Éireann publicly to raise the issue of Church-State relations in Ireland.

Just over a month following his Tramore speech, Browne returned to the topic of Church-State relations, particularly in relation to education. Addressing a public meeting on democracy in education and community schools, in Liberty Hall, on 1 June 1971, probably organised by the LCLL, Browne said that the Catholic Church was inalienably opposed to all ideas of socialist change, and that this opposition was transferred to Irish people through the influence of religiously controlled schools. He continued:

> It is in these schools that our electorate has learned its attitudes to land usage and the right to private property, and its hostility to radical change," he said. "As long as the Catholic Church continues to maintain its role in the structure of the educational system, there is no possible hope of creating a Socialist society."

> None of the issues in which the Church had been concerned recently were the real issues. They were subordinate to the critical issue of education. Education is indoctrination. It is propaganda. It is the making of men's minds. Education was the one section of life for the control of which, in any country in the world, the Catholic Church was prepared to put its hand in its pocket. It was the area which determined the type of men who controlled and dominated society, and to control education was to control society.

> It is no accident that there are no radical parties in Ireland. It is no accident that the three main political parties are extremely conservative. It is no accident that none of them intends to overthrow a rigid class structure which is in control of a majority.

> We are subjected to a rigid didacticism on the education front which has denied to all of us the right to question, and even the opportunity of the right to question. It is our unhealthy, monosexual and sectarian schools that we learned our social attitudes, and any proposal to extend the control of the Church over education should be strongly resisted.

Declaring that it was the role of the religious orders to play their part in perpetuating this structure, Browne stated:

> …They [the religious orders] have created a society in which we have a puppet Parliament, a House of Bishops which has the right of veto over the Parliament if it digresses and above all is Cardinal Conway, exercising the 17th and 18th century royal veto over the elected Parliament. You are fooling yourself if you think you have a serious parliamentary democracy in Ireland.

> What the dispute over the community schools signified was a struggle between the right of the State over the right of an external, clerical, obscurantist theocracy.[16]

A fortnight later, on 15 June, Brendan Scott, Conor Cruise O'Brien and David Thornley were the speakers at a symposium on Community Schools, organised by the Glasthule Branch of the Labour Party, in the Victor Hotel, Dún Laoghaire. Scott said that after fifty years of self-government, Pearse's 'murder machine' still dominated Irish education, turning out middle class civil servants and middle class parish priests, all with smug, closed minds.' Scott continued:

> Fifty years of sectarian education was reaping its inevitable harvest of bitterness and tragedy. The only way to remove this legacy of hatred was by having non-sectarian schools. If we do not educate our children together we will never produce a united Ireland, he said, adding that the Catholic Hierarchy was fighting as bitterly as the Orange Order to protect its education machine. 'The Irish Hierarchy, he said, had fought as bitterly and as arrogantly as either Craig or Paisley in opposing any possible changes. He said Cardinal Conway had been particularly stubborn because he saw community schools as a threat to the breeding grounds for vocations.

> It was necessary for the Labour Party to state clearly where they stood in relation to these schools. The Labour Party wanted an end to ghetto education, not simply a bigger slice of the cake for any particular sect.[17]

In a further contribution to the debate on sectarian education and community schools, apparently in 1972, Scott said:

> Fifty years on [presumably fifty years of Irish independence] and the only sin we worry about in this Gombeen Gomorrah is a sin against the 6th Commandment. No wonder a foreign commentator could mistake the symbolism of our tricolour by explaining the white & orange as the Vatican colours turned inside out and the green as expressing the condition of the majority of our people.

> The situation would be cynically amusing except for its most tragic consequences. On the one hand are the personal tragedies like that of John McGahern who had to leave Irish teaching for writing a novel which painted an aspect of Irish reality while others who savagely beat young children are protected by their colleagues and their Union. On the other hand is the massive Greek tragedy of the 6 Cos. [Counties] where 50 years of Ghetto education, 50 years of sectarian education is reaping its inevitable harvest of hatred & killing and the division of the Catholic and Protestant working classes away from their real interests into the paths of sectarian violence.

> How can we remove this legacy of hatred without non-sectarian schools: if we do not educate our children together we will never produce a united Ireland. Tone saw this, the Young Irelanders saw this and they were attacked in exactly the same way as the defenders of community schools are to-day. The Catholic Hierarchy have fought just as viciously as the Orange Order to preserve their control of the Catholic machine. Even the arrogance is not new. When asked to-day to make sacrifices to achieve a sane non-sectarian community the hierarchy have not given an inch on either civil rights or educational control...[18]

Meanwhile, on 21 May 1971, Scott and John de Courcy Ireland were the speakers at a lecture, 'The Origins of Socialism', in the Coliemore Hotel, Dalkey. Apparently, the event was sponsored jointly by the Labour Party's Glasthule and Dalkey Branches and the Socialist Labour Alliance.[19]

Returning to the issue of Church-State relations, the controversy over this topic may have prompted the BBC *Panorama* television programme on Catholic Church influence in Ireland, which was transmitted on 26 July 1971. 'If the Catholic Church dominated the Republic of Ireland, it was because it predominated in the minds of the people', said a BBC reporter. Concluding a thirty-five-minute film on the Catholic Church in the Republic of Ireland, Nick Sharman, the presenter, said that for the time being it was impossible to imagine an Ireland – even a united Ireland – in which the Catholic Church would agree to be just another organisation among many. Earlier, the programme described the Irish Republic as 'the most Catholic country in the world.' Among interviewees was Dr. Cathal Daly, Bishop of Ardagh and Clonmacnoise, later Catholic Primate of All Ireland and Archbishop of Armagh, and later still a Cardinal, who said regarding the Hierarchy's attitude to proposed changes in the law on contraceptives, that the bishops had felt pressure was being put on people by the media to make changes. One of the sponsors of the Bill introduced in the Senate, Dr. Daly said, had gone on record as stating that he did not see any way in which the availability of contraceptives could be restricted to married couples. The bishops were aware of the 'grave disquiet' this had caused. 'This was not the sort of society Irish people wanted. The legislators had been reminded of this. We wanted to be the voice of the silent majority,' Dr. Daly said. Challenging Daly's contribution, Austin Flannery, OP, said that the bishops had an outmoded view of the role of the State. Noël Browne stated that since there were so many instances of laws in the South being determined by the Catholic Church it was logical to assume that Church control would continue in a united Ireland.[20]

Coinciding with the BBC *Panorama* programme was an article titled, *Ireland's Changing Church,* in the leading American magazine, *Newsweek.* Contending that 'The winds that have buffeted Catholicism elsewhere are at last reaching Irish shores,' the article went on to state:

> The Republic of Ireland has long been the favourite retreat of Irish-American priests who, like combat soldiers, feel a periodic need for rest and rehabilitation in a battle-free zone. Nowhere in the world are Roman Catholics more docile towards their bishops than in Ireland, and nowhere is a priest more powerful than in an Irish pulpit.

> But clerical visitors to Ireland this summer are discovering that they really can't go "home" again – at least not without confronting on Irish soil the same troublesome questions of sexual freedom, priestly dissent and social unrest that currently plague the US Catholic Church.[21]

Notes

1   *Irish Times,* 24 April 1971.
2   ibid., 30 April 1971.
3   ibid., 1 May 1971.
4   ibid.
5   ibid., 27 April 1971.

6   ibid., 3 May 1971.
7   The Fethard-on Sea boycott was a controversy in 1957 involving Seán and Sheila Cloney (née Kelly), a mixed marriage couple (he was Catholic, she was Church of Ireland) from the village of Fethard-on-Sea, County Wexford. It involved a sectarian boycott led by the local Parish priest, Father Stafford, of some members of the local Protestant community. Rejecting Father Stafford's instruction to raise the couple's three daughters as Catholics, Sheila Cooney left the village with the three children, residing initially in Northern Ireland and later in Orkney. Eventually, Seán traced her to Orkney and the couple were reconciled. They returned to Fethard-on-Sea where their daughters were taught at home.
8   *Irish Times*, 1 May 1971.
9   *Irish Press*, 4 May 1971.
10 *Evening Herald*, 15 May 1971; *Sunday Independent*, 16 May 1971; *Irish Times*, 17 May 1971.
11 *Sunday Independent*, 16 May 1971.
12 *Irish Times*, 22 May 1971.
13 *Irish Socialist*, No. 105, May 1971 and No. 106, June 1971.
14 ibid., No. 107, July-August 1971, p. 2.
15 John P. Swift (Anon), 'Christianity?', *Forward*, 28 August 1971.
16 *Irish Times*, 2 June 1971.
17 *Irish Independent*, *Irish Press*, 16 June 1971.
18 Brendan Scott, fragment of unpublished article or speech, undated, circa 1972.
19 *Evening Herald*, 12 May 1971, *Irish Times*, 21 May 1971; The Socialist Labour Alliance was a 'far left' political alliance, seen by some of its members as a political party in process of formation. Initiated in 1970 by the Socialist Labour Action Group, it was composed of Labour Party members, including the Young Socialists who were campaigning for a more left-wing programme. The Alliance included individual members as well as People's Democracy, the Young Socialists, the League for a Workers' Republic and the Waterford Socialist Movement. Individual and affiliated members subsequently played a leading role in founding the Socialist Workers' Movement and the Revolutionary Marxist Group.
20 *Irish Times*, 27 July 1971.
21 ibid.

CHAPTER 21

Sacrificing Socialism

The combination of the Parliamentary Party's failure to promote the more radical socialist policies and the reversal of Labour's anti-coalition position led to the resignation of hundreds of left-wing members of the Labour Party.[1] In Limerick City alone, there was the mass resignation of thirty-nine members in January 1972, including Jim Kemmy, LCLL Vice-Chairman, former Administrative Council (AC) member and future TD; and Tony Crowley, an AC member and Secretary of St. Mary's Branch. The disenchanted members formed a new body, the Limerick Socialist Organisation. In a statement, the thirty-nine members said they included people who had served the Labour Party in every office from the Administration Council, Constituency Council, Director of Elections to Branch Secretary and rank-and-file status. The statement continued:

> From close contact and study of the Labour Party, its structures, policies and political methods, they had reached the conclusion that the party was not a socialist party and that it would not lead the Irish working class to state power.
>
> To remain in the party, while being fully conscious of this fact, would not serve the workers' interests and could only confuse and mislead people

The statement added that in the event of the Labour Party forming a government here, it was certain that it would not even be as liberal or as democratic as the British Labour Government in such areas as education, social welfare and health. It would basically settle for the role of minor reforms while basically accepting the status quo.[2]

However, the majority of those associated with the LCLL, including Dermot Boucher, Noël Browne, Pat Carroll, Matt Merrigan, David Neligan, Brendan Scott and John Swift, decided to remain in the Party working for its re-dedication to the 1969 policies. In an election 'manifesto', the LCLL strongly criticised 'the failures' of the Labour Parliamentary Party over the previous year and set out the socialist policies 'which alone could guarantee the future progress of both the nation and the party.'[3] Issued at Labour's Annual Conference, in Wexford, in February 1972, the manifesto laid bare some of the damage inflicted by the leadership on the Party:

> The Labour Party lies in ruins and the hopes and aspirations of many of those who built the organisation are shattered beyond repair. Hundreds of members have resigned or drifted away, and in many areas the party organisation has disintegrated.
>
> The Administrative Council has become a mere rubber stamp for the pre-determined decisions of the Party officers – except in the matter of the new Party constitution, which threatened local vested interests.

With expulsions and resignations, the loss to Labour was enormous, and at least a dozen constituencies had been in a state of continuous civil war.

The Liaison Committee asserts that even at the "eleventh hour" the party's "shattered morale" could be repaired if a seven-point radical programme of action was agreed to.[4]

The LCLL called for a new Party constitution that would transfer power from head office and the Parliamentary Party to the rank and file membership, and the introduction of a 'just system' of disciplinary action to protect ordinary members from 'the arbitrary judgement of authoritarian bureaucrats.' There was also a demand that all party members associated with the Socialist Labour Alliance should be re-instated, and the Council of Labour should be reconstituted to work for a 'genuine All-Ireland Socialist Party' with the aid of the Derry Labour Party, the Mid-Ulster Independent Socialists and the People's Democracy.[5]

Turning to the issue of contraception, prior to Labour's 1972 Conference, the Labour leadership had failed to table legislation on the matter in the Dáil, leaving it to a private members' Bill in the names of the TDs, Noël Browne and John O'Connell. A first reading of their Bill to liberalise the availability of contraceptives and birth control literature, on 9 February 1972, was defeated by 75 votes to 44, with three Labour TDs, Stephen Coughlan, Michael Pat Murphy[6] and Dan Spring, failing to support the proposed legislation.[7]

Addressing the 1972 Annual Conference, on this and other matters, Scott said:

...The people who should be condemned were those in the parliamentary party; they had shown their contempt for any kind of civil rights by voting against the recent Contraceptive Bill in the Dáil.

He hoped that the procedural motion brought by Mr. James Tully, T.D., which had allowed those three deputies to avoid censure or expulsion from the party, had been a mistake.

The party should oppose the idea of sectarian schools which divided people. There was only one creed which would remove spurious differences in the North and that was Socialism. The party should not be content with putting patches on the existing constitution. What was needed was a blueprint for a Workers' Republic. They should activate the committee which had drawn up the 1969 Labour Party policies and set up other committees as well as to make blueprints of a 26 County and a 32-County Constitution.

The people who would draft the constitution should be given the right to consult all sections and groups to find out what their needs were and those persons who had been forced in disgust out of the Labour Party because of the actions of some deputies should be asked to return to it...[8]

It was also at that 1972 Conference that the LCLL contested nine positions on the AC: Matt Merrigan, Brendan Scott and Pat Carroll for Chairman, Vice-Chairman and Financial Secretary, respectively; and the following for non-officership positions: Des Bonass, Dermot Boucher, Tony Dunne, Paddy Leahy, Pat Magner and David Sloane.[9] In the subsequent elections,

Roddy Connolly defeated Merrigan for Chair by 569 votes to 184, Niall Greene was elected Vice-Chairman by 480 votes to 267 for Scott, while Donal O'Sullivan was elected Financial Secretary by 582 votes to 175 for Carroll.[10] With an impressive 37 per cent share of the vote, Scott's performance against the formidable Greene was testament to his standing in the Party. Another manifestation of his standing was his appointment by the AC as Consultative Editor for a series of Connolly publications, the first of which, *Socialism Made Easy*, was launched at the 1972 Annual Conference.[11]

Less than five months later, John Swift publicly raised concerns about an inter-party review of the Constitution:

> ...Regarding the sectarian references [in the Constitution], it is to be assumed that as the Labour Party claims to be a distinctly socialist party its representatives on the committee will urge deletions to give us a wholly secular Constitution.
>
> But deletions, however justified, will hardly be enough to satisfy constitution-makers of a party that only a few years ago made much of new policies, designed, it was claimed, to usher in radical social changes. None will deny our present Constitution is weak in positive social content. Will the Parliamentary Party, using the party's own policy statement, now urge on the inter-party Committee such changes in our Constitution as will make positive provision for the establishment of the social justice which the present document talks glibly about but leaves for the caprice of brute economic forces?..
>
> I suppose one could say the worth of a constitution is to be judged by not only the statement of rights of the individual citizens but the machinery or institutions which it makes available to secure these rights. In this latter regard, bearing in mind our anarchic system of free-enterprise, our present Constitution has little more value than a book of etiquette in the primeval jungle...[12]

Returning to the topic of election strategy, on 2 July 1972, the LCLL called on the Labour Leader, Brendan Corish, TD, to resign and rejected his arguments favouring a Fine Gael-Labour Coalition. The LCLL said that while it accepted the need for a credible alternative Government, such a coalition would have no credibility whatever. It added that its rejection of the coalition proposal was based on five separate considerations:

(1) There is no significant common ground between Labour and Fine Gael, particularly with regard to finance and economic policy.

(2) The election to office of a coalition Government at this time would inevitably lead to the introduction of additional repressive legislation, and to further erosion of civil liberties.

(3) A coalition Government would further alienate Labour's traditional supporters in the trade union movement.

(4) The present Labour Parliamentary Party could not be trusted to implement socialist policies.

(5) A formal alliance with Fine Gael would make it impossible for Labour to contest the next general election as a united party.[13]

A major setback for Corish and the Labour leadership occurred on 2 August 1972 when, in the first test of the proposed Fine Gael-Labour Coalition,

Fianna Fáil unexpectedly won the Mid-Cork by-election with substantially more support, while both Fine Gael and Labour lost considerable ground. Describing this 'lamentable' outcome for Labour, the LCLL said in a statement that the result was 'a shattering blow' to the Fine Gael-Labour coalition policy and, because of that policy, Labour had lost hope of gaining seats in two key marginal constituencies – Mid-Cork and Dublin South County. The LCLL called on Corish to abandon his present 'shameful role of abject subservience to Fine Gael and provide the nation with a genuine, alternative, socialist policy.'[14]

By October 1972, it was evident that Corish and his Parliamentary Party colleagues were determined to form a coalition Government with Fine Gael. In his report to an AC meeting on 12 October, Corish said that his decision to accept the invitation of Fine Gael to enter into exploratory talks had been endorsed the previous day at the Parliamentary Party meeting. James Tully and he would be meeting Liam Cosgrave and Tom O'Higgins. He emphasised that the talks would be exploratory and that there had been no talks to date. There would be no formal agenda and he had requested the Party spokesmen to submit ideas for inclusion in further discussion, if any. So far he had received very few replies to this request. Following the exploratory talks he and Tully would report back to the Parliamentary Party and AC. Corish's report, which was seconded by Tully, was unanimously agreed.[15]

If that was a bitter pill for the LCLL to swallow, even more alarming were newspaper reports of a proposal that Fine Gael and Labour should merge to form a social democratic party. In a statement issued on 13 October, the LCLL said it viewed with alarm recent newspaper reports that Corish had taken part in 'secret coalition negotiations' with the Fine Gael Leader, Liam Cosgrave, TD. The statement was signed by Dermot Boucher (Secretary), on behalf of LCLL colleagues, Des Bonass, Frank Butler, John Byrne, Pat Carroll, Tony Dunne, Matt Merrigan (Chairman), Brendan Scott and John Throne.[16]

Corish must surely be aware, the statement said, that the resolution adopted by the Cork Special Conference merely empowered him to negotiate participation by the Labour Party in a government. It did not contain any reference to the formulation of a predetermined electoral pact, nor did it commit the Party to fight elections jointly with other parties as in the disastrous Mid-Cork by-election. Furthermore, the resolution contained no specific reference to the Fine Gael Party, and it also stated that all negotiations should be conducted in consultation with the AC, which he had entirely ignored. The statement continued:

> Corish would no doubt have been informed of the recent aggregate meeting of the Dublin Labour membership which condemned, almost unanimously, the proposal to conclude a pre-election pact with Fine Gael. The meeting in question was attended by representatives of all ten Dublin constituencies, which, it was claimed, returned half of the Parliamentary Party and supplied 40 per cent of the total national Labour vote. Corish, therefore, was not only exceeding the

authority vested in him by the Cork conference, but was also openly defying the clearly expressed view of the Party's rank and file membership.

The LCLL categorically rejected the proposal outlined in several newspapers that Labour and Fine Gael should combine to form a so-called 'social democrat' party. Such a proposal, it said, would be totally incompatible with the aims and objectives of the Labour Party and anathema to the vast majority of Labour members and trade unions. The statement claimed that Party remained essentially the political wing of a broadly-based labour movement. In conclusion, the statement said that the LCLL was prepared to abide by all democratic decisions of the annual conference. It would not consider itself bound by any high-level electoral deals arrived at in a 'blatantly opportunistic and undemocratic manner,' and would take whatever steps were necessary to maintain the socialist integrity of the Party.[17]

A more positive and unexpected development for the left was a particularly strong public statement on housing by Conor Cruise O'Brien. Speaking at a meeting of Labour's Raheny Branch, on 17 November 1972, O'Brien insisted that any Government in which Labour might participate must immediately implement the Labour Party's policy document relating to housing. He added that the only way forward to a united Ireland was to make conditions in the South attractive enough for others to want to join it. Praise for O'Brien's stand on housing came in a statement from Browne, Scott and two others associated with the LCLL, namely, John Byrne and John Throne, who welcomed O'Brien's 'uncompromising ultimatum to Fine Gael, and we suspect, to some of his colleagues of the Parliamentary Labour Party too, in his pre-conditions for coalition.' The statement concluded: 'We hope that we can still depend on all our comrades in the Parliamentary Labour Party in insisting on the presentation by our leadership of this minimum-demand ultimatum to Fine Gael as just one socialist precondition of a coalition.'[18]

In addition to its intensive political activities in the Labour Party, the LCLL was also involved in an education project, a series of ten lectures under the general heading, 'Socialist Education Forum'. These were listed to take place in the ATGWU's Hall, Marlborough Street, on a weekly basis, from 3 October to 3 December 1972, with the following speakers: Dermot Boucher, Andy Boyd, Pat Carroll, John de Courcy Ireland, Michael D. Higgins, John Lennon, Tomás Mac Giolla, Brendan Scott, John Swift and David Thornley.[19] Later press notices announced a talk on 'Socialism and Youth' by Scott and John Throne, on 17 October,[20] and a talk by Scott on 'Whither the Labour Movement?' on 7 November.[21]

Scott was also listed as the lecturer on 'Socialism in the 19th and 20th Centuries,' under the auspices of the History Teachers' Association of Ireland (HTAI), in the Catholic University School (CUS), on 6 November 1972.[23] He was also named as a speaker on the same topic, on 25 November, at a HTAI Teachers' One Day Seminar, at Coláiste Iognáid, Cork. Other listed speakers were Pádraig Ó Snodaigh, Louis Cullen and Ronan Fanning.[23]

On several major issues, at least initially, there were little or no policy differences between the Labour leadership and the LCLL. This was the case, for example, in relation to Ireland's proposed entry to the European Economic Community (EEC) in the early 1970s, the vast majority of Labour members, including those associated with the LCLL, being opposed to entry. Notable LCLL exceptions to that position included Kemmy[24] and Swift,[25] who favoured Ireland's entry.

In *The Common Market – The Socialist Alternative*, an extensive, undated, hand-written script of a talk given to an unidentified body, Scott documented the case against Ireland's entry to the EEC (Appendix 5).

Among speakers against entry at the Labour's 1971 Annual Conference were Scott and the TDs, Browne, Keating and O'Leary. In his contribution, Scott supported working with republicans and other groups who opposed membership. Advocating action now, Scott added: 'We are no longer content to listen to words. We must do what Larkin would have done, and be prepared to take to the streets.' The Conference decisively opposed Ireland's entry to the EEC.[26] Addressing the delegates, Swift stated that the most serious part of both the Common Market and the coalition debates within the Labour Party was the lack of a socialist voice on the part of the Parliamentary leadership. 'If they were less afraid of speaking out on socialist solutions, we might not be so afraid of coalition,' he said.[27]

A press comment that Labour's decision to oppose Ireland's entry 'appears to knock much of the ground from under those people in Labour and Fine Gael who have been putting forward the argument for coalition...'[28] completely misjudged the determination of Labour's leadership to form a coalition government with Fine Gael.

On 15 March 1972, at a meeting of Labour's AC, Justin Keating, TD, and Brendan Halligan, General Secretary, said that consultations had been held with the ITGWU, the ICTU and the Common Market Defence Campaign, through two of its most prominent leaders, Mícheál Ó Loinsigh and Anthony Coughlan.[29] The AC decided that the maximum liaison between the Party and these three bodies in particular, together with other unions in opposing the EEC, should be effected 'so as to achieve economics in cost and effort.'[30]

While the Labour Party was overwhelmingly opposed to EEC entry, the margin against entry in the trade union movement was narrower. An ICTU Special Delegate Conference, in Dublin, in late January 1972, decided by 158 votes to 113 to oppose Ireland's entry.[31] Among unions favouring entry were the WUI and the IBCAWAU. On 10 May, Ireland's referendum on entry to the EEC was carried by 82 per cent in favour and 18 per cent against.

Turning to matters more personal, following a request from a Sutton Park School colleague, Scott co-operated in the execution of 'a sensitive bronze' sculpture of himself by the sculptor, Kieran Kelly. This was exhibited at the Royal Hibernian Academy of Arts exhibition in the National Gallery in 1972. Among those present at the official opening of the exhibition on 29 June were the President, Éamon de Valera; the Taoiseach, Jack Lynch; and the Minister for Foreign Affairs, Patrick Hillery.[32]

Notes

1   *Irish Independent,* 10 February 1972.
2   ibid., 25 January 1972.
3   *Irish Times,* 25 January 1972.
4   *Irish Independent,* 10 February 1972.
5   ibid.
6   For further information on Michael Pat Murphy (1919-2000) see Charles Callan and Barry Desmond, 'Michael P. Murphy (1919-2000)', *Irish labour Lives,* op. cit., p. 192.
7   *Irish Times,* 10 February 1972.
8   ibid., 28 February 1972.
9   ibid., 25 January 1972.
10 *Irish Examiner, Irish Times,* 28.02.1972.
11 Labour Party, Annual Report, 1972-73, p. 23.
12 John Swift, 'Labour and Constitution', *Irish Times,* 26 July 1972.
13 *Irish Times,* 3 July 1972.
14 *Irish Independent,* 4 August 1972.
15 Labour Party, AC, minutes of meeting, 12 October 1972.
16 For further information on John Throne (1944-2019) see Conor McCabe, 'John Throne (1944-2019)', *Saothar* 45, 2020, pp. 163- 164.
17 *Irish Examiner, Irish Times,* 14 October 1972.
18 *Irish Press,* 20 November 1972.
19 LLCL, notice of *Socialist Education Forum* series of lectures, undated, September 1972; *Evening Herald,* 28 September 1972. The specific topics and speakers listed were: 'Parliamentary Democracy & Socialism' by John Lennon, on 3 October; 'Educating for Socialism' by David Thornley, TD, on 10 October; 'Socialism and Rural Problems' by Michael D. Higgins, on 17 October; 'Republicanism/Socialism' by Tomás Mac Giolla, on 24 October; 'Labour Party Perspectives' by Brendan Scott, on 31 October; 'Youth and Socialism' by Pat Carroll, on 7 November; 'Socialism and Ireland's Marine Resources' by John de Courcy Ireland; on 14 November; 'Workers' Democracy' by John Swift', on 21 November; 'Organising for Socialism' by Dermot Boucher, on 28 November; and 'Socialism and the Northern Struggle' by Andy Boyd, on 3 December 1972.
20 *Irish Times,* 17 October 1972.
21 ibid., 7 November 1972.
22 ibid., 6 November 1972.
23 *Irish Examiner,* 17 November 1972.
24 Brian Callanan, *Jim Kemmy, stonemason, trade unionist, politician, historian,* op. cit., pp. 26, 119.
25 John P. Swift, *John Swift: An Irish Dissident,* op. cit., pp. 200-201.
26 *Irish Times,* 1 March 1971.
27 ibid.
28 *Irish Press,* 1 March 1971.

29 For further information on Anthony Coughlan see Frank Keoghan, Ruan O'Donnell, Michael Quinn (Editors), *A Festschrift for Anthony Coughlan: essays on sovereignty and democracy* (Iontas Press, Maynooth, 2018).

30 Labour Party, AC, minutes of meeting, 15 March 1972.

31 *Irish Press, Irish Times,* 28 January 1971.

32 *Irish Times,* 1 July 1972.

CHAPTER 22

Labour's Capitulation

In early 1973, less than nine months prior to his demise, Brendan Scott, along with some fifty colleagues, was effectively expelled from the Labour Party when the Howth Branch, of which he was a member, was dissolved. Earlier, in the summer of 1972, Conor Cruise O'Brien, TD, had resigned from the branch. In a letter to John Medlycott, another branch member and a friend and colleague of Scott's, O'Brien explained his reasons for taking this action:

> ...You know the general pattern behind this but the precipitating causes were:
>
> (a) the fact that the Constituency Council asked the Party Officers to inquire into the conduct of the Branch – as having through its officers, made public anti-Party statements – and that these investigations may, and in my opinion should, lead to sanctions against the Branch as at present constituted and
>
> (b) the fact that I received a letter from the Branch Secretary indicating that henceforth I might be required, as delegate from the Branch, to conform with mandatory instructions.
>
> I hope you realise that my resignation from the Branch was impelled solely by disapproval of the Sinn Fein fellow-travellers who have become dominant in it.[1]

Six months later, at its meeting on 25 January 1973, Labour's Administrative Council (AC) adopted a report by the Disciplinary Committee recommending that the Howth and District Branch be dissolved, that the members be suspended and that former members could apply for re-admission to the Party through the AC. A resolution to that effect, moved and seconded by Dan Browne, Chairman of the Disciplinary Committee and Máire Walshe, respectively, was carried by 13 votes in favour to 3 against. Explaining the Committee's decision, Browne said that the Branch had put a statement in the newspapers and refused to give an undertaking to the Dublin North East Constituency Council to refrain from expressing Party differences in the public press.[2]

Apart from Scott, among the members 'suspended' from the Branch were Geoffrey Coulter, Dorothy Gilmore and John Carroll, Vice-President of the ITGWU.[3] Responding to the dissolution of the Branch, the Chairman and Secretary, Gerry O'Sullivan and Rory O'Rourke, respectively, said in a statement on 31 January 1973:

...This means ...that Dublin North-East Constituency has lost one of its most active branches, with a membership approaching fifty...The decision was the result of disciplinary action initiated by a section of the Constituency Council and supported by the deputy for Dublin North-East, Dr. Conor Cruise O'Brien...[4] It is a cause of regret and some dismay that the Branch should be disciplined in such a severe manner for a relatively minor breach of discipline. In fact the severity of the decision tends to support the view that democracy in Dublin North-East allows for only one point of view.[5]

A week or so later, on 9 February, Matt Merrigan, Chairman of the Liaison Committee of the Left (LCLL), wrote to all Labour Party branches asking them to demand a specially convened meeting of the AC by 15 February to lift the suspension of the Howth Branch. In a strongly-worded statement on the same date, Merrigan said the AC should be asked to lift the suspension on the Howth Branch or suspend Deputies Stephen Coughlan, Michael Pat Murphy and Dan Spring who had voted against the John O'Connell-Noël Browne Bill on contraception in the Dáil the previous year; Deputy James Tully who had publicly repudiated the Party's policy on public ownership of the mines; and Councillor McAuliffe, 'who thumbed his nose at the party and joined the stooge RTE Authority.' 'Liaison was appalled at the continued harassment of persons and bodies inside the Party who still interpreted the role and policies of Labour as being Socialist,' Merrigan said.'[6]

For the following six months or so, the Howth Branch controversy lay dormant. Then, at a private session of Labour's Annual Conference, in October 1973, it was decided to restore the Branch.[7] An unnamed delegate at that conference has placed that development in context. After stating that this clearly was not the delegates' conference, but a well-staged public relations job, the delegate added that the agenda was carefully planned to suit the Ministers, who spoke for thirty minutes, and live TV coverage. The delegate continued:

> There was no discussion on education, and the Offences Against the State Act, and 198 resolutions were never reached. The only debate that went against Head Office and the platform was that to re-admit the Howth Branch, of which the late Brendan Scott was a member.
>
> It was a victory which will bring joy, hope and encouragement to those who still battle for Socialism in the Party. The position in Cork [Labour Party's Special Conference on coalition in December 1970] can be very discouraging but not unchangeable and it is the beliefs and ideas of Brendan Scott which we must unite around and adopt as our goal for Conference 1974.[8]

Many years later, following his death, Brendan Scott was honoured when Labour's Howth Branch was re-named as the Scott-Gilmore Branch; Gilmore as a tribute to its former members, the Gilmore brothers Charles (Charlie), George and Harry.[9]

The Howth Branch was not the only Labour branch to be dissolved in the early 1970s. Two years earlier, in 1971, for example, the Fintan Lalor Branch, in the neighbouring Dublin North Central Constituency, was also disbanded. It had been charged with continuing the membership of a person whom the AC decided was ineligible for membership. This was a reference to Paddy Healy who was also a member of a separate organisation, Socialist Labour Alliance.[10] The AC's decision to dissolve the Fintan Lalor Branch, whose members included John Swift, followed a resolution to that effect, proposed and seconded by Niall Greene (Vice-Chairman) and Donal O'Sullivan (Financial Secretary), respectively. The resolution was carried by 10 votes to 1 against.[11]

Meanwhile, for Scott and his LCLL colleagues, a more momentous matter than the reinstatement of Labour's Howth Branch was a 'Statement of Intent' to form a National Coalition Government agreed by the leadership of the Labour Party and Fine Gael. This was circulated by the Labour Leader, Brendan Corish, at an AC meeting, on 9 February 1973. By 22 votes to 1, the AC endorsed the Statement of Intent.[12]

The previous day, obviously aware of the Labour leadership's determination, not alone to form a National Coalition Government with Fine Gael, but to campaign on a joint programme, Noël Browne declared that he would not be standing as a Labour candidate in the General Election. He told the Dublin South East Constituency 'Convention' that he could not seek votes to sit as a back-bencher under a Coalition Government. However, he declared that he would still remain a member of the Irish Labour movement and continue to work within that great movement as a rank-and-file member of the Party. Browne, who had refused to sign the Coalition Manifesto drawn up by the party leaders, said in a public statement that he found himself unable to subscribe to the Statement of Intent from Fine Gael and Labour:

> The document in itself was unexceptional in its stated aims. Its social, political and economic objectives were shared by all thoughtful people, in all three political parties, here and in most other countries.

> They represent the humane platitudes of public life anywhere. But they did not attempt to outline the means by which they could be implemented, nor say how the wealth needed to finance the proposals could be created. And also there was a direct conflict of interests between Labour and Fine Gael on the issue of the maldistribution of wealth. Although Fine Gael could be trusted to remain loyal to their conservative policies, the same could not be said for the loyalty of the majority of Labour members to their own socialist policies

> No serious attempt was made by Labour to advocate or defend its socialist principles of the 1969 manifesto, on which all the Labour deputies were returned to the Dáil. These principles would not be pushed in any coalition with Fine Gael. The promises now being made by them to the public are not worth the paper they are written on.[13]

Responding to Browne's decision, Labour's Dublin South-East Constituency 'Convention' unanimously praised 'the priceless work of Dr. Noel Browne for the labour movement in the last twenty-five years' and expressed the hope that he might in future take up that task again 'as soon as he feels in conscience that he can do so.'[14]

Commenting on Browne's decision, Michael McInerney, *Irish Times* Political Correspondent, said Browne's departure from public life, even if only for the period of the next Dáil, was a deep loss to Irish politics and would be viewed with some dismay by liberals and moderates in Northern Ireland where his reputation stood high. Dr. Browne has tried to debunk many attitudes favouring violence and Nationalism. He is deeply critical of the Catholic Church, said McInerney.[15]

For Brendan Scott, this was an inadequate response to Browne's decision not to seek the nomination. A few days later, in a joint letter to the press, undoubtedly written by Scott,[16] Scott and three LLCL colleagues stated:

> Sir, - It would be a pity if the only comments on Noel Browne's decision not to accept a Labour nomination were the shrewish innuendoes of John Healy [*Irish Times* columnist] or the blandiloquent unctions of your Political Correspondent [Michael McInerney].
>
> It will embarrass Noel, but we think it necessary for the honour of the Labour Party to try to express what most of the rank and file feel about him. It was Noel Browne who attracted many of us to Socialism. In an age when McCathyism and Catholic Triumphalism made politicians squabble for philosophical halters, he held a mirror to the nation. He made it possible for many to believe again that Man was rational; that virtues like honesty and moral courage were not mythical. Like [Owen] Sheehy Skeffington, May Keating and John Swift, you could always find him in the high lonely places, championing the just causes made dangerous by the evasive retreat of men who now presume to tender loyalty pledges to him.
>
> He raised his voice in times when a closed mouth was counted a political asset. On Fethard-on-Sea, the Cuban war dogs, community schools, anti-semitism, contraception. In the barren witch-hunting fifties, he said on the hustings what others were content to whisper behind their hands in diplomatic drawing-rooms. While others pondered profoundly on the symbolism of Herod, he was content to be a practical John the Baptist, entering the Labour Party to help "depaltroonise" [sic] it and make it fit for the latter-day ersatz Elijahs to rise to glory.
>
> Browne was not content merely to condemn senseless violence in the North. He tried to make this part of the country into the kind of state which might make reconciliation something other than a pious platitude. While others, who beat their breasts more loudly about reconciliation have been content to leave its achievement to the British Army or repressive legislation, he tried to introduce the first small step against episcopal fiats in the Dail. He had to do so with a single colleague [Jack McQuillan], rather than with his parliamentary party, which was more anxious to placate the backwoodsmen.
>
> The Dublin rank and file could understand why Browne could not accept a document which talks about the rights of women but fails to mention contraception; talks about housing but fails to mention the nationalisation of building land; talks about education and the North but omits non-denominational schools; talks about worker participation but evades our policy on worker democracy. For the majority of us, the policies of 1969 were not a "tactical exercise", but a clear instruction to our parliamentary representatives. Browne has kept faith with us.
>
> There is still a chance to see that Browne's voice is not lost in Parliament. Trades unions and university graduates can nominate to the Senate.

It was difficult to explain to the new recruits of the late sixties the supine invertebrate position of Labour in the fifties. Now they can understand. I hope they will not consider our present sorry surrender as a cause for opting out but rather as a call to battle. Again there has been one man who believes principle more important than the bones contemptuously thrown from the table of power; who values concern about complaisance; who believes that while it is possible to lead people to socialism, it is impossible to fool them into it. Connolly said: "I cannot conceive of a Socialist hesitating in his choice between a policy resulting in such self-abasement and a policy of defiant self-reliance and confident trust in a people's own power of self-emancipation."

By a strange irony, worthy of an interpreter of Maria Cross or Albert Camus, the official standard of Labour has been pawned to the Coughlans, Murphys and Tullys. Those who value Connolly's ideals above Cosgrave's convenience will re-group around Browne. As Connolly said: "We are here because this is our place." Yours, etc., Brendan Scott, Matt Merrigan, John Byrne, Partrick Perry, 8, Shielmartin Drive, Sutton.[17]

A week or so later, twenty-four Labour Party constituency and branch officers and former officers, all members of the LCLL, issued a statement condemning the coalition policy document agreed by the Fine Gael and Labour leaderships. 'The LCLL', the statement said, 'considers the document to be totally unacceptable to socialists, and urges the rank and file of the Labour movement to campaign strictly on the basis of socialist policies and to vote only for the Labour Party candidates.' The Committee declared its 'total opposition' to the coalition plan, which it described as 'a profoundly dishonest document which represents the ultimate betrayal of socialist policies adopted by the Labour Party over the past five years.' The statement said that the Liaison Committee's particular points of criticism included:

(1) Sweeping promises, such as those to 'stabilise prices', 'halt redundancies,' and 'eliminate poverty' are made without specifying how these objectives are to be attained.

(2) The cost of the VAT rates proposals (in excess of €50 million) will presumably be transferred to income tax, as Mr Cosgrave has specifically vetoed a tax on capital gains...

(3) There is no plan to nationalise the banks and other financial institutions – surely a cornerstone of any socialist economic policy.

(4) All controversial matters such as community schools, family planning laws, public ownership of financial resources, building land etc. have been totally ignored.

(5) There is no reference to the repeal of repressive legislation, in particular the Offences Against the State Act: indeed, there is no guarantee that further legislation of this sort would not be introduced by a Coalition Government.

(6) At a time when civil war rages in the northern part of our country, the national question has been devoted precisely to cliché-ridden sentences.

'The LCLL, the statement added, 'did not consider itself bound by the terms of the coalition agreement which represented a major departure from the decision reached at the Cork conference. It fully supported the action of Noël Browne in declining to endorse the agreement and called on all Labour candidates who profess socialist principles to repudiate this 'shameful, anti-socialist document.'

In addition to Brendan Scott, the signatories of the statement were Matt Merrigan (Chairman, LCLL), Dermot Boucher (Vice-Chairman, Dublin Regional Council of the Party and Secretary, LCLL), Des Bonass, John Byrne, J. Carroll [sic, actually Tom Carroll] Patrick (Pat) Carroll, Vera Carter, G. Doyle, Tony Dunne, Fergus Ingram, Marilynn Kearney, Billy Keegan, Jack Loughran, Liam Malone, Denis McNally, Eamon Mullen, David Neligan, Ciaran O'Donovan, Rory O'Rourke, Gerry O'Sullivan, Paddy Perry, Thomas Turner and Ray Wickham.[18]

Asked for his reaction to the rejection of coalition by the LCLL, Corish, said:

> They don't represent any great part of the labour movement in Dublin or in the country. In any case, if they purport to be democrats they should accept the decision of the annual conference and of the administrative council, who endorsed our decision to offer the people an alternative choice of Government..."[19]

Corish was in no position to lecture the left on democracy. He had no mandate from a Party conference to dilute the 1969 socialist policies or to surrender Labour's independence by fighting the 1973 General Election on a joint programme with Fine Gael. Also, he had disregarded a decision of the 1970 Special Conference on Coalition that all negotiations should be conducted in consultation with the AC.[20] Moreover, by deciding to participate in a coalition government with Fine Gael, Corish reneged on commitments that no coalition negotiations would be held before a general election and that 'Labour will fight the next election on its own policies.'[21]

On 24 February, the LCLL's trenchant opposition to the proposed National Coalition found expression in a letter to the press:

> Sir, - As we enter the final stages of the General Election campaign it is increasingly evident that, after sixteen years of corrupt, incompetent Fianna Fail rule, the nation is desperately seeking an alternative government. At the same time, it has become painfully obvious that the so called "National Coalition" has failed utterly to provide a credible alternative. The campaign has unfortunately degenerated into an irrelevant popularity contest between Tweedlejack and Tweedleliam.
>
> The 14 Point Manifesto issued by the Coalition Leadership is a profoundly dishonest document which insults the intelligence of the Irish electorate. It abounds with vague generalisations about "abolishing poverty", "sterilising [sic] prices" and "halting redundancies" without specifying how these worthy objectives are to be achieved. This is scarcely surprising as the measures required eg the nationalisation of the banks and building land, or the introduction of a Capital Gains Tax, would be anathema to the ultra-conservative supporters of Fine Gael.
>
> Where it is specific, the document is either misleading or contradictory. For example, the promise to stabilise prices is scarcely compatible with the proposal

to increase the V.A.T. rates on non-food items. Again, the proposal to transfer health charges to the central exchequer over a period of four years, far from reducing the overall rates burden, will hardly stabilise the Rates at current levels, bearing in mind that the figures [sic] involved – about 10% p.a. – is much lower than the present annual increase of perhaps 15%. Where it is specific, the document is either misleading or contradictory. Dr. Noel Browne…has repudiated the Coalition and has withdrawn from the election campaign. He has sacrificed his seat in Dail Eireann because he knows from bitter personal experience the futility of minority participation in Right-wing dominated coalitions. At an aggregate meeting last September the rank and file membership of the Dublin Labour Party voted almost unanimously to reject any electoral pact with Fine Gael. What a tragedy it is that the Labour Leadership, unlike Dr. Browne, cannot accept the democratic decisions of the Party members.

Despite the shameful sell-out by the Leadership, the Labour Party as a whole remains committed to the radical policies which alone can solve the economic and social problems of the nation. The Liaison Committee of the Left urges all those who support their policies to vote Labour on Wednesday next, and to demonstrate their lack of confidence in the Coalition by withholding preference votes from the candidates of non-socialist parties. Yours etc. Matt Merrigan, Chairman, Dermot Boucher, Secretary. The Liaison Committee of the Left (Labour Party). 112/113 Marlboro Street, Dublin 1.[22]

As an alternative to Fine-Gael-Labour Party 14-Point Manifesto, The LCLL produced its own 14-point Election Programme, much of it based on Labour's socialist policies:

The Labour Party in Government will:

1. Formulate and implement a comprehensive Socialist Economic plan.
2. Establish a National Development Corporation to re-organise inefficient industries and engage in direct state enterprise.
3. Bring into public ownership all financial institutions within the State.
4. Secure the development of our natural resources of oil, gas, and minerals through State enterprise, including the establishment of a state-owned smelter and ancillary industries.
5. Impose limited import controls to protect employment in depressed industrial sectors pending re-organisation of these sectors. Repudiate EEC restrictions if necessary.
6. Launch a crash programme of public works to help reduce unemployment in the short term.
7. Introduce positive measures to stimulate the depressed building industry.
8. Reform the taxation system to include
    (a) The re-introduction of sur-tax on higher incomes,
    (b) Greater increased rates for Wealth Tax and Capital Gains Tax,
    (c) Full taxation of farmers, the self-employed etc.
    (d) Higher V.A.T. rates on luxury goods,
    (e) Increased personal allowances.
9. Introduce more effective controls on price increases.
10. Reverse the National Coalition policy of financing the Social Services through workers' contributions, rather than through general taxation. Provide a firm undertaking to increase all welfare payments and pensions by at least 5% per annum over and above increases in the cost of living.

11. Cancel all cutbacks in the Health Services and in Local Government expenditure. Positive progress towards the establishment of a free, comprehensive Health service.

12. Implement sweeping reforms in education, including
    (a) A Phased reduction in class size,
    (b) an end to the Coalition policy of discriminating against Vocational Education
    (c) Active promotion of non-denominational and/or comprehensive schools,
    (d) Increased student grants,
    (e) Greater democracy in education for parents, teachers and students,
    (f) Apprenticeship schemes designed to benefit students rather than employers.

13. Implement the Kenny Report and all other measures required to end land speculation. Total abolition of ground rents. Public ownership of the building societies. Introduce a just local taxation system instead of Rates, based on the ability of the taxpayer to pay.

14. Repeal of all repressive legislation, including the O.A.S [Old Age Pension) Act, Emergency powers '76 Criminal Law Act, Forcible Entry Act. Legalise Divorce, Contraception.[23]

Notes

1   Conor Cruise O'Brien, TD, letter to John Medlycott, 27 July 1972. [John Medlycott Papers].
2   Labour Party, AC, minutes of meeting, 25 January 1973, Annual Report, 1972/73, p. 19.
3   *Irish Times*, 1 February 1973.
4   *Irish Press*, 1 February 1973.
5   *Irish Times*, 1 February 1973.
6   *Irish Examiner*, 10 February 1973.
7   *Irish Times*, 15 October 1973.
8   *Irish Socialist*, No. 132, November 1973, p. 3.
9   Emails from the author to Francis Devine, and Francis Devine to the author, 13 August 2019.
10 Labour Party, Annual Report, 1971, p. 14.
11 Labour Party, AC, minutes of meeting, 26 June 1971.
12 Ibid., 9 February 1973.
13 *Irish Times*, 9 February 1973.
14 ibid.
15 ibid.
16 Brendan Scott's hand-written version of this letter is extant [Brendan Scott Papers].
17 ibid., 12 February 1973; *Irish Press*, 13 February 1973.
18 *Irish Times*, 20 February 1973.
19 *Irish Press*, 22 February 1973.
20 *Irish Examiner, Irish Times*, 14 October 1972.
21 *Irish Times*, 14 December 1970.
22 ibid., 24 February 1973.
23 LCLL, undated document, circa January 1973.

CHAPTER 23

Keeping the Socialist Flame Alight

The 1973 General Election was held on 2 March. Despite the fact that Fianna Fáil was in disarray following the 1970 Arms Crisis, Labour gained only one seat, bringing its total to nineteen. More significantly, its share of first preference votes fell by 3.3 per cent, from 17 per cent in 1969[1] to 13.7 per cent in 1973.[2] Furthermore, Labour's first preference vote declined by 39,000, or 17.4 per cent, from 224,000 to 185,000.[3]

In an internal Party document, Labour's General Secretary, Brendan Halligan, presumably referring to the additional seat, described the result as a 'success.' However, the 39,000 reduction in first preference votes was not lost on him:

> The success of the party in the General Election should not be permitted to hide the drop in Labour's national vote. It fell from 224,000 to 185,000. Admittedly some 11,000 of the decrease is accounted for in constituencies not contested this time. Nevertheless, the drop in votes in Dublin and Cork cities is cause for concern, particularly as the vote rose substantially in other areas such as Kildare, Kerry, Tipperary and Galway...[4]

Critical of Labour's involvement with Fine Gael, Brendan Scott was unimpressed with Labour's poor election performance, particularly in Dublin and other urban areas:

> The National Coalition was sired by the media. The dams [sic] had experienced the bitter moment of truth when the untiring professional charms of Super Jack [Jack Lynch, An Taoiseach] appeared to ensure that the only reward for long term virtue would be the political menopause. John Healy [*Irish Times* columnist] deserves the right to claim the paternity allowance but there was a host of capable accoucheurs [sic]. Political commentators from Michael McInerney, across the spectrum to Hugh Munroe, have extolled the maturity of the Irish electors in using P.R. to adopt the European system of Coalition government. We were told that the days of ideological politics were over; groups must be centrist to succeed. The election has been portrayed as a triumph for both Fine Gael and Labour; for Liam Brendan Corish Cosgrave [sic]; for moderation; for pragmatism.
>
> It would be wrong to allow the euphoria to develop even further. It would be a pity if the terrible price paid by Labour in Dublin and other urban areas was allowed to go unnoticed and if assertions that the electorate used P.R. to support multi-party government were to go unchallenged.[5]

Scott then offered this analysis of the National Coalition parties' performance in the 1973 General Election, particularly in Dublin:

> Support for the combined National Coalition parties decreased in seven of the ten Dublin constituencies. Whilst there was an increase of 20,621 in the Total

Valid Poll in 1973 there was a DECREASE of 15,084 in the Labour first preference votes.

In 1969 Labour, putting forward a strong socialist platform and projecting a radical image was within 0.03% of being the second largest party in Dublin. In 1973, as the 'hind-tit' party in the National Coalition, Labour only claimed 22.3% of the vote whilst Fine Gael had increased its support to 32.19%. Labour's percentage dropped in all Dublin constituencies except Dunlaoghaire-Rathdown, [sic] where it increased by ½%. Fine Gael gained in all constituencies except South Dublin where its vote dropped by less than 1%.

Where did the Labour vote go? …Except in North West, North Central and South County, it was a case of the Fine Gael laundry taking in its partner's washing.

What were the reasons for this? The 14-point programme was projected as a Fine Gael document. Labour spokesmen admitted that Socialist policies would be put in cold storage. Labour tacticians acquiesced in Presidential-style press conferences where Liam Cosgrave did the talking and James Tully and Brendan Halligan the nodding. As a friend put it "if we have to negotiate with a pantomime horse we must of course converse with the front end".

…the Dublin pattern was repeated in other constituencies with a substantial urban vote, except in Galway West and Kildare.

What is the moral? Coalition has proved a useful electoral strategy for Fine Gael and a dangerous one for Labour. Labour politicians have now two options if the party is to survive. (a) They must seek to have Labour policies not only adopted by the government but seen as adopted as a result of a Labour initiative. (b) They must look for a merger with Fine Gael to form a new Social Democrat or (if Mr. Cosgrave is unwilling) Christian Democratic Party. The 1973 election has shown that while the voters are willing to support an alternative government they are unimpressed by coalition. Labour once helped to put Fianna Fail into power for forty years. Present Labour tactics might be equally generous to Fine Gael.[6]

Following the General Election of 1973, the rift between the Labour leadership and the Liaison Committee of the Left (LCLL) intensified. At an AC meeting, on 15 March 1973, the following resolution, moved by Niall Greene, seconded by Donal O'Sullivan, was adopted:

> That the Administrative Council refer the statement of the Liaison Committee of the Left signed by members of the Labour Party to the Disciplinary Committee and that the Disciplinary Committee report within 21 days on disciplinary action, if any, to be taken against signatories of the Liaison Committee's statement and further decided that the privileges of membership of the Administrative Council be withdrawn from Mr Des Bonass until such time as the Disciplinary Committee has investigate the charges preferred against him and others by the Party Officers and has come to a decision on the matter.

The Party Chairman then informed Bonass that the privileges of membership of the AC had now been removed from him and he would have to leave the meeting.[7]

In a public statement, the four Party Officers, Roddy Connolly (Chairman), Niall Greene (Vice-Chairman), Donal O'Sullivan (Financial Secretary) and Brendan Halligan (General Secretary), said:

The self-described Liaison Committee of the Left published a statement during the election which, in the unanimous opinion of the party Officers, violates the Administrative Council's resolution of 7th September 1972...The Fianna Fail organisation in Dublin North East used the Liaison Committee's statement in its election literature to attack the Labour Party...[8]

A fortnight later, the LCLL called on the Labour Leader, Brendan Corish, to say whether an agreement on policy between Fine Gael and Labour before the General Election had been discussed with a group of bankers, financiers and stock brokers. It also asked for Corish's comments on a report of a 'secret pre-election deal' which had appeared s in the current affairs and arts magazine, *Hibernia*.[9] The statement continued:

> The Committee [LCLL] is grossly concerned at the terms of the agreement which not alone rule out virtually all meaningful Labour financial and economic policies, but even exclude some of the more progressive policies of Fine Gael. The committee is particularly concerned at the proposal to de-nationalise certain semi-State industries such as food processing, chemicals and fertilisers, and deplores the refusal of the Coalition to regulate mergers and take-overs which could cause widespread redundancies and unemployment.

> The Liaison Committee calls upon Mr. Brendan Corish to state whether... this report is authentic, and if so, why the agreement was not made public prior to the election. The [Liaison] Committee also wishes to know whether the other Labour members of the new Government – in particular Mr. Justin Keating and Mr. Michael O'Leary – were aware of the crippling limitations – when they agreed to accept office.[10]

Separately, in a reply to the charges of breach of discipline on behalf of the twenty-four LCLL members, dated 12 April, Merrigan stated:

> We hereby submit our reply to charges of breach of discipline in connection with a statement appearing over our names in the public press for the following reasons:

> (1) It is our understanding that the Leader and the Parliamentary Party in concluding a pre-Election pact and a joint manifesto with Fine Gael before consulting the A. C., acted contemptuously and grossly in excess of the terms of the Cork [Labour Party Special Conference on Coalition, 13 December 1970] resolution, viz.:

> "That this special meeting of National Conference affirms that circumstances exist in which participation by the Labour Party in Government is in both the national interest and the interest of the Labour Party, and pending the return of a majority Labour Party representation in Dail Eireann, which is our aim Conference empowers the Leader and members of the Parliamentary Labour Party, subject to consultation with the Administrative Council on the terms thereof, to negotiate participation by the Labour Party in a Government that would guarantee the implementation of Labour policies and to participate in such Government for such time as it is in the nation's interest to do so and for so long as Labour Party policies are being implemented."

> (2) We further believe that notwithstanding the injunction in the Cork resolution no specific guarantees to implement basic labour policies are contained in the 14-point manifesto. The manifesto is a shameful capitulation to the conservative illiberal and anti-working-class policies of

Fine Gael. The document is silent on such major policy positions of the Party as public ownership of banks and mining; imposition of a capital gains tax; nationalisation of building land; restructuring the constitution and the control of schools and the creation of secular community schools; repeal of repressive legislation.

(3) These criticisms which we made at the times in question were made in the knowledge of the contents of [Garret] Fitzgerald [sic] "black paper" to the bankers, which was carried in the March 30th issue of "Hibernia" but was in our possession at and before the dates of the alleged offending statement.

(4) We further draw attention to the corroboration of the Fitzgerald [sic] position by Justin Keating when question [sic] on the position of mergers and partial denationalisation of state companies in an interview in the "Irish Times" on Wednesday April 4th 1973. We can only conclude that Keating was either privy to the Fitzgerald [sic] document or for misguided reasons of Coalition solidarity adopted the Fitzgerald [sic] stance. However, we note that as a result of a statement from the I.T.G.W.U., we are now to have legislation at some future date on mergers and takeovers.

(5) We challenge the whole selective basis on which the A. C. and the Disciplinary Committee operate. It is our considered conviction that this machinery is to deny the defenders of the Party's socialist policies a public forum for their views whilst those who would subvert those policies would have total access to the media through the Dail and the Party apparatus. We have witnessed inspired leaks in press and on radio/T.V. and statements planted by hack journalists.

(6) To further demonstrate this selective and biased approach we cite the following breaches and violations of one of the two principles on which the Disciplinary Code rests:

(a) Deputy Tully in March 1972 in the "Drogheda Independent" rejected without reservation the Party policy on mining. Documentary evidence will be supplied if required.

(b) Deputies Coughlan, Spring and Murphy voted in the Dail against the O'Connell/Browne motion on the Criminal Amendment Act (Contraception).

(c) Deputy C.C. O'Brien publicly disassociated himself from the A.C. acceptance in principle of the S.D.L.P. policy document "Towards New Ireland".

(d) Councillor McAuliffe joined the stooge R.T.E. Authority after the government dissolved its predecessor.

In conclusion we say that we deplore the activities of this [Disciplinary] Committee and the expulsions and suspension of the Howth Branch and Des Bonass that have emanated from it. We see its continued role as an instrument to be used against those who object to the manipulation of the Party and its policies for "short-term advantages and personal gain". We reject the premise on which the Coalition rests that a segment of the political machine of capitalism can be harnessed for economic and social reform. We would not be parties to such duplicity that has confused and disoriented the Party members and the working class from which we draw our support. We believe that such a view must be accommodated in the Party.

How can the Party disengage honourably from this adventure and still retain any credibility as an independent socialist party?

Signed: Matt Merrigan, Spokesman.[11]

None of this cut any ice with Labour's Disciplinary Committee which subsequently decided unanimously in favour of a six-month suspension from membership of Des Bonass and a three month suspension of Dermot Boucher, Secretary of the LCLL. It was also stated that on resuming Party membership, Bonass and Boucher would be obliged to provide written undertakings that they would abide by the relevant sections on Party discipline passed by the AC on 7 September 1972. In relation to the remaining twenty-two LCLL members charged, including Scott, it was decided that in the event of any further breaches of the relevant sections of the Party's disciplinary code would immediately incur suspension.[12] Interestingly, the Disciplinary Committee and AC treated the LCLL's Chairman, Matt Merrigan, more favourably than its Secretary, Boucher, presumably for fear of prompting the ATGWU's disaffiliation from the Party.

A further attack on Corish and his Parliamentary Party colleagues for entering coalition with Fine Gael came from Noël Browne, then a Senator, in June 1973. Writing in the LCLL's publication, *Liaison,* he said that in entering coalition the Labour leadership 'had traded the Irish Labour Party and Socialism for half a dozen Mercedes and a handful of Senate seats.'

Continuing, Browne said:

> Corish's action, and that of his parliamentary colleagues, is an act of treachery to Irish working class interests, unprecedented in a country where Labour leadership has spawned "its own special brand of political class Quislings more than any other group of Labour leaders anywhere."

> Brendan Corish, in rejecting Coalition in 1969, predicted that the Labour Party could not fight an election as an independent Party if we entered into a coalition under any condition. Now that he has joined such a Coalition on "unconditional surrender" terms, what does he propose for us?

> My three-year membership of the present Parliamentary Labour Party has made it clear to me that, with the possible exception of Justin Keating, there is no Socialist revolutionary within that group. I am not yet sure what Justin is at."

> In March 1969, I tried to warn the Labour Movement that they were entering a political life style where new and unheard of alliances and relationships must be considered and might become inevitable if we were to win power within the limitations of parliamentary politics

Urging the Labour Party to coalesce 'with like-minded people' and the two civil war parties – Fianna Fáil and Fine Gael to come together in coalition, Browne added:

> There is a good case for believing that a totally uncompromising stand by Labour Party, with the rejection of the opportunist Right-Wing merger, might have forced Fianna Fail to accept the inevitability of some form of alliance with Fine Gael in order to preserve the Status Quo...

> I believe coalitions to be divisive in practice, always dangerous and always harmful to the minority member unless rigidly protected. I believe that the Labour Party should, in the first instance, resist a coalition proposal and most certainly the present coalition, which was abject unconditional surrender of our Socialism to Fine Gael.[13]

Reiterating his criticism of Corish, Browne stated:

> Now that he has betrayed the labour movement, Corish may be correct in implying that there is now no alternative for himself, and his Labour colleagues in coalition, but to form a Social Democratic Party with the 'liberal wing' of Fine Gael.

On fellow Labour Party parliamentary members, Browne said: 'There are in the Labour Party members who, because they are born into "safe" Labour seats, are there for sentimental rather than ideological reasons.'[14]

Coinciding with the publication of Browne's *Liaison* article, was the election, on 11 July 1973, of LCLL members to three of the four leading positions on Labour's Dublin Regional Council (DRC): Kieran O'Donovan (Vice-Chairman), Frank Butler (Secretary) and Tony Dunne (Treasurer). Ruairi Quinn[15] was elected Chairman.[16]

Recalling that, in September 1972, the DRC had voted overwhelmingly against coalition with Fine Gael, a LCLL spokesman said that the poor showing of the Dublin organisation in the General Election and its virtual non-appearance for the Presidential election were due to rank-and-file discontent with the Party's electoral strategy. 'These elections indicate a growing disenchantment among Labour members with the performance of the National Coalition Government', the spokesman said.'[17]

For the LCLL, Labour's support for Tom O'Higgins, the Fine Gael TD and former member of the Blueshirts,[18] in the 1973 Presidential Election, was a further betrayal by the Party leadership. As is evident from the statements of several prominent Labour figures, the leadership's objective was to boost the newly-elected Fine-Gael-Labour Coalition Government. Commenting on this matter, Jim Tully, Minister for Local Government, said: 'The Presidential Election simply means you are in favour of the National Coalition, or you are not.'[19] Echoing that view was Michael O'Leary, Minister for Labour: 'An O'Higgins' win would demonstrate the nation's support for the National Coalition's progressive policies.'[20] Similarly, Conor Cruise O'Brien, the Minister for Post and Telegraphs, declared: 'The Presidency is a political contest and should be honestly seen and presented as such...Mr. O'Higgins' victory would indeed be a victory for the National Coalition.'[21] One of O'Higgins' most enthusiastic supporters in that presidential campaign was none other than the Labour Party Chairman, Roddy Connolly. Clearly, O'Higgins' past membership of the Blueshirts posed no difficulties for the founding President of the original Communist Party of Ireland! Paying tribute to O'Higgins, Connolly said: 'If I have one criticism to make of Tom O'Higgins it is that he spoke and acted too much like a Labour candidate'![22]

Notes

1 Labour Party, Annual Report, 1969.
2 *Irish Times,* 3 March 1973.
3 ibid.
4 Labour Party, *Organisational and Financial Planning* document, reference 74/73, prepared by Brendan Halligan for AC meeting on 19 April 1973.
5 Brendan Scott, *The Price Labour Paid For Coalition,* unpublished and undated typed article, probably for consideration by the LCLL, circa March 1973. [Brendan Scott Papers].
6 ibid.
7 Labour Party, AC, minutes of meeting, 15 March 1973.
8 ibid.
9 *Hibernia,* 30 March 1973.
10 *Irish Times,* 31 March 1973.
11 LCLL, submission, signed by Matt Merrigan, Spokesman, on behalf of 24 members, to the Disciplinary Committee of the Labour Party, 12 April 1973.
12 Labour Party, Disciplinary Committee, Report to AC, 19 April 1973.
13 *Liaison,* June 1973, pp. 3-5; *Evening Herald,* 12 July 1973.
14 Noël Browne, 'Revolutionary Socialism in a Parliamentary Democracy', *Liaison,* June 1973, p. 3; *Evening Herald,* 12 July 1973.
15 For information on Ruairi Quinn, see Ruairi Quinn, *Straight Left: A journey in Politics* (Hodder Headline Ireland, Dublin, 2005).
16 *Evening Herald,* 12 July 1973.
17 ibid.
18 *United Ireland,* 27 April 1935; *Irish Socialist,* No. 127, June 1973, p. 1. Tom O'Higgins' brother, Michael O'Higgins, was also a member of the Blueshirts, while their father, Thomas F. O'Higgins, was a leading figure in that organisation.
19 *Liaison,* June 1973, p. 1.
20 ibid., p. 2.
21 ibid.
22 ibid.

CHAPTER 24

The Incomparable Brendan Scott

At the time of the 1973 General Election, few of Brendan Scott's friends or acquaintances were aware that a year or so earlier he had been diagnosed with cancer of the stomach. During that period, he had been a patient, intermittently, in the Bon Secours Hospital, Glasnevin, and later in St. Joseph's Hospice, Raheny.[1] While his immediate family was aware of his condition from the beginning, it was only a month or two before his death that Brendan discovered the serious nature of his illness, having previously believed he was suffering from an ulcer.[2] In the last months of his life, he was in intense pain.[3] To make matters worse, as a consequence of Brendan's terminal illness, his wife, Carol Ann, was stricken with severe depression, a malady she continued to suffer from periodically for the remainder of her life. Such was the severity of her condition prior to Brendan's death that her sister, Dorothy Dowling, and John Medlycott,[4] Brendan's friend and colleague, were appointed legal guardians of a trust fund for the children's education. On quite a few occasions, Dorothy also looked after the children in their family home in Sutton. Her husband, Tony Dowling, a doctor, spent a lot of time with Brendan when he was dying and was with him when he died.[5]

Undaunted by his medical condition during the final year or so of his life, Scott penned his pamphlet, *Labour and Socialism* (Appendix 1), his most significant piece of writing, which was published posthumously by the Liaison Committee of the Left (LCLL) less than a month following his death. Scott also delivered a three-part series of lectures on the history and development of the trade union movement at the ITGWU's College in Palmerston Park, Rathmines.[6] As the *Irish Times* journalist, Mary Maher, observed: 'The time and effort he put into this work is an indication of the importance he attached to the role of the trade union movement in Irish politics.'[7] Scott also provided history notes for the ITGWU's tutors.[8] The labour historian and former ITGWU-SIPTU Tutor, Francis Devine, recalls using some of this material on economic and social development when he first taught in the College in the mid-1970s.[9] Less than two months before his death Scott wrote an extensive document, *Ideologies of the Left*, which apparently was unpublished.[10]

In the month or so prior to his demise, Scott was visited in St. Joseph's Hospice by several senior Labour Party figures. The initial visit of Niall Greene (Vice-Chairman) and Michael O'Leary, TD,[11] was followed by those of Roddy Connolly (Chairman) and Donal O'Sullivan (Financial Secretary),[12] Conor Cruise O'Brien, TD,[13] and, about a week before Scott's death, Roddy Connolly and Senator Brendan Halligan (General Secretary). Prior to that final visit, at a meeting of the Labour Party Officers, on 7 September 1973, a proposal by Connolly, seconded by O'Sullivan, that Scott be made a member of the Labour Party forthwith, was agreed unanimously. This was confirmed in a letter (Appendix 6) from Halligan to Scott, enclosing a fully-stamped membership card for 1973 (Appendix 7). The letter concluded: "The officers hope you will accept this proposal as a simple expression of their affection and respect for you."[14] When Halligan and Connolly visited Scott, Scott politely declined the invitation to re-join the Labour Party.[15] Nevertheless, according to Greene and Halligan, both encounters with Scott were of a friendly nature.[16]

Brendan Scott died on 19 September 1973, at the age of forty, in St. Joseph's Hospice, Raheny.[17] His funeral service, which took place two days later in St Fintan's Church, Sutton, was attended by a huge crowd, including socialists of every persuasion. He was interred in the nearby St. Fintan's Cemetery. In accordance with his wishes, his funeral Mass was celebrated by his friend and colleague in the Irish Anti-Apartheid Movement, the liberal priest, Austin Flannery, OP. Predeceased by his parents, Brendan Scott was survived by his wife, Carol Ann, their three children, Eoin, Melanie and Ivan, and his brother, Basil.

It was also in accordance with Brendan's wishes, that his corneas were donated to the Royal Victoria Eye and Ear Hospital, Dublin.[18]

While the death of Brendan Scott was obviously devastating for his widow and children, there was also on the left a palpable sense of loss, a stark realisation that, politically, he was simply irreplaceable.

Brendan's reasons for choosing a Catholic funeral ceremony are unknown. What is known is that the Scott family attended Mass regularly up to the First Holy Communion of their second child, Melanie, in the mid-1960s. Subsequently, for reasons unknown, the family was uninvolved in the Catholic Church and, indeed, in any religion, and the children, all pupils of Sutton Park School, were never confirmed.[19] In an observation on this particular matter, Melanie Scott said: 'I do not recall any indications that he was religious – until just before he died when he asked Eoin and I to make our confirmations – which we never did.'[20] Following Brendan's death, his former friend and colleague, Ruarc Gahan, wrote: 'He was one of the least religious people I have known.'[21] Incidentally, Carol Ann Scott's funeral service in 2018 was a humanist one.[22]

John Horgan recently stated: 'I knew Brendan S. [Scott] only very slightly, but everyone I know who knew him couldn't speak too highly of him.'[23] That impression of Scott is borne out by many of the tributes paid to him almost half a century earlier. One of the earliest of these came from his Labour adversary, Conor Cruise O'Brien, TD: '...Brendan's death deeply felt by all who knew him and who will never forget the magnanimity and integrity of his character and his courage in upholding the causes in which he believed.'[24] Another early tribute was that of John de Courcy Ireland: 'He was one of the few irreplaceables but the inspiration he leaves will last.'[25]

Announcing a memorial service for Scott, in St. Saviour's, Upper Dorset Street, Dublin, on 7 October 1973,[26] the Irish Anti-Apartheid Movement said his 'unswerving dedication to the cause of liberation movements of Southern Africa will be sadly missed.'[27]

An earlier tribute to Scott, less than three months before his demise, came from the directors of Sutton Park School:

> The Directors have known for some little time that you have not enjoyed the best of health, and…have expressed their admiration of your resolution in carrying on for so long so that the pupils could have the benefit of your teaching until exam time.[28]

For an opinion on Scott as a teacher, we can turn to one of his former Sutton Park pupils:

> He put himself out to teach us Latin for the Leaving Cert. in two years as we girls all gave up maths after the Inter [Intermediate Certificate examination]… Then we discovered we couldn't go to Trinity [College] unless we had maths or Latin. We frequently had classes outside where Brendan smoked constantly. I always felt he was teaching Latin in his spare time but with hindsight that was unlikely.[29]

A wider view of Scott as a teacher or lecturer was provided by Sister Miriam Thérèse of Our Lady of Mercy College, Beaumont:

> I had the good fortune of being one of his students in UCD some years ago, and though not a very brilliant one, yet I was capable of being inspired by a superior mind…I followed one of his history lessons on the television in 1969, and found his presentation imaginative and inspirational. His rich resonant voice and poetic flavour gave much enchantment to these…The influence which he exerted during his teaching years must have been tremendous.[30]

Scott's contributions as a teacher and an educationalist were the themes of an appreciation by Ruarc Gahan, the former Headmaster of Sutton Park School:

> He was an outstanding teacher. The least among his gifts was his versatile breadth of interest: I remember that one year he successfully taught five subjects to Leaving Certificate honours level…But Brendan's most valuable characteristic as a teacher was his warmth, his ability to like all his pupils, to make good personal relationships with boys and girls of all sorts, to make each pupil feel equally valued. He had great compassion; the pupil who had any special disadvantage, the misfit, the rebel – these he gave the affection and understanding they needed; he was always on their side.
>
> Brendan had none of the absurd "dignity" associated with the profession. His pupils knew him, not as "sir" or as Mr. Scott, but as Brendan or "Scottie." He demanded none of the phoney "respect" often valued by teachers, but got real respect because he was a real person. He had no use for hypocrisy or double-think…
>
> Brendan was an especially active participant in the search for a humane, tolerant,

loving and truly democratic type of school community, which was our main concern at Sutton Park. His death is a loss, not only to his pupils, but to the advancement of educational practice that puts children first and theories about them (what they should think, how they should dress, and so on) second." [31]

In a more general tribute to Scott, Kader Asmal, said:

Brendan Scott…combined a remarkable range of qualities in his commitment to his work and the causes he passionately believed in…He was caught up in the ferment of progressive ideas that affected so many of his contemporaries in the early 1950s in Ireland…

As a brilliant teacher he developed in his students the belief in self-enquiry and democratic self-government.

His abiding interest in history was reflected in his work as a history tutor at UCD and as a lecturer in history methodology in the School of Education at St. Patrick's College, Maynooth. In 1969 he wrote and presented a pioneering series of programmes on Irish social history for Telefís Scoile which gave him great pleasure and satisfaction. His creative talents were seen at their best during this period.

But his greatest passion was for politics. He threw himself into the changing Labour Party of the sixties and played a great and important part in the formulation of the exciting new policy document that emerged before the General Election of 1969. A superb platform speaker and an incisive writer he drew the admiration of even those who disagreed with him but who could not gainsay his wit and style.

Within the Labour Party he was elected to the Dublin Regional Council and the Administrative Council: on these bodies he acted as the conscience of what he considered to be right for the Labour Party. For him, James Connolly was not a figurehead to whom one paid the traditional obeisance once a year….

Out of his socialism and identification with the oppressed emerged his great commitment to the struggles being conducted in the Third World for justice and social progress. He was undeviating in his opposition to racialism …

Anyone who heard Brendan speak will never forget his unique brand of wit and passion, which often struck hard blows but was always based on such a deep and warm commitment to the human values of socialism that it never left behind any feeling of rancour… [32]

A 1973 appreciation of Scott by Matt Merrigan was published posthumously forty-one years later in 2014:

When we think of Brendan Scott, we are compelled to dwell on the inspiration for life that springs from his work…He had a brilliant mind and an impeccable eloquence and wit. Add to these integrity, honesty of purpose and commitment to his ideals and we have a complete human being a Socialist.

Mankind in its struggle from a primitive lifestyle to the space age was to Brendan an inspiration and challenge to build on these human and technical achievements, a system of society that would also free mankind from the relentless exploitation of those who own and control the economic forces and thereby control and limit the social and cultural progress of that large section of the human race the socially deprived and underprivileged…

He fought the good fight with passionate concern. He imparted knowledge and a consciousness where there was ignorance and indifference. He irrigated with his eloquence and intellect the arid minds of a generation of youth moving to Socialism for the first time in a reactionary period of the fifties and sixties...

He was a good comrade, husband, father and he illuminated all of our lives with his brilliance and compassion [33]

In a further tribute, also published posthumously in 2014, Merrigan stated:

One other founding member [of the Liaison Committee of the Left] should be mentioned specially. Brendan Scott was always seen in the lonely political places in the Labour Party as we battled on against its bureaucracy and its running-dogs for a committed and principled socialist and independent thrust for a Labour Government. His long battle with cancer over 1972/73 was interspersed with moments of high political activity, writing a pamphlet and articles for Liaison and speaking at meetings of LCLL and the Labour Party.[34]

Paying tribute to Scott, Des Bonass, Merrigan's LCLL and ATGWU colleague, said:

We were all in the Labour Party, Young Socialists, Republicans or whatever, attempts were made to bring the left closer together with the Liaison Committee of the Left. Among those involved were great people like Brendan Scott...[35]

Alluding to Scott's outstanding communications skills, the journalist and former Secretary of Official Sinn Féin, Máirín de Burca, recalled that Scott once acted as MC at a concert she had organised and that a colleague said to her: 'Who is that man doing MC, he speaks amazingly.'[36]

On the posthumous publication of Scott's pamphlet, *Labour and Socialism,* the LCLL stated:

This essay is published as a simple tribute to Brendan by his comrades in the Labour Party Liaison Committee of the Left. His great impact in the party was through his speeches and lectures as he was primarily a teacher. This booklet will recall the fundamentals of what he taught to those who knew and learned from him. For a new generation it will start again the debate and action on those ideas. In that way it will be his epitaph.[37]

Another trade unionist to pay tribute to Scott was Des Geraghty, then an official of ITGWU and subsequently Editor of the Union's monthly periodical, *Liberty* and General President of SIPTU:

Brendan Scott...was an extraordinarily active man who spent most of his free time working in politics. He was full of energy and threw himself into battle with vigour... He was concerned about people on a world-wide basis and was concerned about the oppressed everywhere.[38]

In another appreciation of Scott, the *Irish Times* journalist, Mary Maher, said:

...He founded and was joint-editor of..."Action", which called for militant action to highlight the appalling housing conditions in the city, and in which he tried to propagate Socialist ideas into the Labour Party.

His writings and speeches were trenchant and witty. He despised hyprocrisy [sic] and never lost an opportunity to expose the right-wing of the Labour Party and all those who gave lip–service to Connolly's teachings. His deep commitment to Socialism, for which he worked actively, forced him to resign from the Administrative Council of the Labour Party. Later he was expelled from the Party by those who feared his vision and ability.

Although already quite ill, he fought vigorously with the Left-Liason [sic] Group to prevent the Coalition between the Labour Party and Fine Gael. At the same time he advocated the unity of the Labour Left, Communist and Republican forces in the country. His study of Marx and Lenin convinced him that such unity was the only effective way to bring about real change...[39]

Amid frequent interruptions by left-wing delegates shouting: 'Salve your conscience', 'Traitor' and 'You stabbed him in the back', Roddy Connolly, the Chairman of the Labour Party, delivered a tribute to Scott at the Party's Annual Conference in Cork, on 12 October 1973. The disturbance had its origin in the disbandment of the Party's Howth Branch earlier that year and the expulsion of its members, including Scott. Apparently unperturbed by the protest, Connolly proceeded with this tribute:

> He was a brilliant teacher not only of academic subjects, but of those progressive political ideas in which he fervently believed and to which he felt a passionate dedication. He was a Marxist of high order, with Irish social history as the major field for his penetrating analysis. He was forthright in his beliefs and in his telling of them he was lucid, witty and vigorous; his courage was an inspiration. When in company of the Financial Secretary I visited him a few weeks before his death, his humanity and understanding stood out supremely. He confirmed in trenchant manner that his ideal was socialism, based on the fundamental principle which had so dominated the life and thoughts process of his hero and mentor, James Connolly...It gave him the greatest satisfaction, he said, to ask me to pass on a last message to all of us in the socialist movement; that outside the Labour Party, there is no hope for the working class.[40]

While there is no doubting the generous nature of Connolly's tribute, the final statement attributed to Scott is puzzling. After all, not only had Scott on his death bed, in the presence of Connolly and Halligan, declined reinstatement in the Labour Party,[41] he had, earlier that year criticised the Party's move towards social democracy.[42] Nevertheless, there is no reason to doubt Halligan who confirmed that, in quoting Scott, Connolly had been 'reported accurately'.[43]

In a somewhat controversial appreciation (Appendix 1, pp. 15-16), Noël Browne, the Irish parliamentarian Scott most admired, stated:

> ...He [Brendan Scott] was a revolutionary Marxist in the barren political wasteland of this Republic.

> Brendan hated the privileged life of the capitalist world – he hated the vulgarity and the greed of capitalism as a system of organised society, for the pain and misery it meant to so many innocents. Like any good hater – I use that word hate, without reservation, - he did what he could to destroy it. He was the only true safe socialist revolutionary, soft on the outside, but hate-hard on the inside. He never faltered in his conviction that socialism must come, even to Ireland...

He knew that socialism must come to Ireland in a way special and unique to Ireland, and that only those who know their Ireland well could help to create it…

Socialist politics was his tribute, simply to being alive with others with whom he suffered, anywhere men were in distress. He had an original creative mind, and all of this fine talent he related to our Irish needs. He learnt from the success and failures of socialist revolutions from Moscow to Santiago de Chile. He learnt from the diversity of our comrades' experience through history, that our own struggle would finally succeed or fail because of what we do here, to encourage an understanding as a prelude to a demand for socialism…

His, as is the life of each of us, I suppose [is] a tiny silken thread, working together and being woven from that part of us all which each of us gives to socialism, into a powerful single rope with which so much can be done, and remains to be done, before our job is finished here.

Brendan's last political act of infinite dignity and characteristic restraint was to decline the unspeakable gaucherie of an invitation by the bureaucrats of the Labour Party, two days before he died, to lift his expulsion so that he could die in that organisation in which these same officials did not consider him fit to live during his lifetime. He could not prevent them from attending his funeral; at last they felt safe from his acid tipped tongue…[44]

Although Scott was trenchantly opposed to capitalism, Browne's contention that he was 'hate-hard on the inside' is inaccurate and unsustainable. It was simply not in Brendan Scott's nature to hate. Other sections of Browne's appreciation prompted Scott's friend and colleague, Julian Walton,[45] to write to Browne on behalf of Carol Ann:

Carol Ann's attention was drawn to the remarks made by the Party Chairman about Brendan on the Friday evening of the Labour Party Conference, and the disturbance with which these remarks were greeted by a certain section of the audience…I myself was present as one of the delegates from Kilbarrack. She also read your remarks about Brendan which appear as an epilogue [Browne's appreciation of Scott] to the pamphlet "Labour and Socialism", by Brendan Scott…

…Carol Ann stresses that Brendan was most concerned towards the end of his life to be reconciled with those with whom he had had personal or political differences. He was able to meet most of these people before he died. The inference to be drawn from your remarks is that he in fact wished to perpetuate these differences to the last. This has greatly upset Carol Ann, who would not like to think that her husband died at enmity with anyone…[46]

Walton's account has been verified by Brendan and Carol Ann Scott's eldest son, Eoin, and daughter, Melanie (Ivan was only six when his father died), who confirmed that their father wished to die in peace with his political opponents.[47]

In that same letter to Browne, to which there was no response, Walton added:

…I do feel that your resentment of their [the Labour Party officers] presence at his [Brendan Scott's] funeral is unworthy. I regard Brendan's funeral as a profoundly moving tribute to his amazing warmth of personality; I can think of no one else who could have aroused friendship and respect from so many people of such a variety of political hues (and there were some present at the funeral with considerably less commitment to socialism than the "bureaucrats" of the Labour Party). Those who had been in disagreement with him attended his funeral as a mark of sincere respect – not from a feeling of obligation, and not because they needed to convince themselves that they were safe from his "acid tipped tongue".[48]

Some eighteen years following his death, this tribute to Scott was published in a biography of John Swift:

> ...Regarded by Swift and many others as one of the finest socialists of his time, Scott was as well as being an active Labour Party member, a founder of both the Irish Anti-Apartheid Movement and the Ireland-USSR Friendship Society [sic]... Intelligence, integrity and modesty were among the qualities Swift admired most in Scott. Scott earned the respect of the Irish Left for his tireless commitment to numerous progressive causes and his unceasing efforts to encourage Left unity.[49]

It was John Horgan who recorded this concise description of Scott: 'Brendan Scott...was a beacon on the left...a charismatic figure who attracted huge personal loyalty but who gave his support selflessly to [Noël] Browne.'[50] Also concise was the *Irish Times* journalist, James Downey, who described 'the lovable' Brendan Scott as 'a pillar of the left and of the anti apartheid movement.'[51]

The most recent tribute to Scott came, in September 2020. in the form of a poem by the labour historian and former ITGWU-SIPTU Tutor, Francis Devine:

September Song, 1973

for Brendan Scott, died 19 September 1973

Though terminal and fighting
for breath, he saluted Jara
whose body, riddled by forty bullets,
knuckles smashed, lay dumped
in the bloody football stadium,
guitar placed as triumphant
trophy of a terrible tyranny.

Despite the morphine,
he knew to champion Sisulu,
ceaselessly spalling stones
after Rivonia's crude show,
an island internment designed
to demoralise and degrade
by those with no morality.

Thinking of Uncle Ho, he drew
strength from an embryonic peace,
a defeat for imperialist might
that indicated that victory was
possible against any odds
if belief were strong enough.

In his dying moments, he politely
declined a request to re-join
a Labour Party whose leaders
welcomed him only in death,
preferring instead to stand
shoulder-to-shoulder with those
whom he had marched alongside
and who march with him still.

Taken collectively, these many tributes to Brendan Scott by trade unionists, students, teachers, lecturers, journalists, authors and politicians, reveal a great deal about Scott and his legacy.

Scott once said: 'It was Noël Browne who attracted many of us to Socialism.'[52] The same could truly be said of Brendan Scott. Pat Carroll, a close socialist ally of both Scott and Browne, has pointed out that Scott's admiration for Browne was reciprocal. Elaborating, Carroll said:

> Scott was well informed about many matters, including, for example, education and labour history, and Browne, who was less well informed on such issues, was dependent on Scott in that respect.[53]

Little wonder, then, that Browne, not known for his praise of others, described his socialist and secular friend and colleague as 'the incomparable Brendan Scott.'[54]

That unique tribute is unlikely to be challenged by anyone who knew Brendan Scott.

Notes

1   Interviews with Eoin Scott, 27 January 2019, and Melanie Scott, 6 May 2019.
2   Interview with Melanie Scott, 6 May 2019.
3   Kader Asmal, 'Brendan Scott: An Appreciation', *Irish Times*, 21 September 1973; Interviews with Eoin and Melanie Scott, 23 August 2019.
4   John Medlycott, a history teacher, was a colleague of Brendan Scott's in Sutton Pak School and in the Labour Party.
5   Email from Melanie Scott to the author, 29 November 2019.
6   Des Geraghty (Anon) 'Brendan Scott', *Liberty*, October 1973; Mary Maher (M.M.), 'Death of Brendan Scott', *Irish Socialist*, No. 131, October 1973, p. 3.
7   Mary Maher (M.M.), 'Death of Brendan Scott', op. cit.
8   Des Geraghty (Anon) 'Brendan Scott', op. cit.
9   Francis Devine, email to the author, 13 August 2019.
10 Brendan Scott, *Ideologies of the Left*, undated and apparently unpublished article, circa July 1973.
11 Interview with Niall Greene, 16 November 2018.
12 *Irish Times*, 13 October 1973.
13 Interview with Pádraig Ó Snodaigh, 11 June 2020.
14 Labour Party, letter to Brendan Scott, signed by Senator Brendan Halligan, General Secretary, 10 September 1973 (Appendix 6), with a fully-stamped Labour Party membership card for 1973 (Appendix 7).
15 Interview with Brendan Halligan, 16 November 2018; email from the author to Brendan Halligan, 23 August 2019; Email from Brendan Halligan to the author, 24 August 2019.
16 Interviews with Niall Greene and Brendan Halligan, 16 November 2018.

17 *Irish Times,* 21 September 1973.
18 Royal Victoria Eye and Ear Hospital, letter, to Carol Ann Scott, 21 September 1973 [Brendan Scott Papers]; interviews with Michael Williams, 10 December 2018, and Eoin and Melanie Scott, 23 August 2019.
19 Interviews with Eoin Scott, 23 August 2019; Melanie Scott, 23 August, 29 November
20 Melanie Scott, email to the author, 20 August 2020.
21 Ruarc Gahan, 'Brendan Scott: An Appreciation', *Irish Times,* 24 September 1973.
22 John [P.] Swift, 'Carol Ann Scott (née O'Rourke) (1937-2018)', *Sound Post,* Vol. 16, No. 2, Summer 2018, p. 18.
23 John Horgan, email to the author, 3 May 2020.
24 Conor Cruise O'Brien, telegram to Carol Ann Scott, 19 September 1973.
25 John de Courcy Ireland, post card to Carol Ann Scott, 22 September 1973.
26 *Irish Times,* 6 October 1973; *Amandla* [IAAM], Vol. V111, No. 6, October 1973.
27 *Amandla,* op. cit.
28 F. Gully, Chairman, Sutton Park School, letter to Brendan Scott, 28 June 1973.
29 Richard Pine, email to the author, 8 August 2018, recording former, unnamed Sutton Park School pupil's recollections of Brendan Scott.
30 Sister Miriam Thérèse, letter to Carol Ann Scott, 27 September 1973.
31 Ruarc Gahan, 'Brendan Scott: An Appreciation', op. cit.
32 Kader Asmal, 'Brendan Scott: An Appreciation', op. cit.
33 Matt Merrigan, *Eggs and Rashers: Irish Socialist Memories,* Edited and Introduced by D. R. O'Connor Lysaght, op. cit., pp. 190-191.
34 ibid., p. 115.
35 Des Bonass, 'The Matt Merrigan I knew', in Des Derwin, "Memories of a Marvellous Legacy", in Matt Merrigan, 1921-2000', in Francis Devine and Kieran Jack McGinley (Editors), *Left Lives in Twentieth Century Ireland,* Volume 2, op. cit., p. 119.
36 Mairín de Burca, email to the author, 27 July 2020.
37 LCLL, untitled tribute to Brendan Scott, in Brendan Scott, *Labour and Socialism,* op. cit., unpaged, page 2.
38 Des Geraghty (Anon.), 'Brendan Scott', op. cit.
39 Mary Maher [M.M.], 'Death of Brendan Scott', op. cit.
40 *Irish Times,* 13 October 1973.
41 Interview with Brendan Halligan, 16 November 2018; email from the author to Brendan Halligan, 23 August 2019; Brendan Halligan, email to the author, 24 August 2019.
42 Brendan Scott, *Labour and Socialism, op. cit.*
43 Email from the author to Brendan Halligan, 23 August 2019; Brendan Halligan, email to the author, 24 August 2019.
44 Noel Browne, 'Brendan Scott' in Brendan Scott, *Labour and Socialism,* op. cit., pp. 15-16.
45 Julian Walton was a colleague of Brendan Scott's in Sutton Park School and in the Labour Party from 1970.
46 Julian Walton, letter to Noël Browne, 21 October 1973. [Julian Walton Papers]
47 Interviews with Eoin Scott and Melanie Scott, 23 August 2019.
48 Julian Walton, letter to Noël Browne, op. cit.
49 John P. Swift, *John Swift: An Irish Dissident,* op. cit., p. 195.
50 John Horgan, *Noël Browne: Passionate Outsider,* op. cit., pp. 183, 248.
51 James Downey, *In My Own Time: Inside Irish Politics and Society,* op. cit., p. 154.
52 Brendan Scott. Matt Merrigan, John Byrne, Patrick Perry, 'Dr. Noel Browne', letter to the Editor, *Irish Times,* 12 February 1973.
53 Interview with Pat Carroll, 30 October 2018.
54 Noël Browne, *Against the Tide,* op. cit., p. 267.

CHAPTER 25

Labour's Lost Leader

In any assessment of Brendan Scott account must to be taken of the fact that he was a socialist and not a social democrat. This is evident from many of his political statements and particularly from his pamphlet, *Labour and socialism:*

> Basically there is a very wide gulf between egalitarian social and meritocratic social democracy. The former wants to get rid of privilege – the latter wants to change the rules on how privileges are allocated. Socialism seeks classlessness, Social Democracy is content with class mobility. Socialism wants industrial democracy, Social Democracy is prepared to live with a private-sector dominated economy, provided there is a welfare service safety net. Socialism sees the cause of inequality as the capitalist system – Social Democracy believes it can be run the system better than the capitalists...[1]

Obviously unimpressed with the performance of social democracy in Western Europe in the field of education, Scott quoted some revealing statistics:

> Education must be the escalator in a meritocratic society. Yet in the 1960's these were the percentages of university students of working class origin: Great Britain, 25%; Norway 25%; Sweden, 16%; Denmark, 10%, France and Austria, 8%, Netherlands, 5%; West Germany, 5%. The percentage of working class children doing grammar school courses in the early sixties were: Great Britain, 52%. Sweden, 23%; Netherlands, 19½%; France, 17%; West Germany, 16%. Again the differentials between unskilled workers and white-collar professionals have increased rather than decreased in the 1960's. In Sweden and in Denmark, there were wider differentials than in the U.S. or Germany. Or look at the percentage of G.N.P. allocated to welfare services. In the 1960's, Sweden was allocating 12.4%; Denmark, 11.1%, Great Britain, 11%; Norway, 10.3%, West Germany, 16.1%; France, 14.9%.[2]

In a more general analysis of social democracy, Scott stated:

> Today the most deadly threat to socialism in Ireland comes not from without the Movement, but from within. It comes from the ultra-democratic, new wave social democrats whose constant battle-cry is "The people have spoken." We will now of course do what they have told us to do...One must first see that a politician can take very different views of his role in the liberal –bourgeois democracy. He can see his role as the shaper of public opinion, right out in front of the herd, trying to steer it in a particular direction. Or he can seek the safe middle of the herd and go where the leaderless majority are heading. The ultra-democrats who are at present claiming to be the leadership of the Labour Movement forget that Socialism cannot and must not claim to be a national party representing all the people. Socialists by definition are a sectional party representing the majority Have-nots in society, and, by definition, wishing to abolish the minority Haves. Newspaper owners and columnists, television programmers, bishops, also

represent minority interests. They have a very good reason for advocating consensus politics because they control the media which produce the consensus. Yet the Labour Party's actions since 1969 at least, have been reactions to prodding from newspapers and bishops on issues such as coalition, the North, etc.[3]

Again we are entitled to ask the ultra-democrats this question – what profound or significant or lasting change was ever initiated or brought to fruition by a majority? The Christian religion? The Reformation? The French or Russian Revolutions? The abolition of slavery? The vote for women? Should Larkin have waited for the majority of the Irish people to back him in 1913? Behind the ideology of the ultra-democrats is a profound conservatism. The Civil Rights Movement in the North, street action of any kind, even if non-violent in theory, we are told, are violent in practice because they stir up a reaction of violence from those against whom the protest is aimed…[4]

Scott's criticism of sections of the left was not confined to social democrats:

…Those who most detest the smug establishment Lefties in Leinster House are often their best, if unwitting, accomplices. How many people are there who say "I'd join the Labour Party or Sinn Fein if they really were socialist? "I'll join them when they say they are…" and there follows a string of conditions. There are others who seek the seamless garment of doctrinal purity in the wilderness…[5]

There is the profound hatred of our socialist sects that assures victory to the new breed of social democratic organisation man….We have forgotten that the purpose of our organisations is to achieve socialism, and instead consider them ends in themselves, and their immediate triumph over other sects to be more important than furthering socialism. Thus we find we spend more time disrupting the activities of other Left-wing groups than we do in fighting the enemy. Hold a meeting on the North in the Mansion House and we will all be there savaging one another. Yet how many of us join Fianna Fail dominated tenants' associations, conservative dominated debating societies, or even trade union meetings. Are we so busy taking in each's other's washing that we do not even know where the launderettes patronised by the uncommitted are situated?[6]

Scott had some insightful things to say about politics in Ireland:

We need to know the leverage points if we want to overthrow the existing society. We cannot ignore any form of protest. For example Women's Liberation could have a far more profound effect on overthrowing our present society than any strike. Contraception and divorce can force the Establishment in the South into the open. The disciplined action of Sinn Fein on issues such as mining, fisheries and housing action caused more pain to the Establishment than activity on the border…We must make the decision on whether action on Southern streets on issues like housing might be of more assistance to both communities in the North than a string of resolutions condemning the role of the British Army.

At the time of Scott's death, the Irish State had been in existence for just over half a century. He was conscious that the capitalist parties that had held power during that era had failed to resolve many major economic and social problems, particularly unemployment, emigration and housing. Socialism had never even been tried. He was acutely aware, too, that coalition governments involving Labour with Fianna Fáil or Fine Gael would never implement fundamental socialist policies.

For Brendan Scott, the transformation, in terms of policy, of the most conservative Labour Party in Western Europe into arguably the most radical one, in the late 1960s, in which he played such a prominent role, was the pinnacle of his involvement in politics. Another highlight for him was Labour's successful 1969 General Election result, when the Party secured its highest share of first preference votes for almost half a century. That result was perceived by the left as an opportunity to develop and promote the socialist policies, while continuing to eschew coalition with conservative political opponents. For Scott, that opportunity was squandered when Labour not only formed a coalition government with Fine Gael in 1973, but contested the General Election, not on its own socialist policies, but a joint, largely superficial programme with Fine Gael.

From the left's perspective it appeared that the Labour leadership was prepared to facilitate the adoption of socialist policies and to quote Connolly *ad nauseam,* provided the Parliamentary Party would not be obliged to advance such radical ideas. Consequently, from the left's perspective, the Party's annual conferences were largely a discussion forum in which radical resolutions could be adopted with no prospect of being pursued by the Party leadership. How many genuine socialists were lost through this cynical and undemocratic approach to politics? The damage this has done to the Labour Party and, more important, to socialism, is incalculable.

The late Brendan Halligan, then General Secretary of the Party, stated that, in determining Labour's decision to form a coalition government with Fine Gael, the Arms Crisis was a consideration.[7] However, Halligan also acknowledged that his pro-coalition stance pre-dated both the Arms Crisis and the rise of the Provisional IRA. Referring to Labour's 1969 General Election results, he said: "I certainly changed my mind about coalition. I changed it in the television studios looking at seats tumbling all around me."[8] It was not long before Corish followed suit as did many other prominent figures in the Party, including the TDs, Desmond, Keating, O'Brien, O'Connell and Thornley, all of whom had ministerial aspirations. In any event, it is highly questionable that the State was actually under threat at that time. Even O'Brien, who was particularly exercised about such matters, acknowledged as much when he said in May 1970 that 'he did not question the loyalty of the Army which had a fine record of responsibility to the lawfully elected Government.'[9]

For Scott and his LCLL colleagues, the raising of the State's security as a consideration in determining Labour's coalition policy was a pretext to justify the suppression of Labour's more radical policies and participation in a coalition government with Fine Gael. Labour's failure to return to its independent, radical position, even when the threat, real or perceived, to the State no longer existed, is highly revealing. It is also a vindication of Scott and the LCLL on this issue.

Scott's total opposition to Labour coalescing with capitalist parties has also been vindicated by subsequent events, and not simply because of the abandonment of the radical policies. A key question that arises is this: What electoral benefits has Labour gained from its involvement in five coalition governments since 1973? The answer is a resounding none. Actually, the reverse is the case. As the following table reveals, in the five general elections following Labour's participation in coalition governments since then, the Party's first preference vote declined by an average of 99,000, its share of first preference votes fell by an average of 5.4 per cent, while there was an average loss of 10.2 Dáil seats.

Labour Party, Changes in General Election Results immediately following participation in Coalition Governments

General Election	Change in first preference votes	Change in percentage share of first preference votes	Change in number of Dáil seats	Change in percentage share of Dáil seats
18.06.1977	+1,754	-2.1	-2	0
18.02.1982	-18,115	-0.8	0	0
18.02.1987	-45,364	-3.0	-3	-1.8
06.07.1997	-146,969	-8.9	-16	-9.7
26.02.2016	-290,898	-12.9	-30	-17.9
Average	-99,184	-5.4	-10.2	-5.9

Sources: *Irish Independent* and *Irish Times*, 1973-2016 and *Irish Press*, 1973-1992

Leaving aside the principle of coalition, is it not reasonable to assume that Scott and the LCLL would have wondered how Labour had such little influence in subsequent coalition governments when the former, economically right-wing party, the Progressive Democrats, with significant less electoral support, could determine the economic policy of this country?

In the most recent General Election of February 2020, the Labour Party recorded its worst ever result, securing a paltry 4.4 per cent share of the first preference vote and six Dáil seats. If Labour is to recover electorally and reclaim lost ground it could learn a great deal from Scott and the LCLL by formulating a distinctive, radical socialist programme and abandoning coalition government with conservative opponents. In fact, in an increasingly competitive electoral field, that may be its only viable option if it is to remain a relevant political force.

In evaluating Scott's legacy, it is evident that, aside from his roles as a husband and a father, his life was dominated by two things: his career as a teacher in Sutton Park School and his voluntary involvement in the Labour Party and numerous other progressive organisations and campaigns. With his exceptional communicating skills, both as a writer and public speaker, his outstanding integrity and deep knowledge of such subjects as philosophy, history, politics education and literature, he was particularly well equipped for his roles as a teacher and a political activist. Among Irish socialists, Scott stands out as one of the very few to write, not alone about socialism, but on many other topics such as secularism, republicanism, nationalism and left unity.[10]

While the greatest political disappointment of his life undoubtedly was Labour's failure to retain ad develop its radical, independent position of the late 1960s, Scott undoubtedly would have welcomed progressive developments in Ireland and internationally, particularly those relating to campaigns in which he had been actively involved. He would, for example, have been pleased that, in the year of his death, agreement on the principal objective of the Ireland-USSR Society, the establishment of diplomatic relations between Ireland and the USSR, had finally been concluded.[11] He would also have rejoiced in the ultimately successful, international campaigns against oppression in South Africa and American military involvement in Vietnam. While much remains to be achieved in the secularisation of Irish society, particularly with regard to education and health, Scott would have welcomed the progress that has taken place since his era in relation to such matters as contraception, divorce, abortion and gay rights.

Although, for many years, Scott served the Labour Party in a part-time, honorary capacity, as a branch and constituency council[12] officer and Dublin Regional Council[13] and, briefly, Administrative Council[14] member, he neither sought nor secured high office in either the Labour Party or the LCLL. Nor did he ever express any interest in contesting either a council or a Dáil election. Yet, from the mid-1960s to the early 1970s, he was arguably the most influential figure of his generation on Labour's left and a central figure in the formation of a significant left-wing presence in the Labour Party. That development did not go unnoticed: Writing about Labour's 1967 Annual Conference, leading *Irish Times* journalist and columnist, Donal Foley, stated:

> The most significant fact which emerged from this conference, more so than last year, was that the Labour Party now has an articulate tightly-knit Left-wing. It is small as yet but will increase in significance...[15]

Scott was also, of course, involved in the formulation of Labour's 1969 socialist and secular education policy, and a leading figure in the adoption and promotion of the suite of socialist policies ratified that year. He was also centrally involved in the subsequent struggle for the retention and development of those policies and for an independent, radical Labour Party, undiluted by coalition with capitalist parties.

For his consistent and cogent advocacy of socialism, left unity, human rights and secularism, Scott earned the respect and admiration of many on the left, not only in the Labour Party, but in other left-wing parties and in none.

Brendan Scott's early death robbed the labour movement of an outstanding, visionary and inspirational leader

Notes

1   Brendan Scott, *Labour and Socialism*, op. cit., p. 8.
2   ibid.
3   ibid., p. 9.
4   ibid.
5   ibid., p. 10.
6   ibid.
7   Interview with Brendan Halligan, 16 November 2018.
8   Stephen Collins, *The Cosgrave Legacy* (Blackwater Press, Dublin, 1996), pp. 102-103.
9   *Irish Times*, 13 May 1970.
10 Brendan Scott, *Labour and Socialism*, op. cit.
11 Michael Quinn, *Irish-Soviet Diplomatic and Friendship Relations, 1917-1991*, op. cit., p. 249.
12 Interview with Máirín Johnston, 30 October 2018.
13 *Irish Times*, 21 August 1971.
14 Kader Asmal, 'Brendan Scott: An Appreciation', *Irish Times*, 21 September 1973; Des Geraghty (Anon), 'Brendan Scott', op. cit.
15 *Irish Times*, 16 October 1967.

LABOUR and SOCIALISM

by

Brendan Scott

This essay is published as a simple tribute to Brendan by his comrades in the Labour Party Liaison Committee of the Left. His great impact in the party was through his speeches and lectures as he was primarily a teacher. This booklet will recall the fundamentals of what he taught to those who knew and learned from him. For a new generation it will start again the debate and action on those ideas. In that way it will be his epitaph.

"We know that the evolution of a phenomenon in movement, no matter what its external appearances may be, depends upon its internal characteristics. And we know that on the political level our own reality — no matter how fine and attractive the reality of others may be — can only be transformed by detailed knowledge of it, by our own efforts, by our own sacrifices . . . The ideological deficiency within the national liberation movements, not to say the total lack of ideology reflecting as this does an ignorance of the historical reality which these movements claim to transform — makes for one of the greatest weaknesses in our struggle against imperialism, if not the greatest weakness of all."

The speaker, the late Amilcar Cabral; the occasion, the first Tricontinental Conference at Havana in 1966. Perhaps a far cry from the Irish Labour Party and all it stands for. But in this brief article I wish to investigate, not just the perspectives for the Labour Party, but the perspectives for socialism in Ireland, and, putting aside slogans and dogmas, to examine at least some of the fundamentals of the Irish political scene.

My first question is this: What stage of development has now been achieved by the Irish people? Connolly distinguishes three stages in the struggle of subject classes. In the first stage the eyes of the subject class are always turned towards the past — they want to march backwards to re-establish the social order of ancient times — "the good old days". In the second period the subject class tends "to believe that the social order in which it finds itself always did exist, and to devote all its energies to obtaining such amelioration of its lot within existent society as will make that lot more bearable". "At this stage of society," Connolly says, "the subject class, as far as its own aspirations is concerned, may be reckoned a conservative force." "In the third period the subject class becomes revolutionary, seeks little of the past for inspiration, but building itself upon the achievements of the present, confidently addresses itself to the conquest of the future".

By arguing that by virtue of their founders, the Irish Labour Party, the S.D.L.P., the N.I.L.P., the Republicans, or any other group, are non-sectarian, and that therefore any apparent sectarian conflict in the North is purely coincidental and will vanish when British troops are withdrawn, are we in the first stage — the nostalgia for the past. By saying that the armed struggle against the British Army is of paramount importance and that

3

other issues will be settled when they have gone, or that any talk of unity is wicked and will merely precipitate civil war, are we in the second stage, i.e. strait-jacketed by a static social order. On a real issue when the neo-colonial sub-structure was unveiled — the E.E.C. issue — unity prevailed between Hume, Faulkner, and our spokesmen in the Labour Party — they all wanted in. They all know that to achieve unity with the alienated Protestant working class, the benevolent hot-line to Cardinal Conway must disappear. The conflict in the North is not a unique one, and its dynamics have parallels elsewhere.

My next question is this: What kind of socialist party do we want? There are as many signposts to socialism as there are roads to heaven, but most of them fall into four categories. Category 1 rests on two foundation stones, firstly, that "without revolutionary theory there can be no revolutionary movement", and secondly, to produce a revolutionary movement there must be a "small, compact core", a revolutionary, disciplined, trained élite.

"The history of every country teaches us," Lenin wrote in **What is to be Done** in 1903, "that by its own ability the working class can attain only a trade-unionist self-consciousness, that is to say an appreciation of the need to fight the bosses, to wrest from the government this or that legislative enactment for the benefit of the workers. The Socialist doctrine, on the other hand, is the outgrowth of those philosophical, historical, and economic theories which have been developed by the representatives of the well to do, the intellectuals". In his essay 'For Twelve Years' published in 1906, he says: "The blind unfolding of the Labour Movement can lead only to the permeation of that movement with a bourgeois ideology because the unconscious growth of the labour movement takes the form of trade unionism . . . therefore our tasks as Social Democrats is to oppose this blind process, to divert the labour movement from the unconscious tendency of trade unionism to march under the protective wing of the bourgeoisie, and to bring it under the influence of social democracy instead." Trotsky, in his preface to the **History of the Commune of 1871,** states: "As we page through the history of the Commune one conclusion is inescapable: the party needed a firm command (a strong revolutionary leadership). Those who fought in 1871 did not lack heroism; what they lacked was a singleness of purpose and a centralised leadership — and this is precisely why they were beaten."

The Second Category is also revolutionary but it looks for revolution from below, wants the complete destruction of the state, and is not only suspicious of a disciplined party of revolutionaries, but distrusts all ideas of parties and tight organisation. "The advent of the social revolution is in no country nearer than in Italy", wrote Michael Bakunin in 1860, "there does not exist as in other countries of Europe a privileged class of workers who, thanks to their considerable wages, pride themselves on

4

the liberal education they have acquired; they are dominated by the principles of the bourgeois, by their ambition and vanity to such an extent that they are only different from the bourgeois by their situation and not in their way of thinking." "Many of the good bourgeois socialists", wrote Bakunin in **Statism and Anarchy,** "are always telling us: let us instruct the people first and then emancipate them. We say, on the contrary, let them emancipate themselves first and they will instruct themselves of their own accord."

The Manifesto of the Maknovite Army — a Russian anarchist group of the Revolutionary Civil War period — states: "Ours is the purest form of socialism; anti-authoritarian, and anti-government, it calls for the free organisation of the social life of the workers . . . the workers themselves must choose their own councils to express the will and carry out the orders of these self-same workers. The soviets or councils will be the executive organs of, and not the authorities over the workers." The modern theorists of the anarchist ideal, Daniel and Gabriel Cohn Bendit, in their book **Obsolete Communism — the Left Wing Alternative** state: "Far from having to teach the masses, the revolutionary's job is to try to understand and express their common aspirations . . . The setting up of any party inevitably reduces the freedom of the people to agree with the party. In other words, democracy is not suborned by bad leadership, but by the very existence of leadership. Democracy cannot even exist within the Party because the Party itself is not a democratic organisation, i.e., it is based upon authority and not on representation." The Cohen Bendits state that "the revolutionary cannot and must not be a leader." They are "a militant minority drawn from various social strata, people who band together because they share an ideology . . . . to dispel the mystification of the ruling classes and the bureaucrats, to proclaim that the workers can only defend themselves and build a socialist society by taking their fate in their own hands, believing that political maturity comes only from revolutionary struggle and direct action."

The Third Category is similar to anarchism in that it distrusts the idea of parties. Syndicalism also believes in direct action. Trade Unionists organise themselves to secure the ownership of the industry in which they work, then gradually a government of the Trade Unionists emerges. Both Connolly and Larkin were aware of this strand in the thought of the American Industrial Workers of the World, and were influenced by it.

The Fourth Category — the Gradualists — the modern Social Democrats believe in achieving socialism through the parliamentary process, by, in Sydney Webb's phrase, "the inevitability of gradualness." I think the best exposition of the dogma of social democracy is still to be found in Bernard Shaw's **The Intelligent Woman's Guide to Socialism, Capitalism, Sovietism and Fascism:** "In the long run you must have your parliament and your settled

5

constitution back again, and the risings and coup d'etat with all
their bloodsheds and burnings and executions might as well have
been cut out as far as the positive and constructive work of
socialism is concerned." Again, "Sooner or later the irreconcil-
ables exterminate one another like the Kilkenny Cats; for when
the toughest faction has exterminated all the other factions, it
proceeds to exterminate itself." Or again Shaw says: "It is far
more likely that by the time nationalisation has become the rule
and private enterprise the exception, Socialism will be spoken of,
if at all, as a crazy religion held by a fanatical sect in that dark-
est age, the Nineteenth Century; and I who said forty years ago
that we should have had Socialism already but for the Socialists,
am quite willing to drop the name Socialist if dropping it will
help me get the thing. What I meant by my jibe at the Socialists
of the 1880's was that nothing is ever done, and much is prevented by people who do not realise that they cannot do everything
at once."

I have dealt at length with the four roads to socialism — the
disciplined party of trained professionals, the anarchist anti-
establishment, the Syndicalist trades unionist, and the gradualist
parliamentarian — for a special reason. Because of our colonial
past, but also because of our nearness to the imperialist heart-
land, all sections of the Labour Movement — even the Labour
Party — has both a revolutionary and a evolutionary past in the
realm of theory. Within almost any Labour Party Dublin branch
you will hear all four ideologies expressed. This is not necessarily
a bad thing but what causes confusion is that there is little if any
attempt to adapt the sacred texts to modern conditions. Too
often the thought of Connolly or Lenin or Trotsky is not a
spring-board but a pair of cement boots. This is what Cabral
means when he says that on the political level our own reality,
no matter how fine and attractive the reality of others, can only
be transformed by detailed knowledge of it.

Take, for example, the quiet but effective way in which the
Labour Party has begun to refer to itself as a "European Social
Democratic Party." There have been no voices raised about
this, no debate, no consideration of the implications. In a vague
sort of way we are led to believe that this is a very good thing,
a slipping off of the old Nationalistic garments. There has been
no mention of the fact that all the modern Social Democratic
parties owe their origin to the triumph of chauvinism in the
First World War situation; that Social Democratic parties have
cheerfully backed imperialistic nationalism in colonial situations,
e.g. Mollet and Algeria. We are also told time after time by
Coalition Europeans, "Seven Days", John Healy, Michael Mc-
Inerney etc., that all the Social Democratic parties have been in
coalitions; that in fact coalition is almost a sacred principle of
social democracy. If we oppose coalition we are narrow Nationalists, Little Irelanders, swimming against the world tide, etc. I
want us, therefore, to take a long hard look at the Brave New

6

World of Social Democracy and see if indeed its record is one which should make us anxious to imitate it.

Frank Parkin, in his excellent book, **Class Inequality And Political Order,** states: "Socialist parties were initially committed to abolishing the system of ownership and rewards of capitalist society, and replacing it with a system based on egalitarian principles. All the major Social Democratic Parties in Western Europe have now abandoned this aim. This process of de-radicalisation has occurred over an extensive period of time, but in most cases the final break with traditional egalitarian socialist doctrines occurred in the 1950's coinciding with the first European taste of affluence." "One implication of this," Parkin says, "is that wherever Social Democrats form the main party of the subordinate class, there is no major political force in society which represents a radical challenge to the reward system of modern capitalism." Indeed, European Social Democracy has taken part in many coalitions with Conservative groups. Ralph Miliband in his book **The State in Capitalist Society** says: "Social democratic ministers have generally been able to achieve little inside these hybrid formations. Far from presenting a threat to the established order, their main function has been to contain their own parties and to persuade them to accept the essentially conservative policies which they themselves have sanctioned. For the most part, participation on this basis has been a trap not a springboard."

Robert Michels in his book **Political Parties** probes for the reasons for revisionism and de-radicalisation within the European Social Democratic Parites. He argues that this is due to the bureaucratisation of the party machine. As the socialist movement grew in numbers the influence of the Party officer grew in importance. He was committed to the routines of organisation rather than to the radicalisation of society. "Those who controlled and prospered by the party machine took a more cautious attitude to social and political change." David Childs in his book on German socialism **From Schumacher to Brandt** states: "The S.P.D. is ruled by a coalition of thoroughly expert, but thoroughly middle class functionaries, managers, professional Lander politicians, and dominated by the federal parliamentary wing . . . Although manual workers make up a majority of ordinary members they find no representation at the top of the Party." Parkin says: "Once the Party has accepted the rules of the parliamentary game, the way is then open for the second phase of de-radicalisation —that brought about by the influx of 'moderate' middle class leaders and cadres. The process then becomes a cumulative one. The greater the inflow of bourgeois recruits the less militant the party becomes so making it even more attractive to those who favour the interpretation of equality along meritocratic and welfare lines. And so on . . ." Here is perhaps the kernel of difference between **socialism,** which is **egalitarian,** and **social democracy,** which is meritocratic. What

7

do we mean by meritocratic? I let Tony Crosland define it. He says in **The Future of Socialism** published in 1956: "The essential thing is that every citizen should have an equal chance — that is his basic democratic right; but provided the start is fair, let there be maximum scope for individual self-advancement. There would be nothing improper in either a high continuous status ladder, or even a distinct class stratification, since opportunities for attaining the highest status or topmost stratum would be genuinely equal."

Basically there is a very wide gulf beween egalitarian social and meritocratic social democracy. The former wants to get rid of privilege — the latter wants to change the rules on how privileges are allocated. Socialism seeks classlessness, Social Democracy is content with class mobility. Socialism wants industrial democracy, Social Democracy is prepared to live with a private-sector dominated economy, provided there is a welfare service safety net. Socialism sees the cause of inequality as the capitalist system — Social Democracy believes it can run the system better than the capitalists.

Let us now look at some figures to see how in fact meritocratic social democracy has been performing. Education must be the escalator in a meritocratic society. Yet in the 1960's these were the percentages of university students of working class origin: Great Britain, 25%; Norway 25%; Sweden, 16%; Denmark, 10%; France and Austria, 8%; Netherlands, 5%; West Germany, 5%. The percentages of working class children doing grammar school courses in the early sixties were: Great Britain, 52%; Sweden, 23%; Netherlands, 19½%; France, 17%, West Germany, 16%. Again, the differentials between unskilled workers and white-collar professionals have increased rather than decreased in the 1960's. In Sweden and in Denmark, there were wider differentials than in the U.S. or Germany. Or look at the percentage of G.N.P. allocated to welfare services. In the 1960's, Sweden was allocating 12.4 %; Denmark, 11.1%; Great Britain, 11%; Norway, 10.3%; West Germany, 16.1%; France, 14.9%.

Perhaps the most dangerous aspect of Social Democratic involvement in coalitions is the tether which this places on affiliated trade unions. The unions are urged to be adult, responsible, and to look to the "national" interest rather than to the class interest. Parkin says about this: "The tendency for underclass leaders in socialist parties or trade unions to redefine their duty as the protection of the national interest obviously undermines their position as class representatives. To withdraw pressure for redistribution in favour of some other abstract principle is to confer an advantage on the dominant class. Clearly in a class — stratified society the very notion of a "National" interest is highly problematic. In terms of income distribution what does not go to the subordinate class goes to the dominant class instead." As Galbraith points out in **The Affluent Society**, pressure

8

to increase G.N.P. has often been used as an alternative to the re-distribution of the national wealth by believers in the merito-cracy. In other words, Don't talk about better slices of the National Cake for the workers; talk instead about baking a big-ger cake so that you can give a bigger share to the workers without letting Rockefeller, Krupps, or Onassis go hungry.

Today the most deadly threat to socialism in Ireland comes not from without the Movement, but from within. It comes from the ultra-democratic, new wave social democrats whose constant battle-cry is "The people have spoken." We will now of course do what they have told us to do — go into Europe, lock up Republicans, accept the meritocracy, etc. Let us examine the case of the ultra-democrats very carefully. One must first see that a politician can take very different views of his role in a liberal-bourgeois democracy. He can see his role as the shaper of public opinion, right out at the front of the herd, trying to steer it in a particular direction. Or he can seek the safe middle of the herd and go where the leaderless majority are heading. The ultra-democrats who are at present claiming to be the leader-ship of the Labour Movement forget that Socialism cannot and must not claim to be a national party representing all the people. Socialists by definition are a sectional party representing the majority Have-nots in society, and, by definition, wishing to abolish the minority Haves. Newspaper owners and columnists, television programmers, bishops, also represent minority in-terests. They have a very good reason for advocating consensus politics because they control the media which produce the con-sensus. Yet the Labour Party's actions since 1969 at least, have been reactions to prodding from newspapers and bishops on issues such as coalition, the North, etc.

Again we are entitled to ask the ultra-democrats this question — what profound or significant or lasting change was ever ini-tiated or brought to fruition by a majority? The Christian re-ligion? The Reformation? The French or Russian Revolutions? The abolition of slavery? The vote for women? Should Larkin have waited for the majority of the Irish people to back him in 1913? Behind the ideology of the ultra-democrats is a profound conservatism. The Civil Rights Movement in the North, street action of any kind, even if non-violent in theory, we are told, are violent in practice because they stir up a reaction of violence from those against whom the protest is aimed. We get the same kind of reaction from coursing and hunt-ting enthusiasts who claim that it is unfair to spoil the sport of the dogs and horses and hunters. Institutionalised violence has received the sacred seal of approval at the ballot box — in time the masters would have had a change of heart. 1916 was unnecessary — in time John Dillon would have persuaded both Carson and England, perhaps because of the legitimate (because blessed by the majority) carnage in Flanders, that Home Rule

9

was permissible. 1913 was doubtless unnecessary because in time William Martin Murphy would have recognised that Larkin was a fine chap to contest the election in North East Dublin, and would have invited him into the confraternity. The ultra-democrat is lavish in spending one commodity — time. Perhaps his prodigality is due to the fact that the time he is spending is not his own. Those who are most keen on cautioning others to wait are usually not the people who are suffering under the disabilities.

But those who most detest the smug establishment Lefties in Leinster House are often their best, if unwitting, accomplices. How many people are there who say "I'd join the Labour Party or Sinn Fein if they really were socialist?" "I'll join them when they say they are . . ." and there follows a string of conditions. There are others who seek the seamless garment of doctrinal purity in the wilderness. In the early days of Christianity there were many zealots who, rather than besoil themselves with contact with the less pure, choose instead to climb their individual pillars in the desert and denounce the world to the empty air. The history of socialism is studded with the pillars of ultra-pure Simon Stylites — perfectly happy to be always right and also seemingly happy to remain ineffective.

There is the profound hatred of our socialist sects that assures victory to the new breed of social democratic organisation man. Laszek Kolakowski, in his profound and moving denunciation of Stalinism, says: "For centuries death by fire was reserved for heretics rather than for pagans and the proscribed books on the Catholic Church's Index are rarely those of non-Catholics. That special merciless hatred which almost every organisation with a political ideology bestows on its heretics, dissidents, apostles or renegades, a hatred surpassing a hundredfold the most violent revulsion felt toward the recognised enemy, is in reality an understandable product of all such social conditions . . . in which a specific political or religious organisation, originally intended by its authors only as a means to an end, becomes an end in itself." In other words we have forgotten that the purpose of our organisations is to achieve socialism, and instead consider them to be ends in themselves, and their immediate triumph over other sects to be more important than furthering socialism. Thus we find we spend more time disrupting the activities of other Left-wing groups than we do fighting the enemy. Hold a meeting on the North in the Mansion House and we will all be there savaging one another. Yet how many of us join Fianna Fail dominated tenants' associations, conservative dominated debating societies, or even trade union meetings. Are we so busy taking in each other's washing that we do not even know where the laundrettes patronised by the uncommitted are situated?

Has our thinking progressed in the last twenty or thirty years? How often do we talk of the masses, the working classes, the

10

workers, as if we were still back in the days of Engels, as if the meritocratic one-hundreth of a revolution had not happened. Take Ireland today and a fairly typical siuation. One factory may contain workers on £18 per week and workers on £60 per week. Rationalisation may produce a situation like this: the boss says to X — "Look, we feel you can handle twice the commodities you do if they are loaded in this way; we are prepared to give you an extra £10 per week for doing it." X hears later that Y, who was paid £20 per week as a loader has been declared redundant. X has a sheaf of H.P. commitments. Is he always ready to declare his solidarity with Y by voting for strike action?

Herbert Marcuse says: "If the worker and his boss enjoy the same television program and visit the same resort places, if the typist is as attractively made-up as the daughter of her employer, if the Negro owns a Cadillac, if they all read the same newspaper, then this assimiliation indicates not the disappearance of classes but the extent to which the needs and satisfactions that serve the preservation of the Establishment are shared by the underlying population." "Indeed", he continues, "in the most highly developed areas of contemporary society the transplantation of social into individual needs is so effective that the difference between them seems to be purely theoretical. Can one really distinguish between the mass media as instruments of information and entertainment, and as agents of manipulation and indoctrination?" Marcuse concludes: "The people recognise themselves in their commodities; they find their soul in their automobile, hi-fi set, split-level house, kitchen equipment. The very mechanism which ties the individual to his society has changed, and social control is enclosed in the new media which it has produced."

Have we, as socialists, done any real research on the subversion of society by affluence? In America the "Hard Hat" workers were amongst the most fervent supporters of the Vietnam War. In England Powellism thrives on the fears of workers enmeshed in higher purchase affluence. In Ireland, the interests of the Northern working-class Catholic and Protestant victims are not foremost in the thoughts of many engaged in tourism and British-owned industries.

We need to know the leverage points if we want to overthrow the existing society. We cannot ignore any form of protest. For example Women's Liberation could have a far more profound effect on overthrowing our present society than any strike Contraception and divorce can force the Establishment in the South into the open. The disciplined action of Sinn Fein or issues such as mining, fisheries and housing action caused more pain to the Establishment than activity on the border. Consider the circumstances leading up to the split in Sinn Fein. We must make the decision on whether action on Southern streets or issues like housing might not be of more assistance to both

11

communities in the North than a string of resolutions condemning the role of the British Army.

The same men who claim to be the real voice of democracy in Ireland, who see our role as the extension of European Social Democracy, are also the men who are causing the most confusion in the North. If you claim to be the voice of majority democracy how can you justify the Unionist Statelet of the North which was imposed upon the geographical entity of Ireland? You can do so by claiming that there are two nations or two states, and thus you can have two majorities. We must differentiate between a state and a nation. We can see the state in Marxist terms as the institutionalised means of coercion of the dominant class, or in liberal terms as simply a legally defined territory. A nation on the other hand, is a human group which identifies as such, has cultural similarities, its own political system, perhaps its own language. We can have a state which contains several nations, eg., Britain which contains the English, Welsh and Scots. We can have a nation divided between states, e.g., the Kurds or the Armenians. We can have a nation without a state, e.g., the Jews before the foundation of Israel.

There are several examples of modern states where different groups co-exist, e.g., Belgium or Yugoslavia. There are clashes between the groups making up the states on matters such as language, religion, etc., but these are not major clashes. There are a number of states which had their statehood imposed upon them, e.g., Nigeria and the Congo. They have been scenes of major conflict, and it is interesting to speculate why the Labour Party spokesman was so keen on smashing Katanga and yet so keen on defending Biafra. Katanga was a classic case of colonial manipulation, but was Biafra free from colonial manipulation?

One can see a whole layer of states where tension between groups was the result of the colonising power's manipulations in trying to maintain its stranglehold. Take the cases of India-Pakistan, Palestine, Cyprus, Algeria and the Congo, where invariably the conflict was fanned by the colonial power. Then there is another layer of states with inbuilt national problems, of which South Africa and Rhodesia are the best examples. What differentiates Belgium and South Africa, or Czecho-Slovakia and Yugoslavia? Is it just numbers? The groups are fairly well balanced in both Belgium and Czecho-Slovakia and Yugoslavia. Is it purely a division between colonist and native? When does one cease to be a colonist and become a native? Both the Boer in South Africa and the planter in Ulster have been there for a longer period than most of the world's states have been in existence. There is one factor absent in the constitution of the Czecho-Slovak, Yugoslav and Belgian states, but present in South Africa and Rhodesia — the assertion of the superiority of one group. If we examine the present status of the Six-County State one finds more similarities to the Rhodesian and South

12

African model than to the Belgian one. There is the difference that within the Six-County area there is a majority — but the doctrine of ascendancy was conceived when the group who fathered Ulster was in a minority. The ascendancy doctrine anywhere in the world has little to do with numbers; it is concerned with holding on to power, both economic and political. What has happened in Ulster is reverse Bantustanisation — withdrawal to the laager.

Now, let's get this one clear, I would be — and I am sure that any Republican or Socialist would be — ready to fight for the rights of conscience of either Catholic or Protestant. In historic terms the Protestant ehtos is more favourable to the growth of socialism as both the thesis of Capitalism and the antithesis of socialism grew out of the Reformation. I think it would be an abmonation to force any Protestant group into a theocratic Catholic republic — and I think the present Irish Republic is such a state. But I feel equally strongly about the principle of Ascendancy — whether it be in Ulster or Rhodesia. Socialism cannot co-exist with 'this principle. The one virus which, whenever it has infected Socialism, always kills or maims it, is Nationalism. In Ireland we have the healthy differeniation between Nationalist and Republican. The Nationalist is the believer in Ascendancy — be he Northern or Southern Catholic, or Northern or Southern Protestant. The Republican in French or Irish history is the assimilationist — he believes in creating new conditions to solve old equations, e.g., Tone's famous definition of an Irishman.

The Two Nations theory, and especially its conclusions, strikes me as being dangerous opportunism. Pandering to Ascendancy nationalism has always lead to disaster for socialism. Remember that the Hitlers, Mussolinis and Mosleys began their careers as socialists. Today, also, it is very easy to involve workers in defence of Ascendancy, e.g., the "Hard-Hats" and poor whites of the States, the White miners of South Africa, the white workers in Rhodesia. Again, not all the South Vietnamese army are conscripts. I would like to ask the believers in the Two Nations theory, and especially those who believe that it should lead to the support of a Northern State, the following questions:

(a) Do they believe that separate development is ever likely to lead to socialism in South Africa or Rhodesia.

(b) Are they supporting separate development in Wales, Scotland and Brittany — why the British and Irish Communist Party? Why the British rather than the British, Irish, Scottish and Welsh Communist Party?

(c) If it is a question of a majority within the boundaries of the state supporting the borders of the state, then why not support Israel and Formosa?

I feel that the hypothesis that all violence in the North is the

13

result of the presence of the British Army is equally wrong. This is not 1920. Violence in the North comes from the imposition of, the reaction to, Ascendancy Orange Nationalism. It was the simple bourgeois civil rights demands which toppled the Unionist Party and opened up the cracks in the structure. It was the return to armed confrontation which facilitated the rise of William Craig and his brigades.

Where does this leave us in the South? I think we do not further the cause of socialism in the South — or the North — by wasting time and energy supporting or rejecting the wish fulfilments or dream fantasies of the S.D.L.P., or the pious "Hear no evil, see no evil, do no evil" conservatism of the Labour Party Establishment. We can profoundly affect the Northern situation by changing the Southern situation.

We can only do this by making a real effort to come together, plan together, at least consent to work for short term objectives together. Stalinist, Trotskyist Independent Socialist thought they could afford the luxury of internecine squabbles in the Weimar Republic. Eventually Hitler united them — in a pile of ashes in the contentration camps.

As Connolly said in 1909: "Now the problem is to find a basis of union on which all these sections who owe allegiance to one or other conception of Socialism may unite. My position is that this union or rapproachement cannot be arrived at by discussing our differences. Let us rather find out and unite upon the things upon which we agree. Once we get together, we will find that our differences are not as insuperable as they appear whilst we are separated. What is necessary first is a simple platform around which to gather . . . As each section has complete confidence in their own doctrines, let them show their confidence by entering an organisation with those who differ from them in methods, and depend upon the development of events to prove the correctness of their position."

BRENDAN SCOTT
January 1973.

14

Brendan Scott
by
Dr. Noel Browne

'It's hard to write about a dead friend — stone crosses, long low lumps of earth, weeds, the perished, once lovely, flowers of withered wreaths — pitiful human artifacts. How trite are words like humane, compassionate, warm, loving life and mankind, unpompous, gentle man, courage in the last agonising months of dying. They are said about nearly anyone who dies, and so are meaningless, except to each of us, privately, who mourn.

Brendan was something more than all these platitudes tell us about any man. Does man, with Beckett, simply "pass the time which would have passed anyway?" With Brendan this could not be said. He was a revolutionary Marxist in the barren political wasteland of this Republic, with its thousands of one-time socialists with nothing but guilty consciences to show for it. Luckily his comrades are of all colours and races who now people one third of the world, a member of a powerful, growing more powerful, wonderful socialist world community — this he never forgot. Heaven forbid that the watching capitalist world could ever learn the truly lethal danger to the revolution of simple ostracism and its loneliness, and the attractive warm cosiness, to the weak in spirit, of the herd; even when simply headed over the next cliff. Such is the simplicity of man's emotions that the romantic murdered revolutionary, fathers a thousand sons to avenge his end. No one mourns the revolutionary who gives up because he cannot wait, ceases to believe any more, or simply cannot stand the awful loneliness and isolation of being only a few, on his own, or seemingly ignored. There is no romance, no anger.

Brendan hated the privileged life of the capitalist world — he hated the vulgarity and the greed of capitalism as a system of organised society, for the pain and misery it meant to so many innocents. Like any good hater — I use that word hate, without reservation, — he did what he could to destroy it. He was the only truly safe socialist revolutionary, soft on the outside, but hate-hard on the inside. He never faltered in his conviction that socialism must come, even to Ireland.

Unlike so many of our intellectually pedestrian doctrinaire imitators, those dogmatic political theologians who have replaced the Roman variety, he built onto his profound knowledge of Marxist Leninism. He knew that socialism must come to Ireland in a way special and unique to Ireland, and that only those who know their Ireland well could help to create it.

15

I loved Brendan as a friend. As a comrade in politics, over the years we met in basements, backrooms, meetings and conference halls all over Ireland. Socialist politics was his tribute, simply to being alive with others with whom he suffered, anywhere men were in distress. He had an original creative mind, and all of this fine talent he related to our Irish needs. He learnt from the successes and failures of socialist revolutions from Moscow to Santiago de Chile. He learnt from the diversity of our comrades' experience through history, that our own struggle would finally succeed or fail because of what we do here, to encourage an understanding as a prelude to a demand for socialism. Each community's socialist struggle supports, compliments and slowly guarantees the other. All that is certain is that we cling to our socialism, we owe this to our comrades everywhere in completing the giant jigsaw of world revolution. Our struggle could be the most difficult of all, a thing of the mind, against the wonderfully well-equipped, well dug-in and resourceful enemy, instead of the much easier and appealing to the romantic, of the bomb and the bullet struggle. Is it not its own tribute to the intricate genius of capitalism in Ireland that socialism should still be so weak here without the help even of a serious Fascist dictatorship.

His, as is the life of each of us, I suppose a tiny thin silken thread, working together and being woven from that part of us all which each of us gives to socialism, into a powerful single rope with which so much can be done, and remains to be done, before our job is finished here.

Brendan's last political act of infinite dignity and characteristic restraint was to decline the unspeakable gaucherie of an invitation by the bureaucrats of the Labour Party, two days before he died, to lift his expulsion so that he could die in that organisation in which these same officials did not consider him fit to live during his lifetime. He could not prevent them from attending his funeral; at last they felt safe from his acid tipped tongue.

We mourn him with Carol Ann and their children, and we are grateful to have known him.

16

Appendix 2

The Labour Party And The North

By Brendan Scott

[Text of type-written, unpublished paper submitted to the Labour Party spokesmen [on Norther Ireland], undated, circa September 1971]

I fully accept the overall strategy of the party and congratulate its spokesmen on their courage and activity. Physical force tactic can only lead to civil war and fascism.

I have reservations on the tactics we are using but I am writing this not as criticism but rather as an attempt to help to achieve the objectives we share. My main reservation is to the tactical wisdom of the frontal attack on Sinn Fein (both streets) while you are trying to carry the party rank and file on a subtle and complex policy.

The dangers I see are as follows:

(a) Irish left-politics, like its episcopal equivalent, has over used the exhortation 'Shun them – have nothing to do with them'. Reaction to this built up the Maoists, the S.L.A. [Socialist Labour Alliance] etc. Better to pose a positive course, expose the opponents weaknesses by forcing them to publicly answer a series of questions.

(b) The danger of the 'Dulles' [John Foster Dulles, USA Secretary of State, 1953-1959] attack i.e. painting our opponent as a monolithic group and by doing so, creating what we picture. Many Irish political activists remind me of chameleons in nostalgic search of a stereotype. We could easily provide them with a mould in which they would happily ossify.

I have nearly two decades of contact in street and cellar politics with people who claim to be Sinn Feiners. I believe that there is not one or even two Sinn Feins but several dozens.

The following are some of the species of the genus Provo:

(i) Political Brando:- an inarticulate, mother-pecked psychotic for whom the gun is a penis substitute. A 'hard man', he will die but not live in the bosom of mother church. At public meetings he bears a shaggy breast and roars that he has not got the power of words of ye shyster politicians but by God he's got the feelings in there (the region slightly above the area where ten pints were recently entombed for Ireland). He is basically anti-political.

(ii) Reversed or mirror image Paisleyite:- Revolver in right hand, rosary beads in left, pioneer pin and Fáinne on breast, chastity belts locked firmly on midriff and mind, he is prepared to 'drive the settlers into the sea'.

(iii) The Green Muslim:- related to the above but has reached his position through despair rather than religious zeal. He is defensive rather than offensive and is group motivated rather than seeking his own salvation.

(iv) Chatterton or 'Marvellous Boy' type:-The Irish version of the Buddhist monk who burns himself. Partly motivated by St. Aloysius symbolism of his schooling and partly by images of Kevin Barry he has his eye fixed on the tombstone, the annual commemoration and the ballad in his honour. Finds it easy to die for Ireland.

(v) The Military Transvestite: Loves the uniforms, flags, parades but as a hobby rather than a profession. Found at the G. P. O. (Dublin) rather than in areas of conflict.

(vi) The Napoleonic Marshall. Feels that in every irregular's knapsack lies a future Pigs and Bacon Commission Chairman's gavel.

(vii) The Fianna Fail apprentice: Give him his chance of a 'national record' and in ten years he will be chairman of a Cumman. [sic].

I feel that the whole of the genus Provo is beyond political redemption. It would be less wearing to conduct dialogue with a platoon of pneumatic drills. To protect against infection it would be necessary to change the education & social systems.

THE GENUS OFFICIAL

Here the position is more complex. There are some near Provos, some traditionalists, but I am convinced that the majority of the rank and file and many of the upper cadres are socialists, near socialists or potential socialists. Among species are:

(i) Cheists or Hoists [sic]:- Watched Vietnam and South American developments. Connected the progress of socialism with nationalism. Willing to experiment with these ideas here.

(ii) French 68ers:- Feel that Dail parties here are corrupt and inactive. Sinn Fein gives them street action and the feeling of being involved in activity in the destruction of the system.

(iii) Czech-ists:- Strong on the role of Imperialism. Would be in C. P. only for suspicion of Russian Imperialism.

(iv) Socialist 'Realists':- Don't defend violence as a positive tactic but feel that neither the Unionists or F. F. will surrender power peacefully.

WHY WE SHOULD DIFFERENTIATE BETWEEN THE PROVOS AND OFFICIALS

After the disasters of the fifties a discredited Republican movement was wide open to new ideas. A group of very bright tough people e. g. Roy Johnston, Tony Caughlin [sic] and others who sat at the feet of the guru Des Greeves [sic] saw in nationalism a dynamo to power the advance of socialism. Events in China, Laos, Vietnam, Africa, the Arab world, Cuba etc. seemed to bear out their analysis. There was a sincere effort to play the game according to Marx's rules and to push the gun well up into the thatch. They didn't behave badly during the civil rights build up. They were not sectarian in the religious war sense and they did not cross the Dail Rubicon.

<u>Why did they fail?</u> (i) After '69 shootings (not started by them) they were accused of leaving the North defenceless. (ii) The Blaney, Haughey, Boland, Kelly promise of guns to the 'Movement' if they reverted to traditional tactics. (iii) Failure to get any type of serious debate or co-operation on even limited issues from parties like ourselves. (Perhaps I am too much of an optimist but I have always felt that it was possible to drag them into realistic politics by the simultaneous use of the carrot of support when they were fighting on social issues like housing and the stick when they 'stunted' as in the E. I. affair).

I think it is the loss of support to the Provos and loss of nerve on the failure to win our support on Housing Action etc which has led to the stupid tactics of the Mogul attack etc.

If we make a frontal global attack on all Sinn Feiners we lose the chance to wean away the younger members from sterile violence, we risk the increase of violent stunting north and south and we may drive the officials into the arms of the Provos.

One Dangerous Possibility

After the death of the 30th or 50th British soldier or a single incident when 15 or 20 British soldiers lost their lives, English public opinion demands a very quick pull out as in Palestine or Cyprus. Provo gunmen (Officials have improvised or are completely discredited) claim to be the victors. Civil War or a splintering into armed enclaves has taken place. As the Provos have no real politics, negotiations are conducted by Boland, Blayney, Conway and Dr. Pill Bin. In this pre or post Civil War situation a Lynchless, Haugheyised southern government can easily be pressurised into making its play for the Sudeten enclaves. Enter the Catholic-Fascist state.

OBJECTIONS AND INITIATIVES AT THE REGIONAL COUNCIL AND CONSTITUENCY "MASS" MEETINGS

These meetings could be dodgy. There is a certain amount of 'Provo' sympathy and a good deal of emotion which needs to be diverted into useful action.

(i) Our main trouble is that while we now function very efficiently at parliamentary level we have never been able to function effectively at the level where the ordinary branch member can feel involved in the action. At this time we need street demonstrations like we need a hole in the head but we could devise collections, secretarial teams, news sheets etc. Some of the suggestions I make later on would involve the activity of quite a number of people, and perhaps keep with us many members who are likely to head for the groups who appear to be active.

(ii) You will be accused that our present policy is too reliant on British initiatives and this will be tied in with the assertion that the British army is the main enemy. Many don't see that the army is an instrument of policy and won't concede that its role changed with the advent of Nautical Nero [Edward Heath] and the exit of James C. [Callaghan] and that its role can be modified most easily by a British initiative.

(iii) The role of N. I. C. R. A., P. D., Derry Labour, Bernadette etc.

I think it is essential that we persuade them to co-operate with the S. D. L. P. in some kind of popular front on peaceful action.

Easier said than done but there is one possibility. If we can persuade the member parties of the Socialist International to send observers who would talk to these groups the pressure of international opinion may force them to co-operate. Such fact finding missions might be also introduced to the Officials who might tone down their force calls in a bid for international sympathy. Recent statements of the C. P. suggest that they are also worried about the way the situation is developing. What are the possibilities of unofficial contacts with Mick O'Riordan to get the Tass [Soviet News Agency] men and other contacts to play along with this.

(iv) The party calls for and assists in the formation of a journal to propose socialist solutions North and South. This journal would have an editorial committee outside of party affiliations e. g. Peadar O'Donnell, George Gilmore, Terence McCaughey, Owen Dudley Edwards. Its space could be open to any group claiming to be socialist and/or to others like Garret [FitzGerald]. One number would carry three or four long articles and the next would be devoted to correspondence on the articles. The journal would be financed by the Trade Unions and distributed by any of the parties who contribute as well as normal channels of distribution. (I doubt if Irish lefties can talk to each other but they might read each other).

(v) An appeal by the party for a New Departure (see page 6) It would be nice if it were accepted – I doubt it – but at least it might help to smoke out the hard liners in each camp and might help to educate our party members in the intransigecies [sic] of other groups.

POSSIBLE OUTCOMES OF PRESENT SITUATION

1. Lengthy Civil War, with or without a British Army presence. In such a situation the Labour Party would be irrelevant.
2. Short Civil War. Won by northern Israel [sic] Arabisation of South. Saudanisation of Labour Party.
3. Short Civil War. Won by Provos. Haughey-Blayney south. Outflow of Prod [Protestant] refugees, world revulsion. Greek colonel type south and ditto north. For Labour same result as 2.
4. Success of security forces in North. Border raids Jack interns. Chaos and Arabisation. See role of T. U.s [trade unions] and Left in Cyprus, Israel and Algeria.
5. Present situation continues but escalates. F. F. Parliamentary Party Putsh [sic]. Enter Blayney, Haughey, Boland and Colonel Boom-id-again O'Malley. Greek or Sudan type government. Labour for Curragh.
6. Tensions increases. Lynch calls an election. Loses. Coalition in power. F. F. in opposition now able to do a soft-shoe Grivas shuffle. Border raids supported by B&B and Hoch-ey. Great pressure for internment. F. G. keen – their supporters even more so. L. P. goes along with this and alienates its support. Resignations from P. P. [Parliamentary Party] within a few weeks. Coalition collapses. F. F. in opposition are able to get rid of Jack. Same solution as 5.

7. Jack negotiates. Gets Nyrere [Julius Nyrere, President of Tanzania] reception. Dev.-Churchill ballet sequence repeated. Jack calls election. Strong pressure on Labour to get under Papas wing in 'national interest.' S. F. campaign that as Coalition would be soft on Britain Jack must be backed. Jack returned with much the same crowd plus several seats picked up from Labour (but not F. G.) (Certain Unions would have had a good excuse for openly backing Charlie and Jack). Jack claims he has now a mandate for internment. Back to fifties.

8. Jack negotiates. Gets some kind of deal with Dead Heat. Captain Kelly and Big Ed. Ride at the head of Jack's band in the north. Back to square one plus the possibility of Prod, [Protestant) Provos.

9. Crisis election leads to F. G. government. Confrontation on historic treaty debate lines. Labour may also be squeezed back into its twenties position.

10. We buy an end to violence by getting a breathing space for Civil Rights campaign. We stress need to prepare the South's legal and social position in order that we can seriously begin dialogue with Unionists. Radical campaign for Civil Rights NORTH & SOUTH has advantage of wrong footing all brands of nationalists plus F. F. & F. G. and for creating the climate necessary for changing the parameters of Irish politics. I think we could only do this if we can get an S. D. L. P. – N. I. C. R. A. popular front.

N. B. WE IGNORE REPUBLICANISM AT OUR PERIL. WE CANNOT IRRADICATE IT BY CONDEMNING IT OR LEGISLATING AGAINST IT BUT WE MIGHT SUBLIMATE IT (is Republicanism the Irish form of sex? Totem and Taboo in search of a couch?

Scenario for the 'New Departure'

1. Appeal to Republicans (emotional – made by Roddy, Dennis [sic] Larkin, George Gilmore? Mick Mullen??? Bernadette??? [sic] President of Congress. Once before the activists stood back to give non-violence a chance. It was a great success. You also would prefer to bring all Irish to-gether. State publicly oh pure souled men of the dynamite that you will postpone the claim for national state for 50 or 25 or 10 or even five years and that you will renounce the use of force for this period (They have been told before the appeal of the other stage of the plan.)

   Harold [Wilson] and Jeremy T. [Thorpe] make approving noises and call for the release of the interned and detained as an answering gesture.

3. [There is no '2'] Pressure backed by Labour Party in Britain for a representative conference on re-organisation of Stormont, British Labour pledge to introduce P. R. Committee to examine Swiss referendum – canton system and adapt it to housing, job allocation, local gov. Such committee to include some of the great populists' e. g. Fr. McDyer, Paisley, Mickey [Mullen], Joe Costello, Craig, Bernadette, Michael Farrell, John McC. etc. Glamourous chairman of this group, e. g. 'Cyprus' Foot [Hugh Foot, last British Governor of Cyprus], Butler, Ted Kennedy, Galbraith.

4. Pressure for removal of discriminating legislation in the South.

5. Committee similar to the one formed in number 3 to supervise thorough arms collection from ALL sections of the community by BRITISH Army.

6. At same time Irish government to ask U. N. to send observer force to supervise our border area.

7. Gradual withdrawal of British army to barracks. Their role taken over by Community Defence Force drawn from Trades Unions and officered by U, N. (Mainly Swedes Dutch and Canadian).

8. Abolition of Special Powers Act, North & South.

9. Trade Unions finance a faculty of Community relations in Coleraine or Queens.

10. Appeal to U. N. E. S. CO [sic] to assist in production of new history and civics text to be used in schools both north and south.

11. Setting up of committee to devise a new system of community inter-denominational schools, both north and south. First steps to be exchange of teachers and then pupils in the present schools.

12. Tourist schemes to encourage northerners to holiday in south and vice versa.

13. Social reconstruction teams (southern Irish and foreign) to aid in physical reconstruction of Belfast and Derry.

14. Establishment of North – South joint T. U. committee on new industries, tourism, etc. organisation of radical priest group (Jack Dowling?) to press for abolition of Ne Temere.

[text missing] <u>COUNCIL AID COMMITTEE FOR THE NORTH</u>

<u>Projects which we might ask the constituencies to subscribe:-</u>

(a) CASE histories of internees, for distribution to British Labour ad T. U. [Trade Union] branches and to European Socialist Organisations. (The appeal to be for funds...resistance) Ditto for political detainees.

(b) Printing and distribution of L. P. [Labour Party], S. D. L. P. and N. I. C. R. A. statements to the same sources as in (a).

(c) Fund to send northern representatives to key centres like Brussels, U. N.

(d) Fund to aid production of handbills, posters, circulars etc. for civil... campaign.

(e) Fund to be administered by Belfast Trades Council to provide assistance for dependants of internees.

(f) Fund to provide legal expenses for detainees.

(g) There is great confusion within the party as to who the various left-wing groups in the north are and what they stand for. Therefore we produce short duplicated accounts to be circulated to each Dublin branch for the information of our members.

(h) Ditto for the various Unionist groups.

(i) Compiling a list of party members who would be willing to give accommodation to a refugee family in the event of a further exodus.

(j)   Contingency plans for relief teams in the event of another mass flight. Each constituency to provide a number of key telephone numbers. Each member, when contacted to be able to provide at short notice a team of five with its own transport, first aid and tea and sandwich-making facilities to assist in transit camps.

(k)   Constituency groups to visit boarding schools in their areas and ask them to take (if necessary the groups finance this) some children who are under nervous strain in the riot areas. Belfast Trades Council to choose the children.

(l)   Each branch takes a street in Belfast, finds out about conditions there, finds funds to support whatever is the most urgent need in the area.

(m) Each branch twins with a branch of the British Labour party and also a branch of one of the European socialist parties and keeps it informed of northern developments.

(n)   Each branch contacts a protestant worker, finances a trip to Dublin and a meeting at which he puts his point of view.

(o)   Each branch to list in order of priority its suggestions for solving the northern crisis. These suggestions to be processed by a committee and the resulting information re-circulated for further discussion.

Appendix 3

The Trial of Richard M. Nixon

By Brendan Scott

[Text of mock trial of USA President Richard M. Nixon, held adjacent to the
USA Embassy, Ballsbridge, Dublin, on 4 October 1970,
during his visit to Ireland]

Judge: I declare this court now open.

Prosecutor: Citizens of Dublin, you are summoned to appear at this open air court before the Silo to act as jury in the trial of Richard Milhaus Nixon, salesman of second-hand ideas, character assassination, the man who once turned the proud office of U.S. Vice President into a lavatory for liberalism. The man who pulled the chain and flushed idealism down the drain and left Spiro Agnew alone floating in the bowl. The current President of the United States - the half way house between L.B.J. and George Wallace.

Why did he come here? Why did Jack Lynch tour the convents? There is an election pending. The sacred strings must be plucked. The Italians, the friends of the Greek Colonels and the militant mums in the Daughters of the Daughters of the Revolution - with sons in the Sixth Fleet - must be whipped into enthusiasm. How can you bring a sentimental tear to the eyes of Mayor Daly's police force? How can you bulldoze your way into the Bronx? How better than a visit to the ould sod - the never-never land of middle class, middle aged nostalgia - the Green island safely Intercontinentalised by the Green Property Company. Who can think of a better obscene joke than to meet your peace-talks stooge in the middle of an Irish Quaker graveyard. Where else in the world could you meet a government of more servile mercenaries. If they could hand over Bantry Bay to Gulf Oil for a world tour, what might they not give for a good C.I.A. grant?

But citizens, remember you are not only the heirs of a gombeen tradition as old as Diarmuid MacMurrough. You are also the heirs of a greater tradition - that of an economically weak but proud nation which struggled to be free. You are the heirs to a people once put to the sword as the Vietnamese people are now being put to the sword. Your ancestral memories are not that of an Imperialist power but of an oppressed subject people. The murderer of Vietnam is walking on the bones of the victims of the same type of war as he is now waging. To-day it is Mai Lai yesterday it was Balbriggan and Bachelor's Walk. Nixon, there is the smell of blood on your hands - the blood of a small nation. Nixon, there is the smell of burning from your clothes - the smell of napalm. Nixon, we remember that smell of blood and that smell of burning. Don't look to us for support, we of all European peoples should remember the smell of Imperialism.

Judge: We don't want sentiment, citizen Prosecutor, we want facts. The Jury want to know what charge you are going to bring against Nixon. What witnesses you will call.

Prosecutor: To avoid sentiment I intend to call only American witnesses - lest anybody should think Vietnamese witnesses prejudiced - though it is hard to see why one should not be prejudiced if one's country is being raped. The first charge we bring against Nixon is that he knowingly and willingly continues to wage a war of aggression against the people of Vietnam. Article 2, Section 4, of the U.N. Charter stipulates that "all members shall refrain in their international relations from the threat or use of force against the territorial integrity or political independence of any state." Article 6 (a) of the Nuremburg Tribunl defines as a crime against peace "planning, preparation, initiation or waging a war of aggression or a war in violation of international treaties, agreements or assurances or participation in a common plan or conspiracy for the accomplishment of any of the foregoing war crimes." The defence will probably plead first that Nixon is saving democracy in Vietnam, and secondly that he is protecting South Vietnam from being taken over by the North. I call my first witness. You were present in Geneva in 1955?

Witness: Yes.

Prosecutor: Did the final Declaration of the Conference state that there should be general elections for the whole country in July 1956, under international supervision?

Witness: Yes, but the U.S. did not want this.

Prosecutor: Just answer the question, please. Did Article 17 (a) prohibit the "introduction into Vietnam of any reinforcements in the form of all types of arms, munitions and other war material such as combat aircraft, naval craft, pieces of ordnance, jet engines, jet weapons and armoured vehicles?

Witness: Yes, but ever since, the U.S. has poured weapons into the country.

Judge: I insist that witnesses confine themselves to straight answers.

Prosecutor: Yes, citizen Judge. I call upon my second witness. You are Ex-President Dwight D. Eisenhower?

Eisenhower: Yes, but please don't ask where I've just come from - as a good Southern gentleman I don't want to have to use the word.

Prosecutor: You know R. M. Nixon?

Eisenhower: Oh, Dickie? Yes, he was my roll of Bronco - the blank paper with which I wiped away my more olfactory political indiscretions.

Prosecutor: Did you write the "Mandate for Change"?

Eisenhower: Well, me and my political caddies did - I put my thumb print on it.

Prosecutor: Would you quote from page 102 please.

Eisenhower: "I have never talked or corresponded with a person knowledgeable in Indochinese affairs who did not agree that had elections been held...possibly eighty per cent of the population would have voted for Ho Chi Minh as their leader rather than Bai Dai.

Prosecutor: Thank you. I now call Donal Duncan. You, Mr. Duncan are the author of "The New Legion". You served in Vietnam and received the Bronze Star for valour, the U.S. Army Silver Star and the U.S. Air Medal, etc.

Duncan: Yes. During the 1964 election when Johnson was asking the people to support his policy - which is now Nixon's policy - I had visual proof that he knew he was talking crap. He was complaining about infiltration from North Vietnam. At the time I was closely involved with an operation where we were infiltrating North Vietnam. Project Delta was initiated for the initial purpose of infiltrating Laos. Project Omega was formed, its duty being to infiltrate teams into Cambodia. They also infiltrated people into Laos and Cambodia from Thailand - a combined CIA and military operation.

Prosecutor: Thank you. Call Peter Martinson from Berkeley, California. Again, a much decorated Vietnam veteran.

Martinson: When I went to Vietnam I was for the Vietnam war. I thought it was an open case of Communist aggression and that the majority of the Vietnamese people wanted us in Vietnam. I developed a small knowledge of Vietnamese and I understood that the Government in Vietnam which states that it supports the Vietnamese people does not really. If this government wants us there the people don't. I know this and the Vietnamese people have told me this.

Prosecutor: Our next charge is that Nixon's forces were launched against the civilian population of Vietnam and Cambodia, which is directly forbidden by the 1923 Convention of the Hague which prescribed "aerial bombings destined to terrorise the population." Again, the Nuremburg Tribunal considers as a war crime "the wanton destruction of cities, towns and villages or devastation not justified by military necessity." The Geneva Convention of 1949 states that "civilian hospitals organised to give care to the wounded and sick, the infirm and maternity cases, may, in no circumstances, be the object of attack. Call our statistician as next witness.

Statistician: In the month of February, 1967, ninety-five hospitals and medical institutions were destroyed. The Quinh Lap leper colony - known throughout the world - was attacked three days running, even though there was a large red cross on top of the hospital. Eighty churches and thirty pagodas were attacked and destroyed in one offensive.

Prosecutor: Call Sergeant J. Weeks of the 1st Infantry Division.

Sergeant Weeks: "Another important thing to realise is when every day, week after week, month after month you hear the bombs, thousand tons a day dropping, the artillery firing all night, you know the bombs are landing in some place and they are not saying 'you are a woman, you are a child' - they're just pulverising everything out of sight."

Prosecutor: Our third charge is that in Vietnam Nixon's troops are using weapons made illegal by international law. The 1925 Geneva Protocol forbids the use of asphyxiating, poisonous or other gases. The U.S. has been using, CN, CS and DM gases in such repeated and massive doses that they become fatal. They are therefore combat gases which come under the prohibitions of international law. Besides gas and defoliants Nixon's air forces use napalm and phosphorus bombs. Our next witness - doctor- will briefly describe their effects.

Doctor: Both napalm and phosphorus inflict unheard of suffering. Phosphorus in particular continues to burn in the skin for many days, and the organism, in absorbing it, undergoes poisoning which damages the liver. Then there are the pineapple and guava bombs. Each bomb contains 300 to 400 smaller bombs. In the smaller ones are about 300 steel pellets. When the mother bomb is exploded more than a hundred thousand pellets are released. They are of little value against military objectives but very effective against civilians caught in the open.

Prosecutor: Re-call Donald Duncan. Donald Duncan, can you tell us about white phosphorus?

Duncan: White phosphorus is standard basic load in all C.I.D.G. camps. The effect on people is devastating and there's a terrible moral issue involved in the use of white phosphorus against personnel. It's extremely painful, painful to the highest degree, essentially because it doesn't stop burning after it gets on the body; it continues to burn until the substance itself has completely dissipated.

Prosecutor: The Geneva Conventions outlaw the torturing of prisoners. The Nuremburg Tribunal adjudged torture a war crime. Everyday torture is practised in Vietnam. Did you witness the use of torture?

Duncan: We used the double E.A. telephone - just a standard Army field set - battery-operated, attaching the lead wires to the genitals for shock. But we were encouraged to use our imagination - the specific thing that was always suggested was that you do not mark a person. In other words don't leave physical evidence on his body.

Prosecutor: Call Peter Martinson again.

Martinson: The Lieutenant kept interrogating him with the field telephone. Then he inserted bamboo splinters under the man's fingernails. This annoyed our field commander because it left marks. Electrical torture does not leave marks. Beating generally does not leave marks, but the use of bamboo was forbidden because it left marks and there was blood. It was understood that if we did not leave marks, we could do exactly as we pleased.

Prosecutor: Call Donald Duncan again.

Duncan: A Lieutenant had a Kabar knife which has a blade on it about nine inches long. The knife was pushed straight through the prisoner's stomach. Then another platoon leader jumped on the prisoner who was now in a state of shock and inserted the knife in the cavity and extracted the gall bladder which he treasured as a trophy.

Prosecutor: The main charge against this man Nixon is the charge that he is still conniving with the main crime of his predecessor - the crime which links them both with Hitler - the crime of genocide. Genocide has only been in the dictionaries for the last twenty-five years, so let's define it. It comes from the Greek peprefix [sic] "geno" meaning race and the suffix "cide" meaning to kill. Its political roots today are imperialism - the stage of capitalism where national or racial groups are oppressed for profit and in racism- the system of white supremacy which justifies the oppression of non-whites on the basis that they are "inferior" or less human.
My first witness on this charge is Sgt. James Weeks.

Sergeant Weeks: In Operation Junction City it was explained to us that anything alive was supposed to be dead. We were told that if we saw a "gook" no matter how big or small we shot first, man, woman and child. At that time men, women and children were all part of the "body count". No preference made at all - the farmer in the field, the girl at the stream. They were all classified as "gooks".

Prosecutor: Call William Witmeyer.

Witmeyer: When you're in a tank the people you're shooting at are not real people, they're dots in your sight - they're just gooks. To the G.I. mind, the gooks are running, they're V.C. Later, the men dismounted from the tanks and counted the bodies. They got a lot of laughs out of that. The slaughtered Vietnamese were all women or men over sixty.

Prosecutor: Call James McLean.

McLean: In classroom training they tell us these gooks are all stupid, it's just a matter of shooting them down. Our Lieutenant told us "when I hear you guys talking about these Vietnamese, I want to hear you calling them gooks, dinks or slopeheads. I don't want to hear you calling them Vietnamese."

Prosecutor: Call Peter Martinson.

Martinson: I remember a helicopter door gunner who liked to kill people on the ground but only after playing with them like a cat plays with a mouse with his machine gun, chasing them around. The Vietnamese hate us also because the whole thing is turning into a big brothel..... we're corrupting the whole country. The money a prostitute in Vietnam can make is 300 dollars a day where the average wage is 30 or 40 dollars a month.

Prosecutor: Call David Tuck.

Tuck: It was common practice that if we received any shots from a village to have what we call a Mad Minute. This means that for one minute everybody could cut loose, tanks, machine guns and everything else into this village.

It was the practice in the 173 Airborne Brigade and in the 25th to cut off the ears of dead Vietnamese to use them as souvenirs. The person who had the most ears was considered Number One VC Killer and also he would get all the free beer and whiskey that he could drink. When we went on our first combat operation our commander, Lt. Col. Saul A. Jackson, gave us what he considered an inspiring speech: He said "I want you to keep the Vietnamese on the run so much and so hard that I want to see Vietnamese blood flowing upon the earth".

Prosecutor: We could go on hour after hour piling on evidence like this, but we will rest our case on what you have already heard. To sum up, let me just quote what International law considers to be war crimes. They include murder, ill-treatment or deportation to slave labour, or for any other purpose, of civilian population; murder or ill-treatment of prisoners of war, killing of hostages, wanton destruction of cities, towns or villages or devastation not justified by military necessity. I want to remind you that the principles of International law recognised in the Judgement of the Nuremburg Tribunal states: "The fact that a person who committed a crime an act which constitutes a crime under International Law acted as Head of State or responsible government official does not relieve him from responsibility under International Law." I therefore ask the supreme penalty against Richard Milhous Nixon. The Prosecution rests.

Judge: Has the Defence anything to say?

Defending Counsel: Yes, my lord. We have indeed. I am not going to even try to plead the truth or untruth of what the prosecution has said. I plead a higher necessity for my client. My client is defending the Western way of life – defending Western Democracy. If Vietnam were to have the right to govern its own destinies today, Watts or Harlem, or Birmingham Alabama may demand those same rights tomorrow. If a war like this is successful in Asia, today, why should Latin America not try it tomorrow? If all those yellow and black and brown men demand the right to reject our guided democracy, what will happen to our economic interests? Our oil, our raw materials must come in large measure from the Third and even the Fourth World. Therefore we must not only have but be seen to have, dominance in those areas over our suppliers. This we have been doing culturally; Hollywood has been a great help, and even more so has television – as you have indeed seen for yourselves here.

But cultural dominance alone will not secure our business interests, or will help us with our population problems or our surplus labour pool. What then must we do? The answer is simple. War is the most labour-intensive industry of our time. The problem is solved; and it makes good sense too. Do you here in your smug little island want to lose this business too? Do you refuse the factories George Colley persuades our war-machine to give you? Who hands over your city to the speculators? Who votes in the government? Will you not vote again for the government which plans to bring you into N.A.T.O. so that your economy may also boom? Surely, citizens, you can see that my client's policies and those of his predecessors in office, are those of the greatest good for the greatest number? What is the population of one small Asian enclave in comparison with the 280 million great U.S. citizens – or with that of the Congo compared with your new about-to-be Federal Europe? It is after all meet [sic] that one man should die for the community. But let me call some witnesses. Call a leader-writer from the Independent Group.

Leader Writer: My name is never known, but I have welcomed Richard Milhous Nixon to Ireland - with a token few words of our ancient language, and fulsome praise in English. I am paid to believe that any opposition to his visit will be from godless athiests in the pay of the Kremlin (or somewhere) and I nearly do believe it myself now. There are the blue tailed flies of our society, and I will brush them away – I and my colleagues - just as we got rid of that Scottish meddler Connolly and the other quack who was fond of illegitimate babies. Course our U.S. Information Service hand-outs are a boon: we can tell you what colour underpants the pilot of "Air Force One" is wearing. Isn't that great?

Defence Counsel: My next witness is a prominent ex-politician from the opposition.

Politician: Just call me Sandiman, friend. I'm rather like Spiro Agnew would be if he had a public school education. I say "Thank God for Vietnam, America. If the Americans were not in Vietnam how could I sleep easy in my bed? And sleeping easy in my bed is a lot more important than the lives of a lot of little yellow heathens who never even heard of Molly McGuire.

Defence Counsel: My next witness. Your Excellency, you are Patrick Hillery, Minister for External Affairs.

Hillery: Well now, I think I am, at least Jack and Maureen say I am, so I must be. You want to know about what I think of the President's visit? Well now, of course I welcome it; at least Jack says I do, and what Jack says I think, I think – I should think, don't you think? Sure every time we have an election here we do the same. I rush up to the Falls to see the Curate's mother - Jack rushes down to the convents to see the Reverend Mothers. So who should think it wrong that Dick should come over here to see ould Mother Ireland? Think of the boys in Chicago weeping with emotion as they club the livin' daylights out of some negroes to honour the traditions of the ould sod. I mean the country, of course, not the President. Sure isn't he a republican of the same kind as Jack and myself?

Defence Counsel: So the leaders of public opinion not only condone but welcome my client. My client is the product of his environment. He doesn't know any better. Call the Historian.

Historian: The crime of murder by government is as American as Apple Pie. Take the students of Kent State University – murdered by the National Guard. The six black workers shot from 2 to 9 times by police in Augusta, Georgia. The history of organised labour in the U.S. is filled with the killings of leaders of the people, by government assassins or by corporation assassins. Take Joe Hill as an example. Or the men whom Nixon forced to jump from windows. Take Malcom X, John F. and Bobby Kennedy, Martin Luther King.

Defence Counsel: Historian, would you tell us something about the doctrine of White Supremacy?

Historian: White supremacy? Vietnam is Asian, Yellow, inferior. What is a Vietnamese death? What does the destruction of a Vietnamese matter? Or the starvation of a Vietnamese child? They are Asian and their lives are cheap. Their homes, their crops, their aspirations are cheap. This is the ideology of White Supremacy.

Defence Counsel: My Lord, need I say more? I am confident that the enlightened self-interest of a true white jury of Irishmen, who are true cousins of my client's Chicago friends, will find Richard Milhous Nixon innocent.

Judge: Before I ask for your verdict gentlemen of the jury, it is my solemn duty to sum up. Let the facts of what is happening in Vietnam speak for themselves. But, I will remind you that we are not trying the American people - the men who have testified before you are also American – we are trying, in the person of this Richard Milhous Nixon, the American Ruling Class, and, because of their welcome for this visit, our own rulers as well. I will read to you the statement of another of those American G.I.'s. He says: "I don't think it gives anybody any great pleasure to say things against their own country. I happen to love the U.S. very much. Things are being done in its name and I must say something. I feel that what we are doing in Vietnam, as horrible and tragic for what it is doing to our society at home. I feel very strongly about this – that we are in fact dangerously close if we have not already arrived at that point, to becoming a military nation that thinks and can only think in military terms."

Have we a duty and a right to try Richard Milhous Nixon? I will quote for you the opinion of John Paul Sartre. "The current genocide is conceived as an answer to people's war and perpetrated in Vietnam not against the Vietnamese alone but against humanity. When a peasant falls in his rice paddy, mowed down by a machine gun, every one of us is hit. The Vietnamese fight for all men the American forces against all. Neither figuratively nor abstractly. And not only because genocide would be a crime universally condemned by International Law, but because little by little the whole human race is being subjected to this genocidal blackmail piled on top of atomic war. This crime carried out every day before the eyes of the world renders all who do not denounce it accomplices of those who commit it, so that we are being degraded to-day for our future enslavement. In this sense, imperialist genocide can only become more complete. The group which the U.S. wants to intimidate and terrorise by way of the Vietnamese nation is the human group in it entirety."

Citizens of the Jury, do you find the defendent Richard Milhous Nixon guilty or not guilty?

[Published originally in the *Irish Socialist,* No. 100, November-December 1970, pp. 7-8]

Appendix 4

Text of Resignation Statement by twenty-three members of the Communist Party of Ireland

17th December 1975

We the undersigned are resigning from the Communist Party of Ireland for the following reasons:

The Communist Party is increasingly moving away from the ideas set out in the programme 'Ireland Her Own' and the Northern equivalent. This perspective was for the building of a broad democratic movement, North and South, as the first step towards a united socialist Ireland. Lip service is being paid to these ideas, but they have in fact now been replaced by an ultra-dogmatic pseudo-ideology, which, while ignoring reality, implies the seizure of power by the Communist Party alone. This idea has been expressed by leading members and culminated in the statement by the General Secretary at the Area Conference that Ireland, 'like Portugal', was in an exceptional situation, and that the only road forward was a non-parliamentary one.

'Democracy' and 'independence' have become dirty words among the dominant section of the leadership. To stand for these is now categorised as 'social democracy' or 'liberalism'. Democracy is categorised as being simply a tactic. In fact the attitudes and statements of many leading members of the Party are irreconcilable with the concept of broad movements provided for in policy statements of the party.

Ideas which were denounced at the 20th and 22nd Congresses of the CPSU for the horrors and crimes committed against the Soviet people which they had led to [sic]are now being put forward in the CPI as 'true Marxism'.

Present policies are leading to complete political bankruptcy in relation to the critical situation in Ireland. Utterly irrelevant, ideal perspectives for new types of state structures, approximating to Soviets, are being seriously put forward as a solution to the situation in the North. Sectarianism is now taking over the CPI rendering real discussion on any major issue ever more difficult.

We believe that Socialism is the highest form of democracy and will extend and develop the democratic rights won by the working class under capitalism. We agree with the statement issued by the Italian and French Communist Parties that freedom of opinion, publication, organisation and opposition must arise under Socialism. We also agree with the type of perspectives put forward in the 'British Road to Socialism', and with the Spanish Communist Party's concept of socialism through democracy.

We believe that socialism can only be achieved through the consent of the majority of the Irish people, and that such consent will only be won for a perspective of Socialism that clearly includes democracy and freedom – including freedom of artistic creation, which the CPI rejected as its 16th National Congress. We are convinced that a Communist Party that does not project such a concept of Socialist Society can only hinder the achievement of the widest unity of class forces, led by the working class, which alone can bring about Socialism in countries of developed capitalism.

Typical of the type of atmosphere which now exists in the CPI is the treatment of the decisions of the 16th Congress in March 1975. An amendment from the Political Committee, recognising two viewpoints on Czechoslovakia in the CPI, was unanimously accepted on the assurance of the Chairman that it would become part of the political resolution. When that resolution was published, a new section, which had not been passed by Congress, and which completely omitted the main points of the NPC amendment, was substituted.

These developments have occurred since 1968 and the invasion of Czechoslovakia. Some leading members refused to accept the decision to oppose the invasion and have devoped [sic] themselves up to the 16th Congress to overturning it. This so-called ideological line sees certain other Communist and left wing parties as enemies. The fight is less and less against imperialism, but against the Chinese Communist Party in the first place, and after that against the Italian, French, Rumanian, Yugoslav and other 'revisionist' parties. This was highlighted in the joint communique issued by the CPI and the CPSU which made no mention of US imperialism while denouncing China. This is presented as internationalism. Real internationalism is support fro [sic] the working class and progressive movements of all countries, in spite of differences.

The Party is relating less and less to the real problems in Ireland. For [text missing] has been made, not by open political debate but through intrigue and rumour, to isolate all those who stood for the original Party programme. This culminated in the organised defeat of the panel for the AC at the Area Congress. These are the same tactics that were used in the Connolly Youth Movement and which have reduced it to a shadow of what it was.

In these circumstances we can see no other way of continuing to put forward the ideas of a Socialism based on the Marxism of James Connolly but to resign and find other means of expression. The whole trend within the Party has been an orientation away from thinking based firmly on Irish condition [sic].

We wish to state that the slander which is being spread that some of us formed a faction before the Area Congress is utterly without foundation. The ways in which we voted prove that. It was only after the Congress that the realisation came to us individually that there was no place in the CPI for us so long as it pursues its present policies.

A Boucher	M Dowling	L Mulready
B Browne	D Fitzgerald	F Murray
G Byrne	J Flood	J McDonnell
P Carmody	G Jeffares	S Nolan
P Clarke	M Jeffares	M O'Reilly
F Collins	J Kelly	N Wayne
B Deasy	M Kelly	E Dillon
J Deasy	P Mew	

Appendix 5

The Common Market - the Socialist Alternative
By Brendan Scott

[Text of hand-written, unpublished speech delivered to unknown body,
undated, circa 1972]

I have been asked by the organisers to talk about the socialist alternatives to the Common Market. In a sense this is like asking a redemptorist father to provide the alternative to sin or the learned Doctor Paisley to provide an alternative to the Papacy. The short answer to the question what is a better alternative for Ireland to the Common Market would be "almost anything".

Yet I suppose it is true to say that the argument used by many pro-marketeers to bolster our entry is, "we don't like the market. We don't think it will do Ireland much good but we have no alternative. To stay out would be much worse than to go in."

So in order to see what are the alternatives to the Common Market, we must look first at what the CM is. Firstly, to describe it as the European Common Market is erroneous, it consists of just six European states. It does not include the very sizable socialist bloc in Eastern Europe nor does it wish to include these countries.

As an organisation, the EEC is best suited to forwarding the interests of its larger members. Lenin, writing long before even the idea was mentioned predicted that monopoly capitalism on an international scale would be the next stage for the development of national capitalism. What brought the market into being was the pressure towards supernational integration by some of the giant firms in key areas. Having outgrown their national markets these firms sought expansion. These giant firms in the car, electronics, computer, aircraft and petro-chemical industries required, in order to maximise their profits, to gain huge markets and mobilise vast amounts of capital. Freedom to take goods and capital across national frontiers, and freedom from the control of national governments. To meet the challenge of the supra-national American firms they had to have the most favourable conditions for international mergers and amalgamations. In the words of Hans von der Groeben an EEC commissioner, the aim of freeing movements of capital from control can be achieved only "if steps are taken to remove the impediments which company and tax laws place on mergers and the acquisition of holdings across the internal frontiers of the Common Market".

In short, for the big firms to grow, state interference from national governments must be cut to a minimum. There must be a return to the hayday of nineteenth-century laissez faire capitalism. The Rome Treaty forbids most forms of government interference with "free" competition; its main purpose is to bring

232

into being uniform conditions of competition so that all firms are treated in the same way, whether they are run by nationals or non-nationals. Governments are forbidden to support national industries and must abandon economic development powers.

"Planning" in EEC terms is essentially planning to enforce uniform conditions. As far back as 1962 Harold Wilson said, "the plain fact is that the whole conception of the Treaty of Rome is anti-planning or at any rate, anti-national planning". "The whole philosophy," he goes on, "of the relevant articles show a dedication to one principle and this is the principle of condition. What planning is contemplated is supranational not national, but it is, planning for the purpose of embracing free competition".

Thus my first point is - the Common Market was not the creation of European workers it was the creation of financiers and monopoly capitalists. Its ideal is not the union of European workers but the creation of a giant laissez faire labour and money basin.

The only advantage which small nations have with regard to trading with bigger ones is the existence of democratic governments with the power to defend their interests. If we join the C.M. we lose the power to impose quotes and tariffs to protect sensitive sectors of our economy. We lose the power to give tax reliefs to keep our capital at home. We lose the power to give state grants to Irish industry. We lose the power to establish new state industries or to sign trade treaties with other countries. We lose the power to prevent Irish savings or capital flowing abroad. We lose the power to prevent non nationals buying Irish land and so go back to the position before the bloody land battles of the last century. As Douglas Jay says, "If Ireland joins the EEC her future will be determined not in Dublin, nor in London, but in Brussels. In the Common Market Ireland would not be an independent country but would simply become one state in a union like Texas or Pennsylvania".

If you accept my argument so far, you will agree that no socialist could abandon an economic framework which allows even the limited amount of state control and state finance we have in exchange for a tiny fistful of chips at a laissez faire roulette wheel. The central core of any socialist system is the ability for state control of economic life. No socialist can willingly abandon this right. Whatever we may have in common with a German or a French worker we have nothing in common with I G Farben, Krupps, or the Union Minière. We cannot as socialists barter a future socialist government's power to control and manipulate our economy for any mess [sic] of Potez.

If the Common Market is a laissez faire super national cartel the socialist alternative or negation is the national democratic state. What do I mean by the national democratic state? I mean by this a state that consistently defends its political and economic independence and fights against imperialism and its military blocs, against military bases on its territory, one that opposes the new forms of colonialism and foreign capital penetration, one that rejects dictatorial and despotic forms of government; one that ensures the people broad democratic rights and freedoms, the opportunity of having land and housing reforms carried into practice.

Thus the socialist alternative is both old and new. Old in the sense that it fits into the long Republican tradition of this country and new in that it means the struggle to change the jerry built state we have into the Workers Republic of James Connolly.

The opposing of CM entry by the demand for a democratic workers state has the additional advantage that it forms a theoretical basis for a united front with other progressive groups fighting against entry like the progressive elements in the Sinn Fein and the C. P. [Communist Party]. Indeed the programme of the CPSU [Communist Party of the Soviet Union] states, "The political basis of a national democracy is a bloc of all progressive patriotic forces fighting to win complete national and broad democracy and to consummate the anti imperialist, anti feudal democratic Revolution.

Besides, the one issue in which the militant Paisleyite sees his class interest as being at one with the workers of the South is in opposition to the market. This does not apply to the Unionist members of Westminster whom Ted Heath is wooing for their pro- market votes. So if we now stand up for the rights of the Irish worker to keep his job, we will be showing to the Belfast industrial worker of the Shankill that we care more for our fellow worker Pope-Head or Prod than does the country gentlemen whom the Unionist Rank and File now elect. By joining the market we make Irish unity much more difficult to achieve because within the market frontiers will become ossified. The only thing we are likely to achieve is to create several more Celtic Rangers punch ups in Hamburg, Rotterdam and Milan. By staying out we expose the real contradiction between Heath's European ambitions and his support for the empty symbols of Orange Unionist domination.

I am sure that many sincere believers in European Union would want to object to my thesis which counterposes the national democratic state to the Common Market. One objection would be, "but most of the socialist parties in Europe support the market". My answer to that is twofold. Sweden, which has a Social Democratic government is so gravely disturbed that she does not want to enter. British, Norweigan, Finnish, Austrian and Swiss socialists are against as are the struggling opposition groups in Spain and Portugal. The second part of my answer is that the European Social Democratic Record in the fight to build socialism is not a very good one. In 1914 they supported their national governments' war policies and earned the scorn of both Connolly and Lenin. Their opposition to the rise of Fascism was also not very effective. Since the last war their record on the freedom of small colonial peoples has been abysmal (eg. Mollet and Suez, the French S.D.s and Algeria and arms sales to South Africa.

Another objection would be that we are too small to go it alone. To this one can point out that the Swiss, the Spaniards, the Austrians, the Finns, the Icelanders and the Portuguese are also small. They do not give into despair. Cuba was a smaller island being strangled in the apron strings of a much bigger financial sugar daddy and she went it alone, as did Yugoslavia, Hong Kong, Singapore and now Malta. Of course this would mean sacrifice on our part. Whether we join or whether we stay out we will suffer. There is no easy, economically safe course for us.

Another objection would be that as socialists we must be internationalists and that now we are falling back on an outmoded narrow nationalism. As socialists we should be internationalists in the sense that we should recognise the brotherhood of workers throughout the world. Does the Common Market and the socialists within it do so? The Common Market discriminates against the agricultural exports of the Third World as indeed does the supra-national American companies. Common Market countries supply the bulk of the hardware of repression to the oppressors of the African and Middle Eastern countries - France is the largest supplier of arms in the world. There has been precious little opposition from the socialist groups within the market. Swedish and Yugoslav socialists have shown far better solidarity with the oppressed of the world and they have done so from outside the market.

I would go even further than this by stating that even if the Common Market were controlled and dominated by socialist parties. I would still be reluctant to advocate joining it. I say this because I have reluctantly had to accept the validity of Marcuse [sic] gloss on Marxism. You will recall that Marcuse expressed extreme pessimism about the likelihood of the working class in the industrialised Western World supporting revolutions in less developed countries. His argument is that much of the high standard of living of Western workers depends upon the exploitation of workers in less developed countries. That in fact the workers wage packet is part of the establishment structure. Let me give some examples American workers - the hard hats - were Johnson's staunchest supporters on Vietnam. A British labour government contemplated selling arms to South Africa. French socialists assisted in the invasion of Egypt when oil supplies were threatened. It would, I think be asking too much of human nature to expect even a socialist centralised common market to worry too much about providing jobs for Irish workers in Ireland when the bulk of their support would come from the iron triangle London - the Ruhr - Milan. Let's illustrate this by an Irish example. Our nationalist bourgeois parties have always paid fanatical lip service to the virtues of the Irish speaking Western sea-board but have they provided more jobs there? Why has Cork got more new industries than Galway?

Which underlines the importance and relevance of Ireland's geographical position in any supra-national model. We exist on the rim of a Europe whose hub is the Franco-Belgian coal field - Ruhr - Milan - Turin industrial complex. Even the most elementary study of geo-economics demonstrates that it does not make economic sense to site industries on the rim. "Why," goes the old question, "is the East coast of Ireland more industrialised than the West?" It may make socialist sense to provide jobs for people where they were born but no Social Democratic government that I have heard of have yet preferred socialist sense to economic logic. Take Clydeside Wales and Derry under Wilson. Brittany under Mollet. Sicily under the Social Democrats.

As part of the socialist alternative I would propound the following axiom - the bigger the economic-political sphere of influence the more neglected the periphery and the collolory [sic] to that axiom the smaller the economic political unit the more influence of the periphery will be felt.

But one cannot of course propose the pure Sinn Fein theory of ourselves alone in this modern world. As Galbraith points out with frightening clarity - capitalism has developed more swiftly than Trades Unionism. Today many international corporations have larger budgets and work forces than national governments. As we saw on a small scale during the Cement dispute it is very difficult for a national trade union to beat an international corporation. The international company can afford to stick out a national strike, even make a profit by black marketing its product from abroad - as Cement Ltd did. To fight this we must try to build up closer links between the T.U.s [Trade Unions] of national states but this cannot replace strong national unions and socialist planning for national areas.

Which brings me to another major consideration. Socialism is not only concerned with national economic control, it is also vitally concerned with democratic rights and the importance of each individual having a say in government. The E.E.C. has a most undemocratic and bureaucratic constitution in which the power rests not with any Parliament or government elected by the people but rather with a commission and officials who are outside the control of any elected authority.

The Rome Treaty established the following bodies a Commission, a Council, a Court and a Parliament. The Commission is the executive and civil service it which has 9 commissions appointed by member governments for 4-year terms. Once appointed they are not responsible to their governments or recallable by them. They can issue <u>decisions</u> which are binding in every respect, <u>recommendations</u> which are binding as to ends but <u>not</u> to means and <u>opinions</u> which are not binding. The Commission is the only body with powers of initiate [sic]. It can make proposals to the Council which cannot initiate proposals. The Commission runs the 6,000 strong Common Market civil service and administrates the multi million dollar budget. One trembles to think that the Irish names mentioned for the Commission were Charlie Haughey and Paddy Hillary [sic]. Remember once they are appointed they are not recallable or answerable to our government.

The Council of Minsiters has one member from each state and there is a weighted voting system. Britain, Germany, Italy and France would have 10 votes each. Belgium and Holland, 5, Ireland, Denmark and Norway, 3 and Lux [sic], 2. That means Ireland would have 3 votes out of 61, which would mean we would be a kind of European equivalent to Frank Sherwin. The proceedings of the Council are confidential. We wouldn't know how our men voted. We could recall them but the decisions of the meeting would still be enforceable in the Irish courts.

The Parliament - which is a kind of expense a/c junket for willing hacks - meets once a year. Its only power is to pass a vote of censure on the Commission by a 2/3 [sic] majority which entails the Commission's resignation. The Court's interpretation of the Rome Treaty override national law and National Supreme Courts.

Thus compared to the E.E.C's political structure Stormount [sic] in its hey-day would be the epitome of dcmocracy and the powers of Basil Brooke would be pitiful compared to that of the Commission. It would be worse than returning to system of 1800.

What is the socialist alternative? As socialists we must also be democrats. We must fight for the right of people to control their destinies and for the answerability of every official and bureaucrat to the people. We must recognise that most important of modern developments the demand for more control by the people for the decentralisation of decision-making for the reduction in scale of the decision making authority. Throughout the world the demand is for more power _to_ the people for more control _by_ the people. In America the young have spearheaded this demand. In France they have taken to the streets for it as they have done and are doing in Derry and Belfast. Tupamaros claim their right as do Clydeside shipyard workers and Gaeltacht workers. American negroes, women's rights, hippies, gay liberation movements all echo the demand for decentralising and their rehumanising the political structure. The Common Market structure is thus running right against the trend of history.

We must counter the control of the Common Market bureaucracy with the demand for small decision making units, for the Yugoslav type worker control.

How can we keep financial [sic] afloat if we don't join. We have already been in a supra-national union 1800-1921. How did we do then? Are we worse off now? Our position between Russia and America - how African states keep afloat. Mintoff in Malta. Castro in Cuba. Yew in Singapore.

CM at present [has] dear food but the logic is cheap food. Gearing our industry to food production [sic]. Third world 250m in Europe but 3,600m outside then cut off from us. Is the North any better off by living in the Common Market with Great Britain for the last 150 years.

To sum up, by entering the Common Market we abandon control of our own economic destiny, we surrender the possibility of socialist national planning we surrender control of our political destiny N and S and we gain in exchange a better income for a handful of big farmers.

By staying out we will have to conquer a 7-8% E.E.C. external tariff which will mean that there will be great hardships to many of our inefficient small capitalist industries. This in turn can lead to intensification of worker militancy and a socialist government. Under socialist government planning in the state our standard of living will be no worse than today and certainly a lot better than it would be inside the E.E.C. and we will be in control of our own destiny. Therefore I submit that the socialist alternative to the E.E.C. is no more or no less revolutionary than the vision of the founder of our party - the Workers Socialist Republic.

The offer of re-admission to the Labour Party
which was declined by Brendan Scott

1/1/17/bd

The Labour Party
20 Earlsfort Terrace Dublin 2
Phone 63445 · Grams 'Labour'

10 September 1973

Mr. Brendan Scott.
8 Sheilmartin Drive,
Sutton,
Co. Dublin.

Dear Brendan,

At a meeting of the Labour Party Officers on Friday
7 September it was proposed by the Chairman R.J.
Connolly and Financial Secretary Donal O'Sullivan that
you be made a member of the Labour Party forthwith.
This proposal was agreed unanimously.

It gives me great personal pleasure to inform you
accordingly and to enclose a Labour Party membership
card for the year 1973.

All the officers hope you will accept this proposal as
a simple expression of their affection and respect for
you.

Best personal regards,

Brendan

Senator Brendan Halligan.
General Secretary.

Appendix 7

Labour Party, fully-stamped 1973 membership card enclosed with letter to Brendan Scott of 10 September 1973 (Appendix 6)

The Labour Party

20 Earlsfort Terrace
Dublin, 2.

Membership Card

Branch _____ No. _____

Name BRENDAN SCOTT.

Address 8 Shielmartin Dr.

Co. Dublin.

Signature _____

Constituency NORTH EAST.

Branch
Secretary _____

Address _____

HEAD OFFICE REGISTRATION 1973

JANUARY	FEBRUARY	MARCH
R LABOUR PARTY	R LABOUR PARTY	R LABOUR PARTY
APRIL	**MAY**	**JUNE**
R LABOUR PARTY	R LABOUR PARTY	R LABOUR PARTY
JULY	**AUGUST**	**SEPTEMBER**
R LABOUR PARTY	R LABOUR PARTY	R LABOUR PARTY
OCTOBER	**NOVEMBER**	**DECEMBER**
R LABOUR PARTY	R LABOUR PARTY	R LABOUR PARTY

Bibliography

Select Published Writings by Brendan Scott

'You Don't Beat Communism by Starting Witch Hunts', *Sunday Independent,* 2 December 1962.

'Congo Hangings', *Irish Times,* 10 June 1966.

'Rhodesia', *Irish Times,* 2 January 1967.

'Olympic Games', *Irish Times,* 9 April 1968.

'Olympic Games', *Irish Times,* 23 April 1968.

'Small 'p'', *Irish Times,* 25 September 1968.

'Press and Apartheid', *Irish Press,* 27 September 1968.

Summary of Lecture on Soviet Education, 5 March 1969, an edited version of which was published in the *Irish Times,* 7 March 1969.

'Housing and Violence', *Crisis,* Bulletin No. 1, March-April 1969.

'Tshombe', *Irish Times,* 14 July 1969.

'Springboks Tour', *Irish Times,* 3 December 1969.

'The Springboks', *Irish Times,* 8 December 1969.

'The Springboks', *Irish Times,* 17 January 1970.

'The Trial of Richard M. Nixon', *Irish Socialist,* No. 100, November-December 1970. [Appendix 3].

'Arms sales to South Africa', *Irish Independent,* 8 January 1971.

'Where Healy Stands', *Irish Times,* 3 August 1971.

Labour and Socialism (Liaison Committee of the Left – Labour Party or LCLL, Dublin, 1973). [Appendix 1].

Select Published Writings in the name of Brendan Scott and Others

'Arms sales to South Africa', *Irish Independent,* 8 January 1971.

'Anti-Apartheid Movement', *Irish Times,* 20 November 1971.

'Asking the Provos to stop bombing', *Nationalist and Leinster Times,* 18 August 1972.

'Dr. Noel Browne', *Irish Times,* 12 February 1973.

Select Unpublished Writings by Brendan Scott
[Brendan Scott Papers]

Steam Power and the factory, hand-written article or talk, undated, circa 1960s.

Changing Patterns in Education, talk, undated, circa 1960s.

The Maze and the New Minotaurs: A "New Left" Look at the Irish Socialists' Dilemma, article or talk, undated, circa 1960s.

Ideologies of the Left, article or talk, undated, circa 1960s.

Marxism in Underdeveloped Economy, text of hand-written article or speech, circa 1960s.

Untitled speech delivered at public meeting on the Vietnam War, Mansion House, Dublin, on 6 May 1968.

Untitled hand-written text of speech on socialism, nationalism, etc., undated, circa late 1960s- early 1970s.

Untitled, text of hand-written article or talk on the challenges for socialists in Ireland and the NICRA, Late circa late 1960s-early 1970s.

The Labour Party and the North, typed submission to Labour Party spokesmen on Northern Ireland, circa September 1971. [Appendix 2].

The Common Market – the Socialist Alternative, text of hand-written talk, undated, circa 1972. [Appendix 5].

The History of Irish Trades Unionism, hand-written text of lecture delivered to ITGWU members, Dublin, circa 1973.

The Union in the Modern World, hand-written text of lecture delivered to ITGWU members, Dublin, circa 1973.

The Price Labour Paid For Coalition, typed article, undated, circa March 1973.

Select Published Writings about Brendan Scott

Asmal, Kadar, 'Brendan Scott: An Appreciation', *Irish Times,* 21 September 1973.

Browne, Noël, 'Brendan Scott', appendix in Brendan Scott, *Labour and Socialism* (Liaison Committee of the Left – Labour Party, Dublin, 1973, pp. 15-16.

Connolly, Roddy, untitled tribute to Brendan Scott at Labour Party Annual Conference, in Cork, on 12 October 1973], *Irish Times,* 13 October 1973.

Devine, Francis, *September Song 1973,* poetical tribute to Brendan Scott, September 2020 (published in Chapter 24 of this volume).

Gahan, Ruarc, 'Brendan Scott: An Appreciation', *Irish Times,* 24 September 1973.

Geraghty, Des [Anon], 'Brendan Scott', *Liberty,* Vol. 28, No. 3, October 1973, p. 12.

Maher, Mary [M.M.], 'Death of Brendan Scott', *Irish Socialist,* No. 131, October 1973, p. 3.

Merrigan, Matt, 'Brendan Scott: An Appreciation', published posthumously in Matt Merrigan, *Eggs and Rashers: Irish Socialist Memories,* edited and introduced by D. R. O'Connor Lysaght (Umiskin Press, Dublin, 2014), pp. 190-191.

Merrigan, Matt, untitled tribute to Brendan Scott in Matt Merrigan, *Eggs and Rashers: Irish Socialist Memories,* edited and introduced by D. R. O'Connor Lysaght (Umiskin Press, Dublin, 2014), p. 115.

Swift, John P., untitled tribute in *John Swift: An Irish Dissident,* (Gill and Macmillan, Dublin, 1991), p. 195.

Labour Movement Records

DTUC, minutes of council meetings.

DTUC, minutes of executive committee meetings.

DTUC, annual reports.

DTUC, minutes of Council of Action's Standing Committee, 2 June 1941 to 24 July 1941.

DCTU, minutes of council meetings.

DCTU, minutes of executive committee meetings.

DCTU, annual reports.

ITUC, annual reports.

CIU, annual reports.

ICTU, Annual reports.

Labour Party, Annual Reports, 1950-1974. [NLI].

Labour Party, Minutes of Executive Board [sic], 1969-1973. [NLI].

Labour Party, Minutes of the Central Council [sic], 1969-1973. [NLI].

Labour Party, Minutes of Party Officers' Meetings, 1971-1973. [NLI].

Labour Party, Minutes of Standing Committee Management, 1967-1973. [NLI].

Labour Party, Minutes of Standing Committee Organisation, 1972-1973. [NLI].

Labour Party, report, recommendations and draft policy document of sub-committee on Industrial democracy, 1968.

Labour Party, *The New Republic* [Address by Brendan Corish, T.D., Leader of the Labour Party at Annual Conference, Liberty Hall, October 1967]. [Niall Greene Papers].

Labour Party, *Labour Party Outline Policy, Annual Conference 24-26 Jan.'69'* (Labour Party, Dublin, 1969) [Swift Papers].

Labour Party, certificate of ballot for chairman, vice-chairman and financial secretary at 1971 annual conference, February 1971.

Labour Party document, Ref. H.O. 74/73 *Organisational and Financial Planning* from Brendan Halligan to AC, 19 April 1973.

Labour Party, Disciplinary Committee, Report to AC, 19 April 1973.

Labour Party, Letter from General Secretary, Senator Brendan Halligan, to Brendan Scott, 10 September 1973. [Brendan Scott Papers].

LCLL, Pat Carroll, Election Address for AC position of the Labour Party, 1971. [Swift Papers].

LCLL, John Swift, Election Address for Chairman of the Labour Party, 1971. [Swift Papers].

LCLL, *Manifesto Liaison of the Left Committee* [sic], 1972. [Brendan Scott Papers].

LCLL, List of candidates, including Brendan Scott, for Vice-Chairman, sponsored by the Liaison Committee of the Left for positions on the Labour Party's Administrative Council, 1972. [Brendan Scott Papers].

LCLL, Submission to Disciplinary Committee, Labour Party, on behalf of twenty-four Liaison Committee of the Left members, 12 April 1973. [Brendan Scott Papers].

Other Records

CSO, estimated net migration, 1927-1986.

CSO, Live Register of unemployment, total live register, 1923-1986.

Dáil Éireann. Parliamentary Debates, vol. 125, col. 668, 12 April 1951; vol. 125, col. 951, 17 April 1951; Vol. 138, Col. 839, 29 April 1953.

Gahan, Ruarc, Sutton Park School: The First Fifteen Tears, a personal memoir, undated, but 1975. [John Medlycott Papers].

College of Industrial Relations, Growth from Strength, unpublished report of the working party to advise the Jesuit Provincial on the future of the College of Industrial Relations, 1 May 1983.

Ireland-USSR Society, minutes of committee meetings. [Angela McQuillan Papers].

Labour Movement and Republican Movement Publications

Action (Labour Party, Sean Heuston Branch).

Civil Service Review (Civil Service Executive Association).

Forward (Connolly Youth Movement).

Irish Labour History News (ILHS).

Irish Socialist (Irish Workers' League-Irish Workers' Party-Communist Party of Ireland).
Labour History News (ILHS).
Labour (Labour Party).
Liaison (Liaison Committee of the Left – Labour Party) [Brendan Scott Papers and Irish Labour History Society Archive].
Liberty (ITGWU).
Newsline (SIPTU).
Obair (ILHS).
Plough (Independent socialist) [ILHS Archive].
Report (WUI).
Saothar (ILHS).
SIPTU Report (SIPTU).
Sound Post (Musicians' Union of Ireland).
Treoraí (Scéim na gCeardcumann).
United Irishman (Sinn Féin and Sinn Féin-The Workers' Party).

Other Publications

*Crisis (*Dublin Housing Action Committee) [Fergal Costello Papers].
Harkin, Nora; McQuillan, Angela; Edwards, Sean; Kavanagh, Brian (Editorial Board), Ireland USSR: 21st Anniversary Ireland-USSR Society 1987 (Ireland-USSR Friendship Society, [sic] Dublin, 1987). [John P. Swift papers].
Irish Anti-Apartheid Movement 1964-1994 (Irish Anti-Apartheid Movement, Dublin, undated, but probably 1994) [Gearóid Kilgallen Papers].
Irish Catholic Directory.
*Report (*Ireland-USSR Society).

National and Local Newspapers and Periodicals

Anglo-Celt	*Irish Independent*	*Sligo Champion*
Ballina Herald	*Irish Press*	*Southern Star*
Connacht Sentinal	*Irish Times*	*Standard*
Dublin Evening Mail	*Leinster Express*	*Sunday Independent*
Evening Echo	*Longford Leader*	*Sunday Press*
Evening Herald	*Monaghan Argus*	*Sunday Tribune*
Evening Press	*Nationalist and Leinster Times*	*This Week*
Hibernia	*Nenagh Guardian*	*United Ireland*
Irish Catholic	*Nusight*	*Western People*
Irish Examiner		

Interviews

In addition to numerous interviews with Eoin Scott, Melanie Scott and Ivan Scott between 2018 and 2020, the following individuals were interviewed by the author:

Susan Boland (née O'Rourke), 7 March 2019.
Frank Buckley, 6 November 2018.
Brendan Byrne, 2 July 2020.
Charles Callan, 28 July 2020.
Pat Carroll, 11 May, 30 October 2018, 24, 25 September 2020.

Aidan Clarke, 14 January 2019.
Fergal Costello, 5 November 2018, 31 October, 20 December 2019, 20 July 2020.
Francis Devine, 23 July 2020.
Michael (Mick) Dowling, 19 and 26 June 2020.
Gerard Duffy, 25 February 2019.
Patsy Duffy (née Burke), 25 February 2019.
Eithne FitzGerald (née Ingolsby), 6 November 2018.
Eric Fleming, 16 and 22 June 2020.
Ita Gannon (née McGrath), 1, 2 July 2020.
Jack Gannon, 30 June, 1, 2 July 2020.
Des Geraghty, 1 May, 6 December 2018, 20 June 2020.
Tom Geraghty, 7 November 2018.
Niall Greene, 16 November 2018, 16 June 2020.
Brendan Halligan, 16 November 2018.
John Horgan, 22 January 2019.
Máirín Johnston (née Mooney), 30 October 2018, 12 February, 31 October 2019, 24 September 2020.
Gearóid Kilgallan, 24 July 2018.
Raynor Lysaght, 20 January 2019.
Kieran Jack McGinley, 1 August 2020.
Catherine McGuinness (née Ellis), 11 June 2019.
John Medlycott, 1, 22 November 2018, 29 January 2020.
Bob Mitchell, 9 February 2019.
David Neligan, 24 May 2018.
Sam Nolan, 24 May 2018, 20 December 2019.
Michael (Mick) O'Reilly, 24 May 2018, 16 December 2019, 24 September 2020.
Pádraig Ó Snodaigh, 3 December 2018, 11 June 2020.
Dermot Quish, 12 November 2018.
Mary Sealy (née Simms), 27 January 2019.
Yseult Thornley, 1, 19 February 2019.
Julian Walton, 23 January 2019.
Michael Williams, 10 December 2018.

Select Books, Pamphlets and Articles

Allen, Kieran, *Fianna Fáil And Irish Labour, 1926 To The Present* (Pluto Press, London, 1997).
Anon, 'The Blessing and Official Opening of the New Liberty Hall', *Liberty,* May 1965.
Anon, 'Bobbie Edwards', *Irish Socialist,* No. 305, December 1988.
Anon, 'Labour politician who had life-long commitment to social justice: Brendan Halligan', *Irish Times,* 15 August 2020.
Bacik, Ivana, 'Labour and the Liberal Agenda', Paul Daly, Rónán O'Brien, Paul Rouse (Editors), *Making the Difference?* (Collins Press, Cork, 2012).
Bergin, Paddy, 'Ruaidhrí Roberts', *Saothar* 12, 1987 (ILHS, Dublin, 1987).
Bolster, Evelyn, *The Knights of St Columbanus* (Gill and Macmillan, Dublin, 1979).
Bonass, Des, 'Des Bonass: The Matt Merrigan I Knew', in Des Derwin, 'Memories of 'A Marvellous Legacy': Matt Merrigan, 1921-2000', Francis

Devine and Kieran Jack McGinley (Editors), *Left Lives in Twentieth Century Ireland*, Volume 2 (Umiskin Press, Dublin, 2019).

Boyd, Andrew, *The Rise of the Irish Trade Unions 1729-1970 (Anvil Books,* Dublin, 1972).

Boyle, John W., *The Irish Labor Movement in the Nineteenth Century* (Catholic University of America Press, Washington, 1988).

Breathnach, Niamh, 'Norah O'Neill', *Saothar* 28, 2003 (ILHS, Dublin, 2003).

Brown, Michael, *The Irish Enlightenment* (Harvard University Press, Cambridge Massachusetts and London, 2016).

Brown, Tony, 'Ambition to Serve', *Saothar* 43, 2018 (ILHS, Dublin, 2018).

Brown, Tony, 'Brendan Corish on Social Welfare, Combating Poverty and Social Inclusion', in Francis Devine & Kieran Jack McGinley (Editors), *Left Lives in Twentieth Century Ireland*, Volume 2 (Umiskin Press, Dublin, 2019).

Browne, Noël, *Against the Tide* (Gill and Macmillan, Dublin, 1986).

Browne, Noël, 'Brendan Scott', appendix in Brendan Scott, *Labour and Socialism* (Liaison Committee of the Left, Dublin, undated, 1973).

Byers, Seán, *Seán Murray: Marxist-Leninist and Irish Socialist Republican* (Irish Academic Press, Sallins, County Kildare, 2015).

Byers, Seán & Devine, Francis, *William Walker 1870-1918: Belfast Labour Unionist Centenary Essays* (Umiskin Press, Dublin, 2018).

Callan, Charles, *Painters in Union* (Watchword, Dublin, 2008).

Callan, Charles, 'We got it for everybody': the Irish National Painters' and Decorators' Trade Union and the 40-hour-week strike of 1964', *Saothar* 30, 2005 (ILHS, Dublin, 2005.

Callan, Charles, *50th Anniversary 40-Hour, 5-Day week Building Workers' Strike, 18th August –19th October 1964 (Irish National Painters' & Decorators' Craft Group – SIPTU & ICTU Construction Industry Committee, Dublin, 2014).*

Callan, Charles and Desmond, Barry, *Irish Labour Lives: A Biographical Dictionary of Irish Labour Party Deputies, Senators, MPs and MEPs* (Watchword, Dublin, 2010).

Callanan, Brian, *Jim Kemmy, stonemason, trade unionist, politician, historian* (Liffey Press, Dublin, 2011).

Cody, Seamus, 'May Day in Dublin, 1890 to the Present', *Saothar* 5 (ILHS, Dublin, 1979).

Cody, Seamus; O'Dowd, John, Rigney, Peter, *The Parliament of Labour: 100 Years of the Dublin Council of Trade Unions* (Dublin Council of Trade Unions, Dublin, 1986).

Collins, Stephen, *The Cosgrave Legacy* (Blackwater Press, Dublin, 1996).

Coolahan, John, *The ASTI and Post-primary Education in Ireland, 1909-1984* (Association of Secondary Teachers in Ireland, Dublin, 1984).

Cooney, John, 'Michael Sweetman', *Sunday Tribune,* 27 October 1996.

Cooney, John, *John Charles McQuaid – Ruler of Catholic Ireland* (O'Brien Press, Dublin, 1999).

Corish, Brendan, *The New Republic* [Address to 1967 Labour Party Annual Conference] (Labour Party, Dublin, 1967).

Cronin, Mike, *The Blueshirts and Irish Politics* (Four Courts Press, Dublin, 1997).

Cullen, Louis, 'Six Generations', *RTÉ Guide,* 26 September 1969.

Cullen, L. M. [Louis] *Six Generations: Life and Work in Ireland from 1790, Based on R. T. É Television Series* (Mercier Press, Cork, 1970).

Cullen Owens, Rosemary, *Smashing Times: A History of the Irish Women's Suffrage Movement 1889-1922* (Attic Press, Dublin, 1984).

Cullen Owens, Rosemary, *Louie Bennett* (Cork University Press, Cork, 2001).

Cullinane, Liam, 'A Happy Blend'?: Irish republicanism, political violence and social agitation, 1962-69', *Saothar* 35, 2010.

Cunningham, John, *Unlikely Radicals: Irish Post-Primary Teachers and the ASTI, 1909-2009* (Cork University Press, Cork, 2009).

Curran, Owen A., *Two Hundred Years of Trade Unionism 1809-2009* (Irish Print Group, SIPTU, Dublin, 2009).

Curtis, Maurice, *The Splendid Cause: The Catholic Action Movement In Ireland In The Twentieth Century* (Original Writing Ltd., Dublin, 2008).

Curtis, Maurice, *A Challenge To Democracy: Militant Catholicism In Modern Ireland* (The History Press, Ireland, Dublin, 2010).

Daly, Paul; O'Brien, Rónán and Rouse, Paul (Editors) *Making the Difference?: The Irish Labour Party 1912-2012* (Collins Press, Cork, 2012).

D'Arcy, Fergus A., 'The Irish Trade Union Movement in the Nineteenth Century', Donal Nevin (Editor), *Trade Union Century* (Mercier Press, Cork, in association with the Irish Congress of Trade Unions and Radio Telefís Éireann, 1994).

D'Arcy, Fergus A. and Hannigan, Ken (Editors), *Workers' in Union* (Stationery Office, Dublin, 1988).

Deasy, Joseph [Joe], *Fiery Cross: The Story of Jim Larkin* (New Books, Dublin, 1963).

Deasy, Joe, 'Noel Browne', *Saothar* 22, 1997.

Derwin, Des, 'Memories of 'A Marvellous Legacy': Matt Merrigan, 1922-2000, in Francis Devine & Kieran Jack McGinley (Editors), *Left Lives in Twentieth Century Ireland*, Volume 2 (Umiskin Press, Dublin, 2019).

Desmond, Barry, *Finally and in Conclusion – A Political Memoir* (New Island, Dublin, 2000).

Desmond, Barry, *No Workers' Republic: Reflections on Labour and Ireland, 1913-1967* (Watchword, Dublin, 2009).

Devine, Francis, 'Socialist trade unionist: Matt Merrigan's political formation', *Saothar* 12, 1987.

Devine, Francis, 'A Dangerous Agitator': John Swift, 1896-1990, Socialist, Trade Unionist, Secularist, Internationalist, Labour Historian', *Saothar* 15, 1990 (ILHS, Dublin, 1990).

Devine, Francis, 'Paddy Bergin', *Saothar* 16, 1991 (ILHS, Dublin, 1991).

Devine, Francis, 'Trade Union Records in the Registry of Friendly Societies, Dublin, and the National Archives', *Saothar* 19, 1994 (ILHS, Dublin, 1994).

Devine, Francis, 'George Jeffares', *Saothar* 20, 1995 (ILHS, Dublin, 1995).

Devine, Francis (Compiler and Editor), *Acting for the Actors: Dermot Doolan and the Organisation of Irish Actors and Performing Artists, 1947-1985* (ILHS, Dublin, 1997).

Devine, Francis, 'Jim Kemmy', *Saothar* 22, 1997 (ILHS, Dublin, 1997).

Devine, Francis, 'J. W. Boyle', *Saothar* 24, 1999 (ILHS, Dublin, 1999).

Devine, Francis, 'Micheál O'Riordan', *Saothar* 31, 2006 (ILHS, Dublin, 2006).

Devine, Francis, 'John de Courcy Ireland', *Saothar* 31, 2006 (ILHS, Dublin, 2006).

Devine, Francis, 'Hugh Geraghty', *Saothar* 32, 2007 (ILHS, Dublin, 2007).

Devine, Francis (Compiler and Editor), *Understanding Social Justice: Paddy Cardiff and the Discipline of Trade Unionism* (ILHS, Dublin, 2008).

Devine, Francis, 'Make way for the Incomparable Luke Kelly', *Sound Post,* Vol. 6, No. 4, Winter 2008.

Devine, Francis, *Organising History: A Centenary of SIPTU 1909-*2009 (Gill and Macmillan, Dublin, 2009).

Devine, Francis, 'Justin Keating', *Saothar* 35, 2010 (ILHS, Dublin, 2010).

Devine, Francis, *A Unique Association: A History of the Medical Laboratory Scientists' Association 1961-2011* (Medical Laboratory Scientists' Association, Dublin, 2012).

Devine, Francis, 'Andrew Boyd (1921-2011)', *Saothar* 37, 2012 (ILHS, Dublin, 2012).

Devine, Francis, 'Joe Deasy (1922-2013)', *Saothar* 38, 2013 (ILHS, Dublin, 2013).

Devine, Francis, 'Donal Nevin (1924-2012)', *Saothar* 39, 2014 (ILHS, Dublin, 2014).

Devine, Francis, 'The Catholic Workers' College: Some Data From 1951-1961', *Saothar* 40, 2015 (ILHS, Dublin, 2015).

Devine, Francis, *Communicating the Union: A History of the Communications Workers' Union* (CWU, Dublin, 2015).

Devine, Francis, 'Paddy Behan (1938-2016)', *Saothar* 42, 2017 (ILHS, Dublin, 2017).

Devine, Francis, 'John Carroll (1925-2018) Trade Unionist', *Saothar* 44, 2019 (ILHS, Dublin, 2019).

Devine, Francis, 'Dermot Doolan (1926-2019)', *Sound Post,* Vol. 17, No. 4, Winter 2019.

Devine, Francis, 'Dermot Doolan (1926-2019) Trade Unionist', *Saothar* 45, 2020 (ILHS, Dublin, 2020).

Devine, Francis; Lane, Fintan and Puirséil, Niamh (Editors), *Essays in Irish Labour History: A Festschrift for Elizabeth and John W. Boyle* (Irish Academic Press, Dublin, 2008).

Devine, Francis and McGinley, Kieran Jack (Editors), *Left Lives in Twentieth Century Ireland,* Volume 1 (Umiskin Press, Dublin 2017).

Devine, Francis and McGinley, Kieran Jack (Editors), *Left Lives in Twentieth Century Ireland,* Volume 2 (Umiskin Press, Dublin 2019).

Devine Francis & Smethurst, John B. (Compilers), *Historical Directory of Trade Unions in Ireland* (ILHS/Working Class Movement Library, Dublin/Salford, 2017).

Devine, Francis & Smylie, Patrick (Editors), *Left Lives in Twentieth Century Ireland – Communist Lives,* Volume 3 (Umiskin Press, Dublin, 2020).

Devlin, Paddy, *Straight Left – An Autobiography* (Belfast, 1993).

Downey, James, *In My Own Time: Inside Irish Politics and Society* (Gill and Macmillan, Dublin, 2009).

Dunne, Tony, 'Veteran Activist who didn't suffer fools gladly', *Liberty,* Vol. 17, No. 1, February 2018.

Dunne, Tony, 'Bernard Browne (1944-2017) SIPTU', *Saothar* 44, 2019 (ILHS, Dublin, 2019).

Edwards, Frank, 'Frank Edwards: Lieut. Waterford City Battalion IRA Sergt. XV International Brigade, Spain', interviewed by Uinseann MacEoin (Editor), *Survivors* (Argenta Publications, Dublin, 1980).

Edwards, Ruth Dudley *James Connolly* (Gill and Macmillan, Dublin, 1981).

Elliott, Marianne, *Wolfe Tone: Prophet of Irish Independence* (Yale University Press, New Haven and London, 1989).

Finlay, Fergus, *Snakes and Ladders* (New Island Books, Dublin, 1998).

Fox, R.M., *Jim Larkin: The Rise of the Underman*, London, 1957).

Fox, R.M., *Louie Bennett: Her Life and Times* (Talbot Press, Dublin, 1958).

Fuller, Louise, *Irish Catholicism Since 1950: The Undoing of a Culture* (Gill and Macmillan, Dublin, 2002).

Gahan, Ruarc, *Sutton Park School: The First Fifteen Years, a personal memoir*, undated, 1975. [John Medlycott Papers].

Gallagher Michael, *The Irish Labour Party in transition 1957-82* (Gill and Macmillan, Dublin, 1982).

Gannon, Jack, 'Why the Labour Party is Against Coalition: A Reply to Dr. Noel Browne', *Irish Socialist*, No. 81, October 1968.

Gaughan, J. Anthony, *Thomas Johnson* (Kingdom Books, Dublin, 1980).

Gaughan, J. Anthony, *Olivia Mary Taaffe 1832-1918: Foundress of St. Joseph's Young Priests Society* (Kindgom Books, Dublin, 1995).

Geraghty, Des, *Luke Kelly – A Memoir* (Basement Press, Dublin, 1994).

Geraghty, Hugh, *William Partridge and his times (1874-1917)* (Curlew Press, Dublin, 2003).

Gilmore, Eamon, *Leading Lights: People Who've Inspired Me* (Liberty Press, Dublin, 2010).

Gilmore, George, *The Republican Congress 1934* (Dochas Co-Op. Society, Dublin, undated, circa 1970.

Greaves, C. Desmond, *The Life and Times of James Connolly* (Lawrence and Wishart, London, 1961).

Greaves, C. Desmond, *The Irish Transport and General Workers' Union: The Formative Years, 1909-1923* (Gill and Macmillan, Dublin, 1982).

Greene, Niall, 'The Administrative Committee of the Labour Party in the 1960s', in Francis Devine & Kieran Jack McGinley (Editors), *Left Lives in Twentieth Century Ireland*, Volume 2 (Umiskin Press, Dublin, 2019).

Halligan, Brendan (Editor), *The Brendan Corish Seminar Proceedings* (Scáthán Publications, Dublin, 2006).

Halligan, Brendan, 'Michael O'Leary', *Saothar* 31, 2006 (ILHS, Dublin, 2006).

Halligan, Brendan, 'A Noble Adventure': The New Republic Speech in Retrospect', in Francis Devine & Kieran Jack McGinley (Editors), *Left Lives in Twentieth Century Ireland*, Volume 2, op. cit.

Hanley, Brian, 'The IRA and Trade Unionism, 1922-72', in Francis Devine, Fintan Lane and Niamh Puirséil (Editors), *Essays in Irish Labour History: A Festschrift for Elizabeth and John W. Boyle* (Irish Academic Press, Dublin, 2008).

Hanley, Brian, 'The needs of the people': the IRA considers its future, 1967-68', *Saothar* 38, 2013.

Hanley, Brian, 'We mourn our brothers…': Workers respond to Bloody Sunday and the conflict in Northern Ireland 1969-72', *Saothar* 42, 2017 (ILHS, Dublin, 2017).

Hanley, Brian, 'The Impact of the Troubles on the Republic of Ireland 1968-79, Boiling Volcano', *Saothar* 44, 2019 (ILHS, Dublin, 2019).

Hanley, Brian and Millar, Scott, *The Lost Revolution: The Story of the Official IRA and the Workers' Party* (Penguin Ireland, Dublin, 2009).

Hannigan, Ken, 'British Based Unions in Ireland: Building Workers and the Split in Congress', *Saothar* 7, 1981 (ILHS, Dublin, 1981).

Hazelkorn, Ellen, 'The Social and Political Views of Louie Bennett 1870-1956', *Saothar* 13, 1988 (ILHS, Dublin, 1988).

Heney, Michael, *The Arms Crisis of 1970: The Plot that Never Was* (Apollo, London, 2020).

Heron, Marianne, *Sheila Conroy: Fighting Spirit* (Attic Press, Dublin, 1993).

Higgins, Michael D. (MHD), 'John Swift - An Appreciation', *Irish Times*, 16 April 1990.

Hoar, Adrian, *In Green and Red: The Lives of Frank Ryan* (Brandon, Dingle, County Kerry, 2004).

Horgan, John, *Labour: The Price of Power* (Gill and Macmillan, Dublin, 1986).

Horgan, John, *Noël Browne: Passionate Outsider,* (Gill and Macmillan, Dublin, 2000).

Horne, John, 'Charles McCarthy', *Saothar* 12, 1987.

Johnston, Andy; Larragy, James; McWilliams, Edward, *Connolly: A Marxist Analysis* (Dublin, 1990).

Johnston, Roy H. W., *Century of Endeavour: A Biographical & Autobiographical View Of The Twentieth Century In Ireland* (Tyndall Publications, Carlow in association with Lilliput Press, Dublin, 2003).

Jones, Mary, *These Obstreperous Lassies, A History of the Irish Women Workers' Union* (Gill and Macmillan, Dublin, 1988).

Jordan, Anthony J., *To Laugh or to Weep: A Biography of Conor Cruise O'Brien* (Blackwater Press, Dublin, 1994).

Kearney, Ben, 'Matt Merrigan', *Saothar* 25, 2000 (ILHS, Dublin, 2000).

Keating, Justin, edited by Barbara Hussey and Anna Kealy, *Nothing is written in Stone: The Notebooks of Justin Keating* (Lilliput Press, Dublin, 2017).

Kenny, Brian, *Joe Deasy: A Life on the Left* (Hugh Geraghty–Crumlin, Drimnagh, Walkinstown Branch, Labour Party, Dublin, 2009).

Kenny, Brian, *Sam Nolan: A Long March on the Left* (Brian Kenny in association with Personal History Publishing, Dublin, 2010).

Kenny, Brian, 'A Long March: Sam Nolan, 1930-' in Francis Devine & Kieran Jack McGinley (Editors), *Left Lives in Twentieth Century Ireland*, Volume 2 (Umiskin Press, Dublin, 2019).

Keogh, Dermot and McCarthy, Andrew, 'Limerick Boycott, 1904: Anti-Semitism in Ireland' (Mercier Press, Cork, 2005).

Keoghan, Frank; O'Donnell, Ruan; Quinn, Michael (Editors), *A Festschrift For Anthony Coughlan: essays on sovereignty and democracy* (Iontas Press, Maynooth, County Kildare, 2018).

Keohane, Leo, *Captain Jack White: Imperialism, Anarchism & The Irish Citizen Army* (Merrion Press, Newbridge, County Kildare, 2014).

Kilmurray, E., 'Joe Deasy: Evolution of an Irish Marxist 1941-50', *Saothar* 13, 1988.

Lane, Fintan, *The Origins of Modern Irish Socialism 1881-1896* (Cork University Press, Cork, 1998).

Larkin, Emmet, *James Larkin-Irish Labour Leader 1876-1947* (Rutledge and Keegan Paul, London, 1965).

Larkin, Jim, *In the Footsteps of Big Jim: A family Biography* (Blackwater Press, Dublin, 1996).

Lee, J.J., *Ireland 1912-1985 Politics and Society* (Cambridge University Press, Cambridge, 1989).

Levenson, Samuel, *James Connolly: A Biography* (Martin, Brian & O'Keeffe, London, 1973).

Logan, John (Editor), *Teachers' Union: The TUI and its forerunners 1899-1994* (A. & A. Farmer, Dublin, 1999).

Lynch, Gilbert, *The Life and Times of Gilbert Lynch*, edited by Aindrias Ó Cathasaigh, *Studies in Irish Labour History* 13, 2011 (ILHS, Dublin 2011).

Lyons, F.S.L., *Ireland Since the Famine* (Weidenfeld and Nicolson, London, 1971).

MacBride, Seán, 'Sean MacBride', interviewed by Uinseann MacEoin (Editor), *Survivors* (Argenta Publications, Dublin, 1980).

MacEoin, Uinseann (Editor), *Survivors* (Argenta Publications, Dublin, 1980).

Madden, Gerard, 'Bishop Michael Browne of Galway and Anti-Communism, 1937-1976', *Saothar* 39, 2014.

Maguire, Martin, *Servants To The Public: A History of the Local Government and Public Services Union 1901-1990* (IPA, Dublin, 1998).

Maguire, Martin, *Scientific Service: A History of the Union of Professional and Technical Civil Servants 1920-1990* (IPA, Dublin, 2010).

McCabe, Anton, 'The Stormy Petrel Of The Transport Workers': Peadar O'Donnell, Trade Unionist, 1917-1920', *Saothar* 19, 1994 (ILHS, Dublin, 1994).

McCabe, Conor, 'Someone Who'll Carry On The Fight When I'm Gone', Michael O'Riordan, 1917-2006, in Francis Devine and Patrick Smylie (Editors), *Left Lives in Twentieth Century Ireland – Communist Lives*, Volume 3 (Umiskin Press, Dublin, 2020).

McCabe, Conor, 'John Throne (1944-2019) Marxist, activist, writer', *Saothar* 45, 2020 (ILHS, Dublin, 2020).

McCamley, Bill, *Dennis Dennehy – Socialist Agitator* (Labour History Workshop, Dublin, 1985).

McCartan, Eugene, 'Tom Redmond', *Saothar* 41, 2016 (ILHS, Dublin, 2016).

McCarthy, Charles, *The Decade of Upheaval: Irish Trade Unions in the Nineteen Sixties* (IPA, Dublin, 1973).

McCarthy, Charles, *Trade Unions in Ireland 1894-1960* (Institute of Public Administration, Dublin, 1977).

McCarthy, Charles, 'The Impact of Larkinism on the Irish Working Class', *Saothar* 4, 1978 (ILHS, Dublin, 1978).

McGarry, Fearghal, 'Catholics First and Politicians Afterwards: The Labour Party and the Workers' Republic, 1936-1939', *Saothar* 25, 2000 (ILHS, Dublin, 2000).

McGarry, Fearghal, *Frank Ryan* (Historical Association of Ireland, Dublin, 2002).

McGinley, Dr. Jack (Editor), *Dear Comrade SIPTU 1990-2010* (Watchword, Dublin, 2010).

McGinley, Kieran Jack (Editor), *Cluskey: The Conscience of Labour* (Uimskin Press, Dublin, 2015).

McGinley, Kieran Jack, 'Frank Cluskey – A Man of Principle', in Francis Devine and Kieran Jack McGinley (Editors), *Left Lives in Twentieth Century Ireland*, Volume 1(Umiskin Press, Dublin, 2017).

McGonagle, Owen, *Stephen McGonagle: Ombudsman, Trade Unionist, Senator* (Umiskin Press, Dublin, 2018).

Maguire, Charlie, 'Roddy Connolly and the Workers' Party of Ireland in 1926', *Saothar* 30, 2005 (ILHS, Dublin, 2005).

McGuire, Charles, *Roddy Connolly and the Struggle for Socialism in Ireland* (Cork University Press, Cork, 2008).

McGuire, Charlie, 'Builders of Ireland's First Communist Party: Roddy Connolly, 1901-1980, and Seán McLoughlin, 1895-1960', in Francis Devine and Patrick Smylie (Editors), *Left Lives in Twentieth Century Ireland – Communist Lives,* Volume 3 (Umiskin Press, Dublin, 2020).

McInerney, Michael, *Peadar O'Donnell: Irish Social Rebel* (O'Brien Press, Dublin, 1974).

McInerney, Michael, 'A Lifetime in the Service of Labour' [John Swift], *Irish Times,* 31 July 1975.

McInerney, Michael, 'Roddy Connolly, Sixty Years of Political Activity', *Irish Times,* 27 August 1976.

McKay, Enda, 'Changing with the Tide: The Irish Labour Party, 1927-1933', *Saothar* 11, 1986 (ILHS, Dublin, 1986).

McLoughlin, Barry, 'Left to the Wolves: Irish Victims of Stalinist Terror', *Saothar* 32, 2007 (ILHS, Dublin, 2007).

Mecham, Mike, *William Walker: Social Activist & Belfast Labourist 1870-1918* (Umiskin Press, Dublin, 2019).

Mecham, Mike, 'For Quality of Life and Brotherhood': John W. Boyle, 1914-1918', in Francis Devine and Patrick Smylie (Editors), *Left Lives in Twentieth Century Ireland – Communist Lives,* Volume 3 (Umiskin Press, Dublin, 2020).

Merrigan, Matt, *Eagle or Cuckoo?: The Story of the ATGWU in Ireland* (Matmer, Dublin, 1989).

Merrigan, Matt, *Eggs and Rashers: Irish Socialist Memories,* Edited and Introduced by D. R. O'Connor Lysaght (Umiskin Press, Dublin, 2014).

Millar, Scott, 'Paddy Behan (1938-2016)', *Saothar* 42, 2017 (ILHS, Dublin, 2017).

Millotte, Mike, *Communism in Modern Ireland: The Pursuit of the Workers' Republic Since 1916* (Gill and Macmillan, Dublin, and Meier, New York, 1984).

Mitchell, Arthur, *Labour in Irish Politics 1890-1930* (Irish University Press, Dublin, 1974).

Morrissey, Thomas J., *William Martin Murphy* (Dundalgan Press/Historical Association of Ireland, Dundalk, 1997).

Morrissey, Thomas J., *William O'Brien* (Four Courts Press, Dublin, 2007).

Muldowney, Mary (Editor), with Ida Milne, *100 Years Later: The Legacy of the 1913 Lockout* (Seven Towers, Dublin, 2013).

Murphy, Michael, 'Gerry Fitt', *Saothar* 32, 2007 (ILHS, Dublin, 2007).

Myers, Kevin, 'An Irishman's Diary' [on Louie Bennett], *Irish Times,* 13 March 1990.

Myers, Kevin, 'The maritime man' [John de Courcy Ireland], *Irish Times,* Weekend, 24 August 1991.

Nevin, Donal (Anon), *1913 Jim Larkin and the Dublin Lock-Out* (WUI, Dublin, 1964).

Nevin, Donal (Editor), *Trade Union Century* (Mercier Press, Cork, in association with the Irish Congress of Trade Unions and Radio Telefís Éireann, 1994).

Nevin, Donal (Editor), *Lion of the Fold* (Gill and Macmillan, Dublin, 1998).

Nevin, Donal (Editor), *James Connolly: A Full Life* (Gill and Macmillan, Dublin, 2005).

Newsinger, James, 'As Catholic as the Pope': James Connolly and the Roman Catholic Church in Ireland', *Saothar* 11, 1986 (ILHS, Dublin, 1986).

Ní Choncubhair, Sinéad, 'Brendan Corish: a life in politics, 1945-1977', *Saothar* 39, 2014 (ILHS, Dublin, 2014).

Nolan, Seán (Johnny) (Anon), (Editor), *Communist Party of Ireland-Outline History* (CPI, Dublin, undated, 1975).

O'Brien, Conor Cruise, *Memoir: My Life and Themes* (Poolbeg Press, Dublin, 1999).

O'Brien, May, *Clouds on My Windows: A Dublin Memoir* (Brandon, Dingle, County Kerry and London, 2004).

O'Brien, Máire Cruise, *The Same Age As The State* (O'Brien Press, Dublin, 2003).

O'Brien, William (as told to Edward MacLysaght), *Forth the Banners Go: Reminiscences of William O'Brien* (Three Candles, Dublin, 1969).

Ó Broin, Eoin, *Sinn Féin and the Politics of Left Republicanism* (Pluto Press, London, 2009).

Ó Cathasaigh, Aindrias, *The Life and Times of Gilbert Lynch* (ILHS, Dublin, 2011).

O'Connell, T.J., *100 Years of Progress – The Story of the Irish National Teachers' Organisation 1868-1968* (INTO, Dublin, 1968).

O'Connor, Éimear, *Seán Keating in Context: Responses to Culture and Politics in Post-Civil War Ireland* (Carysfort Press, Dublin, 2009).

O'Connor, Éimear, *Seán Keating: Art, Politics and Building the Irish Nation* (Irish Academic Press, Dublin, 2013).

O'Connor, Emmet, *A Labour History of Ireland 1824-1960* (Gill and Macmillan, Dublin 1992).

O'Connor, Emmet, *James Larkin* (Cork University Press, Cork, 2002).

O'Connor, Emmet, *Reds and the Green: Ireland, Russia and the Communist Internationals 1919-1943* (UCD Press, Dublin, 2004).

O'Connor, Emmet, 'The age of the red republic: the Irish left and nationalism', *Saothar* 30, 2005 (ILHS, Dublin, 2005).

O'Connor, Emmet, *Big Jim Larkin: Hero or Wrecker?* (UCD Press, Dublin, 2015).

O'Connor, Emmet, 'Persona Non Grata: Andrew Boyd, 1921-2011', Francis Devine & Kieran Jack McGinley (Editors), *Left Lives in Twentieth Century Ireland,* Volume 2 (Umiskin Press, Dublin, 2019).

O'Connor, Emmet, 'Greater Son: James Larkin Junior, 1904-1969' Francis Devine and Patrick Smylie (Editors), *Left Lives in Twentieth Century Ireland – Communist Lives,* Volume 3 (Umiskin Press, Dublin, 2020).

O'Connor Lysaght, D. R., 'The Rake's Progress of a Syndicalist: The Political Career of William O'Brien, Irish Labour Leader', *Saothar* 9, 1983 (ILHS, Dublin, 1983).

O'Connor Lysaght, D. R. (Editor), *100 Years of Liberty Hall: Papers on the history of SIPTU, given at the Irish Labour History Society Conference, 22 October 2009* (ILHS, Dublin, 2013).

O'Connor Lysaght, D. R., 'From the GPO to the Winter Palace: how a Workers' Revolution was lost and how a workers' revolution was won', *Saothar* 38 (ILHS, Dublin, 2013), pp. 119-130.

O'Connor Lysaght, D. R., *From the GPO to the Winter Palace: How a Workers'*

Revolution Was Lost & How a Workers' Revolution Was Won (ILHS Studies in Irish Labour History, No. 15, Dublin, 2016).

O'Donnell, Peadar, 'Peadar O'Donnell: Commandant General Irish Republican Army', interviewed by Uinseann MacEoin (Editor), *Survivors* (Argenta Publications, Dublin, 1980).

O'Leary, Don, *Vocationalism and Social Catholicism in Twentieth-Century Ireland* (Irish Academic Press, Dublin, 1999).

O'Reilly, Mick, 'Matt Merrigan: a marvellous legacy', *Red Banner,* Issue 8, November 2000.

O'Reilly, Mick, *From Lucifer To Lazarus* (Lilliput Press, Dublin, 2019).

O'Riordan, Manus, 'Larkin in America', *Saothar 4,* 1978 (ILHS, Dublin, 1978).

O'Riordan, Manus, 'Portrait of an Irish Anti-Fascist: Frank Edwards, 1907-1983', *Morgen Freiheit,* New York, 1983, reproduced in Labour History Workshop, Dublin, 1984.

O'Riordan, Manus, 'James Larkin Junior and the forging of a thinking intelligent movement', *Saothar* 19, 1994.

O'Riordan, Manus, 'The Voice Of A Thinking Intelligent Movement: James Larkin Junior & Ideological Modernisation Of Irish Trade Unionism (Studies in Labour History 2, ILHS, Dublin, 1995), reprinted in updated edition 2001.

O'Riordan, Michael, 'Industrial Democracy is all a cod', *Irish Socialist,* No. 83, January 1969.

O'Riordan, Michael, *Pages from History on Irish-Soviet Relations* (New Books, Dublin, 1977).

O'Riordan, Michael, *Connolly Column: The Story of the Irishmen who fought in the ranks of the International Brigades in the national-revolutionary war of the Spanish people, 1936-1939 (*New Books, Dublin, 1979).

O'Toole, Fintan, 'Swift and Sure', *Sunday Tribune,* 5 November 1984.

Parr, Connal, 'Left From the Margins': Paddy Devlin, 1925-1999, in Francis Devine & Kieran Jack McGinley (Editors), *Left Lives in Twentieth Century Ireland,* Volume 2 (Umiskin Press, Dublin, 2019).

Parr, Connal, 'Other People's Struggles – Kader, 1934-2011, and Louise Asmal, 1939-, in Francis Devine and Patrick Smylie (Editors), *Left Lives in Twentieth Century Ireland – Communist Lives,* Volume 3 (Umiskin Press, Dublin, 2020).

Patterson, Henry, 'James Larkin and the Belfast Dockers' and Carters' Strike of 1907', *Saothar 4,* 1978 (ILHS, Dublin, 1978).

Puirséil, Niamh, 'Labour and coalition: the impact of the first inter-party government, 1948-51', *Saothar* 27, 2002 (ILHS, Dublin, 2002).

Puirséil, Niamh, *The Irish Labour Party 1922-73* (University College Dublin, 2007).

Puirséil, Niamh, 'Catholic Stakhanovites? Religion and the Irish Labour Party, 1922-73', in Francis Devine, Fintan Lane and Niamh Puirséil (Editors), *Essays in Irish Labour History: A Festschrift for Elizavbeth and John W. Boyle* (Irish Academic Press, Dublin, Portland, Oregon, 2008, in association with the Irish Labour History Society).

Puirséil, Niamh, "If it's socialism you want, join some other party": Labour and the Left', in Paul Daly, Rónán O'Brien and Paul Rouse (Editors), *Making the Difference?* (Collins Press, Cork, 2012).

Puirséil, Niamh, *Kindling the Flame: 150 Years of the Irish National Teachers' Organisation* (Gill Books, Dublin, 2017).

Purdie, Bob, *Politics in the Street: The Origins of the Civil Rights Movement in Northern Ireland* (Blackstaff Press, Belfast, 1990).

Quinn, Michael, *The Making of an Irish Communist Leader: The life and times of Michael O'Riordan 1938-1947* (Communist Party of Ireland, Dublin, 2011).

Quinn, Michael J., 'The Ireland-USSR Society, 1966-92', *Saothar* 38, 2013 (ILHS, Dublin, 2013).

Quinn, Michael, *Irish-Soviet Diplomatic and Friendship Relations 1917-1991* (Umiskin Press, Dublin, 2016).

Quinn, Michael, 'Angela McQuillan, née Nolan', *Sound Post*, Vol. 18, No. 2, Summer 2020.

Quinn, Ruairi, *Straight Left: A Journey in Politics* (Hodder Headline Ireland, Dublin, 2011).

Rafter, Kevin, *The Clann: The Story of Clann na Poblachta* (Mercier Press, Cork, 1996).

Rafter, Kevin, *Democratic Left: The Life and Death of an Irish Political Party* (Irish Academic Press, Dublin, 2011).

Redmond, Seán, *The Irish Municipal Employees' Trade Union 1883-1983* (IMETU, Dublin, 1983).

Redmond, Tom, 'Sean Redmond (1936-2012)', *Saothar* 29, 2014 (ILHS, Dublin, 2014).

Renshaw, Patrick, *The General Strike* (Eyre Methuen, London, 1975).

Roberts, Ruaidhri, *The Story of the People's College*, Edited and additional material incorporated by R. Dardis Clarke (O'Brien Press, in association with the People's College, Dublin, 1986).

Scott, Brendan, *Labour and Socialism*, (Liaison Committee of the Left – Labour Party, Dublin, 1973).

Seery, Aidan; Liam McKenna, S.J., 'The Catholic Workers' College Dublin – a personal history', *Saothar* 39, 2014 (ILHS, Dublin, 2014).

Sheehan, Helena, *Navigating the Zeitgeist: A story of the Cold War, the New Left, Irish Republicanism, and International Communism* (Monthly Review Press, New York, 2019).

Sheehy Skeffington, Andrée, S*keff: A life of Owen Sheehy Skeffington 1909-1970* (Lilliput Press, Dublin, 1991).

Siggins, Lorna, 'An Irishwoman's Diary' [on Nora Harkin], *Irish Times*, 23 September 1992.

Simmons, Sheila and Devine Francis, 'Evelyn Owens', *Saothar* 36, 2011 (ILHS, Dublin, 2011).

Swift, John, *History of the Dublin Bakers and Others* (IBCAWAU, Dublin, 1948).

Swift, John, 'How Labour Relations Work in Russia – 1', *Irish Times*, 7 November 1967.

Swift, John, 'Labour Relations in Russia (2): A Choice of Systems', *Irish Times*, 8 November 1967.

Swift, John, 'Looking for Connolly and the Dread of Finding Him', *Irish Times*, 23 July 1968.

Swift, John, 'Looking for Connolly – 2, Labour and the Development of the State', *Irish Times*, 24 July 1968.

Swift, John, 'Industrial Democracy: A Reply by John Swift', *Irish Socialist*, No. 84, February 1969.

Swift, John, 'We Need a School of Socialism', *Irish Socialist*, No. 97, July-August 1970.

Swift, John, 'Commemorating Hegel', *Irish Times*, 6 November 1970.

Swift, John, 'Vocationalism Last Time', *Irish Times*, 12 January 1971.

Swift, John, 'Labour and Workers' Democracy – 1, Connolly Revisited', *Irish Times*, 22 February 1971.

Swift, John, 'Labour and Workers' Democracy – 2', The Silence on Socialism'. *Irish Times*, 23 February 1971.

Swift, John, 'The Political Strike', *Irish Times*, 12 April 1971.

Swift, John, 'Sources of Irish Secularism – 1', *Irish Times*, 14 May 1971.

Swift, John, 'Sources of Irish Secularism – 2', *Irish Times*, 15 May 1971.

Swift, John, 'Labour and Constitution', *Irish Times*, 26 July 1972.

Swift, John, 'Ireland's Soviet Friends', *Irish Times*, 8 November 1972.

Swift, John, 'The March of Organised Labour', *Irish Times*, 9 August 1973.

Swift, John, 'Report of the Commission on Vocational Organisation (and its times, 1930-'40's)', *Saothar*, Vol. 1, No. 1, May Day 1975 (ILHS, Dublin, 1975).

Swift, John: 'Trade Union Leader and Pacifist' [sic], interviewed by Uinseann MacEoin (Editor), *Survivors* (Argenta Publications, Dublin, 1980).

Swift, John, 'Trade Unions Under Socialism', *Irish Times*, 17 December 1982.

Swift, John, 'Daily Life in the USSR', *Irish Times*, 30 April 1983.

Swift, John, 'The "holy" crusade for the Corporate State', *Irish Socialist*, No. 240, May 1983.

Swift, John, 'Pius Memories', *Sunday Tribune*, 21 August 1983.

Swift, John, 'Noel Browne And The defects In Our Education System', *Sunday Tribune*, 29 January 1984.

Swift, John, 'The De-Politicalisation of Big Jim Larkin', *Irish Socialist*, No. 256, September 1984.

Swift, John, 'How Larkin Died on His Knees', *Irish Socialist*, No. 260, January 1985.

Swift, John, 'The Launching of the People's College', *Irish Socialist*, No. 261, February 1985.

Swift, John, 'The fight to make the trade unions turn to a political direction', *Irish Socialist*, No. 268, September 1985.

Swift, John, 'How the Bakers' Library Came to be "Blessed"!, *Irish Socialist*, April 1986.

Swift, John, *Told in Toberona – A Memoir* (Watchword, Dublin, 2008).

Swift, John P. (Anon), 'Christianity?', *Forward*, 28 August 1971.

Swift, John P., 'Irish Labour's Living History', *Sunday Tribune (Colour Tribune)*, 23 August 1987.

Swift, John P., *John Swift: An Irish Dissident* (Gill and Macmillan, Dublin, 1991).

Swift, John P., 'SIPTU: An Inspirational Development', in Dr. Kieran Jack McGinley (Editor), *Dear Comrade* (Watchword, Dublin, 2010).

Swift, John P., *Striking a Chord: A Trade Union History of Musicians in Ireland* (Watchword, Dublin, 2012).

Swift, John P., 'A Solitary Voice That Echoes Still: John Swift 1896-1990', in Francis Devine and Kieran Jack McGinley (Editors) *Left Lives in Twentieth Century Ireland*, Volume 1 (Umiskin Press, Dublin, 2017).

Swift, John [P.], 'Carol Ann Scott (née O'Rourke) (1937-2018)', *Sound Post*, Vol. 16, No. 2, Summer 2018.

Thornley, Edward, *Lone Crusader: David Thornley and the Intellectuals* (Ashfield Press, Dublin, 2012).

Thornley, Yseult (Editor), *Unquiet Spirit: Essays in Memory of David Thornley* (Liberties Press, Dublin, 2008).

Tobin, Fergal, *The Best of Decades: Ireland in the 1960s* (Gill and Macmillan, Dublin, 1984).

Tormey, Bill, *Ten Years Hard Labour: A Personal Political Odyssey* (Blackwater Press, Dublin, 1994).

Treacy, Matt, *The Communist Party of Ireland 1921-2011: Vol. 1: 1921-1969* (Brocaire Books, Dublin, 2012).

Ward-Perkins, Sarah, *Select Guide to Trade Union Records in Dublin with details of Unions Operating in Ireland to 1970* (Irish Manuscripts Commission, Dublin, 1996).

White, Trevor, *Alfie: The Life and Times of Alfie Byrne* (Penguin, Dublin, 2017).

Whyte, J.H., *Church and State in Modern Ireland, 1923-1970* (Gill and Macmillan, Dublin, 1975).

Wickham, James, 'The New Irish Working Class?, *Saothar* 6, 1980 (ILHS, Dublin, 1980).

Yeates, Pádraig, *Lockout Dublin 1913* (Gill and Macmillan, Dublin, 2000).

Yeates, Pádraig, 'Tomas Mac Giolla', *Saothar* 36, 2011 (ILHS, Dublin, 2011).

Yeates, Pádraig, *A City in Wartime: Dublin 1914-18* (Gill and Macmillan, Dublin, 2011).

Yeates, Pádraig, *A City in Civil War: Dublin 1921-4* (Gill and Macmillan, Dublin, 2015).

Index

British Army, 43-45, 47-49, 170, 193, 210,
212, 217-218, 220
British Embassy, Dublin, 23, 85-86, 82-83
British Labour Party, see Labour Party,
British
British Road to Socialism, 230
Brittany, 49, 235
Brockway, Fenner, 18
Brooke, Basil, 236
Brooks, J. A., 84
Brown, Christy, 18
Browne, Bernard, 65, 74, 114-115, 231
Browne, Dan, 53, 114, 129, 131, 167
Browne, Noël, 7-10, 13, 15-16, 18, 23-25, 36,
38-39, 44, 46, 50, 53-54, 71,74, 85, 87,
93, 105-106, 11, 115, 117-118, 122-123,
128-129, 131, 133-137, 149-155, 157,
159, 163, 167-173, 178-180, 187-190,
213-214
Mother and Child Scheme, 7-8, 117
eradication of tuberculosis, 9
socialism, views on, 9-10
secularism, views on, 9-10
liberalism, views on, 9-10
TD of five political parties, 10
Independent TD, 10
Labour Party admission opposed by
Labour Leaders, 10
Fine Fail and Fine Gael, views on, 13
National Progressive Democratic Party
(NPD) progenitor and co-founder,
15
Labour Party member, 16, 38
The Plough, contributor, 18
Irish Left, criticism of, 18
Campaign for Nuclear Disarmament
activist, 23-24
nuclear tests, opponent of, 23-25
CND-NPD demonstration against USA
blockade of Cuba, participant in ,
25
Provisional IRA, opponent of, 44, 46
May Day demonstrations, participant
and/or speaker, 53-54
Springboks Rugby tour of Ireland,
1970, opponent of, 85, 87
Vietnam War, opponent of, 93
elected Labour Party Vice-Chairman,
1967, 105
Labour Party radical 'Outline Policy',
1969, contributor to and supporter
of, 106, 213
Labour Party coalition policy, views on,
111, 122, 133, 169, 179-180

supports expulsion of Stephen
Coughlan, TD, over anti-Semitic
statement, 129
Liaison Committee of the Left – Labour
Party, associated with, 136
contraceptive legislation, advocate and
supporter of, 137, 149-150, 160,
168, 178
Tramore landmark speech on
separation of Church and State,
149-150
Catholic Hierarchy influence in
education, opponent of, 149, 155
Ireland's EEC entry, opponent of, 164
Decision not to stand as Labour
candidate in 1973 General Election,
1973
Tributes to Brendan Scott, 187-188,
190, 212-213
Browne, Vincent, 71
Brussels, 220, 233
Brutus, Dennis, 83
Buckley, John, 127
Bulgaria, 98
Buswells Hotel, Dublin, 76
Butler, Frank, 47, 162, 180
Butler, Hubert, 18
Butler, Rabb, 219
Byrne, Brendan, 28
Byrne, Catherine, 22
Byrne, G., 231
Byrne, Hugh, 85
Byrne, John, 125, 129, 136, 152, 162-163,
171-172
Cabral, Amílcar, 201, 204
Callaghan, James (Jim), 217
Cambodia, 93, 224
Campaign for Nuclear Disarmament,
British, 22, 24
Campaign for Nuclear Disarmament, Irish,
22-25
Cape Clear Island, 27
Cape Town, South Africa, 84, 88
Carmody, Paddy, 17, 98, 231
Carpenter, Wallie, 30
Carr, Bunny, 84
Carr, Justice, 68
Carroll, John, 167
Carroll, Mick, 29, 30
Carroll, Patrick (Pat), 136, 159, 160, 162-
163, 190
Carroll, Tom, 136, 172
Carson, Edward, 207
Carter, Vera, 172

Castro, Fidel, 237
Catholic Hierarchy, 7-8, 149, 152, 156
Catholic University School, 163
Catholic Workers College, 9
CCL, see Citizens for Civil Liberties
Celtic Football Club, 234
Central Hotel, Dublin, 99
Central Intelligence Agency, 222
Ceoltóirí an Chaisleáin, 30
Chambers, Maura, 28
Change or Chains?: The Civil Wrongs of Irish Women, IWLM Manifesto, 52
Chekhov, Anton, 100
Chenevix, Helen, 22-24
Chi Minh, Ho, 223
Chicago, 228
Chieftains, The, 28, 35
Childers, Erskine, 70
Childs, David, 205
China, 216, 231
Churchill, Winston, 219
CIA, see Central Intelligence Agency
Citizens Advice Bureau, see Sinn Féin Citizens Advice Bureau
Citizens for Civil Liberties, 74-79
CIU, see Congress of Irish Unions
Civil Rights Campaign, Northern Ireland, 34, 193
Civil Rights Campaign, USA, 34, 219
Civil Rights Movement (Northern Ireland), 207
Civil War, see Irish Civil War
Claffey, Una, 135
Clancy Brothers and Tommy Makem, 35
Clann na Poblachta, 8, 10, 14
Clarke, Aidan, 3, 13, 76
Clarke, Austin, 3, 18
Clarke, John, 28
Clarke, Paul, 231
Clerkin, Andrew (Andy), 36
Cloonin Mór, Co. Sligo, 1
Cluskey, Frank, 44, 85, 87, 99, 129
Clutton-Block, Guy, 86
Clydeside, 235, 237
CND, see Campaign for Nuclear Disarmament
Cohen, Issac, 129
Cohn Bendit, Daniel, 203
Cohn Bendit, Gabriel, 203
Coláiste Iognáid, Cork, 164
Coleraine University, 220
Colimore Hotel, Dalkey, 156
Colley, George, 227
Collins, Fred, 231

Collins, John, 24
Comhaltas Ceoltóirí Éireann, 35
Comhar Fhollseacháin Teo, 16
Committee to Oppose Repressive Legislation, 74-76, 81
Common Market Defence Campaign, 164
Common Market, see European Economic Community
Communications Workers' Union, 27
Communist Party of China, 231
Communist Party of Czechoslovakia, 34
Communist Party of France, 230-231
Communist Party of Ireland (original, founded 1921), 180
Communist Party of Ireland (1970-), 17, 30, 36-38, 52-54, 66-67, 75 91, 94, 98, 154, 230-231, 234
  resignations, 1975, 98, 230-231
Communist Party of Italy, 230-231
Communist Party of Northern Ireland, 36
Communist Party of Romania, 231
Communist Party of Spain, 230
Communist Party of the Soviet Union, 230-231, 234
Communist Party of Yugoslavia, 231
Community Schools, 78, 155,-156, 170-171, 178
Congo, The, 14-15, 210, 227
Congress of Irish Unions, 8
Conneff, Kevin, 28
Connolly Hall, Limerick, 87
Connolly Youth Movement, 30, 36, 52-54, 66-67, 75, 87, 98-99, 154, 231
Connolly, James, 9, 14, 18, 30, 35, 39, 44, 46-48, 54, 93, 105-107, 109, 138, 161, 171, 185, 187, 194, 204, 212, 227, 231, 234
Connolly, Roderick (Roddy), 74, 138, 153, 161, 176, 180, 182-183, 187, 219
Conradh na Gaeilge, 75-76
Constitution, see Irish Constitution
contraception legislation, 52, 137, 149, 151, 157, 160, 168, 170, 174, 178, 193, 196
Conway, William, 202, 217
Coonan, Charles, 14
Cooper, Ivan, 74, 77-78, 87
Co-operative Publications Limited, see Comhar Fhollseacháin Teo
Córas Tráchtála, 84
Corcoran, Seán, 38
Corish, Brendan, 8, 10, 14, 44, 74, 85, 93, 102-106, 109-110, 114, 117-118, 122, 124, 129, 130-131, 134-135, 137-139, 153, 161-162, 172, 175, 177, 179, 180, 194

Internment, Northern Ireland, 43, 45-46, 79, 86

Ireland, 1-4, 7-8, 13-14m 16-18, 22, 24, 28, 30, 34-37, 44, 46-50 52-54, 66-67, 70, 74, 76, 78, 82-84, 86-87, 91-92, 94, 96, 98-100, 106, 111-113, 117-118, 124-125, 128-129, 138, 149-152, 155-157, 160, 163-164, 178, 180, 185, 188-189, 192-193, 196, 210, 214-216, 219, 222, 227-229, 231-235-236

Ireland Her Own, 230

Ireland-USSR Society, 1, 37, 96, 99-100, 196

IRFU, see Irish Rugby Football Union

Irish Actors' Equity Association, 48, 69, 100

Irish Anti-Apartheid Movement, 37, 81-88, 96, 183-184, 189

Irish Bakers', Confectioners' and Allied Workers' Amalgamated Union, 8, 83, 96, 164

Irish Campaign Nuclear Disarmament, see Campaign for Nuclear Disarmament

Irish Civil War, 1

Irish CND, see Campaign for Nuclear Disarmament

Irish Communist Organisation, 49, 66, 211

Irish Congress of Trade Unions, 14, 34, 45, 74, 87, 164

Irish Constitution, 7, 78, 128, 160-161, 178

Irish Independent, 3, 84, 115, 137

Irish Labour History Society, 17

Irish Marxist Society, 98

Irish Press 105, 123

Irish Rugby Football Union, 82, 84, 87

Irish Socialist, 37-38, 40, 98, 154

Irish Student Movement, 67

Irish Students' Campaign for Nuclear Disarmament, 23

Irish Times, 13, 40, 68-69, 97-98, 105, 110, 114, 118, 122, 124, 127, 129, 139, 170, 175, 178, 182, 186, 189, 196

Irish Trade Union Congress, 9

Irish Transport and General Workers' Union, 8-9, 27, 30, 36, 38, 54, 67, 78, 85, 105, 164, 167, 182, 186, 189

Irish Voice on Vietnam, 1, 37, 91, 93-94,

Irish Women's Liberation Movement, 52-54, 74-76

Irish Workers' League, 17, 52

Irish Workers' Party, 36-37, 46, 52-54, 91, 96, 98, 114

Israel, 49, 210, 218

Istanbul, 40

Italy, 7, 236

ITGWU College, Dublin, 182

ITGWU, see Irish Transport and General Workers' Union

ITUC, see Irish Trade Union Congress

IVV, see Irish Voice on Vietnam

IWL, see Irish Workers' League

IWLM, see Irish Women's Liberation Movement

IWP, see Irish Workers' Party

Jacks, H. B., 4

Jackson, Saul, 226

Jeffares, George, 231

Jeffares, Marion, 231

Johannsburg, South Africa, 84, 86, 88

Johnson, Lyndon, 91-92

Johnston (née Mooney), Máirín, 28, 38, 52-53, 65-66, 69, 71

Johnston, Joseph, 22

Johnston, Roy H. W., 18, 99, 216

Jury's Hotel, Dublin, 36, 96

Katanga, 210

Keane, John B., 82, 93

Keane, Seán, 29

Kearney, Marilynn, 172

Keating, Justin, 17-18, 23, 44, 85, 118, 120, 122, 124, 129, 131, 133, 150, 164, 177-179, 194

Keating (née Wine), Loretta, 18

Keating (née Walsh), May, 16-18, 22, 170

Keating, Seán, 17

Keegan, Billy, 136, 172

Kelleher, Derry, 54

Kelly, Betty, see Hayden, Betty

Kelly, James, 217, 219

Kelly, Jimmy, 231

Kelly, Kieran, 165

Kelly, Luke, 28, 30, 35

Kelly, Máirín, 231

Kemmy, James (Jim), 28, 46, 53, 125, 128-129, 136, 138-139, 152, 159, 164

Kennedy, Edward (Ted), 219

Kennedy, Fintan, 85

Kennedy, John F., 24-25, 27, 37, 228

Kennedy, Robert (Bobby), 228

Kenny, Ivor, 39

Kenny, Mary, 52-54

Kenny Report on teachers' pay, 4

Kent State University, 228

Kevin Barry Hall, 29

Khrushchev, Nikita, 24

Kilduff, Sarah (Colleen), see Scott, Sarah (Colleen)

Killeenduff, County Sligo, 1

Killybegs, Co. Donegal, 40

O'Donovan, Con, 27
O'Donovan, John, 44
O'Faolain, Sean, 93
O'Higgins, Michael, 106, 122
O'Kennedy, Michael, 86
O'Leary, Michael, 10, 15, 28, 39, 44, 69, 85, 91, 194-105, 113, 120, 124, 129, 164, 177, 180, 182
O'Mahony, Flor, 44, 53
O'Malley, Desmond (Des), 75, 218
O'Malley, Donagh, 34
O'Mara, Joan, 17
O'Neill, Mattie, 28
O'Neill, Michael, 91
O'Neill, Norah, 17
O'Rahilly, Alfred, 9
O'Reilly, Michael (Mick), 30, 37, 53, 66, 98, 231
O'Riordan, Michael (Mick), 18, 52, 54, 66-68, 98-99, 218
O'Rourke, Carol Ann, see Scott, Carol Ann (wife)
O'Rourke, Dermod (father-in-law), 2
O'Rourke, Dermot, 114-115
O'Rourke, Dorothy, see Dowling, Dorothy
O'Rourke family, 2
O'Rourke (née Carroll), Martha (mother-in-law), 2
O'Rourke, Rory, 167, 172
O'Sullivan, Donal, 105, 138, 161, 169, 176, 182-183
O'Sullivan, Gerry, 167
O'Sullivan, Maurice, 130
Offences Against the State Act, 78-79, 168, 171
Official IRA, 217
Official Sinn Féin, 45, 47-48, 53-55, 74-76, 87, 94, 125, 138, 167, 186, 193, 208-209, 215-218, 234, 236 (see also Sinn Féin and Provisional Sinn Fein)
Onassis, Aristotle, 207
Orange Order, 1560, 156
Owens, Evelyn, 85, 137

Paisley, Ian, 156, 219, 232
Pakistan, 210
Palestine, 210, 217
Paor, Liam, 93
Parkin, Frank, 205-206
Parnell, Charles Stewart, 93
Patrician College, Ballyfin, County Laois, 2
Patterson, John, 91
Pearse Patrick, 14, 35, 47, 156

Pennsylvania, USA, 233
Penrose, Ed, 66
People's College Adult Education Association, 9
People's College, see People's College Adult Education Association
People's Democracy, 44, 46, 94, 124, 125, 160, 217
Philpott, Tadhg, 27
Phoenix Park, Dublin, 75
Pickard, Yvonne, 30
Pikemen, The, 30
Planxty, 35
Plough, 16-18, 40
Plunkett, James, 16
Poland, 37, 98
POOA, see Post Office Officials' Association
Pope Leo X111, 9
Pope Pius X1, 9
Pope Pius X11, 8-9
Portugal, 113
Post Office Officials' Association, 74
Post Office Workers' Union, 74
Potter, Dudley, 138
Powell, Enoch, 92
POWU, see Post Office Workers' Union
Pratschke, Anthony (Tony), 87, 114, 125
Prentice Folk, 30
Progressive Democrats, 195
Prohibition of Forcible Entry and Occupation Bill, 1970, 53, 74
Provisional IRA, 43-44, 46-47, 79, 194, 217
Provisional Sinn Féin, 45, 125, 138, 167, 193, 208-209, 215-217, 219, 234, 236 (see also Sinn Féin and Official Sinn Fein)
Puirséil Niamh, 134

Quadragesimo Anno, Papal Encyclical, 7
QUB, see Queen's University, Belfast
Queen's Hotel, Dundalk, 83
Queen's University, Belfast, 220
Quinn, Ruairi, 110, 180

Rangers Football Club, 234
Rape Crisis Centre, 52
Ravel, Maurice, 3
Reformation, The, 49, 193, 211
Reilly, Paddy, 30
Rerum Novarum, Papal Encyclical, 7
Rhatigan, Seamus, 53
Rhodesia (now Zimbabwe), 49, 82-84, 86, 113, 210-211
RIAM, see Royal Irish Academy of Music
Rifai, Hishan, 86